# THE ARDEN SHAKESPEARE

GENERAL EDITORS:
RICHARD PROUDFOOT, ANN THOMPSON
and DAVID SCOTT KASTAN

KING JOHN

# The Arden Shakespeare

*Second Series

# THE ARDEN EDITION OF THE WORKS OF WILLIAM SHAKESPEARE

# KING JOHN

Edited by
E. A. J. HONIGMANN

The Arden website is at
http://www.ardenshakespeare.com

The general editors of the Arden Shakespeare have been
W. J. Craig and R. H. Case (first series 1899-1944)
Una Ellis-Fermor, Harold F. Brooks, Harold Jenkins and
Brian Morris (second series 1946-82)

Present general editors (third series)
Richard Proudfoot, Ann Thompson and David Scott Kastan

This edition of *King John,* by E.A.J. Honigmann,
first published 1951 by Methuen & Co. Ltd

Editorial matter © 1981 Methuen & Co. Ltd

Published by The Arden Shakespeare
Reprinted 2002

Arden Shakespeare is an imprint of Thomson

Thomson
High Holborn House
50-51 Bedford Row
London WC1R 4LR

Printed in Singapore

*British Library Cataloguing in Publication Data*
A catalogue record for this book is available from the British Library
*Library of Congress Cataloguing in Publication Data*
A catalogue record has been requested

ISBN 0-174-43639-4 (hbk)
ISBN 1-90343-609-5 (pbk)
NPN 9 8 7 6 5

# CONTENTS

# PREFACE

Ivor B. John's edition has been expanded in the footnotes and the collation: where his footnotes are retained they are acknowledged. The Introduction also departs from the older edition in a number of ways, new appendices are added, and the text reverts to the Folio in many readings.

I am indebted for help of various kinds to Mr J. C. Maxwell, Dr J. G. McManaway, Professor A. Nicoll, and Dr C. T. Onions; and to Mr J. R. Brown and Dr R. A. Foakes for much detailed criticism. Professor C. J. Sisson has kindly allowed me to collate *King John* from the proofs of his forthcoming edition of Shakespeare. Dr H. F. Brooks and the General Editor have spent more time in reading and re-reading my MS. than any reasonable editor could demand, and suggested many valuable improvements. Professor P. Alexander has advised and guided me over a period of years in the study of the King John plays: and not the least of my many debts to him is that he put me in touch with Mrs F. M. H. Bone, who placed all her notes on these plays at my disposal, and most generously allowed me to print some of her discoveries for the first time.

E. A. H.

The Shakespeare Institute
Stratford-on-Avon
*February*, 1953.

## NOTE

In reprinting (1959) only a few minor alterations have been made; in particular the traditional line numbering is indicated in square brackets in this edition where, in Act II. Scene ii and Act III, new act and scene division is introduced.

E. A. H.

# ABBREVIATIONS

| | |
|---|---|
| Abbott | E. A. Abbott, *Shakespearian Grammar* (ed. 1897). |
| Arber | E. Arber, *Transcript of the Registers of the Company of Stationers* (5 vols.) (1875–94). |
| B. & F. | F. Beaumont and J. Fletcher, *Comedies and Tragedies* (1647). |
| Carter | T. Carter, *Shakespeare and Holy Scripture* (1905). |
| Chapman | G. Chapman, *Plays and Poems* (2 vols., ed. T. Parrott) (1910–14). |
| Foxe | J. Foxe, *Actes and Monuments* (Vol. 1) (ed. 1583). |
| Furness | H. H. Furness, *King John* (Variorum ed.) (1919). |
| Heywood | T. Heywood, *Dramatic Works* (6 vols.) (1874). |
| Hol. | R. Holinshed, *Chronicles* (Vol. III) (1587). |
| Kyd | T. Kyd, *Works* (ed. F. S. Boas) (1901). |
| Lyly | J. Lyly, *Works* (3 vols., ed. R. W. Bond) (1902). |
| Nashe | T. Nashe, *Works* (5 vols., ed. R. B. McKerrow) (1904–10). |
| Noble | R. Noble, *Shakespeare's Biblical Knowledge* (1935). |
| On. | C. T. Onions, *Shakespeare Glossary* (ed. 1941). |
| Paris | M. Paris, *Historia Maior* (1571). |
| Schmidt | A. Schmidt, *Shakespeare-Lexicon* (2 vols.) (1874–5). |
| Sidney | P. Sidney, *Arcadia* (ed. A. Feuillerat) (1912). |
| Smith | G. C. Moore Smith, *King John* (Warwick ed.) (?1900). |
| S.R. | Stationers' Registers (see Arber, above). |
| Tilley | M. P. Tilley, *Dictionary of . . . Proverbs* (1950). |
| *T.R.* | *The Troublesome Raigne of Iohn King of England* (2 vols., ed. C. Praetorius) (1888). |
| Vaughan | H. H. Vaughan, *New Readings* (3 vols.) (ed. 1886). |
| Wilson | J. D. Wilson, *King John* (C.U.P. ed.) (1936). |

The customary abbreviations are used for periodicals and well-known works: *D.N.B.* = *Dictionary of National Biography*; M.S.R. = Malone Society Reprint; *O.E.D.* = *Oxford English Dictionary*; *R.E.S.* = *Review of English Studies*, etc. The abbreviations of the titles of Shakespeare's plays and poems follow C. T. Onions, *Shakespeare Glossary*, p. x.

Unless otherwise stated, quotations from the Bible are from the Genevan version; quotations from Shakespeare (except those from *King John*) from *The Oxford Shakespeare* (ed. W. J. Craig) (1907).

References to the first leaf of the gathering and to the recto of the page in early printed books omit the usual "1" and the superior "r": thus in the note on I. i. 17 sig. D = sig. D₁ʳ; in the note on I. i. 110 sig. Eᵛ = sig. E₁ᵛ.

# INTRODUCTION

## I. The Sources

According to the large majority of critics, Shakespeare's *John* is based upon an anonymous play, *The Troublesome Raigne of Iohn King of England* (hereafter called the *T.R.*), which was published in two parts in 1591. Prof. J. Dover Wilson, having examined the claims of all other suggested sources in his valuable edition of *John*, has recently declared that Shakespeare "made use of no other source whatsoever".[1]

Evidence that Shakespeare consulted other authorities besides the *T.R.* is meagre, but Prof. Wilson's pronouncement may fall short of the truth. No one has had sufficient faith in Shakespeare's source-reading to bother to explore the possibilities: yet *John* may turn out to be a good example of his searching thoroughness, the very quality often denied him largely on the strength of this play. For it may be asserted with some confidence that he consulted at least two English and two Latin chronicles, apart from the *T.R.*—and probably more.

Prof. Wilson considered three points where "Shakespeare might appear to have made use of historical or quasi-historical material not found in the source-play" (p. xxxii). In his notes to iv. ii. 120, v. iii. 16, v. vi. 30, he explained away the coincidences that Queen Eleanor "the first of April died", that John is carried in a "litter", that John's poisoner's bowels "burst". Although direct access to the chronicles would account for this agreement between Shakespeare and three different sources available to him, Prof. Wilson disregarded this possible explanation to suit the framework of a larger theory. And we could scarcely blame him, for three such points by themselves carry little weight.

Before Prof. Wilson, Prof. Moore Smith had discussed the

---

1. *John* (1936), p. xxxiv (the C.U.P. Shakespeare).

sources of *John*, without finally hazarding a decision, and cited other instances where Shakespeare seemed to have used the chronicles.[1] One of these was the burial of John, to which Holinshed and both plays allude:[2]

(*a*) [John's men] marching foorth with his bodie . . . conueied it vnto Worcester, where he was pompouslie buried . . . not for that he had so *appointed* (as some write) but bicause it was thought to be a place of most suertie for the lords (Hol., 194, ii).

> Meane while to *Worster* let vs beare the King,
> And there *interre* his bodie, as beseemes  (*T.R.*, II. ix. 38–9)
>
> At Worcester must his body *be interr'd;*
> For so he *will'd* it  (*John*, v. vii. 99–100)

John's appointment (will) to be buried at Worcester may mean that Shakespeare knew Holinshed, thought Smith. The editors have not noticed, however, that Holinshed reverts to John's funeral after a digression:

his buriall, whereof I saie thus much, that whether it was his *will* to *be interred*, as is aforesaid . . .  (195, i)

Even though Shakespeare may have followed the *T.R.* for the other details, the word "will'd" (and "be interr'd"), coupled with the correspondences outlined below, persuades us that he did not neglect his favourite source-book.

In illustration of Shakespeare's dependence upon Holinshed we must compare other similarities between the chronicle and the two plays. Unless otherwise stated, the same context is the subject of the three versions.

(*b*) K. Iohn commeth vpon his enimies *not looked for* (Hol., 164, ii, in the margin).

> How much *unlook'd for* is this expedition  (*John*, II. i. 79)
>
> I rather *lookt for* some submisse reply  (*T.R.*, I. ii. 78)

In both plays King Philip, like Holinshed, comments on John's military speed: but only Shakespeare used "looked for" in the source's sense.

---

1. *John* (1900), p. xxviii ff.
2. For the sake of clarity we have added italics in our quotations from the sources.

(c) Stephan / Langton cho- / sen archbishop ⸗ of Canturbu- / rie (Hol., 171, i, in the margin).

> Stephen Langton, chosen archbishop
> Of Canterbury (*John*, III. i. 69–70)

*Stephen Langhton*, whom his Holines hath elected Archbishop of *Canterburie* (*T.R.*, I. v. 70–1)

Holinshed's gloss precedes Pandulph's appearance, but as the latter's first speech, so remarkably alike in the plays, contains the chronicle's words and perhaps its line-division in *John*, Shakespeare's deviation from the *T.R.* has significance.

(d) great *suit* was made to haue Arthur set at *libertie* (Hol., 165, i).

> our *suit*
> That you have bid us ask his *liberty* (*John*, IV. ii. 62–3)

> your *boone* . . .
> The *libertie* of Ladie *Constance* Sonne (*T.R.*, I. xiii. 114–17)

(e) Other examples of Shakespeare's direct use of Holinshed will be found in many footnotes.

(f) Besides verbal similarities, the action of *John* frequently follows Holinshed more closely than the *T.R.* For instance, *John* (following Hol., 190, ii) reports that Melun crossed the Channel before Lewis to encourage the English nobles (IV. iii. 15–17). The *T.R.* omits this. Again, Melun tells the nobles in his dying speech that Lewis intends to reward their treachery to John with treachery (*John*, V. iv. 37–8). The *T.R.* portrays the French actually planning the coup (II. iii. 237–76); Holinshed, like *John*, reports in Melun's dying speech that Lewis thinks the English barons who support him traitors (193, ii), but the *T.R.* omits this detail in the corresponding passage (II. v. 1–47). Again, John's reactions to the death of Arthur appear to go back to Holinshed.[1]

Secondly, Shakespeare seems to have turned to John Foxe's *Actes and Monuments*.[2] Since *John*, more than any other of his plays, impinges on religious issues, we need not be surprised that Shakespeare glanced at the leading English Church historian, as the following quotations suggest.

1. See notes on IV. ii. 103, 208–14.
2. All our quotations are from the 1583 ed., vol. I.

(*a*) John's submission to the pope.

the king and his heirs should *take againe* these two dominions of the Pope to forme, (Foxe, 253, ii).

Then tooke the King the crowne from hys heade . . . saying in this wise. Here I resigne vp the crowne of the realme of England to the Popes hands Innocent the third (Foxe, 253, ii).

Foxe continues that John was later forced, as the pope's vassal, "to receiue it [the crown] *againe of him, at the handes of an other Cardinall*", and quotes "the letter obligatorie . . . concerning the *yelding vp* of the crowne" (Foxe, 253, ii).

he tooke the crowne from his owne head, and deliuered the same to Pandulph the legat, neither he, nor his heires at anie time thereafter to receiue the same, but at the popes hands (Hol., 177, i).

In the *T.R.* Pandulph orders John to surrender his crown (II. ii. 205), but the surrender is not represented. Later Pandulph is shown returning the crown to John (II. iv. 1 *sqq.*).

In *John*, v. i. 1–4 Shakespeare seems to follow Foxe in (i) giving John a speech as he hands over the crown; (ii) "yielded up"; (iii) "Take again / From this my hand".

(*b*) The death of John's poisoner.—Foxe contains a woodcut of this with the caption "The monke lyeth here burst of the poyson" (p. 256). Compare *John*, v. vi. 29–30: "A monk . . . / Whose bowels suddenly burst out".—The *T.R.* ascribes a similar death to John: "vnhappy Lord, / Whose bowells are deuided in themselues" (II. viii. 111–12). Prof. Wilson, discussing this coincidence, which he thought the only contact with Foxe, suggested that, as both men tasted the poison, "the same effect is naturally transferred".[1] (Query: Is it the same effect?)

(*c*) The Peter of Pomfret material.

Peter . . . an *idle* gadder about . . . a very *idle* vagabund . . . thys *phantasticall* Prophet went all the realme ouer . . . because he was then imprisoned for the matter, the *rumor* was the larger . . . old gossips tales went abroad, new tales were inuented, fables were added to fables, and lies grew vpon lyes . . . [various troubles being only due to Peter's] darke drousy *dreames* (Foxe, 252, ii, 253).

1. See Wilson's note on v. vi. 30.

I find the people strangely *fantasied*;
Possess'd with *rumours*, full of *idle dreams*
(*John*, IV. ii. 144–5)

The *T.R.* parallels Shakespeare's later repetition ["Thou idle dreamer" (*John*, IV. ii. 153)] in an unhistorical meeting between John and Peter on Ascension Day ["*Peter*, vnsay thy foolish doting dreame" (*T.R.*, II. ii. 21)].

Moreover, the *T.R.* (I. xiii. 183–7) follows Holinshed (180, i, ii) in making Peter announce John's deposition to John himself. In *John* (IV. ii. 147–52) as in Foxe (pp. 252–3) Peter publishes this dangerous prophecy before facing John: and only Shakespeare and Foxe mention that the whole realm was disturbed by the consequent rumours.

(*d*) The anti-Roman recriminations in *John*.

charging the suffraganes and Bishops, to *meddle* no more (Foxe, 250, i); what great profite and *reuenewes*, hath proceeded hetherto to them out of the realme of England (Foxe, 250, ii)[1]; the *vsurped power* of the popes bulles (Foxe, 251, ii); the Popish Prelates . . . their crafty *iuggling* by their fained prophet (Foxe, 253, i).

his *usurp'd authority* (*John*, III. i. 86); this *meddling* priest (*ibid.*, l. 89); This *juggling* witchcraft with *revenue* cherish (*ibid.*, l. 95).

This is the standardized anti-papal abuse, but as it is missing in the *T.R.* and in Holinshed, and as Shakespeare has concentrated his echoes into a few lines, just as in (*c*) above, and as these echoes in (*d*) as in (*c*) all come from the same part of Foxe, we ought to take note.

Thirdly, Shakespeare seems to have looked at the *Historia Maior* (1571) of Matthew Paris. Two striking and a number of fugitive resemblances make this more or less certain.

(*a*) The loss of John's carriages in the Wash.

*Mors Regis Iohannis.*
. . . in fluuio qui Wellestrem dicitur, carretas omnes, bigas, & summarios, cum thesauris . . . *inopinato euentu* amisit. Aperta est enim in medijs fluctibus terra, & voragines abyssus, quae absorbuerunt vniversa cum hominibus & equis . . . Rex tamen cum exercitu suo *vix elapsus, nocte sequenti* apud Abbatiam, que Suenesheued dicitur, pernoctauit. Vbi, vt putabatur, de *rebus a fluctibus deuoratis* tantam

---

1. For Foxe's "reuenewes" Holinshed reads "gains" (171, i, 44).

mentis incurrit tristitiam, quod acutis correptus febribus, coepit
grauiter infirmari (pp. 384–5).

> When *in the morning* our troupes did gather head,
> Passing the washes with our carriages,
> The impartiall *tyde* deadly and inexorable,
> Came raging in with billowes threatning death,
> And *swallowed* vp the most of all our men,
> My selfe vpon a Galloway right free, well pacde,
> Out stript the *flouds* that followed waue by waue,
> I so *escapt* to tell this tragick tale   (*T.R.*, II. vi. 46–53)

After a second report of the same disaster, the *T.R.* makes
Lewis exclaim

> Was euer heard such *vnexpected* newes? (II. vii. 42)

When we compare *John*, v. vi. 39–44, v. vii. 61–64 several
points seem noteworthy: (i) Shakespeare's "Devoured by the
... flood" (v. vii. 64) = Matthew's "a fluctibus deuoratis";
the *T.R.* reads "The ... tyde ... swallowed", bringing in
"flouds" further down; (ii) Shakespeare and Matthew make
the disaster itself "unexpected"; in the *T.R.* the *news* of the disaster is "vnexpected"; (iii) Shakespeare's "*hardly* have escap'd" = Matthew's "*vix* elapsus"; the *T.R.* reads simply
"escapt", like Holinshed; (iv) Shakespeare explains twice that
the floods came at *night*, and Matthew seems to imply that; the
*T.R.* gives the time as "morning"; (v) Holinshed and Foxe
report this incident more briefly than Matthew, without any
of the verbal parallels which we have italicized.

    (*b*) The reception of Lewis by the English nobles.

*Barones Angliae in Regem eligunt Ludouicum Regem Galliae.*
CIrca hos dies, cum denique Barones ... tacti sunt dolore cordis
intrinsecus, & quid agerent, ignorabant, maledicentes Regis ver-
sutiam, tergiuersationes & infidelitatem, & dicentes, suspiria ge-
minando: Veh tibi Iohannes Regum vltime, Anglorum Principum
abominatio, Nobilitatis Anglicanae confusio. Heu Anglia iam vas-
tata & amplius vastanda: heu Anglia, Anglia, omnibus bonis
hactenus Princeps prouinciarum, facta es sub tributo ... aduena-
rum imperio subiecta & subpeditata: ... tu Iohannes ... vt alios
tecum traheres in seruitutem, quasi cauda serpentina medietatem
stellarum a firmamento teipsum primo depressisti ... Et sic
Barones lachrymantes & lamentantes, Regem & Papam male-
dixerunt (pp. 372–3).

This passage in Matthew was condensed by Holinshed,[1] who omitted a number of points common to Matthew and Shakespeare (*John*, v. ii. 8–39): (i) Following Matthew's "Barones lachrymantes & lamentantes" Shakespeare makes Salisbury *weep* (v. ii. 45–59), while Holinshed simply said "the Noble men ... sore lamented the state of the realme" (186, ii); (ii) Matthew and Shakespeare apostrophize England ["Heu Anglia . . .", "O nation . . ." (v. ii. 33)], Holinshed cuts out this detail; (iii) the image of the nobles as stars (*John*, v. vii. 74), which has puzzled editors, may well derive from Matthew's allusion to *Revelation*, xii. 4 quoted above: and if so, it is curious that both Matthew and Shakespeare are led to the same image through the idea of servitude. Holinshed dropped the "cauda serpentina" and "stars".

(*c*) Other words and phrases where Shakespeare may be indebted to Matthew will be found in the footnotes.[2]

A fourth source of *John* may be the Latin MS. *Wakefield Chronicle*, from which alone, so far as we now know, Shakespeare could have learned that Queen Eleanor died on the first of April.[3] In the days when Shakespeare was not credited with any first-hand reading of chronicles for *John*, the "first of April" was practically always dismissed as a coincidence. Three reasons dissuade us against this attitude. Firstly, Shakespeare risks, three lines after the "first of April", another statement about dates, which is half-wrong—in the peculiar idiom adopted elsewhere in the play when he feels uncertain about his facts.[4] We suggest, therefore, that in the passage in question Shakespeare was writing from memory. Secondly, there are grounds for thinking that another Latin MS. chronicle was known to Shakespeare—that of Ralph Coggeshall—for the central scene in *John* (IV. i) seems to follow Ralph, who was the principal authority for the story, as Holinshed's margin records.[5] Thirdly, Shakespeare is now generally thought to have consulted MS. sources for *Richard II*—the twin-play to *John*—

1. Hol., 186, ii (cf. Appendix A, p. 159). The parallel scene in *T.R.* omits the lament of the nobles altogether (II. iii).
2. See II. i. 156, 236, 586, III. i. 254, IV. ii. 4, IV. iii. 156, v. i. 44, v. ii. 33, notes.
3. See IV. ii. 120, and W. G. Boswell-Stone, *Shakspere's Holinshed* (1896), p. 61n.
4. See II. ii. 14, III. ii. 7, IV. ii. 123, v. vi. 23, notes.
5. See Hol., 165, i; and Appendix A (2).

which in itself is a sound blow against the old belief that he read as little as possible.

Prof. Wilson, ruling that Shakespeare's "direct access to the chronicles is an illusion", nevertheless cautions us that if he did read the chronicles "the case for his [Shakespeare's] dependence upon it [the *T.R.*] would be weakened".[1] We must pay heed to this warning. Indeed, the possibility that *John* preceded the *T.R.* cannot be ignored, for Prof. Peter Alexander, who revolutionized the interpretation of the early Shakespeare documents twenty and odd years ago, has insisted on many occasions that the *T.R.* follows *John*: and some recent writers have already accepted this view.[2]

Our difficulty in determining the precedence of the two plays arises, in part, from the number of the sources; but the sources also bring us nearer than any other approach to a decision. The authors of both the plays evidently read up their story carefully. *One of them also knew the other's work*—witness the "large body of verbal coincidence or similarity which is one of the most remarkable features of the problem we are studying".[3] Each, in fact, added many details not to be found in the other play.[4]

Having conceded the independent source-reading of both the authors we can still ask how accurately the sources were followed when both plays handle the same material. Does one take over the words of the source and the other paraphrase them?[5] Does one transplant an episode from its correct con-

1. *Op. cit.*, p. xxxii.

2. Notably A. S. Cairncross [*Problem of Hamlet* (1936), pp. 136–43]: cf. v. vii. 84, note. Cf. P. Alexander's *Shakespeare's Life and Art* (1939), p. 85; review in *M.L.R.*, vol. XLIV (1949), p. 263; *Shakespeare Primer* (1951), p. 63; also R. Noble's *Shakespeare's Biblical Knowledge* (1935), p. 113.

3. Wilson, *op. cit.*, p. xxvi.

4. John Elson's 'Studies in the King John Plays' [in *J. Q. Adams Memorial Studies* (1948), ed. J. G. McManaway] drew attention to some *T.R.* sources, among them Foxe's *Actes and Monuments*, which illustrate the *T.R.* author's independent source-reading (Elson did not consider the possibility of the *T.R.* following *John*). Further "source-reading" may be briefly indicated: Melun is a viscount in the *T.R.* (II. iii. 237), as in Hol. (193, ii), but a count in *John* (IV. iii. 15); Pembroke's name "William Marshal" occurs in the *T.R.* (I. i. 1), but not in *John*; Arthur is a youth in the *T.R.*, as in the chronicles, not a boy as in *John*; and so on.

5. See Hol. (*a*), (*c*), (*d*), Foxe (*b*), (*c*), Matthew Paris (*a*), above.

text, the other leave it there?[1] Or do both contain the words of the source, one not using them in the sense of the source?[2] While the second writer could conceivably revert to the source again and again, one is inclined to award the precedence to the accurate man. And, though the *T.R.* includes facts not given in *John*, Shakespeare is the accurate man in all the types of divergence that we have outlined. Upholders of the traditional theory about the relations of the two plays will have to ponder this.

Comparison with the chronicles provides us with no final answer. To penetrate to the heart of the problem we must consider dates. If the majority opinion which assigns *John* to the years 1595/6 be unassailable, little will be gained from a discussion that ignores chronology, since the *T.R.* was printed in 1591. But that part of the "Shakespeare chronology" which supports this majority opinion has been under fire of late from a number of competent authorities. Newly discovered facts, moreover, suggest that, quite apart from the *T.R.*, *John* must probably be dated back to the winter of 1590/1. Our section on Date being, however, the proper place for the discussion of this and the other arguments which can alone unravel the difficult relations of the two plays, we must now momentarily drop the subject. Nevertheless it must be said here that we finally side with Prof. Alexander against the commoner view that the *T.R.* came before *John*: a decision which colours much of our comment in the ensuing pages.

If *John* precedes the *T.R.*, we must next account for the sources of those facts formerly said to be lifted straight out of the "source-play". With the four chronicle sources for which a claim was made above, only details omitted from the *T.R.* were grist to our mill: and only Holinshed and Matthew Paris passed muster with tolerable certainty. As soon as we brush aside the *T.R.*, however, there emerges a new picture. Holinshed, as we expect, turns out to be the primary source. Shakespeare studied his life of John in minute detail, also reading up Richard I and Henry III.[3]

1. See Hol. (*f*), Foxe (*b*), Matthew Paris (*a*), above.
2. See Hol. (*b*), Matthew Paris (*a*), above.
3. The first and last extracts from Holinshed in Appendix A (1) make this plain.

The case for Foxe as a source becomes watertight, which it was not before. For instance, Shakespeare's incorrect form of the name "Swineshead Abbey" follows Foxe's "Swinsted" (Foxe, p. 256; *John*, v. iii. 8 etc.), for Holinshed reads "Swineshead" (p. 194, ii) and Matthew Paris "Suenesheued" (p. 385). Pandulph's mission to John (*John*, III. i. 62–72), again, follows Foxe more closely than Holinshed:

[The pope] sent to ye king two Legates (the one called Pandulph, and the other Durant) to warne him *in the popes name* that he should cease his doinges to *holy church*, and amend the wrong he had done to the Archb. of Cant. . . . These two Legates comming into England, resorted to ye king to Northhampton, where he held his Parliament, & *saluting him*, sayd: *they came from the Pope of Rome*, to reforme ye peace of *holy church*. And first sayd they we monish you in the popes behalfe, that ye make full restitution of the goods & of the land that ye haue rauished *holy church* of: *and that ye receiue Stephen the Archbi. of Cant. into his dignity.* . . . (Foxe, 252, i).

the pope sent two legats into England, the one named Pandulph a lawier, and the other Durant a templer, who comming vnto king Iohn, exhorted him with manie terrible words to leaue his stubborne disobedience to the church, and to reforme his misdooings. The king for his part quietlie heard them . . . when they perceiued that they could not haue their purpose . . . the legats departed, leauing him accursed, and the land interdicted (Hol., 175, i).

Here, as in quotation (*a*) from Foxe above (p. xiv), Foxe and Shakespeare have direct speech as opposed to Holinshed's indirect. Shakespeare also follows Foxe in making John's hostility to Stephen Langton the main business of Pandulph's mission.

Beside Holinshed, Foxe, Matthew Paris, and perhaps the MS. *Wakefield Chronicle* and *Coggeshall Chronicle*, Shakespeare must also have been familiar with one of the Cœur-de-lion romances. We think that the medieval poem printed by Wynkyn de Worde as *Kynge Rycharde Cuer du Lyon* may be a "source", though Richard was so popular a national hero that obviously much literature about him may be lost.[1] Wynkyn's romance, at any rate, must serve as our authority for a number of points in *John* for the time being.

---

1. We use Wynkyn's ed. of 1528 throughout. A lost "boke intituled *kynge Rychard Cur De Lyon*" was entered in the S.R. in 1568–9 (Arber, I, 389).

(a) The identification of Leopold, Archduke of Austria, with Widomar, Viscount of Limoges.—Richard I was killed while besieging Limoges,[1] shortly after building "Chateau Galiard" (Hol., 155, ii), the erection of the castle being otherwise unconnected with his death. In a complete hotch-potch of the facts, the romance (i) supplants Limoges by Austria, (ii) locates the scene at "castell gaylarde":

> And syth he came I vnderstonde
> The waye towarde englonde
> And thorugh treason was shotte alas
> At castell gaylarde there he was
> The duke of estryche in the castell
> with his hoost was dyght full well
> Rycharde thought there to abyde (sig. Q₄)

As in the romance Richard's two enemies in *John* are merged into one, with obvious dramatic advantages. Not through ignorance, but following an established tradition. Characteristically, Shakespeare has not silently *omitted* the name Limoges, but gives the one person both names, an equivocating method of compression used frequently in our play.[2]

(b) The characters of Richard's two principal enemies, Philip Augustus and Austria.—In *John* cowardice is the keynote of Austria, treachery that of King Philip, and the romance emphasizes these qualities above all others again and again. We have only room for two typical quotations:

> (i) Rycharde wende Phylyp had fought
> And he and his men dyde nought
> But made mery all that nyght
> And were traytours in that fyght
> For he loued no crownes to crake
> But to do treason and tresour take (sig. Mᵛ)

> (ii) The duke of estryche hyed faste
> Awaye with his meyne in haste
> And with hym the duke of burgoyne
> The folke of fraunce & the erle of coloyne

---

1. George H. Needler [*Richard Cœur de Lion in Literature* (1890), pp. 56–7] noted that the substitution of Austria for Limoges in Wynkyn's book was the source of their identification in the *T.R.* Cf. P. Simpson in *N. & Q.*, 12 Nov. 1898.
2. See p. xvii, n. 4.

> Kynge Rycharde let breke his baner
> And caste it into the ryuer
> And cryed on hym with voyce stepe
> Home shrewed cowarde and go slepe (sig. N$_6$$^v$)

We gather from (ii) the reasons for Austria's unhistorical association with the French (*John*, II. i. 7); Faulconbridge's treatment of the cowardly duke (*John*, II. i. 135–40, III. i. 57, etc.) reproducing exactly the tone of his father.

(*c*) The invincibility of the Bastard.—

> That misbegotten divel, Faulconbridge,
> In spite of spite, alone upholds the day
>            (*John*, v. iv. 4–5)

It transpires that the superman "devil" appellation, recurring in *John*, II. i. 135, IV. iii. 95, IV. iii. 100 (Faulconbridge taking pride in the name) is part of the Cœur-de-lion heritage:

> The sarasynes as I you tell
> Sayd he was the deuyll of hell (sig. G$_7$$^v$)

> Eueryche sate styll and plucked other
> And sayd this is the deuylles brother (sig. K$_2$)

> The sarasynes sayd than
> He was a deuyll and no man (sig. O$_2$$^v$)

> The englysshe deuyll I come is
> And but we flee out of his waye
> An euyll deth shall we dye to daye (sig. P$_7$)

These are by no means the only instances where Richard is paid the compliment in the romance.

There remain many puzzles in *John* where Shakespeare falls in line with facts or traditions, his authority being disputable. The Cœur-de-lion romance gives help with the most important one.

(*a*) The Faulconbridge story.—Holinshed mentions Cœur-de-lion's bastard son:

Philip bastard sonne to king Richard, to whome his father had giuen the castell and honor of Coinacke, killed the vicount of Limoges, in reuenge of his fathers death (160, ii).

But whence the name Faulconbridge?—An anonymous play,

*Looke About You* (1600), probably written after *John*,[1] exhibits a Sir Richard Faulconbridge (not Sir *Robert* as in *John*) whose wife Prince Richard attempts to seduce. This play must be intimately connected with the Robin Hood plays by Munday and Chettle, written in 1598, and *The Funeral of Richard Coeur-de-lion*, a lost play which followed hard upon the latter,[2] being like them the property of the Admiral's company. If Chambers's date for *Looke About You*, viz. 1599, may be accepted, the play could be a kind of sequel to the two about Robin Hood, for the chief characters—Queen Eleanor, Prince Richard, Prince John, Robin Hood, Gloucester, and other nobles—are repeated in both stories. Richard's wooing of Lady Faulconbridge, moreover, not only resembles John's wooing of the fair Matilda: the *Looke About You* dramatist has made Lady Faulconbridge the (unhistorical) sister of Gloucester—Gloucester being the father of Matilda in the Robin Hood plays—so that the whole Faulconbridge set-up in *Looke About You* seems imitative and unauthentic.

In a second late publication, *The Famous History of George, Lord Fauconbridge Bastard Son to Richard Cordelion* (1616, 1635[3]), a prose pamphlet, Richard begets a son, George, on Austria's daughter, Claribel. The princess's infatuation with Richard goes back to pre-Shakespearean books, such as Warner's *Albions England* (1589), the germ of the idea existing already in the Wynkyn romance[4]: which suggests that the prose pamphlet *combines* two stories, (i) about Richard and the Austrian princess, (ii) about Richard and Lady Faulconbridge. Lord George's favourite garment, the lion-skin of his father, may be the fiction of Shakespeare,[5] like the pamphlet's other fugitive coincidences with *John*. The freedom the pamphleteer allowed himself with names suggests that facts were not his obsession.

But the names of the different versions are a stumbling-block

---

1. E. K. Chambers, *The Elizabethan Stage*, IV, 28.

2. Chambers, *op. cit.*, III, 446–7; W. W. Greg, *Henslowe's Diary*, II (1908), 190, 193.

3. We have only seen the 1635 ed., from which we quote. The copy was entered in 1614 by John Beale (Arber, III, 558), who was buying up the copies of the recently deceased stationer Barley.

4. *Albions England*, sig. P₃; Wynkyn's *Cuer de Lyon*, sig. C₃ᵛ, etc.

5. "Never wearing any other Garment, but that *Lyons skin*, by which his Kingly Father challenged his *Lyon-like* Title" (1635 title-page).

too. Cœur-de-lion's mistresses, christened "Margare" in Wynkyn's romance (sig. C₂ᵛ), "Ladie *Margaret*" (Faulconbridge)
in the *T.R.* (I. i. 222), "Marian" ( Faulconbridge) in *Looke
About You* (sig. B₂ᵛ), may be throwbacks, in the extant treatments, to a lost original.

*Looke About You* and *The Famous History* must be earlier than
1600, 1614 respectively, but the Faulconbridge material in
them seems spurious, not going back beyond Shakespeare.
And that Shakespeare was in fact the inventor of it all the
Faulconbridge elements in his other plays may bear out. For
Shakespeare frequently resorted to the name, and this may
imply some personal relationship. Three "second period"
plays beside *John* use it significantly.[1] In his most topical
comedy, *Love's Labour's Lost*, two allusions to the house of Faulconbridge (II. i. 42, 203), have not yet been pounced upon by
the commentators. In the *Merchant of Venice* the "Baron Faulconbridge" described as the typical Englishman (I. ii. 70–81)
is a "proper" man, but unlanguaged, which reminds one of
the Bastard. In *Henry IV*, Part II, a Lord Faulconbridge was
excised from the Northumberland circle, to which Shakespeare's contemporary Faulconbridge family belonged[2]: and
it is tantalizing that in the same quarto text a Sir John Russell,
bearing the surname of one of Shakespeare's best friends, was
likewise dropped.[3]

Our conjectural solution is that Shakespeare (i) invented
the Faulconbridge story, possibly with some topical innuendo,
(ii) merged the invented bastard Faulconbridge with Holinshed's Philip. If Shakespeare had connections in the north in
the early 1590's, as Dr Hotson has shown to be likely,[4] and
as the theory that he was one of Strange's men confirms,[5] a
Faulconbridge (Belasyse)–Shakespeare contact grows less unlikely, and similarly the possibility that northern MS. chro-

---

1. The historical use of the name does not concern us here, as in *1 H 6*, IV. vii
67, *3 H 6*, I. i. 239.

2. *2 H 4*, I. iii (Q1). The Faulconbridge title came to England with Belasius,
Lord Faulconbridge, in 1066. In Shakespeare's day the Belasyse family of Yorks.
(for which the title of Earl Fauconberg was revived in the 17th century) would be
*the* Faulconbridges. Their circle included the Northumberlands, Rutlands, Lord
Burghley, the archbishop of York (as their and their relatives' wills show).

3. *2 H 4*, II. ii; cf. L. Hotson's *I, William Shakespeare* (1937).

4. *Shakespeare's Sonnets Dated* (1949), p. 127 ff.          5. See pp. xlix–liii.

nicles were sources of *John*. Indeed, stray facts in *John* not available in published sources in 1590 may well go back to the family chronicle of a northern house. Perhaps Shakespeare's Philip Faulconbridge was based (iii) on the historical Philip de Falconbridge, Archdeacon of Huntingdon *anno* 1222,[1] introduced to Shakespeare by such a source: for the historical Philip was successor to William Cornehill, one of King John's right-hand men, and may therefore have been a receiver of Church goods seized by John like William Cornehill,[2] and like his namesake the Bastard in our play (III. ii. 17–23, IV. ii. 141–2).

(*b*) "Cardinal" Pandulph.—Like John Bale in his *King Iohan* and other early writers about John's reign, Shakespeare elevates the papal legate Pandulph to a cardinalate. The historians tripped up first, confusing our Pandulph with Pandulf Masca (created a cardinal in the 1180's): it therefore seems likely that Shakespeare, falling in with an established tradition, knew at least one more "source". Foxe alone among the sources so far identified has one hint to the same effect, but probably too casual to have caused Shakespeare's change. He describes John's surrender of the crown to Pandulph, and John's acceptance of it again later "at the handes of an other Cardinall" (253, ii).

Over and above actual "source-books", plays on familiar subjects also follow the floating knowledge of the age, which may have a bearing on interpretation. Well-known historical facts do not have to be led up to or motivated as conscientiously as unknown ones, the audience being already conditioned to accept them.

That the reign of John was an open book to Shakespeare's first audience there can be no doubt. Ever since Bale's *King Iohan*, a morality written *c.* 1540, which pointed the parallel between the reigns of John and Henry VIII, religious controversialists had publicized John's life. The Protestants praised him as the first English king who tried to throw off the yoke of

---

1. See Browne Willis: *Survey of the Cathedrals of York, Durham, etc.* (1727 etc.), III, 105.
2. See Foxe's *Actes and Monuments* (ed. 1596), p. 227.

Rome, blackened the tale of his perfidious poisoning, and blamed earlier historians for blackening John[1]; the Catholics made much of John's surrender of the crown to the pope, claiming that Henry VIII was only a vassal as a consequence, and his Reformation civil as well as ecclesiastical rebellion. These issues were so dear to Shakespeare's contemporaries that non-specialist books often enter the fray at unexpected moments. Quasi-controversial works such as William Allen's *Admonition to the Nobility and People of England* (1588),[2] Sir Thomas Smith's *Common-Welth of England* (1589),[3] and innumerable others of equal fame, tacitly assume that the reader knows all about John: recurring digressions about him and his problems in, for instance, William Lambarde's *Perambulation of Kent* (1576),[4] might, however, seem less normal than they happen to have been, unless we see John through Elizabethan eyes.

The controversialist interest in John was reinforced, as Prof. Lily Campbell has recently shown, by the addition of the "Homilie against Disobedience and Wylfull Rebellion" to the Elizabethan *Book of Homilies* in 1571.[5] Here the enormity of John's nobles' crime, who aided the invader Lewis, was outlined and chastised at great length in the sixth part. Periodic reading of these homilies was compulsory in all churches.

During the "Armada period" (c. 1583–96), moreover, a new type of patriotic pamphleteering sprang into existence, wherein Englishmen were exhorted to defend their country, should the need arise, by means of plentiful citations of famous English exploits of the past. The sudden cult of the chronicle play in the 1590's was thus prepared for by a revival of interest in wars of long ago, and we deduce that the sermons and more ephemeral literature teaching history left an impression. Indeed, the unheralded historical allusion, so common in these pamphlets, makes this quite plain:

1. "Verelie, whosoeuer shall consider the course of the historie written of this prince, he shall find, t lat he hath beene little beholden to the writers of that time in which he liued: for scarselie can they afoord him a good word... The occasion whereof (as some thinke) was, for that he was no great freend to the clergie" (Hol., 196, i).
2. Sigs. A₈ᵛ, C₇.          3. Sig. Cᵛ.
4. See pp. 132–5, 217, 328, etc.
5. *Shakespeare's "Histories"* (1947), p. 143.

Let vs deale but with our selues, and with our owne feeling, knowledge and memorie. The accursing of King *Iohn*: the receyuing him
vassaill: the making his Realme subiect and feudatorie to the Pope:
the arming his Subiects against him: the poysoning of him at
length: the giuing the Land to the French Kinges sonne: the in-
uading thereof by the *Dolphin* of *Fraunce*: his so long possessing a
great part of it: the rebellion of the Barons to take the French mens
part: all the mischeefes that fell in all this whyle, were they not the
good workes of Popes and Papistes?[1]

It has been fashionable of late to condemn the motivation of
the last third of *John*.[2] Yet just the last third deals with the
events peculiarly fascinating for Elizabethans: the rebellion of
the nobles, John's surrender of the crown, the poisoning of
John. It is no accident that just these events are so often the
target of modern criticism. But perhaps Shakespeare expected
his first audience to look forward to them avidly, to accept
them unhesitatingly.

The story of John was familiar as a parallel to Elizabeth's.
Perhaps Shakespeare chose it on that account to mirror certain problems of the queen which he forced into the super-
structure of historical truth. For the Armada period itself is
another source of *John*. In 1874 this was strongly urged by
Richard Simpson, some of whose arguments we must recapitulate.[3] Eleanor, for instance, tells John that he holds the throne
through "strong possession", not through right (1. i. 40). While
the legitimacy of Elizabeth's title to the succession was in hot
debate, because the pope did not recognize it, John's "usurpation" is Shakespeare's fiction, for his "right" is not seriously
questioned in the chronicles. Again, Shakespeare seems to
think of Tudor rather than Plantagenet history when he mentions a will (II. i. 192–4) that bars Arthur's right to the throne.
Henry VIII left a will barring the right of Mary Queen of
Scots to the throne of England (the argument is that John =

1. A(nthony) M(unday)'s *Watch-Woord to Englande* (1584), sigs. L₄, L₄ᵛ.
2. "the hero, without rhyme or reason, dies . . . murdered by an anonymous
monk, who . . . is not shown to have any motive whatever for his deed" (Edward
Rose, quoted approvingly by Wilson, p. xxi); "Shakespeare huddles together
and fails to motivate properly the events of the last third of his play" [Tillyard:
*Shakespeare's History Plays* (1944), p. 215].
3. Cf. 'The Politics of Shakspere's Historical Plays' (in the *Transactions* of the
New Shakspere Society, 1874).

Elizabeth, Arthur = Mary). Another of Simpson's points was that Lewis's treachery to the English nobles (v. iv. 10 ff.) parallels that contemplated by Medina Sidonia, commander of the Spanish Armada, to the English Catholics who were ready to aid him against the Queen.[1] But, as the chronicles already provided the last two "parallels", we must not dwell unduly upon them, except to observe that elements in John's real story may have been emphasized in our play in order to underline the contemporary resemblances.

Simpson also followed up a suggestion of Warburton that John's order to Hubert to murder Arthur, and his violent recriminations when he thinks his rival dead (III. ii. 29–79, IV. ii. 208–48), have, on the one hand, no direct source in the chronicles, but on the other a curious likeness to Elizabeth's treatment of Secretary Davison. Elizabeth asked Davison to have Mary Queen of Scots murdered, so the rumour went, to save political unpleasantness. Entrusted at last with a warrant for the execution of Mary, Davison was made the queen's scapegoat when it was found that Mary's death afforded Elizabeth's enemies first-rate opportunities for propaganda. He was put on trial and fined a very large sum for his "fault"—modern historians agreeing that, in fact, he only carried out his duties. Though Shakespeare and Davison may well have known each other as fellow-members of the Essex-circle, and though Hubert's fate in *John* does resemble Davison's, many another cat's-paw has fared similarly and therefore it is now usual to belittle the "Davison parallel".

But the question of topicality is still not closed. Prof. L. Campbell has discovered that the right of Mary to the English crown was actually argued in at least two books in terms of Arthur's right to John's crown.[2] Whether Shakespeare knew

1. The significance of the Melun parallel only dawns on us as we recognize that even Roman Catholics believed that the Spaniards intended treachery [v. W. W., *Important Considerations* (1601), sig. E]. The treachery of foreign Roman Catholics had, curiously, been argued a little before Shakespeare through the very story of Melun: "Wil *Israell* trust to a reed? can Papists imagine that strangers will doe them good? . . . do they remember, or haue they forgotten, or haue they not reade county *Melunes* most memorable counsel to our English nobles?" [J. Prime, *Sermon* (1585), sig. B₆ᵛ]. Prime subjoined the whole of Melun's death-speech—as in *John*, v. iv—from M. Paris.

2. *Op. cit.*, p. 142. The two books were by John Leslie, Bishop of Ross. There were in fact more than two books: Leslie says that the Mary-Arthur parallel was

these books or not, the comparison may have reached him orally, and has importance. Again, the Davison-Hubert correspondences were even more pointed than has yet been shown. Shakespeare draws attention to the king's "hand and seal" (IV. ii. 215–17) which authorized the murder of Arthur: yet the chronicles do not mention them, nor does Shakespeare in any murder scene in his other plays drag in "hand and seal". The trial of Davison, however, revolved round the fact that Elizabeth *signed* the death-warrant, but that he then prematurely *sealed* it and sent it to Fotheringhay. John's very language, reproaching Hubert that he should have demanded "*express* words" (IV. ii. 234) when he "spake *darkly*" (IV. ii. 232), echoes the main issue of the Davison trial: "That she [the Queen] had *darkely* signified, but not *expressely* commanded" the sealing.[1]

Shakespeare's manipulation of the historical facts brings out the similarities of the reigns of John and Elizabeth excitingly, almost dangerously. An English sovereign, said to be a usurper (I. i. 40), and perhaps a bastard (II. i. 130), defies the pope (III. i. 73), becomes "supreme head" (III. i. 81), is excommunicated (III. i. 99), imprisons his rival (IV. i), who was barred from the crown by a will (II. i. 192); the pope promises his murderer canonization (III. i. 103), invites another king to invade England (III. i. 181), the English sovereign darkly urges the murder of the rival "pretender" (III. ii), then needs a scapegoat (IV. ii. 208), a foreign invasion is attempted (IV. ii. 110), the invaders intending to kill the Englishmen who help them (V. iv. 10), their navy is providentially wrecked off the English coast (V. v. 12), English unity being finally achieved through the failure of the invasion (V. vii. 115):—frequent "Armada idiom" hammering home the topicality of the play.[2] That Shakespeare found *some* of these facts in the chronicles does not detract from the overwhelming effect of the parallel, which is entirely due to the selection of incidents relevant to a particular purpose.

Not only does Shakespeare carefully guide his story towards the "disconnected" incidents of Act V, ineffective in the eyes

---

not his invention, but that of his "Aduersaries" [*Treatise Touching the Right* (1585), sig. D₇].

1. Camden's *Annales*, tr. Darcie (1625), p. 211.
2. See p. xlvi, n. 2.

of some modern critics, but possibly inevitable in those of his first audience: he also makes a sincere attempt to interpret the major facts as he found them as regards character. As in most of Shakespeare's plays, the hero seems to step straight out of the source (lesser characters are slightly altered to suit the more subtle dramatic plot). Certain repetitions in Holinshed must have suggested John's significant moodiness to Shakespeare, indeed "la psychose périodique" which Charles Petit-Dutaillis diagnosed in the historical king.[1] And beside many remarks about John's sudden fury, Holinshed also emphasized the king's power of self-restraint when intent on deception, the two polarities of his personality:

the king in a great rage sware, that . . . he would put out their eies, and slit their noses (172, i).

These words being signified vnto the king, set him in such an heat . . . (172, ii).

they were much deceiued, for the king hauing condescended to make such grant of liberties, farre contrarie to his mind, was right sorowfull in his heart . . . he whetted his teeth, he did bite now on one staffe, and now on an other . . . with such disordered behauiour and furious gestures (186, ii).

[Pandulph and Durant] exhorted him with manie terrible words to leaue his stubborne disobedience. . . . The king for his part quietlie heard them . . . (175, i).

Shakespeare adapts history by portraying in John's early career a suave man of the world, in the later acts expressing the king's consciousness of his helplessness through his moody outbursts: Act III being the transition. John's degeneration is reinforced by means of the symbol of military speed, with which he surprised the French,[2] only to be taken unawares by them himself in Act IV[3]; Holinshed, again, having signalized the extraordinary dualism of John's capacity for expedition and sluggishness:[4]

1. *Le Roi Jean et Shakespeare* (1944), chap. 1.
2. II. i. 79, III. iii. 10–14.
3. IV. ii. 110–16.
4. Holinshed often mentions John's *haste*: "hasting towards Ireland" (174, i), "he brake foorth of Winchester, as it had beene an hideous tempest of weather" (193, ii), "the king hasted forward till he came to Wellestreme" (194, i), etc.

[King John] in all possible hast speedeth him foorth . . . he was vpon his enimies necks yer they could vnderstand any thing of his comming . . . (164, ii).

All this while king Iohn did lie at Rouen . . . and would saie often-times to such as stood about him; What else dooth my coosen the French K. now, than steale those things from me, which hereafter I shall indeuour my selfe to cause him to restore with interest? (166, ii).

Recreating the essential John, Shakespeare has, however, violated facts again and again, subordinating dates and like details to the truth of character, the credibility of climaxes. *John* has been called his most unhistorical play. Act iv, Sc. ii alone fakes the sequence of events more cleverly than perhaps any other part of the canon. John's new coronation (l. 1) and the rumoured death of Arthur (l. 85) took place in 1202; the landing of the French (l. 110) in 1216; the death of Eleanor (l. 120) in 1204; the death of Constance (l. 122) in 1201; the Peter of Pomfret episode (l. 131) belonging to the year 1213; the five moons (l. 182) to 1200: practically the whole span of John's reign being crammed into one scene and made to seem simultaneous, for the dramatic advantage of heaping up John's troubles and omens of misfortune.[1]

Compression must obviously be the historical dramatist's first thought, and there is a great deal of it in *John*. But to say that the story falls apart and dies in the author's hands because he attempted to concentrate too many unrelated events into five acts[2] is to ignore Acts i and ii, where Shakespeare has liberally invented and added without worrying about retailing facts. Act i, indeed, a prelude to the main theme, is entirely

---

1. P. A. Daniel's "time-scheme" for *John* (in the *Transactions* of the New Shakspere Society, 1877-9, pp. 257-64) shows how the whole reign has been made to seem a matter of a few months, the action requiring only seven separate days (with intervals). Day 1 is Act i, day 2 is Act ii—Act iii, Sc. ii, day 3 is Act iii, Sc. iii, day 4 is Act iv, day 5 is Act v, Sc. i, day 6 is Act v, Sc. ii-v, day 7 is Act v, Sc. vi-vii.—As in *Oth.*, *Troil.*, etc., Shakespeare probably intended a "double time-scheme", viz. John should seem to age, to lose physical vigour, in the two last acts—despite the "few months" duration, the purpose of which was simply to interlock causes and effects.

2. E. K. Chambers called *John* "incoherent patchwork" [*Shakespeare: A Survey* (1925), p. 105]; Brander Matthews said "the action is wandering and uncertain" [*Shakespeare as a Playwright* (1913), p. 97]. Equally typical condemnations are quoted on p. xxvii, n. 2, and p. lxvi.

original so far as we can tell. John judges the legality of a "usurper", the Bastard, who took possession of his younger and physically weaker relative's inheritance. A will is appealed to (I. i. 109) and rejected (I. i. 116, 132), anticipating the main story's will (II. i. 191-4), the Faulconbridge family quarrel heralding that of the Plantagenets. Here Shakespeare has amplified history for the sake of thematic iteration. Similarly, purely artistic reasons dictated the compression of source-book facts in the later acts, for, loosely as the later episodes may seem to cohere at first glance, a moment's reflection about the meaning of the play assures us that structural compactness might have been Shakespeare's aim. The fourth section of our Introduction resumes this topic, and here it remains only to indicate how the plot has been tightened. Arthur's plight, for instance, becomes more clear when he accepts help from Limoges–Austria, the two traditional enemies (compressed into one) of his "great forerunner" (II. i. 2).—Angiers, where Eleanor was almost taken by Arthur's men, and Arthur later captured, is identified with Mirabeau,[1] the unhistorical location symbolizing the whole of the disputed Angevin inheritance.—Cœur-de-lion's bastard son Philip may be partially identified with Faukes de Breauté, the soldier of fortune, also a bastard, to whom John entrusted the leading of an army towards the end of his life[2]; and Shakespeare's Bastard Faulconbridge must almost certainly be a distillation from half a dozen sources, inorganically related in so far as some are famous bastards, or part of a topical story, or otherwise associable as "Faulconbridges"[3]—which makes clear the meticulous instincts behind the play, ranging beyond history in pursuit of satisfactory tone and balance.

To sum up: Shakespeare sifted so many sources in order to find incidents germane to his purpose. His drama was made to

---

1. See Hol., 164, ii.     2. Cf. *John*, v. ii. 77 and Hol., 189, ii.

3. See pp. xxii, lii. W. G. Boswell-Stone [*Shakespere's Holinshed* (1896), p. 48, etc.] cited various views about the origins of Faulconbridge—who may be modelled on Faukes; on the "Stern Faulconbridge" of *3 H 6*, I. i. 239, another famous bastard known to Shakespeare; and perhaps on Dunois (whose story Shakespeare read while writing *1 H 6*), who declared that his "noble corage" assured him he was the bastard of Orleans, and that he scorned to be "the lawful sonne of that coward cuckolde Cauny" despite the financial loss to him. Cf. also G. Kopplow, *Shakespeares "King John" und seine Quelle* (1900), p. 14.

follow the *outlines* of a familiar story, but he nevertheless searched painstakingly for dramatic *details* to build up his idea of
John—because contemporary ignorance allowed him freedom
of detail. Fugitive facts are thrown at the audience to give the
effect of authenticity, while at the same time larger truths are
outraged. The ultimate purpose was a "truthful" interpretation of behaviour in peculiar circumstances according to Elizabethan lights—consequently the truths of time and place and
historical identity were sacrificed to the superior needs of the
total impression.

## 2. THE TEXT

*The Life and Death of King John* was first published in the
Folio of 1623, at the head of the Histories. The copy for the
text was once thought to be a prompt-book,[1] but Prof. J. D.
Wilson detected certain non-theatrical features,[2] and Sir
Walter Greg, following up, finally proposed foul paper prove-
nance,[3] a theory which at present holds the field.

Greg's attitude was determined by "inconsistency in the
directions and speech prefixes—which McKerrow overlooked".[4] Stage directions that follow the action they are supposed
to herald indicate a non-theatrical origin:

> The interruption of their churlish drums
> Cuts off more circumstance, they are at hand,
> > *Drum beats.* (F1, II. i. 76–7)

Because these late directions occur only in the first half of *John*
(for others see I. i. 49, I. i. 220) Dr Alice Walker has suggested
that Acts I–III may have been printed from foul papers and
Acts IV–V from prompt-copy.[5] Greg disagreed with Dr Walker,
however, declaring that a composite MS. would be very unusual.[6]

1. Cf. E. K. Chambers, *William Shakespeare* (1930), I, 143, *sqq.*
2. Cf. his C.U.P. *John*, pp. 92–4.
3. *The Editorial Problem in Shakespeare* (1951), pp. 142–3.
4. *Op. cit.*, p. 142; cf. R. McKerrow: 'A Suggestion Regarding Shakespeare's
Manuscripts' [*R.E.S.* (1935), p. 463].
5. Greg, *op. cit.*, p. 143n.
6. Some editors thought that at III. i. 81, v. vii. 60 "God" was altered to
"heaven" in conformity with the Act of Abuses, 1606. But the F1 editor probably

Inconsistency in the speech headings which, according to McKerrow,[1] was foul paper rather than prompt-book practice, frequently confronts us in *John*. Queen Eleanor appears as *Elea.* (i. i. 5), *Ele.* (i. i. 31), *Eli.* (i. i. 40), *Queen* (ii. i. 120), *Qu. Mo.* (ii. i. 166), *Old Qu.* (ii. i. 468); the French king is *King* until John appears, then becomes *France* (ii. i. 37, 89); the Citizen of Angiers is *Cit.* from ii. i. 201 to ii. i. 281, and from ii. i. 325 is *Hubert*, and so on.

Act ii, more inconsistent in its speech headings than the rest of the play, also contains

some confusion in the use of the names in the text, which must be due to the author: the French king, whose name is Philip, sometimes appears as Lewis by confusion with the Dauphin. Modern editors have generally corrected this, and so doubtless would a playhouse scribe have done had he noticed it.[2]

If it is possible, as we think, to rationalize these confusions, the case for foul papers becomes even stronger.

(*a*) The first line of Act ii provides the first probable "speech heading confusion". Although the Folio gives the speech to Lewis, line 7 can hardly be ascribed to anyone but the French king, as editors have realized.

(*b*) ii. i. 149–51 brings further complications. The Folio reads:

> King *Lewis*, determine what we shall doe strait.
> *Lew.* Women & fooles, breake off your conference.
> King *Iohn*, this is the very summe of all:

Does Austria here appeal to the king *and* Lewis, or does Shakespeare confuse Lewis and Philip?[3] If the former, why does the king not answer?

(*c*) In ii. i. 368, the speech heading *Fra.* has been generally rejected in favour of Hubert, the citizen, the speech being obviously his.

---

reformed profanity as well as the prompter (Greg, *op. cit.*, p. 155n.), as various non-theatrical F1 texts show (cf. *Oth.*, ii. iii. 106, *1 H 4*, ii. iv. 213, 523 etc.).

   1. *Op. cit.*    2. Greg, *loc. cit.*

   3. It is probably irrelevant to observe that Holinshed mistakenly names the king "Lewis" in one passage (Hol., 161, i).

Either through his absence where he should be present, or *vice versa*, France is the common factor in these three cruxes. Until John's entry (II. i. 84) the speeches of France are consistently headed *King*: thereafter the form *France* replaces *King*. This *France* may well derive from Shakespeare himself. If, however, we assume that *King* was used throughout the act in the author's copy, and that an editor or compositor, attempting to clarify, reheaded the king's speeches *France* after John's entry, the three cruxes easily explain themselves. The coincidence of *King* and a proper name may have caused (*a*) and (*b*). France and Austria enter "at several doors" at the opening of Act II: Lewis could say II. i. 1, as the Folio directs, walking towards Austria and bringing him back to France. We suggest that a speech heading *King* was dropped before l. 2 because it seemed to be part of the text and was (i) hypermetrical, (ii) apparently nonsensical, i.e. Arthur is not a king. A similar confusion may be postulated for II. i. 149–51, where the speech heading *King* was made part of the text (l. 149), and again dropped (l. 151). The MS. reading may be reconstructed thus:

> King. Lewis, determine what we shall doe strait.
> Lew. Women & fooles, breake off your conference.
> King. King Iohn, this is the very summe of all: (II. i. 149–51)

If the stops had faded, the metre of l. 149 would be "improved" by the tenth syllable ("Lewis" was monosyllabic). In l. 151 dittography may have been diagnosed.[1]

This explanation is less far-fetched than appears at first sight. We refer to the last scene of the Folio *Henry V*, where two kings are on-stage as in *John*: sometimes the forms *France* and *England* are used, but plain *King* (for King Henry) occurs nine times without causing trouble. Again, compare the famous line

1. We have followed Capell's note on II. i. 149–51: "The father, indeed, may very reasonably make his son the declarer of a thing praeconcerted . . . it shews the son's consequence, and weight with the father; and . . . rescues him from the state of a cypher in a scene of great length. . . [Capell is led to the same conclusion by the "free manner of opening" of l. 150] which has a juvenile air with it: The correction . . . [is] a slight one; for 'tis founded on the only supposal that the copy had "King" for French King, without scoring or stopping it, and that the printer was too faithful." Capell read as we do, but kept ll. 150–4 as one speech (Lewis's). But the *I* claiming *In right of Arthur* (l. 153) can only be Philip, and confusions (*a*) and (*c*) also weigh against Capell's reading of II. i. 151.

*Nath.* Of persing a Hogshead (*LLL.*, Q1, iv. ii. 89)

which, as many editors agree, corruptly represents

Holof. Persing a Hogshead

Shakespeare, it seems, did not always use Italian script for speech headings, nor carefully distinguish speech headings and text.

Our contention that *King* was a speech heading throughout Act II gains strength from crux (*c*). *Hu*[*bert*] misread as *Fra.* looks improbable: *Hu* misread *Ki*[*n.*], or Hu. as Ki[n.] (Secretary hand)—normalized to *Fra.*—would be a simple error. Misreading of this kind, rather than a compositor's muddle-headedness, seems a safe guess where three different types of confusion can be linked by a common thread.[1]

Conjecture though it be, we depart from the *textus receptus* six times on the strength of our hypothesis. *K. Phi.* gives way to Folio *Lewis* at II. i. 1, 18, 150; new speech headings are allotted to *K. Phi.* at II. i. 2, 149, 151. Moreover, II. i. 368 *Fra.*, if we are right, no longer stands alone as a freak error. These corruptions, cutting deeper than has been suspected, point to a foul paper origin rather than prompt-copy—just like the parallel corruptions in other Shakespeare plays.

Like Prof. J. D. Wilson we detect two textual strata in *John*. Prof. Wilson defined these as (*a*) prompt-book, (*b*) Shakespeare's revision of the prompt-book[2]; we suggest that they are (*a*) foul papers, (*b*) printing-house interference in 1621. Hair-splitting such as this has even its practical rewards. Prof. Wilson, though the first to show that Hubert and the Citizen of Angiers were intended to be one person,[3] could not identify them in his text. The foul paper theory, on the other hand, allows us to scrap the Citizen as Shakespeare scrapped him during composition, and to reintroduce Hubert with all

---

1. Compare also *Ham.*, I. ii. 58 where Q2 reads "*Polo.* Hath", as against F1 (and Q1 and modern texts) "*Pol.* He hath". Prof. J. D. Wilson explains that Shakespeare wrote "Pol a hath" [*The Manuscript of Shakespeare's Hamlet* (1934), i, 110]. The speech heading *Kin.* (for *King*) is frequent in Shakespeare, and Elizabethan plays generally, occurring also in the Folio *John* (II. i. 79).

2. Cf. Wilson's note on the copy, pp. 91–4.

3. *Op. cit.*, pp. xlv–xlvii; cf. also Charles Petit-Dutaillis: *Le Roi Jean et Shakespeare* (1944), pp. 70–1. The speech heading *Cit.* (for *Citizen*) is replaced by *Hubert* and *Hub.* from II. i. 325.

his lines for the first time since the original prompt-book.[1]

Naturally the merging of the Citizen and Hubert startles one at first. The Citizen speaks impersonally throughout Act II; Hubert's test in IV. i is very personal indeed. But as *John* is full of impersonal "official" language cheek by jowl with other types, the important contrast of formality and passion being thus brought out (cf. p. lxvi), we must not take this too seriously. As Hubert still speaks impersonally in III. ii, where his presence cannot be disputed, Shakespeare may have decided to heighten the "impersonal" impression through identification with the Citizen, so that Hubert's thawing out in IV. i, his slow and reluctant recognition of a personal problem behind an official duty, would give edge to that central scene. Be this as it may, our conviction is strengthened by two other points. First, Shakespeare renamed many minor characters as he saw their places in their plays more clearly—a foul paper practice conspicuous in *Love's Labour's Lost* and *Much Ado*; while the favourite explanation of the Hubert-Citizen tangle (first advanced by Collier)—namely, that one actor doubled the two parts—has no comparable parallel in the canon.[2] Second, there is Hubert's "voluntary oath" (III. ii. 33). As the two other voluntary oaths (v. i. 29, v. ii. 10) show, a vassal's oath of allegiance is meant. John's thanks are not altogether too extravagant if *Hubert* swore on behalf of Angiers. The *Citizen* had repeatedly refused to pay allegiance on behalf of Angiers till one king should prove greatest: as John did prove greatest, and Angiers did submit to him (III. iii. 6), continuity of character seems to be urged by the action quite apart from the essential corroboration of the text.

A foul paper theory for the text also urges us to return to the Folio for our act and scene division. Greg, contending that

1. Though Wilson proves Hubert's mean birth (cf. IV. iii. 87, note) he describes him as "a burgher de Burgh", Shakespeare undoubtedly saw the name "Hubert de Burgh" in Holinshed, but, degrading the great justiciar of history, dropped the "de Burgh". Hubert becomes an *arriviste* like Faulconbridge, dependent on John, so that the murder of Arthur tempts him more searchingly.

2. See Greg, *The Editorial Problem in Shakespeare*, under "doubling of parts". In those plays where doubling is thought to have caused confusion of names only *isolated* instances of confusion are known (in the Folio *MND.*, v. i, Philostrate disappears altogether, which is a different matter): in *John* Hubert takes over the Citizen's part *systematically* from II. i. 325.

these divisions are "unlikely to have been made by the folio editor" because of the shortness of *Actus Secundus*, confirmed the impression of E. K. Chambers and Prof. Wilson that clearly "something has gone wrong".[1] Though erratic, these divisions conceal a five-act structure much like that of Shakespeare's other plays.[2] If Greg is right, and we are right about two textual strata, Shakespeare himself may be responsible for these curious divisions: that is, Shakespeare as interpreted by the Folio compositor.

We suggest that the compositor read certain numbers at the head of the scenes and interpreted these unmethodically, confusing acts and scenes. Thus "ɪɪ" or "2" (for Act ɪɪ?) he made *Scaena Secunda*; "2" (for Act ɪɪ, Sc. ii?) he made *Actus Secundus*. Prof. J. D. Wilson has recently explained the ludicrously short *Actus Quintus* (Act v, Sc. v in modern texts) of *Henry VI*, Part ɪ, on the same surmise, viz. that Scene v was "presumably labelled 'scena quinta' (or merely '5')".[3] Despite such progressive corruption earlier, the complete form *Actus Tertius, Scaena prima* in our play ought, we think, to be reconsidered with renewed faith.

Ever since Theobald, Act ɪɪɪ, Sc. i replaces the Folio *Actus Secundus*, the Folio *Actus Tertius, Scaena prima* being dismissed as a mistake. Theobald's rearrangement must be attributed to his desire to spite Pope: his only argument of note, that Faulconbridge, being the poet's favourite character, very properly closes the act with his soliloquy on commodity, loses all its force once we recall the soliloquy in Act ɪ. R. G. White, one of the few who preferred the Folio division to Theobald's, rejoined vigorously:

according to Theobald's disarrangement . . . when *Salisbury* delivers his message to *Constance* . . . the ceremony has already taken place; . . . the royal trains enter the tent . . . they have made some hasty preparation for the marriage, gone to Saint Mary's Chapel

---

1. *Loc. cit.*

2. Folio *Actus Primus, Scaena Prima* = Arden Act ɪ, Sc. 1; *Scaena Secunda* = ɪɪ. i; *Actus Secundus* = ɪɪ. ii (ɪɪɪ. i. 1–74 in *textus receptus*); *Actus Tertius, Scaena prima* = ɪɪɪ. i (ɪɪɪ. i. 75–347 in *textus receptus*); *Scaena Secunda* = ɪɪɪ. ii (ɪɪɪ. iii in the *textus receptus* begins at Arden ɪɪɪ. ii. 11); other divisions as in Arden, except that the Folio repeats *Actus Quartus* for Act v.

3. The C.U.P. *1 H 6* (1952), p. 104, following P. Alexander, *Shakespeare's Henry VI and Richard III*, p. 185.

in the town, had the ceremony performed, and come thence to the very place whither their "hasty messenger" (*sic*) was sent![1]

White clinched his argument by emphasizing that "consciousness that the ceremony awaited his return" must lie behind Salisbury's line

> I may not go without you to the kings (II. ii. 62)

Theobald's division was perpetuated rather because the Folio is obviously wrong than because he is obviously right. The present-day sources of editorial misgivings are (i) the shortness of the Folio *Actus Secundus*; (ii) the absence of an exit after *Actus Secundus*; (iii) the typographical suspiciousness of *Actus Tertius, Scaena prima*, which lacks the usual rule beneath it; (iv) the apparent continuity of the action. These reasons have not all the same weight. We may disregard (i), if the compositor has misinterpreted "II" or "2", and also (iii), since the absence of a rule recurs in the next scene (III. ii) and need have no connection with the copy. Reasons (ii) and (iv) cause the real trouble.

(ii) The absence of a Folio exit coincides with Constance's declaration that she will not exit (II. ii. 73–4). Probably there was no exit in the copy, and the compositor (a careful worker) took a hint from the text and did not insert an exit. Dramatists sometimes ended scenes with no more than a line across the page, i.e. the printing-house must sometimes be responsible for end-of-scene exits.[2]

Besides Constance, Arthur and Salisbury appear in *Actus Secundus*; unlike her, they are not made to enter again in *Actus Tertius, Scaena prima*. Though their absence may be due to the fact that they have nothing to say in III. i, Arthur's absence in the *scene* would explain why Constance speaks throughout of herself, of *her* side,[3] and, a more difficult teaser, why John's side captures Arthur (III. ii. 1) and not Constance as well.

(iv) Since a new act must begin somewhere between the

1. See Furness's *John*, pp. 174–8, where the commencement of Act III commands a lengthy footnote.

2. Bald "*Exeunt*", so common in old plays where only some of the characters go off and a "*Manet*" also seems necessary (as in *John*, II. i. 560, IV. ii. 102), may at times be a similar printing-house interpretation of a line.

3. Arthur's presence is not necessitated by "our oppression" (III. i. 32) or "my child" (III. i. 113).

first Folio *Scaena Secunda* (= the Arden II. i) and the second
(= III. ii), and only two possible places recommend themselves,
namely *Actus Secundus* (II. ii. 1) and *Actus Tertius, Scaena prima*
(III. i. 1)—which would be more likely? Surely White interpreted Shakespeare's idea of continuity more soundly than
Theobald's silent followers. The logic of time seems to support
the Folio beginning for Act III.

The logic of the action suggests that Constance still sits on
the stage at the opening of *Actus Tertius, Scaena prima*. But the
more briefly she sits there, the less effective the device. May
Shakespeare not have intended her to remain thus for the
whole length of the ceremonies? Salisbury could take Arthur
by the hand and walk off with him, or leave by himself; while
the time-lapse would be conveyed by the formal procession
opening *Actus Tertius*.

Four arguments persuade us that *Actus Tertius, Scaena prima*
is a reliable notation. First, the madness of the Folio divisions
seems to follow some (misunderstood) authority. Whereas
*Scaena Secunda* (II. i) and *Actus Secundus* (II. ii) stand apart, perhaps because only one number could be deciphered, the complete form here inspires more confidence. Second, the support
of the time-scheme. Third, if no break was intended at III. i. 1,
the entry for Constance, who would be on-stage already,
would be unnecessary. Whether Arthur and Salisbury be on
or off, Constance is certainly on—if the stage direction goes
back to Shakespeare, this would establish the break. If "*Constance*" was added to the stage direction by the act division
"interpolator" we would expect this individual to have clean-
ed up the other loose ends—in brief, the state of the text as a
whole confirms that the "interpolator" may be a superfluous
fiction, that a sincere attempt to reproduce copy could have
caused all these textual difficulties.[1] Fourth, the *T.R.*, though
diverging in detail, introduces a division at this very juncture
(I. v–vi)—strong collateral evidence for a break. In accordance
with these arguments we revert, for our Act II, Sc. ii, Act III,

---

1. The *John* Act II–III transition can be parallelled, e.g. in the end of *Ham.*,
Act III. In the (prompt-copy) Folio text Gertrude remains on-stage, there being
an exit for Hamlet and Polonius's corpse, an entry for Claudius. In the (foul
paper) Q2 the exit probably covers Gertrude as well—at any rate, she is made to
re-enter for IV. i. 1. In (foul paper) *John* Constance is given an entrance for III. i. 1,
though likewise on-stage.

Sc. i, to the divisions contained—or concealed—in the Folio. Similarly, our Act III, Sc. ii reverts to the Folio. Although modern editors start a new scene after III. ii. 10 (Arden text) the sense does not require it, and authority of weight, as we think, contradicts it.[1]

This brings us to the problem of textual integrity. Prof. Wilson claimed *John* as "an indisputable example of textual revision".[2] E. K. Chambers had cautiously suggested the cutting of a scene,[3] and Prof. Wilson submitted that a scene with Hubert's "voluntary oath" has been dropped[4] between *Actus Secundus* and *Actus Tertius*. But this oath, less mysterious than he makes out, the 1591 audience would take for granted—the oath of allegiance of a new vassal (*v.* p. xxxvii). As the *T.R.* here follows the scene-sequence of *John* without trace of a "voluntary oath" scene, we cannot agree with Prof. Wilson.

Prof. Wilson's "most striking evidence of textual disturbance" comes from III. iii. 68, where Constance's "To England, if you will" replies to King Philip's "I prithee, lady, go away with me" (III. iii. 20). Aldis Wright long ago suggested that III. iii. 21–67 may be an interpolation.[5] Prof. Wilson took up the revision theory, rejecting Wright's alternative solution, that Constance relapses into apathy, because

it is unworkable on the stage, inasmuch as no audience after forty-six (*sic*) lines of dialogue would be able to associate Constance's reply with Philip's original question.[6]

But the resumption of momentarily dropped subjects forms part of Shakespeare's standard "frenzy technique" (compare especially *King Lear*). If Philip beckoned Constance to follow him, the audience would not forget his question: Constance may disdain to answer, until *he* temporarily forgets his question (ll. 61–7)—whereupon she turns upon him bitterly with "To England, if you will".[7]

1. The traditional act, scene, and line numberings are given in brackets.
2. *Op. cit.*, p. viii.      3. *William Shakespeare*, I, 365.      4. Cf. III. ii. 33.
5. Quoted Furness, *John*, p. 264.      6. *Op. cit.*, p. l.
7. Furthermore, the *T.R.* seems to echo this "interpolation" in 1591 already. Compare "all *counsel*, all *redress* . . . all *counsel*, true *redress*" (*John*, III. iii. 23–4), Death "Which *cannot hear* a lady's feeble voice, / Which *scorns* a modern invocation" (III. iii. 41–2)—and "counsell", "redresse" (*T.R.*, II. v. 51, 61), "Why dye I not? *Death scornes* so vilde a pray", (I sue to Life and Death) "But both are *deafe*, I can be heard of neither*" (*T.R.*, II. vi. 8, 11).

Although the evidence does not seem quite strong enough to warrant disintegration, signs of foul paper hurry, which may have been obliterated in the fair copy, litter the text. Words repeat themselves uneconomically, bad or weak lines crop up now and then. We are even led to wonder whether some of the grand lines in the *T.R.*, few though they be, represent Shakespeare's second thoughts as he copied out his play, and echo the *John* prompt-book: for instance, whether Shakespeare added two lines after II. i. 192 such as

> *K. Philip* But heres no proof that showes your son a King.
> *K. Iohn.* What wants, my sword shal more at large set down.
>
>                                             (*T.R.*, I. iii. 125–6)

Again, the part of the Earl of Essex (who appears only in Act I with one short speech) may have been expanded in the theatre to include Lord Bigot's, whose first entry comes at IV. iii. 11. Perhaps Shakespeare forgot the name of his third earl—he often forgot the names of his minor characters, an easy matter if one writes on odd scraps of paper—mistakenly called him Bigot, correcting the error when he prepared his fair copy. In the *T.R.*, at any rate, Essex continues to make a third with Salisbury and Pembroke, where in *John* Bigot takes over.[1]

Even if very minor alterations such as we suggest were introduced, the play as a whole cannot be further disintegrated. Its best poetry the *T.R.* author knew in 1591 already—including the soliloquies.[2]

Obviously the *T.R.*, if indeed derivative, helps us with many cruxes in *John*. Problems of scene-division, textual integrity, and character-parts it illumines to advantage. But how far may we trust its apparent substantiation of "doubtful readings" in *John*? Only two lines are the same in the two plays,[3] and, though the *T.R.* reproduces Shakespeare faithfully by

---

1. When *John* was thought prompt-copy, F. G. Fleay [*John* (1878), p. 24] suggested that Essex "was intended to be struck out altogether", since no other Essex appears in the canon and the contemporary earl fell out of favour in 1596. Cf. also Fleay's *Life and Work of Shakespeare* (1886), p. 197.

2. Wilson noted the connection between *John*, I. i. 182, 183, 206 and *T.R.*, I. i. 291 ("I haue no lands, honour is my desire"), I. i. 295 ("foote of land"), I. i. 261 ("this monnting minde"); again, between *John*, II. i. 561, 573, 598 and *T.R* , I. iv. 112–13 ("To fill and tickle their ambieious eares, / With hope of gaine").

3. Cf. *John*, II. i. 528, v. iv. 42, notes.

and large, much telescoping and reshuffling vitiates its authority for questions of detail.[1] None the less, the *T.R.* compels us
on occasion to part ways with the *textus receptus*—especially
when it vindicates the Folio.[2]

As regards general textual procedure, the present edition
follows the Folio as closely as possible, collating all significant
changes. Thus variant word-forms are retained (e.g. vild,
winch), the modernized forms of the *textus receptus* (vile, wince)
not being collated; and some cases of hyphening are passed
over silently. No "normalization" of the metre is attempted,
except that verbs ending in "-ed" are contracted to "-d"
according to the requirements of scansion (the "-ed" form was
used indiscriminately for accented and unaccented syllables
in the Folio). False concords are not emended, as they were
common in the Elizabethan period. The punctuation of the
Folio has had to be modernized, our text being probably far
more heavily stopped than Shakespeare's MS. was (the Folio
punctuation must often be editorial). Literals, turned letters,
etc., are not collated unless some significance might attach to
them.

## 3. THE DATE

*John* was known to Francis Meres in 1598. Previous writers,
accepting the *T.R.* as its source, have therefore championed
every year between 1591 and 1598 as the date of composition.[3]
The death of Shakespeare's son Hamnet in 1596 once inclined
the sentimental to suspect autobiography in Constance's la-
ments for Arthur (in Act III, Sc. iii); and Prof. G. B. Harrison
has recently argued for this year because, in his opinion, topical preoccupation with war finds an echo in the play.[4] D. F.
Ash, discussing 'Anglo-French Relations in "King John"',[5]

---

1. The reader may dismiss as chop-logic our reliance upon the *T.R.* where it
agrees with *John* together with our inattention to it where it disagrees. We ignore
disagreement between the texts because the *T.R.* often disagrees intentionally:
derivative plays usually "embellished" their originals, even to the extent of
adding new characters.
2. Cf. I. i. 44, III. i. 185, IV. iii. 8, notes.
3. See the list of dates in Furness's *John*, pp. 443–4.
4. 'Shakespeare's Topical Significances' [*T.L.S.* (1930), p. 939].
5. *Études Anglaises*, III (1939), 349 ff.

suggested that the play parallels the political scene in 1595. Earlier chronologers sometimes favoured 1593, because the conversion of Henry IV to the Roman faith—"Paris vaut bien une messe"—seemed to them to have inspired the tergiversation of Shakespeare's King Philip, and the Bastard's censure of commodity.

Prof. J. D. Wilson ignored vague topicality and reinterpreted a known *John–Spanish Tragedy* contact which moved him to propose a new date. Steevens had noted the similarity between *John*, II. i. 137–8, and the *Spanish Tragedy*:

> He hunted well that was a Lyons death,
> Not he that in a garment wore his skin:
> So Hares may pull dead Lyons by the beard.[1]

Wilson declared that here Kyd "is clearly alluding . . . to Austria's wearing of Richard's lion's-skin",[2] dated the *Spanish Tragedy* 1590 not 1589 (the usual *terminus ante quem*), and assigned a first draft of *John* to 1590. Since this dating is backed by the definite allusion in *John* to *Soliman and Perseda* discovered by Theobald, this play being generally dated 1590,[3] and by an allusion to the defeat of the Spanish Armada,[4] Wilson's date deserves at least as much consideration as any other.

Although the *Spanish Tragedy* "contact" admits of more than one interpretation, our belief that *John* precedes the *T.R.* (1591) naturally leads us, with Wilson, to prefer the year 1590. Unlike Wilson we think that the whole Folio text belongs to this year[5]: and this early date can be supported by other evidence hitherto unnoted.

(*a*) A contact between *John*[6] and stanza 12 of Samuel Daniel's *Complaint of Rosamond* (1592). Though we have no sure

1. I. i. ii. 170–2.
2. C.U.P. *John*, pp. liii–liv.
3. See *John*, I. i. 244, II. i. 75, notes; E. K. Chambers, *The Elizabethan Stage*, IV, 46.
4. Armada allusions are more important than Wilson suggests: see pp. xxix, xlvi, n. 2.
5. Wilson assigns the Folio *John*, the revision of a postulated 1590 draft, to the year 1594 (C.U.P. *John*, pp. lv–lvii). We disagree with his disintegration of the play into two drafts since the *T.R.* author knew the whole of *John* in 1591 already: see p. xlii.
6. See *John*, II. ii. 52, note.

indication who borrowed from whom, the persisting "correspondences" in the works of Shakespeare and Daniel leave no room for doubt that contact there was, as in their sonnets, their treatments of the stories of the civil wars and of Cleopatra. Daniel, it is widely held, altered his *Cleopatra* with one eye on Shakespeare's play. It seems reasonable to suppose that the *Rosamond* contacts with *Richard 3*, *Romeo*[1] and *John* likewise refer back to the greater poet's current stage successes, rather than that Shakespeare should recall one much less notable work on three separate occasions.

(*b*) A joke about the actor John Sincklo going the rounds in 1590. Sincklo's "thin-man" roles were detected in the plays of Shakespeare and others by Prof. A. Gaw,[2] and Prof. J. D. Wilson has argued that Robert Faulconbridge in *John* was one of these.[3] In *An Almond for a Parrat*, a pamphlet often credited to Thomas Nashe, which McKerrow convincingly dated early 1590,[4] we read, after a dedication to William Kempe (Shakespeare's later "fellow"), and constant allusions to the contemporary stage, the following:

Doest thou feare God in deede...? What, by the smoothing of thy face, the simpering of thy mouth, or staring of thy eies? Why, if that be to feare God, Ile haue a spare fellowe shall make mee a whole quest of faces for three farthinges.[5]

Here only an actor could be meant, and amongst actors Sincklo was the notorious "spare fellowe". The joke, also reproduced in *John*, I. i. 143, turns on the commonplace jibe that actors were such poor rogues that they gladly played for *a penny*,[6] making of Sincklo's thinness a symbol of his more abject poverty.[7]

(*c*) Correspondences with other early books.—(i) Fortune's "golden hand" (*John*, II. i. 57) we find also in Peele's *Descensus Astraeae* (written for October, 1591), perhaps echoing *John* as

---

1. See A. Thaler, 'Shakspere, Daniel, and *Everyman*' [*Philological Quarterly*, xv (1936), 217 ff.].

2. 'John Sincklo as one of Shakespeare's Actors' [*Anglia*, XLIX (1926), 289 ff.].

3. *Op. cit.*, p. lii.   4. See McKerrow's Nashe, IV, 461.   5. Nashe, III, 349.

6. See quotations from *Theses Martinianae* (1589) and from *Martins Months Minde* (1589) in Chambers, *The Elizabethan Stage*, IV, 230.

7. Poverty attaches to Sincklo also in *Rom.*, v. i. 68–76, *Err.*, v. i. 238 *sqq.*

Peele's *Honour of the Garter* (1593) echoes *Titus Andronicus* (*c.*
1588).[1] (ii) Shakespeare may imitate the *Heroicall Devises* of
C. Paradin (1591, S.R. August 1590) in III. iii. 164–8 (see note).
(iii) *Arden of Feversham* (1592) seems to imitate *John*, II. i. 463,
III. i. 126–7 (see notes). (iv) The two pre-Shakespearean giants
of Elizabethan literature, Sidney's *Arcadia* and Spenser's *Faerie
Queene* (Bks I–III) were published in 1590. *John* may echo both,
in III. ii. 35, IV. i. 102, and in II. i. 63, v. vii. 36 (see notes).

(*d*) Correspondences with topical events.—(i) Armada
idiom and allusions are more frequent in *John* than has been
suspected.[2] (ii) The murder of a king by a fanatical Roman
Catholic was topical after August 1589, when Henry III of
France was killed by Jacques Clement. The League agitated
for some time for canonization for Clement, to the indignation
of French and English Protestants. Pandulph's promise of
canonization for regicide (*John*, III. I. 102–5) perhaps took
back Shakespeare's first audience to the Bull excommunicat-
ing Elizabeth (see our note), but the canonization of Clement
was the burning question in 1589–90[3]; in his *Fig for the Spaniard*,
1591, one G. B. in fact lumped the murderers of John and
Henry together, perhaps because the John plays were already
popular:

> Such Hypocrites in Fryers habites lurke,
> That rapines, rapes, treasons, guyles, murders worke.
>
> Aske *France* heereof, such Hypocrites they rue,
> And *England* when king *Iohn* was poysoned[4]

(iii) Throughout 1590 the friends of Secretary Davison made
many efforts to bring him back to the queen's favour, the most
strenuous campaigner being the Earl of Essex.[5] John's repudi-

---

1. See C. Crawford, 'The Date and Authenticity of Titus Andronicus'
[*Shakespeare Jahrbuch* (1900), p. 109].

2. See p. xxix, and notes to II. i. 23, 26, III. iii. 2, v. i. 65, v. ii. 151, 154,
v. vii. 117.

3. See A. Colynet, *True History of the Ciuill Warres of France* (1591), p. 419;
P. Le Roy, *Catholicon of Spayne* (1595), sigs. B, M₃.

4. Sig. A₄ᵛ.

5. See E. M. Tenison, *Elizabethan England*, vol. VIII (1947), p. 248 ff., and
Davison in *D.N.B.* Lord Strange, to whose company of actors Shakespeare, in
our opinion, belonged while writing *John* (cf. p. xlix), was a close friend of
Essex.

ation of Hubert may be a reflection of Elizabeth's repudiation of Davison.[1] The other surprising topicalities in *John* make Shakespeare's "collaboration" with the Essex circle,[2] to which he certainly belonged a little later, quite plausible: but as Davison abandoned all hopes early in 1591, and agitation on his behalf then ceased, we must consider 1590(–91) as a possible date of composition for *John*.

Miss F. A. Yates has argued that the Traveller satire in *John* (I. i. 189–204) is bound up with the "school of night" controversy of the early 1590's, and imitates John Eliot's *Ortho-Epia Gallica* (1593).[3] A map in a painter's shop called forth, in one of Eliot's dialogues, the following eulogy:

Seest thou the Fennes of Nyle? Lo here the red Sea. Looke vpon the great Caire! ... Here are the Alpes, ouer which we go downe into Italie. There are the Appenines: and here are the Pyrenaean hilles, by which you may go directly into Spaine.

That the Bastard has in mind "modern language manuals" in his soliloquy, as Miss Yates contended, we find hard to believe. Indeed, the necessity of a connection between Eliot's and Shakespeare's Alps-Apennines-Pyrenean seems small. On the one hand alliteration would draw the words together, on the other both writers follow a type of geographical description familiarized by the classics.[4]

(*e*) A further topical reflection in *John* which, though now first suggested, may provide an upper and lower limit for dating quite independent of the otherwise all-important *T.R.*

In November 1590, a long-standing family-quarrel between

1. See p. xxix.
2. See pp. l–li. For backing up of Essex in *John* and other Shakespearean plays, see E. M. Albright: 'Shakespeare's *Richard II* and the Essex Conspiracy' [*P.M.L.A.*, XLII (1927)].
3. *A Study of Love's Labour's Lost* (1936), p. 64.
4. Compare Ovid, *Metam.*: "Caucasus ardet, / Ossaque cum Pindo maiorque ambobus Olympus, / Aëriaeque Alpes et nubifer Appenninus" (ii. 224–6); and the translation of Claudian's *Rape of Proserpine* (1617) by Shakespeare's friend Leonard Digges: "The poore cold dweller on steepe *Appenine*, / And frozen passengers, that slowly climbe / The hoary *Alpes*, amazed stand, and doubt / Of some new broile 'twixt *Ioue* and *Gyant* rowt: / Those that (along thy streames) with naked limbe / Perpetuall trophie bearing *Tyber*, swimme, / And those that to thy current famous *Po* / Launch out their little barkes ..." (sig. F₃).

James Burbage and the widow of his brother-in-law John
Brayne (or Braynes) reached a temporary peak-point.[1] Having together built the Theatre (the first English play-house) in
1576, the in-laws fell out in 1578, and, after John Brayne's
death in 1586, the widow Brayne, together with one Robert
Miles, whom John Brayne had charged with being the cause
of his death,[2] continued litigation. As this centred on the receipts for the Theatre's galleries, not only the Court of Chancery would cause publicity, since the suit was dealt with there
on 4, 13, 28 November 1590: but events at the Theatre itself,
where, on 16 November (beside other days unspecified[3]) the
Burbages fought the widow and her friends with words and
blows before the assembling audience, would familiarize
*theatre-goers* in particular with it.

On the eventful 16 November the widow, with Robert
Miles, Ralph Miles (the son of Robert), Nicholas Bishop (a
friend of the Miles's), and others, took up stations at the gallery
entrance, determined to collect her due share. On the 13th
Chancery had awarded her an order that she might enjoy her
moiety of the gallery receipts, and when James Burbage called
her a "Murdring hor",[4] Miles produced it. Burbage was not at
a loss: "hang her hor qd he she getteth nothing here",[5] declaring that he would commit twenty contempts of court rather
than lose his possession.[6] Mrs Burbage and her eldest son Cuth-
bert also helped to rail. The hero of the day, however, was
Richard, the second son (the principal "fellow" of Shakespeare from 1594 onwards), whom one witness found

wt A Broome staff in his hand of whom when this depot asked what
sturre was there he answered in laughing phrase hew they come for
A moytie But qd he (holding vppe the said . . . broomes staff) I haue,
I think deliuered . . . him A moytie wt this & sent them packing[7]

N. Bishop, besides many others, made a deposition about this
unhappy visit to the Theatre:

1. See C. W. Wallace, *The First London Theatre* (1913) (The University Studies
of the University of Nebraska, vol. xiii).

2. "Braine . . . at his deathe . . . charged Miles wth his deathe, by certaine
stripes geven him by Miles" (*op. cit.*, p. 86).

3. *Op. cit.*, pp. 97, 100, 105.     4. *Op. cit.*, p. 105.     5. *Op. cit.*, p. 100.
6. *Op. cit.*, p. 101.     7. *Loc. cit.*

And by cause this depot. spake then somewhat in the favor. of the por womman . . . Ry. Burbage scornfully & disdainfullye playing wt this depotes Nose sayd that yf he delt in the matter he wold beate him also and did chalendge the field of him at that tyme[1]

The upshot was that James Burbage was cited to answer for contempt of court. He denied the "odious termes" against Chancery and religion of which he was accused, pulling wool over the court's eyes with seeming humility. Furthermore, he had trouble with his actors. Two companies, Lord Strange's men and the Lord Admiral's men, had amalgamated to play at the Theatre.[2] When John Alleyn, who had pleaded with Burbage on behalf of Mrs Brayne, asked Burbage for money due to the Admiral's men, and he refused to pay, Alleyn "told him that belike he ment to deale wt them as he did wt the por wydowe"[3]: and some time thereafter the Admiral's, with several of Strange's men, left Burbage's management.[4]

Much has been written about Shakespeare's first company. If *John* precedes the *T.R.* the orthodox Shakespeare chronology necessarily falls, and with it most of our conjecture about the first company. Fresh speculation gets a good start, in recompense, through John Sincklo's part in our play. It is generally agreed that Sincklo was playing with the combined Admiral's and Strange's men in 1590, together with Edward Alleyn, the leading actor of the day, Richard Burbage, and others whose names are preserved in an old dramatic plot.[5] Possibly, then, *John* was written for Alleyn, Burbage, Sincklo, and the rest—written, if *John* precedes the *T.R.*, for the Theatre just as the Burbage-Brayne suit was approaching a new crisis.

Though not concerned with *John*, Prof. Wallace believed that the Brayne litigation, so annoying to the close business associates of Shakespeare, "can hardly have failed to leave a residuum of human experience plastic to the hand of the poet".[6] The possibility deserves exploration, for the resem-

---

1. *Op. cit.*, p. 115.    2. See Chambers, *The Elizabethan Stage*, II, 120.
3. Wallace, *op. cit.*, p. 101.
4. In May 1591, according to Chambers (*loc. cit.*).
5. The plot of Part II of *The Seven Deadly Sins*; cf. Chambers's *The Elizabethan Stage*, III, 497.
6. *Op. cit.*, p. 157.

blances between the Burbage suit and some *fictitious additions* to the story of John are quite extraordinary.

(i) A widow appears with the man accused of the death of her husband to claim her possession.—In *John*, II. i. 2, 6, 13, Arthur is made the "off-spring" of Richard I, an intentional ambiguity reinforced later by the assertion that Arthur is Eleanor's "eldest son's son" (II. i. 177)—which creates the impression that Constance is aided by the man (Austria) who killed the father of her son, i.e. her husband. This impression Aldis Wright denounced as Shakespeare's "strange careless-ness". Once we realize, however, that Shakespeare may not have been revising an old play in great haste, but probably checked his story in half a dozen chronicles, reading up the accounts of other Plantagenets beside John, Wright's view, approved by so many editors, no longer satisfies. When we re-call, further, that Shakespeare has unhistorically resurrected Austria to champion Constance, the double violation of his-tory leads us, in the first place, to expect an overriding *purpose* rather than carelessness.

(ii) Richard Burbage browbeats the widow's secondary protector Nicholas Bishop, and later is himself largely respons-ible for the flight of her party.—In *John*, the Bastard bullies Austria as superciliously (II. i. 290; III. i. 57, etc.),[1] and later emerges as the strong man of the day (III. ii. 7). As well as Austria, the Bastard is Shakespeare's fiction.

(iii) The two parties quarrel outside the Theatre, disputing their rights to it.—In *John*, the blockade and abusive quarrel outside Angiers—which symbolizes the whole of the English inheritance—is Shakespeare's fiction.

(iv) James Burbage scornfully rejects the court order, but later knuckles under to Chancery.—In *John*, King Philip de-clares that he has a "commission" from "that supernal judge" (II. i. 110, 112) to call John to restitution. John derides this (but later submits to the pope: Act v, Sc. i).

(v) The Admiral's men fear similar treatment to the

1. In the *T.R.* the Bastard actually challenges Austria (I. v. 23), as R. Burbage did N. Bishop: the challenge being declined in both cases. Perhaps the *T.R.* here echoes an addition to the *John* prompt-book (cf. p. xlii above).

widow's and finally leave Burbage.—In *John*, the nobles are dismayed by John's treatment of his rival (IV. ii. 47–66), fear for themselves (IV. iii. 11–13), and likewise leave. Though Shakespeare's *English* nobles react to Arthur's murder as Holinshed's nobles of *Brittany*, historical truth has again been abandoned, and Burbage and his men certainly provided a situation similar to that of John and his men.

(vi) Since *John* describes a quarrel of in-laws in the first acts, the Burbage–Brayne relations are again reproduced; the widow being helped in both cases by a father and son (Robert and Ralph Miles, France and Lewis) and *their* friend (N. Bishop, Austria).

(vii) Minor coincidences may still be mentioned. Austria's over-confident promise that he will maintain Constance's quarrel (II. i. 19–31) corresponds to a report

that the said Myles hath made great boast, that it is he, that will maynteyne and defend her herin, al be it she did procure his trouble before the coroners enquest, and did impute to him the deathe of her husband[1]

Again, it was said that Robert Miles declared that the Theatre was his

and that he would spend all that he had but he would pull the defendt out of the said Theatre by the eares[2]

Compare *John*, II. i. 263–6, and King Philip's other asseverations of his unshakable purpose (II. i. 41–3, 343–9).

Although the correspondences are not consistent—Robert Miles being reproduced, if we are right, both in King Philip and in Austria, N. Bishop being likewise caricatured in Austria, and so on—we know that such disguised lampooning was the fashion on the Elizabethan stage.[3] We suggest that at certain points, especially in Act II, Shakespeare saw the resemblances in his story to a real-life drama with which he knew his audience to be familiar, and distorted history in details to enrich his play with a topical back-cloth. He seems to celebrate the victory of young Richard Burbage consciously; in other details

1. Wallace, *op. cit.*, p. 88.   2. *Op. cit.*, p. 119.
3. For proofs of this see C. J. Sisson's *Lost Plays of Shakespeare's Age* (1936), pp. 57–71, 97–110, and *passim*.

he may sometimes be plastic to contemporary events unconsciously, because of the similarity of the action.

If the Bastard was created for swashbuckling Richard Burbage, the part of John, unless we are mistaken about the company, must have been meant for Edward Alleyn. Thus the age-
old question—why does the Bastard almost oust John from the
centre of interest in the play?—may partly reflect the growing
challenge of young[1] Burbage to the theatrical supremacy of
Alleyn. If this conjecture be correct—and it is no more than
conjecture—we are bound to recall that Alleyn left the
Theatre with the Admiral's men early in 1591. We cannot say
for certain what happened to Sincklo, but Richard Burbage,
with some of the principal actors of the 1590 amalgamation,
perhaps including Shakespeare, seems not to have gone with
Alleyn, probably staying on at the Theatre.

The suggested allusion to the Burbage–Brayne suit fits in
perfectly, of course, with the new theory about the *T.R.* Since
so much other evidence assigns *John* to the same year, we are
tempted to submit as the precise date of composition—which
the suit alone can indicate within that year—the winter/spring
of 1590/91. The squabbles in November 1590 would be the
*terminus a quo* for Act II at any rate—Act I might have been
completed before Shakespeare altered his plans—and the
secession of the Admiral's men the *terminus ante quem*.

Our impression that Shakespeare was writing for the amalgamated Strange's and Admiral's men gains further strength
from the 1594 quarto title-page according to which "the Earle
of Darbie, Earle of Pembrooke, and Earle of Sussex their
Seruants" had performed Shakespeare's *Titus Andronicus*. That
Sussex's were the last owners can scarcely be disputed, since
they played *Titus* as "ne" for Henslowe on 24 January 1594,
and on 6 February *Titus* was entered in the Stationers' Regis-
ter, while the theatres closed down for some months on account
of the plague.[2] Pembroke's must have been the previous
owners, since they were compelled to pawn their apparel in the

1. He was about 22 years old in 1590 (E. K. Chambers: *The Elizabethan Stage*,
II, 307): and the Bastard, though often played as an older man, must be of roughly
this age, in Act I at least, as "thou unreverend boy" (I. i. 227) and "thou most
untoward knave" (I. i. 243) indicate.
2. Chambers, *The Elizabethan Stage*, II, 95.

autumn of 1593, and apparently they sold other plays at this time.[1] Thus the *Titus* title-page seems to give the right sequence of ownership for Pembroke's and Sussex's. Unless we resort to far-fetched hypotheses,[2] we can hardly refuse to admit that Derby's (= Strange's)[3] must have owned *Titus* before Pembroke's, exactly as the title-page avers. We know, too, that the combined Strange's and Admiral's men were called simply Strange's in contemporary documents: and since Ben Jonson in the well-known quotation implied that *Titus* was written between 1584 and 1589,[4] we infer that the combined companies at the Theatre owned *Titus c.* 1590 *and employed Shakespeare.* Sincklo's part in *John*, the allusion to the Burbage lawsuit in *John*, and the *Titus* title-page testify independently and therefore the more persuasively concerning Shakespeare's first London company, if *John* may indeed be dated 1590.

But may it? The orthodox chronologers will hardly rush in at this stage to agree. Other plays seem so much less mature, eight or ten being practically always said to precede *John*: and yet, we are told, Shakespeare only began his writing career in 1590. Fortunately for us a distinguished body of critics, who believe that Shakespeare's first plays have been badly postdated, now counterpoises the authority of the formidable Malone and Chambers.[5] Our only possible attitude to the chronologers' *impasse* must therefore be to disregard dates. For, since the debated *John–T.R.* relationship must necessarily be a mainstay of either chronological theory, it would be illogical in any discussion of this relationship (which we now resume from p. xix) not to suspend preconceptions about dates until all the other evidence, judged *per se*, can be weighed against them.

We must now look a little more closely at the *T.R.* Thanks

1. See Chambers, *op. cit.*, II, 128.

2. That *Titus* is a revision of an older lost play *Titus and Vespasian*, etc. See E. K. Chambers, *William Shakespeare*, I, 316–21.

3. Title-pages usually gave the company's current name even though it had performed under another one. Lord Strange became the Earl of Derby in 1593.

4. See Chambers, *William Shakespeare*, I, 316.

5. See A. W. Pollard's review of Chambers' *William Shakespeare* (in *Library*, XI (1931), 380); T. W. Baldwin's *Shakspere's Five-Act Structure* (1947), chap. 33; L. Hotson's *Shakespeare's Sonnets Dated* (1949), pp. 32–6; P. Alexander's *Shakespeare Primer* (1951), p. 33.

to a notable work by Sir Walter Greg, we can fit this play into a general picture of theatrical dishonesty, which, precluding an unprofitable study in isolation, takes us a good step forward with most of its difficulties.[1]

For, on its title-page, the *T.R.* proclaims that it was "publikely acted by the Queenes Maiesties Players". Having been the principal company in the later eighties, the Queen's men had gone steadily downhill after the death, in 1588, of their chief comedian Richard Tarlton. In the nineties a number of their plays appeared in print in debased texts,[2] in a study of one of which Greg showed that the company itself was probably responsible for the perversion of the original sense. Greg suggested that, driven to the last extremes, the Queen's men sold their prompt-book to another company, then reconstructed a prompt-book for themselves from memory, with alterations to suit the taste of a lower class of audience, continuing to act the "sold" play—and finally sold the second prompt-book to a printer for a second fee.[3]

From the reconstruction of their own plays it would be a small step, for a hard-up company, to the "plagiarism" of the successes of other companies. Word for word reconstruction would, of course, save time where the company remembered the words of a play it had once possessed. Pirating another company's get-penny would make accuracy difficult, since the words would have to be learned first, or written down in the theatre. To surmount these obstacles, the Elizabethan pirate would probably anticipate the methods of Tate Wilkinson, who reconstructed Sheridan's *Duenna c.* 1777:

I locked myself in my room; set down first all the jokes I remembered, then I laid a book of the songs before me; and with magazines kept the regulation of the scenes; and by the help of a numerous collection of obsolete Spanish plays, I produced an excellent comic Opera.[4]

1. *Two Elizabethan Stage Abridgements: The Battle of Alcazar & Orlando Furioso* (The Malone Society Extra Volume, 1922), 1923.

2. About a dozen Queen's plays were sold in the 1590's (Chambers, *The Elizabethan Stage*, IV, 382–6), some certainly in "bad" texts, others in doubtful ones.

3. Greg, *op. cit.*, section VI.

4. Quoted by Prof. Alexander in illustration of the composition of *The Taming of a Shrew* [*Shakespeare's Henry VI and Richard III* (1929), p. 69].

That the *T.R.* is a hotch-potch of a numerous collection of old plays Prof. Rupert Taylor has already demonstrated in an article listing its correspondences with Marlowe.[1] Shakespeare, too, was put to good account, contacts with his early histories being particularly common; lesser dramatists were likewise pillaged.[2] Though it contains no extended borrowings such as *The Taming of a Shrew* (1594) took from *Tamburlaine* and *Faustus*, imitation runs riot in the *T.R.*, so that obvious suspicions gather head in the reader.

Rewriting the plays of other companies—a simple matter before the copyright laws—was not restricted to the John plays, whichever came first. G. B. Churchill has proved that there was contact one way or the other between Shakespeare's *Richard III* and the Queen's men's anonymous *True Tragedie of Richard the Third* (1594)[3]; and L. Kirschbaum has classed this *True Tragedie* as a "bad quarto".[4] *The Taming of a Shrew* —hereafter *A Shrew*—connects similarly with Shakespeare's *The Taming of the Shrew*—hereafter *The Shrew*. Though ascribed on the title-page to Pembroke's company, H. Dugdale Sykes has argued that the prose of *A Shrew* is the work of S. Rowley,[5] and critics of weight have approved.[6] Two other "Rowley plays", following Sykes's definition, *Orlando Furioso* (1594) and *The Famous Victories of Henry V* (1598), we know to have been Queen's men's plays. Sykes thought all the "Rowley plays" the property of the Admiral's men, since Rowley is first heard of as a member of that company in 1597–8. But as Rowley's earlier affiliations remain a mystery, and as several of the "Rowley plays" date from before 1594, it is more logical to associate him with the only company known to have possessed more than one of his plays. As this company (the Queen's) admittedly passed on plays to other companies and reconstructed them for itself, if Greg is right, it seems possible that

1. *P.M.L.A.*, vol. LI (1936), p. 633 ff.

2. H. Dugdale Sykes [*Sidelights on Shakespeare* (1919), p. 99 ff.] argued strongly on stylistic grounds for Peele's authorship of the *T.R.*; but more probably Peele was only imitated, like Shakespeare and Marlowe.

3. 'Richard the Third up to Shakespeare' [in *Palaestra*, x (1900)].

4. In 'A Census of Bad Quartos' [*R.E.S.*, XIV (1938), pp. 35–6].

5. *The Authorship of 'The Taming of A Shrew'*, etc. (Shakespeare Association Pamphlet), 1920.

6. Greg, *Alcazar and Orlando*, pp. 358–61; E. K. Chambers, *The Elizabethan Stage*, III, 472.

*A Shrew* was written in the first instance for the Queen's men and by them sold to Pembroke's. We suggest, in short, that three early Shakespeare plays—*John*, *The Shrew*, and *Richard III*—may have been rewritten for one company, the Queen's, in the early nineties.[1]

To proceed to the *T.R.* itself. We must glance at its printing-house history. Thomas Orwin, who printed the play, had a suspicious career: his press was seized during part of 1591, the very year the *T.R.* appeared, and had been suspended at least twice not long before.[2] Though the *T.R.* was printed "for Sampson Clarke", it seems to us that Orwin may have been responsible for it[3]: for the possible risks taken with an early "derivative play" turn our thoughts first to the man who lived dangerously. Though of course it would be wrong to exaggerate its bearing on our problem, Orwin's career should be kept in mind.

The shoddy text of the *T.R.* also concerns us. Exits and entrances are omitted, many speeches have no speech headings, speech headings are sometimes ambiguous, stage directions summarize the action or describe it as something already witnessed before.[4] Faults such as these, common in reported texts, can obviously be expected even in derivative plays such as we suppose *A Shrew* and the *T.R.* to be. For derivative plays had to be written in haste after the production of the source-play, if this latter was unprinted: and descriptive directions referring to the source-play would creep in quite naturally if imi-

1. In *Alcazar and Orlando* Greg quoted a private letter from J. D. Wilson suggesting that *A Shrew* was sold to Pembroke's by the Queen's men (pp. 361–2).

2. Orwin became a printer in 1587. In 1587–8 he was in trouble with the Court of Star Chamber; in 1589 the Master and both Wardens of the stationers waited at Lambeth a whole day "about an answere for the staie that came from his grace for Orwyn"; on 30 Aug. 1591 Whitgift wrote to the Stationers asking for the return of his press to Orwin [cf. Arber, 1, 527; 1, 555; v, li; also McKerrow, *Dictionary of Printers and Booksellers (1557–1640)* (1910); Strype's *Whitgift* (1718), p. 303].

3. Clarke's name survives on only three books: Lodge's *Alarum against Usurers* (1584); Greene's *Menaphon* (1589); and the *T.R.* (1591). Lodge's *Alarum* resumed the attack on Gosson for which an earlier book of his had run into trouble (cf. Lodge in *D.N.B.*); Greene's *Menaphon* contained the famous attack on the author of the *Ur-Hamlet*, probably Shakespeare. Thus Clarke's name appears on three potentially dangerous books, and he may have been used as a stooge publisher.

4. See our note on the text of the *T.R.*, Appendix C.

tation was the order. Typical foul paper omission of speech headings and stage directions in company with the above define the text more or less recognizably.

One last approach to the *John–T.R.* problem still remains open to us—a particularly fruitful one. The critics have long been aware that obscurities in Shakespeare's plays can sometimes be explained through his sources: where he has written hurriedly, he is said to have forgotten to transplant motives or other details which would otherwise have smoothed over his "inconsistencies". A large number of such "inconsistencies" has been claimed for *John*. It is possible, however, to turn the argument by pointing out inconsistencies in the *T.R.* which seem due to the precedence of *John*. In Appendix B we discuss the two plays from this angle and conclude, without prejudice we hope, that *John* is less inconsistent than has been thought, while the *T.R.* leaves the field with dishonour.

Let us now recapitulate the more important evidence concerning the *T.R.-John* relationship.

(*a*) *John* is in every way a good text (p. xxxiii ff.).—The *T.R.* features some recognized "bad quarto" characteristics, being (i) a tissue of stolen phrases; (ii) a text much more untidy than "foul paper plays" usually are, which, moreover, contains summarizing and descriptive directions (p. lv; Appendix C).

(*b*) The *T.R.* belonged to a company which, according to a distinguished critic, reconstructed for itself at least one other play just at the time when the *T.R.* came into existence. Three plays, two of which certainly belonged to this company, have curious contacts with three of Shakespeare's plays, and one of these (*A Shrew*) is now generally accepted as "derivative" (p. liii ff.).

(*c*) The writers of the two plays both consulted the chronicles (p. xviii). At one point the *T.R.* paraphrases M. Paris imperfectly, while *John* uses the words of the source in the right context: and whereas the *T.R.* shows no other sign of acquaintance with M. Paris, *John* follows him in at least one more passage (p. xv). Where both plays draw upon the same source material, Shakespeare is usually closer to the words of the source: which the intimate contact of the plays makes doubly interesting, since the second writer evidently thought first of the first play, referring only in the second place to the chronicles (p. xviii ff.).

(*d*) The *T.R.* contains structural inconsistencies which conflate (i) historical truth as retailed in the chronicles, and (ii) deviations therefrom such as appear also in *John* but there moulded into a consistent whole. Being comprehensible only as thoughtless echoing from a previous version, these inconsistencies alone plead strongly for the precedence of *John* (Appendix B).

(*e*) The "dates" of the plays must not enter the argument. We ask for disregard of the traditional "Shakespeare Chronology", since the relationship of the two John plays is part of the evidence (p. liii). New clues for the date of *John* suggest that the two plays were written within a few months of each other at most in 1590-1 (p. xliv ff.).

So far nothing has been said of the "internal evidence" for dating. Kinship of temper and style is generally taken to indicate proximity in composition. This is not necessarily right, but the parallels between *John* and *Richard II* are certainly startling. *Love's Labour's Lost* also has many verbal resemblances, as a glance at our footnotes will show, and likewise *Richard III*.[1] *Richard II* may well have been written within a very short time of *John*; *Richard III* at least a year earlier, and *Love's Labour's Lost* about a year later, in our opinion. *Romeo* and *Midsummer Night's Dream* belong more or less to the same period. To fit *John* into a more clear-cut "chronology" lies outside our present duties.

We believe that *John* was written in the winter/spring of 1590/91. Critics of exceptional authority prefer a date between 1593 and 1596. Students of the period will realize that more is at stake than meets the eye, and that the problem, obscure and elusive though it be, must be faced.

---

1. For the affinities of these plays cf. articles by König, Isaac, Sarrazin in the *Shakespeare Jahrbuch* for 1875, 1884, 1894, 1897-8.

## 4. THE PLAY

To praise the contrivance of a play which deviates very little from its "source-play" would be dangerous. The critics, consequently, have been content to admire the few virtues in *John* not plundered directly from the *T.R.*—the exuberance of the Bastard, the logic of Pandulph, the soliloquies, the verse generally. But if, as we suggest, the plot for *John* was not found ready-made by Shakespeare we must re-examine it with new respect.

An exception to those who saw *John* as a mere shadow was John Masefield. Disregarding sources altogether, he declared that the "great scheme of the play is the great achievement, not the buxom boor who flouts the Duke of Austria".[1] *John* "is an intellectual form in which a number of people with obsessions illustrate the idea of treachery".[2] Masefield's brief summary must be quoted:

John's mother, Elinor, has been treacherous to one of her sons. John has usurped his brother's right . . . [The Bastard's mother] confesses that she was seduced by . . . Coeur de Lion. The Bastard's half-brother, another domestic traitor, does not scruple to accuse his mother of adultery . . .

[In Act II the kings] turn from their pledged intention to effect a base alliance. . . . In the third act . . . the French King adds another falseness. He breaks away from the newly-made alliance at the bidding of the Pope's legate . . .

. . . Hubert fails to blind Prince Arthur. Even in the act of mercy he is treacherous. . . . John, thinking that the murder has been done, breaks faith with Hubert. . . . In the last act, the English nobles, who have been treacherous to John, betray their new master. . . A monk treacherously poisons John. . .[3]

Persuasive as it is, Masefield's thesis that "treachery" is the

1. *William Shakespeare* (1911), p. 81.    2. *Op. cit.*, p. 76.

3. Pp. 78–80.—As all concepts contain their opposites, e.g. treachery supposes loyalty, Masefield's account ignores half the "treachery" theme. Shakespeare emphasizes the bond between Constance and Arthur, Eleanor and John, France and the Dauphin; a messenger professes loyal zeal instead of speaking in formulae (IV. ii. 180); various passages present treachery as the rider to loyalty (e.g. III. i. 253–62, v. ii. 9–44), and not *vice versa*; and so on. The Bastard's extravagant loyalty to the criminal John (cf. IV. iii. 142–4, notes) likewise counterpoises the generalized treachery—being partly a device to preserve the sanity and balance of *John*.

*Leitmotiv* of *John* does not wholly satisfy. Iteration of one topic in a "great scheme" does not necessarily make it central. An analysis of recurring features of style and imagery will show that Masefield's précis covers only a part of the play.

Remarkable in *John*, firstly, are the nicely-argued dsiquisitions on moral concepts, often illustrating the conflict of two value-systems in a finely-pointed dualism. Thus crime and punishment go together (II. i. 184–90), faith and need (III. i. 137–42), law and justice (III. i. 111–16), truth and perjury (III. i. 150–223), truth and deceit (V. iv. 26 ff.), honesty and commodity (II. i. 561–98). And no sooner are these concepts lined up than kindred material clamours for admission amongst them—madness and reason (III. iii. 43–60), perfection (II. i. 423–45), and ceremony (IV. ii. 1–39), that great Elizabethan bugbear. The middle star in this galaxy of elaborated concepts emerges, finally, as the age-old will-o'-the-wisp of right and wrong, or right and might.

A simple count of the frequency of words can often be a valuable first step in an examination of a play's themes, as F. C. Kolbe has shown.[1] Having noted the preoccupation with moral concepts, we are not surprised to find that the word "right" occurs more times in *John* (28 times) than in any other play of Shakespeare (*3 H 6* is next: 21 times).[2] Other words numerous enough to claim attention in *John* are "blood" (40 times, first place in Shakespeare),[3] "hand" (52, second to *Titus*), "eye" (47, third to *MND.* and *LLL.*). And, just as the chopped-off hand in *Titus*, and the symbolism of eyes in comedies of love, is not accidental to the main theme so, in *John* too, repeating words are firmly anchored in the action, they are not slip-shod writing. The dominant image-sequence of the play, with its clear interlocking, resolves all doubt on this head.

(*a*) We take IV. i. to be the central scene,[4] and the spectacle

1. In *Shakespeare's Way* (1930). Kolbe did not discuss *John*.
2. All our figures are based on J. Bartlett's *Concordance* for Shakespeare.
3. Prof. W. Clemen pointed out the significance of blood in *John* [*Developmen: of Shakespeare's Imagery* (1951), p. 86].
4. The action of the play is held together through Arthur, for whom France took up arms (Acts I–III), and whose "murder" caused the revolt of the nobles (Acts IV, V). Shakespeare exaggerates the French concern for Arthur, and the nobles had forgotten Arthur when they revolted in 1215, but Shakespeare's rearrangement of history centres John's problems round Arthur. We suggest in

of Hubert threatening to blind Arthur to be the most exciting picture of the play. What Hubert saw in Arthur's eyes seems to have fascinated Shakespeare particularly, for the image of reflecting eyes gradually deepens in meanings. Fitly enough, in a play where impersonal rhetoric and passionate pleading continually supplant each other, the image first appears in a conventional setting: the lover sees himself mirrored in his lady's eyes (II. i. 496–503). Immediately after IV. i we find John searching the eyes of his lords (IV. ii. 2), while Hubert's eyes reflect the (supposed) blinding scene:

> The image of a wicked heinous fault
> Lives in his eye (IV. ii. 71–2)
>
> . . . foul imaginary eyes of blood
> Presented thee more hideous than thou art
> (IV. ii. 265–6)[1]

The sub-surface significances that gradually attach to repeating images convert eyes into symbols of right, and hands into might. When the "heavy hand" (IV. iii. 58) of might is later equated with "wall-ey'd wrath or staring rage" (IV. iii. 49), a terrible image of distortion and deformity applied to John, these repeating symbols, like the perpetual personifications of Death and Fortune,[2] almost achieve the stature of *dramatis personae*.

(*b*) Closely related to the imagery of blinding is a group denoting outrage to the body generally. The city (and state) conceived as body politic ranges fresh associative fields beside the more literal:

> . . . our cannon shall be bent
> Against the brows of this resisting town (II. i. 37–8)

---

Appendix A (2) that Shakespeare took the pains to look up R. Coggeshall's Latin MS. chronicle, the recognized authority for the death of Arthur, which, if we are right, implies Shakespeare's realization of the importance of IV. i.

1. Cf. also IV. iii. 150, v. iv. 60.

2. Death (II. i. 352, 453, 456, III. iii. 25 ff., IV. ii. 82, IV. iii. 35, v. ii. 177, v. vii. 15) reappears in disguise as War (III. i. 30, IV. iii. 149, v. ii. 74, 164) and Time (especially III. i. 250–1); Fortune (II. i. 391, II. ii. 52 ff., III. i. 44, III. iii. 119, v. ii. 58) as Occasion (IV. ii. 125). Prof. C. Spurgeon's *Shakespeare's Imagery* (1935) discussed personification as a special feature of *John* (pp. 246–53).

> We from the west will send destruction
> Into this city's bosom (II. i. 409–10)

John's first set speech to the men of Angiers is the most sustained expression (II. i. 206–34), but the cluster stands out throughout:

> Whose foot spurns back the ocean's roaring tides (II. i. 24)

> Austria and France shoot in each other's mouth (II. i. 414)

> . . . when I strike my foot
> Upon the bosom of the ground, rush forth (IV. i. 2–3)

Body-images are especially important in *John*, because of their variety and profusion. Apart from eye, hand, blood (cf. above) —mouth (14 times), breath (18), foot (12), bosom (10), brow (11), spleen (4), bowels (3), arm (27),[1] tooth and teeth (5) are all unexceeded in number in other plays of the canon, while some, such as tongue (23 times in *John*, third to *R 2* and *LLL.*), come not far behind. When we recall that *John* is only 2,600 lines long, definitely shorter than the plays that compare with it in the frequency of body-images, these statistics call for attention.[2]

(*c*) After body-outrage the next step is rape-imagery. The naturalness of the transition is best illustrated by the set speeches at the siege of Angiers. John's (II. i. 206–34) is shot through with threats of body-outrage, Philip's (II. i. 235 ff.) implies rape (l. 257), and the Bastard expounds with zestful innuendo (II. i. 381–7). All through *John* we meet this important connective theme:

> Outfaced infant state, and done a rape
> Upon the maiden virtue of the crown (II. i. 97–8)

> . . . on the marriage-bed
> Of smiling peace to march a bloody host (III. i. 171–2)

> And kiss the lips of unacquainted change (III. iii. 166)

Subsidiary here is the blot and stain imagery which, though usually toned down in petrified metaphors—

---

1. Bartlett's "arm" takes armour and arm (the limb) together.

2. Prof. Spurgeon (*loc. cit.*) thought body-images the outstanding device in *John*, apart from personification (cf. p. lxi, n. 2).

To look into the blots and stains of right     (II. i. 114)

The faiths of men ne'er stained with revolt     (IV. ii. 6)

—is highly charged when applied to Arthur (II. ii. 43–54), since a child's "stains" are imagined the equivalent of the rape-fornication qualities of the adults (II. ii. 54–65): physical deformity being equated with the spiritual deformity of adultery, the conceit is that Arthur's beauty (not his age) disqualifies him from the favours of strumpet Fortune. In II. i. 129–33 stain and fornication images are likewise bracketed.

(d) The bastardy-fornication theme proper is a cornerstone of *John*. Act I dwells upon it, and Act II at once resumes it (II. i. 122–33); the Bastard likes to remember his illegitimacy (I. i. 207, II. i. 276, 279), to soliloquize about "That smooth-fac'd gentleman, tickling commodity" (II. i. 573), to threaten to cuckold Austria (II. i. 290–3), and Shakespeare created him partly to fill the needs of this theme. Fortune, not unexpectedly, enters as a strumpet (II. i. 391–4, II. ii. 54–61, v. ii. 58–9). Perhaps the most brilliant jugglery comes in III. iii, where Constance invokes Death as a lover (ll. 25–36), rebukes him for being passionless and sleepy (ll. 39–41), then wonders how she "may be deliver'd" of her woes—her woes being a "child-substitute" (l. 55, note)—and finally brings forth a "babe of clouts" (l. 58). The sexual looseness of the elder Plantagenets had been emphasized to distinguish the correctness of the other party—France staid and cautious, Lewis a formal wooer (II. i. 496 ff.), Arthur a child. Constance believes in chastity (II. i. 124)—unlike Eleanor, who waives such considerations (II. i. 132), or Cœur-de-lion the seducer, or John or Faulconbridge. Constance's frenzy resembles Ophelia's insanity in its sexual prepossessions, but whereas Ophelia, whose mind has snapped, gives voice to something essential to her nature in her bawdy songs, Constance in III. iii is not true to herself, and her ravings show only how far from itself her mind has been bent.

(e) Bridging across to the final element in the sequence, a wealth of "over" and "under" images are clear pictures of suppression. The close affinity to group (d) emerges in verbal echoes,[1] and in the juxtaposition of similar over/under ideas:

1. Cf. I. i. 263–4 and II. i. 41–3.

> Sh' adulterates hourly with thine uncle John,
> And with her golden hand hath pluck'd on France
> To tread down fair respect of sovereignty, . . .
> And leave those woes alone which I alone
> Am bound to underbear! (II. ii. 56–65)

Infrequent and nonce words help to give weight to the group: aloft (IV. ii. 139, note), brawl'd down (II. i. 383), overbear (III. iii. 9, IV. ii. 37), o'ermasterest (II. i. 109), overstain'd (III. i. 162), o'erswell (II. i. 337), supernal (II. i. 112), underbear (II. ii. 65), underprop (V. ii. 99), underwrought (II. i. 95), uphold (III. i. 83, 241, V. iv. 5).

(*f*) The last link in the interlocking group of major images, though not itself imagery, we take to be the device of perpetual analysis of moral concepts (cf. p. lx). Here we expect over/ under pictures, the simplest symbols of right and wrong:

> O then tread down my need, and faith mounts up:
> Keep my need up, and faith is trodden down! (III. i. 141–2)

Since all moral concepts are poor relations of right and wrong, we also expect to recognize the basic dichotomy despite its transmutations:

> . . . when *law* can do no *right*
> Let it be lawful that *law* bar no *wrong*! (III. i. 111–12)

and the two primary concepts, disguised as truth and falsehood, honesty and commodity, faith and need, chastity and unchastity, and so on, thus continually re-enact for us the human drama of Arthur and John.

The key to the major "imagery of oppression" which we have outlined seems to be the theme of "right versus might". This theme also dictated many of the more striking deviations from history in *John*. Arthur, a young warrior in Holinshed, becomes a helpless child in the play; Constance a "widow, husbandless" (II. ii. 14, note); Limoges and Austria, the two enemies *par excellence* of Cœur-de-lion, are made one person, so that Arthur's plight—having to accept aid from Limoges–Austria—seems more abject; and, more significantly still, Shakespeare presents John as a usurper from the start (I. i. 40, note), whereas his right to the throne was declared as strong as Arthur's by the chroniclers.

Especially in the minor imagery the theme of "right versus might" can be shown to have occupied Shakespeare. For *John* follows the "wheel of Fortune" pattern for tragedy[1]—was probably billed as a tragedy in 1591—and various comparisons help to construe the rise and fall of the hero. Fortune's favours before III. ii, and her frowns thereafter, are expressed in different ways. Up to III. iii John's military speed repeatedly contrasts with French caution and slowness[2]; and Fortune helps John with good winds (II. i. 57); in IV. ii. 113 ff. Lewis's military speed surprises John. John recognizes that Fortune has turned against him (IV. ii. 125), now helping Lewis with favourable winds.[3] Various game and gambling allusions are thrown in to underline the participation of Fortune.[4] The antithesis of speed and slowness, again, continues in the parallel one of John's hotness and French coldness.[5] Impetuousness, indeed, may be said to be John's "tragic flaw", and the *burning* fever that kills him (v. vii. 30–48) the final irony of Fate. The story ends when the usurper's vitality has consumed itself, when even his legs fail him (v. iii. 16, v. vii. 10), and a child-figure, Arthur resurrected as Prince Henry, triumphs at last in undisputed "right".

A further stylistic device that requires some attention, being now unfamiliar, may be called "putting the case". In a sense, *John* develops into one continuous debate, broken up into separate issues. In Act I the Faulconbridges argue it out before the king; in Act II follow the twin-speeches of John and King Philip (II. i. 206–66), of the English and French heralds (II. i. 300–24), the twin rebukes of the kings (II. i. 334–49), the contrasting speeches of the Bastard advocating war (II. i. 373–96), and of Hubert advocating peace (ll. 423–55); in Act III King

1. Cf. R. Chapman, 'The Wheel of Fortune in Shakespeare's Historical Plays' [*R.E.S.*, I (1950), pp. 1–7], and I. i. 1 note.

2. Cf. also I. i. 178, II. i. 79, 233, 297, III. ii. 16, III. iii. 11, IV. ii. 170, 260–9, IV. iii. 74, v. vii. 50, etc.

3. Shakespeare manufactured a parallel by having the messenger of war delayed with the invading army (II. i. 57–9, IV. ii. 114–15).

4. Cf. II. i. 123, III. i. 144, IV. ii. 93–5, v. ii. 103–7, 118, 141, etc.

5. Cf. II. i. 53, 479, III. i. 31, 49, 243, 266, III. iii. 11, IV. iii. 74, v. iii. 3, etc.

Philip pleads for the sanctity of oaths (III. i. 150–78), and Pandulph's reply (ll. 189–223), the turning-point of John's career, whether *ratiocinatio* or not,[1] is universally acclaimed as wonderfully typical "school-logic", unique in Shakespeare; in III. ii John urges Hubert to kill Arthur, in IV. i Arthur persuades Hubert to let him live (the play's two best scenes); in V. ii. 9–39 Salisbury puts the case for rebellion; and other formal and contrasted speeches abound. Modern critics often condemn the consequent "motiveless zigzagging of the action", which meant that in "almost every act a new side-issue is treated with such breadth as to become the main issue".[2] They forget that the study of rhetoric trained educated Elizabethans in the refinements of debate, and that the "side-issues" in *John* may be viewed as thematic iteration, being always a continuation of the same high debate of right and wrong.

In Act II the soldiering distracts from the possible monotony of "putting the case". Elsewhere diversity of style provides a relief:

one feels at times that here Shakespeare is thinking consciously of the variety of characters and of the language which is appropriate to them[3]

And not only diversity as between individuals. The constant intrusion of formality—in the person of ambassadors, heralds, legates, messengers—extends to the presentation of character generally. Except for the Bastard's circle in Act I, everyone speaks impersonally on first appearance, and it is the doffing and donning of the "official" mask, the interplay of private passion and public duty, that throws a really distinctive light and shade through *John*.[4]

Arthur's conceits in IV. i, often dismissed as unnatural, are

---

1. Cf. III. i. 189, note.

2. Bulthaupt, quoted approvingly in G. C. Moore Smith's *King John* (1900), p. xxxi.

3. B. Ifor Evans, *The Language of Shakespeare's Plays* (1952), p. 44.

4. Cf. the problem of the Identity of Hubert and the Citizen of Angiers (p. xxxvii). Tillyard hinted at the more elaborate "interplay" that we suggest: "John is sometimes a conventionally dignified monarch and at others a mean and treacherous man, realistically portrayed" [*Shakespeare's History Plays* (1944), p. 223].

the pressure-point of the method.[1] For Hubert's short, simple
answers help to heighten the impression of Arthur's artifice:
and the man's uncompromising determination leaves open no
door for the child except verbal wriggling. Perhaps, then,
Shakespeare aimed at preciousness. Sudden necessity similarly
drove Pandulph to verbal tricks in III. i. 189–223, and anger
and despair plunged Constance into involute declamation in
II. i and III. i. By III. iii the reasoning madness of Constance
establishes verbal pyrotechnics as the language of emergency,
so that Arthur in IV. i behaves *conventionally* (as does John in
V. vii, quibbling on his deathbed). And, though some writers
have felt that Arthur should be dumb with fright in IV. i, that
his pleading is unnatural, the convention does not seem to us
to jar with the purely psychological needs of the situation, but
rather to harmonize with them. Arthur darts from conceit to
conceit as from door to door, elaborating any point that might
prize open Hubert's determination. He realizes that his pretty
thoughts undermine Hubert's purpose, and the consequent
wild dash to a new conceit, just as the one in hand fades out,
reveals a more or less conscious *technique of pleading*. His conceits do not ring prettily because "innocent prate" (IV. i. 25)
when turned "crafty" and "cunning" (IV. i. 53–4), like beauty
selling itself, distorts and defaces itself. Hence, we think, the
usual vague diagnosis of "unnaturalness" is only half-right.
Arthur's conceits or contortions are unnatural, as all contortions must be: yet the situation calls for them. Physical dis-
figurement has to be avoided—even at the cost of spiritual
stain. Not his terror, but the sight of a child forced into dupli-
city, produces the more subtle pathos of the scene.[2]

If *John* may not be dismissed as a hotch-potch of alarums

1. Walter Raleigh condemned them as typical of Shakespeare's immature
writing [*Shakespeare* (1916), p. 222]; so Kreyssig (*apud* Furness, p. 291), and
many more. Shakespeare probably remembered the pathos of the Abraham and
Isaac plays while writing this scene.

2. Mark Van Doren treated the stylistic extravagance in *John* somewhat dif-
ferently: "The presence in 'King John' of a certain famous passage about paint-
ing the lily is not accidental but essential, for the theme of the play is excess..."
Van Doren thought many orations of the play "bloated beyond all form", and
that "the pole of hyperbole, the chill Thule of sigh-blasted excess is reached and
passed by Constance. She is the last and most terrible of Shakespeare's wailing
women" [*Shakespeare* (1939), pp. 106, 107, 109].

and excursions, can a good word be said for a "hero" of the play? The few who accept John as hero condemn his colourlessness; some think the Bastard the hero, the majority, that there is none.[1]

Two considerations are usually allowed to stigmatize John as an unsatisfactory hero. Compared with the complementary *Richard II*, Shakespeare's "revision of the *T.R.*" is unambitious, therefore "its straightforward chronicling seems less mature than the psychological study of Richard".[2] In short, the failure of the hero is the fault of the "source-play", and of Shakespeare's neglect of possible improvements. Here the assumption, that an introspective hero imports better psychology or greater dramatic craftsmanship, must not pass unquestioned. Should not an exhibition of minds working on each other enthrall as much as inner conflicts and soliloquies? This elementary principle seems to have satisfied Shakespeare in some of his most mature plays, as in *John*. John explores and exploits his fellow-men. He tries to find everyone's price. The Bastard is bought with a knighthood (i. i. 162), France with five provinces (ii. i. 527 ff.), Hubert with promises (iii. ii. 30–42), Arthur is promised lands (ii. i. 551), the nobles are promised Arthur (iv. ii. 67), John tries to buy them off a second time (iv. ii. 168), buys off the pope with a nominal submission (v. i. 1), in order to buy off Lewis (v. i. 64). The outstanding speech of the play, analysing commodity, is not gratuitous, nor are the psychological implications of "this all-changing word" made a secret.

As John's few distinctive qualities, such as rebelliousness and patriotism, one by one prove to have been inessentials, his wielding of commodity assumes significance. One is tempted to regard the play as a study of a virtuoso politician. For, however short-sighted his strategy, John's tactics are brilliant. Nowhere is this more patent than in iii. ii. Having been tied down by his interfering mother, by the threats of France and the mere existence of Arthur, John throws off his chains for one brief moment with wonderful skill, but disastrous consequences. France has been repulsed. Meanwhile Eleanor lost

1. A. Bonjour gave samples of these various views in 'The Road to Swinstead Abbey' [*Journal of English Literary History*, XVIII (1951), 253–6].
2. M. R. Ridley, *Shakespeare's Plays A Commentary* (1937), p. 85.

face by nearly being captured (III. ii. 7) : John seizes the opportunity to order her to remain in France (l. 11), rubbing in her
failure ("strongly guarded", l. 12) to make sure she does not
answer back. Then he fishes for Hubert's promise to murder
Arthur. Scarcely has the scene ended, however, before Pandulph's strategic commentary (in III. iii) points out the fruit-
lessness of John's tactical master-stroke.

But in the last resort Shakespeare's John is Holinshed's
John (cf. p. xxx), with ungovernable passion as well as cunning dissimulation in his heart. To some degree, therefore, the
psychological interest in him springs from a simple dualism,
a see-saw between seeming irreconcilables. For an audience
he should be a puzzle and a surprise. In the study, of course,
the theatrical trick loses power.

Like his distaste for introspection, John's collapse in Act v
displeases the critics. A hero ought to be heroic, they contend
(ignoring Richard II). But perhaps the very disappointment
of the critics in the heartlessness of a man at death's door is a
measure of unreasonable expectations, and a tribute to a con-
trived effect. Inaction is undramatic, and a heartless hero
must indeed be a disappointment; but John's collapse in v. iii
may be tensely dramatic within the context of the play as a
whole, even if it seems mere inaction within the scene. The
full-circle scheme of *John* demands that the hero who is
Impetuousness must come to a dead stop (v. iii), while the
transformation of his energy into raving madness (v. vii. 11),
like the roaring of a car that will not go, finally brings home to
us the tremendous power of the pent-up forces to which he was
a slave.

Charges that John fails as hero are due to a confusion of
terms. Admittedly, he cannot claim to be a national hero in
Act v. But his personal qualities are one thing, and his structural position as the play's hero (or protagonist) another.
That John occupies the middle of his play need not be labour-
ed, but two series of parallels can help to show how structural
tightening consolidates his position.

Firstly, the fortunes of Lewis are made to resemble John's.
Lewis, dominated by his father (as John by Eleanor at the out-
set), gambles for a kingdom, goes to ruin once his parent's influence is discarded (as John after III. ii), deciding on a coward-

ly murder of the English lords (as John decides on Arthur's, the turning-point in both cases); he is let down by clashing loyalties in Melun (as John by Hubert), defies the pope, and finally, his supplies lost at sea (as John's devoured by the Wash), knuckles under (like John) to—Pandulph and Fortune. Such parallelism Shakespeare used often, most successfully perhaps in the stories of Gloucester and Lear in *King Lear*.

Secondly, John's tragedy is interpreted as a family drama. Three sons of Henry II, beside John, fill in the background. Richard I, crusader and adulterer, symbolizes the conflicting passions of the Plantagenets; Salisbury, his half-brother, almost personifies Nobility ["noble . . . nobility . . . noble" (v. ii. 40–3)], and it may be no coincidence that he alone in *John* expresses a desire to crusade (v. ii. 33–8); Geoffrey seems to have been a nonentity, hag-ridden like his father; Faulconbridge takes over from Richard I ["perfect Richard" (i. i. 90)[1]]; and Arthur resembles Salisbury ["noble boy" (ii. i. 18)]. John fights against "nobility", crusades against Rome, and dies a nonentity, and all the while other *dramatis personae* overshadow him, in one sense. His abuse of the pope cannot rival the railing of Eleanor and Constance; he boasts neither the vigour of Faulconbridge, nor the generalship of Cœur-de-lion, nor the virtues of Salisbury. But, though he appears colourless by comparison, being the centre where all the strong colours of the family meet and neutralize each other, Shakespeare created the family as the complement to John, and not the other way about. That is, John seems to be the product of his family, but really the family was devised as a projection of John.[2]

Structurally John seems to be the centre of his play; if he is not the hero, he is certainly the villain. Nevertheless, the Bastard's ascendancy at the end may still perplex readers. As soon as we view him as one of a type, however, his place in the play becomes more clear. Like Mercutio, Falstaff, Touchstone and Jaques, and Autolycus, the Bastard is a cynic, Shakespeare's

---

1. Cf. ii. i. 294, iii. ii. 1, v. i. 57, notes.

2. Most of the Plantagenets (e.g. Arthur, Geoffrey, Salisbury, Faulconbridge) are given characters which are entirely Shakespeare's fiction, the rest (Eleanor, Constance, Richard I) having subsidiary traits emphasized, new traits added, for the purposes of the play. Only John remains more or less as in Holinshed.

customary addition to the stories that he followed closely. True to type, he stands outside the inner framework of his play, mainly as a commentator. Whether or not he is the chorus,[1] as many have thought, his irrepressible candour, which dovetails with the functions of a chorus, makes him immensely likeable. But, however likeable, the chorus cannot be the hero. It might help, furthermore, to compare the Honesty or Simplicity of the moralities, for the Bastard's expository tirades and various other touches indicate his descent.[2] Indeed, to make his subordinate position crystal clear, Shakespeare has him snubbed again and again—by Eleanor (I. i. 64), by Lady Faulconbridge (I. i. 227, 243), by Austria (II. i. 147), by John (III. i. 60), by Salisbury (IV. iii. 94), by Lewis (V. ii. 160).

Countering the theory that *John* has no hero, Dr A. Bonjour, in a stimulating article, has recently argued that

we have to deal here with a deliberately contrasted evolution. John's career represents a falling curve, the Bastard's career a rising curve; and both curves, perfectly contrasted, are linked into a single pattern. The structure of the play is thus remarkably balanced . . . in very simple terms: decline of a hero—rise of a hero.[3]

This is ingenious, but we feel that Dr Bonjour concedes too much. We cannot accept the Bastard as a hero even in Act v. Nowhere in the play does his interference "make history". Impressed by John's delegation of authority to him (v. i. 77), some take this as a sign of the Bastard's greatness: whereas, we think, it was meant to be only a sign of John's dejection that he hands over to a servant, a bastard, and a boon companion. Modern democratic ideas distort our response to John's action. The immediate result—defeat in battle, and then the loss of John's army in the Wash, an act of criminal stupidity accredit-

1. His chorus duties at times impinge upon his psychological integrity. In II. i. 561–98 he has to denounce that sly devil, commodity, with whom he as a person really sympathizes: the sudden *volte-face* ("And why rail I on this commodity?") makes Shakespeare's machinery creak. In IV. iii. 139–59 Shakespeare walks a tight-rope, bringing Faulconbridge to the verge of recognizing John's usurpation during a chorus (cf. ll. 142, 143, 154, notes); in II. i. 585 the chorus Faulconbridge calls France's support of Arthur "honourable".

2. I. i. 182 ff., II. i. 561 ff., IV. iii. 140 ff., v. vii. 110 ff. are the "choruses"; cf. also II. i. 135, 573, IV. iii. 145, notes.

3. *E. L. H.*, XVIII (1951), 270.

ed to the Bastard by Shakespeare and dwelt upon twice to belittle him[1]—surely proves that this "hero" fails in the higher spheres, despite his triumphs as a bully. Those who find in the Bastard the regal qualities of "the character of the genuine king"[2] seem to us to have overstated their case.

The Bastard's "rising curve" cannot, of course, be denied. But we are doubtful whether it is integral rather than accidental to the structure. If John does not carry the play entirely by himself, the challenge comes not so much from another character as from the spirit of England. Yet England is not on that account the "hero" of the play, nor its structural centre. Various quibbles guide us to the old commonplace of the identity of king and country[3]: in a way John and England are one and the same theme. As in many of Shakespeare's political plays, the tragedy of the hero leads to the regeneration of his country. A further reason for the Bastard's ascendancy towards the end may therefore lie in the fact that "His function is to embody England, to incorporate the English soul".[4] The Bastard is carried upwards by the theme of England, of which he forms so essential a part.

Uncertainty about the hero may be indicative of a larger problem of approach. We no longer feel as did the Elizabethans about some of the subsidiary themes. Horror of rebellion was universal when Shakespeare wrote[5]: we must not forget this when reading the long-winded apology for rebellion in v. ii. Protestantism was still in the balance: a new and greater Armada was expected from abroad, while Martin Marprelate

1. v. vi. 37 ff., v. vii. 59 ff.

2. Tillyard, *Shakespeare's History Plays* (1944), p. 227.—In *John*, even more immediately than in the two historical tetralogies, "Shakespeare's problem is how to legitimize the illegitimate" [J. F. Danby, *Shakespeare's Doctrine of Nature* (1949), p. 75]. Illegitimate kingship plunges John into crime, while the Bastard rises from country boor to national spokesman by dint of his illegitimate birth. Dr Bonjour's theory of a "deliberately contrasted evolution" works in more ways than one. Yet the Bastard fails to develop in personality, he is not "a man whose every syllable makes him better understood", as Van Doren recognized (*Shakespeare*, p. 115), and his consequent failure as general and statesman may not be passed over lightly.

3. Cf. ii. i. 91, 202, iv. iii. 142–3, notes.

4. J. M. Murry, *Shakespeare* (1936), p. 156.

5. Tillyard, *op. cit.*, p. 221 ff.; L. B. Campbell, *Shakespeare's "Histories"* (1947), p. 155 ff.

made the foundations of the Church tremble at home.[1] The
play has topical qualities that may too easily elude us today
(cf. p. xxix). But it is worth the effort to come to grips with it:
not alone because it seems an admirable piece of craftsmanship to a late apologist, but also because it was the first of
Shakespeare's plays which contemporaries thought good
enough for plagiarism.

## 5. The Stage History

*John* was probably the first of Shakespeare's plays to be
pirated. New editions of the *T.R.*, first printed anonymously
in 1591, pay tribute to the popularity of the parent-play, for in
1611 the *T.R.* title-page read "by W. Sh.", and in 1622 "by
W. Shakespeare". In other words, the *T.R.* was being sold
under the pretence that it was *John*, a play in demand.[2] Francis
Meres remembered *John*, though he forgot other early plays of
Shakespeare, when he made his list in 1598. Munday, whether
part-author of the *T.R.* or not (p. 175), alluded to *John* in his
*Death of Robert, Earle of Huntington* (1601), as to a play familiar
to all.[3] Deloney in 1602, writing *The Lamentable Death of King
Iohn*, recalled tags from Shakespeare's play,[4] as did Richard
Niccols in his account of John's life in *A Winter Nights Vision*
(1610).[5] As the text of *John* was not available in print till 1623,

---

1. Many critics debate Shakespeare's religion at great length on the evidence
of *John*. Roman Catholic writers have felt that Shakespeare was pro-Rome, since
he toned down the anti-Roman violence of the *T.R.*, and "eliminated all anti-
Catholic elements"(!) [G. M. Greenewald, *Shakespeare's Attitude Towards the
Catholic Church in "King John"* (1938), p. 179; cf. J. H. de Groot, *The Shakespeares
and "The Old Faith"* (1947), pp. 180–224]. But the Protestant (Armada) bravado
in *John* contradicts such special pleading, and if Shakespeare was not "toning
down" the *T.R.* we can scarcely doubt that he was a Protestant in 1590.

2. The S.R. entry for the Folio (8 Nov. 1623) did not include *John* or *The
Shrew*: apparently the stationers, in whose eyes the possession of a "bad quarto"
gave "copy-right" covering the good text [cf. W. W. Greg, 'The Spanish
Tragedy—A Leading Case?' (in *Library*, VI (1926), 47)] allowed "derivative
plays" to cover their source-plays as well, taking the two as one work.

3. The *John* story is alluded to in dumb show (Austria, Constance and Arthur
appear on sig. D,ᵛ); Hubert is addressed as "*Hubert*, thou fatall keeper of poore
babes" (sig. F₄)—Shakespeare faked Arthur's age, but the *T.R.* left him a young
warrior as in the chronicles (cf. p. xviii).

4. Cf. v. vii. 2, note.

5. Cf. stanza 52 (Niccols), and III. i. 102–5 (Shakespeare).

we infer that the initial success of 1591 was followed by several revivals.

After Shakespeare's death no record of performance remains until the revival at Covent Garden on 26 February 1737. The playbill for the Drury Lane production of 1745 said "Not acted 50 years", but probably this only meant "not acted for a long time".

In the 1720's Colley Cibber (the later poet laureate) rewrote *John*, calling it *Papal Tyranny*; but general ridicule kept the adaptation off the boards until the imminent Jacobite rebellion in 1745.[1] Cibber's play met the opportunity generously: Act I and the parts of Eleanor and Constance were cut completely, to give the "French invasion" more space, and very few lines were left as Shakespeare wrote them. Unfortunately for Cibber, however, Drury Lane managed to put on *John* itself five days after his first night at Covent Garden—with Garrick as John, Delane as Bastard, Macklin as Pandulph, Mrs Cibber as Constance, and Miss Macklin as Arthur.

Another famous adaptation also owed its success to contemporary politics. Valpy, headmaster of Reading School, "refined" Shakespeare's dialogue for his boys, also cut out Act I, so that, with the help of anti-French insertions, his version reached the Covent Garden stage in 1803, and

made so strong an impression on the feelings of an English audience, on the renewal of the War, that the Play was acted in almost every Town in Great Britain and Ireland.[2]

The most famous of all productions of *John* came in 1823–4 at Covent Garden. J. R. Planché (the later Somerset herald) was responsible for the exact imitation of antiquity—"The whole of the Dresses and Decorations being executed from indisputable Authorities, such as Monumental Effigies, Seals, Illumined MSS., &c.", according to the playbill. This was London's first "antiquarian production". The actors were dismayed by Planché's historicity, but the public enjoyed the spectacle. One enthusiastic critic wrote:

1. The story found its way into Pope's *Dunciad* (ed. 1742): "King John in silence modestly expires" (I, 252).
2. John Nichols, *Literary Anecdotes*, vol. IX (1815), p. 758.

Charles Kemble never more distinguished himself than by his powerful personation of the bastard *Falconbridge*. His first and second dresses were particularly graceful and picturesque. We never saw this distinguished actor to greater advantage.[1]

Planché's researches were preserved in an illustrated booklet published in 1823, and historical accuracy became the producers' mania. Kean's *John* (1852) brought theatrical pedantry to its high-point. Only in the present century did simplicity and Elizabethan styles return to favour.

Never a firm favourite, except when the political situation gave it edge again, *John* has usually been produced at regular intervals. Most of the stars of the theatre have appeared in it. But, short as it is, it has practically always been cut. Few producers have dared to retain the scolding of Eleanor and Constance, and the longer speeches have suffered. Often the principal actor played Faulconbridge, not John, which must also have distorted the play. The custom of casting girls to play Arthur seems quite as dangerous.

Harold Child added an excellent section, 'The Stage-History of *King John*', to Prof. J. D. Wilson's C.U.P. *King John* (1936). This supplements Prof. G. C. D. Odell's *Shakespeare from Betterton to Irving* (2 vols., 1920). Productions after 1936 include one by the Old Vic Theatre in Leeds in 1941 (Ernest Milton as John, Lewis Casson as Bastard, Sybil Thorndike as Constance, Renee Ascherson as Blanche, Sonia Dresdel as Lady Faulconbridge); one by the Birmingham Rep. Theatre in 1945 (David Read as John, Paul Scofield as Bastard); one at Stratford in 1948 (Robert Helpmann as John, Anthony Quayle as Bastard); and one on television in 1952 (Donald Wolfit as John).

1. Quoted by G. C. D. Odell, *Shakespeare from Betterton to Irving*, II, 172.

# THE LIFE AND DEATH OF
# KING JOHN

## DRAMATIS PERSONÆ*

KING JOHN.

PRINCE HENRY, *son to the king.*

ARTHUR, *Duke of Brittany, nephew to the king.*

THE EARL OF SALISBURY.

THE EARL OF PEMBROKE.

THE EARL OF ESSEX.

THE LORD BIGOT.

ROBERT FAULCONBRIDGE, *son to Sir Robert Faulconbridge.*

PHILIP *the Bastard, his half-brother.*

HUBERT, *a citizen of Angers.*

JAMES GURNEY, *servant to Lady Faulconbridge.*

PETER *of Pomfret, a prophet.*

PHILIP, *king of France.*

LEWIS, *the Dauphin.*

LIMOGES, *Duke of Austria.*

MELUN, *a French lord.*

CHATILLON, *ambassador from France to King John.*

CARDINAL PANDULPH, *the Pope's legate.*

QUEEN ELEANOR, *mother to King John.*

CONSTANCE, *mother to Arthur.*

BLANCHE *of Spain, niece to King John.*

LADY FAULCONBRIDGE, *widow to Sir Robert Faulconbridge.*

*Lords, Sheriff, Heralds, Officers, Soldiers,
Messengers, and other Attendants.*

SCENE: *Partly in England, and partly in France.*

* The list of *dramatis personæ* does not appear in the Folios. It was first given by Rowe.

2

# THE LIFE AND DEATH OF
# KING JOHN

## ACT I

### SCENE I.—[*The Court of England.*]

*Enter* KING JOHN, QUEEN ELEANOR, PEMBROKE, ESSEX,
SALISBURY, *and Attendants, with them* CHATILLON *of France.*

*K. John.* Now, say, Chatillon, what would France with us?
*Chat.* Thus, after greeting, speaks the King of France
    In my behaviour to the majesty,
    The borrow'd majesty, of England here.
*Elea.* A strange beginning: "borrow'd majesty"!     5
*K. John.* Silence, good mother; hear the embassy.
*Chat.* Philip of France, in right and true behalf

---

ACT I
*Scene* 1

*Act* I *Scene* I.] Actus Primus, Scaena Prima. F1.   The . . . England.] Pope;
om. F1.   S.D.] This ed.; Enter King Iohn, Queene Elinor, Pembroke, Essex,
and Salisbury, with the Chattylion of France. F1; King *John*, discovered upon a
Throne, . . . Bell.   S.D. and Attendants] Om. F1; and Others Capell.   S.D.
with them] This ed.; with Rowe, edd.   1. *Chatillon*] Johnson (throughout);
Chatillion F1 (throughout).

The . . . *of*] *John*, R 2, and R 3 have
the "life and death" formula in F1
(also *Caes.* in the F1 Catalogue). As *R 2*
and *R 3* omit it in their quartos, which
promise *The Tragedy of* —, we assume
that *John* acquired it in F1, and was
first known as a tragedy. Meres in 1598
called it that, and *T.R.* was also described thus (Pt II, sig. A₂).
   S.D. with them *Chatillon*] F1 "the
Chattylion" might be a confusion with
a title ("the Chatelain"): but an omit-

ted suspension-mark (for "m") seems
more likely.
   1. *Now . . . us?*] Cf. Kyd's *Spanish
Tragedy*: "Now say L. Generall, how
fares our Campe?" (I. ii. 1).
   *Chatillon*] Trisyllabic: cf. *H5*, III. v. 43.
   3. *In my behaviour*] In my person:
"the king of *France* speaks in the *character* which I here assume" (Johnson).
Cf. v. ii. 129.
   4. *borrow'd*] stolen, counterfeit.
   6. *embassy*] ambassador's message.

Of thy deceased brother Geoffrey's son,
Arthur Plantagenet, lays most lawful claim
To this fair island and the territories:                              10
To Ireland, Poictiers, Anjou, Touraine, Maine,
Desiring thee to lay aside the sword
Which sways usurpingly these several titles,
And put the same into young Arthur's hand,
Thy nephew and right royal sovereign.                                 15
*K. John.* What follows if we disallow of this?
*Chat.* The proud control of fierce and bloody war,
  To enforce these rights so forcibly withheld.
*K. John.* Here have we war for war and blood for blood,
  Controlment for controlment: so answer France.                     20
*Chat.* Then take my king's defiance from my mouth,
  The farthest limit of my embassy.
*K. John.* Bear mine to him, and so depart in peace.
  Be thou as lightning in the eyes of France,

---

9. *most*] F1; om. Pope.        18. *To*] F1; *T'* Pope.        20. *for controlment*] F1; *for control* Vaughan conj.        22. *farthest*] F1; *furthest* Steevens.

---

10. *territories:*] i.e. dependencies. This "rather odd use of the word" puzzled Wilson (C.U.P. *John*, p. xxv), but, as I. John had noted, the *T.R.* in a later passage reads like Shakespeare: "King to *England, Cornwall* and *Wales,* & to their Territories" (II. iii. 222–3).

12. *Desiring*] Asking; commanding.

12–13. *sword . . . sways*] The usual cliché was "the sceptre which sways" i.e. rules, and Shakespeare's twist emphasizes that John *rules by the sword.* Cf. I. i. 40, note.

13. *titles*] possessions.

14. *young Arthur*] Arthur is called *young Arthur* a dozen or so times (following Hol., 164, ii), to emphasize his helplessness.

15. *Thy . . . sovereign.*] Cf. Appendix A, p. 166.

16. *disallow of*] disapprove of, reject.

17. *proud control*] overbearing mastery, or compulsion. Cf. G. Whetstone's *Censure of a Loyall Subject* (1587): "subiect to the proud controlement

of euery raskal *Spaniard*" (sig. D).

*fierce and bloody*] *fierce* meant "proud, haughty" as well as "wild, excessive", and thus ties *proud* to *bloody* (*bloody* could = "passionate"). Cf. v. ii. 158, III. iii. 17–19, note.

19–20. *Here . . . controlment*] Steevens compared *The First Part of Ieronimo* (1605): "*And.* Thou shalt pay trybute, Portugalle, with blood. / *Bal.* Trybute for trybute, then: and foes for foes. / *And.* I bid you sudden warres" (Kyd, p. 309).

19. *blood for blood*] Cf. II. i. 329, note.

20. *for controlment*] Wilson "restores the metre" with Vaughan, since his reading "gives better sense, i.e. 'a check to your compulsion,'".

22. *farthest limit of*] most extreme course granted me in.

23. *and . . . peace*] Noble cited the Nunc Dimittis in the *Book of Common Prayer:* "Lord, now lettest thou thy servant depart in peace." Also *Luke,* ii. 29.

For, ere thou canst report, I will be there:              25
The thunder of my cannon shall be heard.
So, hence! Be thou the trumpet of our wrath
And sullen presage of your own decay.
An honourable conduct let him have:
Pembroke, look to't. Farewell, Chatillon.                 30

               [*Exeunt Chatillon and Pembroke.*

*Elea.* What now, my son! have I not ever said
How that ambitious Constance would not cease
Till she had kindled France, and all the world,
Upon the right and party of her son?
This might have been prevented and made whole     35
With very easy arguments of love,
Which now the manage of two kingdoms must
With fearful-bloody issue arbitrate.

*K. John.* Our strong possession and our right for us.

*Elea.* Your strong possession much more than your right,  40
Or else it must go wrong with you and me:
So much my conscience whispers in your ear,
Which none but heaven, and you, and I, shall hear.

---

25. *report*,] F1; *report* Capell.     *there:*] F1; *there,* Rowe.     28. *sullen*] F1; *sudden* Collier MS.     30. S.D.] Exit Chat. and Pem. F1.     38. *fearful-bloody*] Craig (*ap.* I. John); no hyphen F1.     40.] F1; [aside to K. John] Dyce ii.

25. *report*] announce; thunder. Ll. 24–6 mean: "Be as swift as lightning in your return to France; [And yet,] before you will be able to *announce* your message, I will be there, and instead of you the *thunder* of my cannon shall be heard." The secondary meaning of *report* was new in 1590.

26. *cannon*] A typical anachronism. Gunpowder was invented about a century later (Z. Grey).

27. *trumpet*] "our tongues are *Trumpets* . . . to giue warning of any euill approching, Esay 58.1" [T. White, *Sermon* (1589), sig. F₄ᵛ]. Delius suggested an allusion to the trumpet of doom, presaging the last judgment.

28. *sullen . . . decay*] "*The sullen presage* . . . means, *the dismal passing bell, that announces your own approaching dissolution*" (Steevens); *sullen* = gloomy, dismal (Malone compared *2 H 4*, I. i.

102); *decay* = downfall, perdition.

29. *conduct*] escort, or safe-conduct.

32. *ambitious Constance*] Cf. II. i. 123, note.

34. *Upon . . . party*] Cf. *R 3*, III. ii. 47 (Furness), *Mac.*, III. vi. 30 (Wilson).

35. *made whole*] "set right" (Smith).

36. *arguments of love*] evidence of your love; "friendly discussions" (Smith).

37. *manage*] government, administration.

39–41. *Our . . . me*] W. Rushton [*Shakespeare's Legal Maxims* (1859), p. 12] thought Shakespeare had in mind the maxim "In aequali jure melior est conditio possidentis" (= Where the right is equal, the claim of the party in possession shall prevail). Shakespeare emphasizes the (unhistorical) illegality of John's kingship: see Introduction, p. lxiv.

*Enter a Sheriff.*

*Essex.*  My liege, here is the strangest controversy,
Come from the country to be judg'd by you,                          45
That e'er I heard: shall I produce the men?

*K. John.*  Let them approach.
Our abbeys and our priories shall pay
This expeditious charge.

*Enter* ROBERT FAULCONBRIDGE, *and* PHILIP
*his bastard brother.*

What men are you?

*Bast.*  Your faithful subject I, a gentleman,                      50
Born in Northamptonshire, and eldest son,
As I suppose, to Robert Faulconbridge,
A soldier, by the honour-giving hand

44. S.D.] F1; om. Rowe; Enter *Essex*. Johnson; Enter the Sheriff of *Northampton-shire*, and whispers *Essex*. Capell; after l. 38 Kemble.        46.] F1; Exit Sheriff.
Capell.        47.] F1; Exit Sheriff; and Re-enters, with *Philip*, the Bastard . . . and
Robert . . . Capell.        49. *expeditious*] F1; *expeditions* F2, edd.        49. S.D.]
Malone; Enter Robert Faulconbridge, and Philip. F1 (after l. 49); Enter . . . the
Bastard. Rowe; after *charge* l. 49 Johnson.        50.] F1; *Scene* II. Pope.        50 . . .
132. Bast.] Rowe; Phil. (Philip) F1.        50. *subject I,*] Capell; *subiect, I* F1.
53. *honour-giving hand*] Honor-giuing-hand F1.

44. S.D.] Various edd. put the S.D.
earlier, to allow a longer whisper before Essex speaks. But the *T.R.* S.D.
"Enter the Shriue, & whispers the
Earle of *Sals* in the eare" (I. i. 66) is
followed immediately by a speech by
Salisbury. The pirate witnessed a very
brief whisper. Surely the Sheriff only
reminds Essex of business already discussed, and a word is enough.

45. *Come . . . country*] John was the
last king to whom a controversy might
come from the country for judgment—
Magna Carta vested this authority in
the Court of Common Pleas (Verplanck). Cf. *T.R.*, I. i. 80.

49. *expeditious*] speedy, sudden; cf.
*Tp.*, V. i. 315. For John's speed cf.
Introduction, p. lxv. The case for
"expedition's", that the adjective was
unknown in the 1590's, is unfounded:
cf. W. R.'s *English Ape* (1588): "The

expeditious practise of vice" (sig. A₂).

*What*] Of what name, who.

50. *I*] From here to the end of Act I
the pronoun *I* is used fifty-eight times,
fifty-one times by Faulconbridge: indi-
cating his self-reliance, and his narrow
limits.

51. *Northamptonshire*] Holinshed often mentions John's stays in Northampton, but *Come from the country*
(l. 45) suggests that we may be in
London, and the county may not have
been guess-work: see Introduction,
p. xxv.

53. *honour-giving hand*] Hyphens
were used to compress into a single
concept. Our reading might suggest a
hand giving honour on a single occasion, the F1 spelling implies one that
gave honour always, as part of its
nature. Cf. II. i. 582, III. iii. 133, IV. ii.
8, IV. iii. 24, V. i. 11, 67.

Of Cœur-de-lion knighted in the field.

*K. John.* What art thou?                                              55

*Rob.* The son and heir to that same Faulconbridge.

*K. John.* Is that the elder, and art thou the heir?
   You came not of one mother then, it seems.

*Bast.* Most certain of one mother, mighty king;
   That is well known; and, as I think, one father:     60
   But for the certain knowledge of that truth
   I put you o'er to heaven and to my mother:
   Of that I doubt, as all men's children may.

*Elea.* Out on thee, rude man! thou dost shame thy mother
   And wound her honour with this diffidence.             65

*Bast.* I, madam? no, I have no reason for it;
   That is my brother's plea and none of mine;
   The which if he can prove, a pops me out
   At least from fair five hundred pound a year:
   Heaven guard my mother's honour, and my land!        70

*K. John.* A good blunt fellow. Why, being younger born,
   Doth he lay claim to thine inheritance?

*Bast.* I know not why—except to get the land—
   But once he slander'd me with bastardy:

---

54. *Coeur-de-lion*] Cordelion F1 (throughout).    64. *rude man*] F1; *rudeman* Walker conj.    68. *a*] F1; *he* Pope; *'a* Capell.    69. *pound*] F1; *pounds* ed. 1735.    73. *why —...land—*] This ed.; *why,...land:* F1.    74. *But once*] F1; *But, once,* Theobald.

54. *knighted ... field*] Knighthoods were at this time conferred (*a*) before or after battle as a rule, and (*b*) "out of warre they [knights] are made for . . . some good hope of vertues that doo appeare in them" [W. Segar: *Booke of Honor and Armes* (1590), sig. Q₂]. Old Sir Robert Faulconbridge was knighted the first way, Philip the second (I. i. 162), and Robert, though son and heir of a knight, remained a squire (I. i. 177).

57. *that*] he.

61. *that truth*] the true facts.

62. *put you o'er*] refer you.

64. *rude man*] = rude-man. Cf. *rudesby* (*Shr.*, III. ii. 10, *Tw.N.*, IV. i. 55). Some think that "man" in compounds had an enclitic force—as in "goodman" (youngman, rudeman). "Rude"

= uncivilized; ignorant, unskilled.

65. *diffidence*] mistrust.

68. *a*] Unstressed form of "he". In ll. 68–9, Shakespeare portrays Faulconbridge's familiarity by means of colloquialisms — *a*, the undignified *pops*, the singular *pound*.

71. *Why*] This must be the exclamation (= "What's this!"), which Faulconbridge pretends to understand the other way.

74. *once*] "in short" or "sometime in the past" (edd.). We suggest "on a single occasion" (viz. Robert did not dare to repeat the slander). Faulconbridge simulates ignorance (*I know not why*) to insinuate that no other claim has been substituted, also to be able to twist into l. 74, answering "why" = "for what end", and = "on what grounds".

But whe'r I be as true begot or no,                          75
That still I lay upon my mother's head;
But that I am as well begot, my liege—
Fair fall the bones that took the pains for me!—
Compare our faces and be judge yourself.
If old Sir Robert did beget us both                          80
And were our father, and this son like him,
O old Sir Robert, father, on my knee
I give heaven thanks I was not like to thee!

*K. John.* Why, what a madcap hath heaven lent us here!

*Elea.* He hath a trick of Cœur-de-lion's face;             85
The accent of his tongue affecteth him.
Do you not read some tokens of my son
In the large composition of this man?

*K. John.* Mine eye hath well examined his parts
And finds them perfect Richard. Sirrah, speak,              90
What doth move you to claim your brother's land?

*Bast.* Because he hath a half-face, like my father!
With half that face would he have all my land:
A half-fac'd groat five hundred pound a year!

*Rob.* My gracious liege, when that my father liv'd,        95
Your brother did employ my father much—

---

75. *But*] F1 ; *Now* Wright conj.    84. *lent*] F1 ; *sent* Heath [*Revisal* (1765), p. 222].
93. *half that face*] F1 ; *that half-face* Theobald.

75. *But*] Not repetitive, as Wright thought, if in l. 74 it is adverbial and in l. 75 conjunctive.

*whe'r*] whether. The monosyllable was a common variant.

76. *lay . . . head*] let my mother answer for.

78. *Fair fall*] Fair hap befall, may good befall. For similar *double entendre* cf. *LLL.*, II. i. 123–5, *Ven.*, l. 472. Possibly Faulconbridge falls heavily on his knee as he speaks, leading up to l. 82.

80. *old*] In *Looke About You* (1600), "olde *Faukenbridge*" (as he calls himself in his first line) is the butt of a cuckold sub-plot. See Introduction, p. xxiii.

84. *madcap*] mad-brained fellow.

*lent*] bestowed upon. Already ar-

chaic, but familiar in wills: "the worldly goods that heaven has lent me".

85. *trick*] characteristic expression, trait.

86. *affecteth*] resembles.

92. *half-face*] profile.

93. *With . . . face*] Probably playing on the familiar exclamation "With that face!" (=You're not the man, not likely), as in *LLL.*, I. ii. 147 (see R. David's note); also punning on *face* as "impudence". Read: "He wants my land—but he's not likely to get it!"

94. *half-fac'd groat*] groat with an effigy in profile. "Half-faced" also meant "imperfect", as in *1 H 4*, I. iii. 208, and *2 H 4*, III. ii. 286 (another part of J. Sincklo, the probable first actor of Robert Faulconbridge).

*Bast.* Well sir, by this you cannot get my land:
    Your tale must be how he employ'd my mother.
*Rob.*  —And once dispatch'd him in an embassy
    To Germany, there with the emperor         100
    To treat of high affairs touching that time.
    Th' advantage of his absence took the king
    And in the mean time sojourn'd at my father's,
    Where how he did prevail I shame to speak;
    But truth is truth: large lengths of seas and shores   105
    Between my father and my mother lay,
    As I have heard my father speak himself,
    When this same lusty gentleman was got.
    Upon his death-bed he by will bequeath'd
    His lands to me, and took it on his death      110
    That this my mother's son was none of his;
    And if he were, he came into the world
    Full fourteen weeks before the course of time.
    Then, good my liege, let me have what is mine,
    My father's land, as was my father's will.      115
*K. John.* Sirrah, your brother is legitimate;
    Your father's wife did after wedlock bear him,
    And if she did play false, the fault was hers;

110. *death*] F1; *oath* Anon. conj. *ap.* Cambridge.

98. *tale*] For the pun cf. *Gent.*, II. iii. 56, *Oth.*, III. i. 6–11, *O.E.D.*, tail, 5c.
  *employ'd*] Could be used like Latin "implicare" (*O.E.D.*, employ, 5).
  99. *dispatch'd*] sent; got rid of.
  *embassy*] Shakespeare's disregard of time has been criticized. Richard I became king in 1189, so that Faulconbridge could be only nine or ten in Act I. But Richard could have sent embassies as Duke of Aquitaine, and be referred to by his latest title. *Looke Ahout You* dates the seduction in the reign of Henry II (see Introduction, p. xxiii).
  105. *truth is truth*] certain facts are beyond argument. A common phrase. Cf. *Meas.*, v. i. 45, *LLL.*, IV. i. 48 (Tilley, p. 686).
  *lengths of seas*] No child born of a married woman could be bastardized in Shakespeare's day—unless the husband was "beyond the four seas during the whole period of the wife's pregnancy" [C. K. Davis: *Law in Shakespeare* (1884), p. 144]. But as Robert admits his father's return before the birth of Philip (l. 113), John rightly ignores the point.
  108. *lusty*] merry.
  110. *took*] took the oath, swore *Wiv.*, II. ii. 13, *1 H 4*, II. iv. 9 have been compared.
  *took . . . death*] swore most solemnly. To swear thus on one's deathbed signified extraordinary conviction [cf. S. Rowlands, *Crew of Kind Gossips* (1613): "But if I were this instant houre to die, / Ile take it on my death, that she doth lie" (sig. Eᵛ)].
  112. *And if*] (= An if) = If. One might read *And, if*—.

Which fault lies on the hazards of all husbands
That marry wives. Tell me, how if my brother,          120
Who, as you say, took pains to get this son,
Had of your father claim'd this son for his?
In sooth, good friend, your father might have kept
This calf, bred from his cow, from all the world;
In sooth he might; then, if he were my brother's,      125
My brother might not claim him; nor your father,
Being none of his, refuse him: this concludes;
My mother's son did get your father's heir;
Your father's heir must have your father's land.

*Rob.* Shall then my father's will be of no force       130
    To dispossess that child which is not his?

*Bast.* Of no more force to dispossess me, sir,
    Than was his will to get me, as I think.

*Elea.* Whether hadst thou rather be a Faulconbridge,
    And like thy brother, to enjoy thy land,            135
    Or the reputed son of Cœur-de-lion,
    Lord of thy presence and no land beside?

134. *Whether*] F1; *Say* Pope; *Whe'r* Staunton conj.    *rather be*] F1; *rather,—be* Capell.

119. *lies . . . hazards*] "belongs to the chances" (Wilson).

124. *calf . . . cow*] "he which maried the woman, shall bee saide to bee the father of the childe, and not hee which did beget the same . . . for whose the cow is, as it is commonly said, his is the calfe also" [H. Swinburne, *Briefe Treatise of Testaments* (1590), sig. Y₆].

127. *concludes*] "This is a *decisive argument*" (Johnson). Wright quoted *LLL.*: "The text most infallibly concludes it" (IV. ii. 171).

130–3. *Shall . . . think.*] Shakespeare reproduces the law for John's reign, not Elizabeth's: "From the time of the Norman conquest, lands in England ceased to be devisable. . . This remained in force until the statute of wills, in 32 Henry VIII" (Verplanck).

135. *like . . . land*] rated the *like* of your brother, so as to enjoy possession of your land. It was thought that a child could resemble a possible adulterer physically, yet the husband be the true father: "Wherein diuerse (I confesse) of no small aucthoritie haue contended mightilie . . . [But] forme or similitude maie happen to the infant by the mothers . . . firme imagination at the time of the conception" (Swinburne: *op. cit.*, sig. Y₇); cf. *T.R.*, I. i. 200–2. Eleanor therefore tests Faulconbridge's spiritual likenesses: Is he mean-spirited like a Faulconbridge, or a gambler like a Plantagenet?

*to*] When two infinitives follow *whether*, a *to* before the second was common (Abbott, sect. 350).

137. *Lord . . . presence*] "Lord of thine own person" (Heath); "master of that dignity, . . . that may sufficiently distinguish thee from the vulgar without the help of fortune" (Johnson). Cf. II. i. 367, 377, notes.

*no land*] Every title had its equiva-

*Bast.* Madam, and if my brother had my shape,
　　And I had his, Sir Robert's his like him;
　　And if my legs were two such riding-rods,　　　　140
　　My arms such eel-skins stuff'd, my face so thin
　　That in mine ear I durst not stick a rose
　　Lest men should say "Look, where three-farthings goes!"
　　And, to his shape, were heir to all this land,
　　Would I might never stir from off this place,　　145
　　I would give it every foot to have this face:
　　It would not be Sir Knob in any case.
*Elea.* I like thee well: wilt thou forsake thy fortune,

138. Bast.] F1 (throughout); Phil. Theobald (throughout).　　139. *Robert's his*]
As F1; Robert *his* Theobald; Robert's, *his*, Hanmer.　　144. *his . . . this*] F1; *this
. . . his* J. M. Mason [*Comments* (1797), p. 35].　　146. *I would*] F1; *I'd* Pope.
*face*] F1; *hand* Fleay.　　147. *It*] F1; *I* F2, edd.　　*Sir Knob*] This ed.; *Sir Nob* F1
(*sir nobbe*), edd.

lent in income: in 1590 a knight had to
have £120 p.a. (Segar, *op. cit.*, sig.
Q₂ᵛ).

139. *Robert's his*] A reduplicated
genitive, *his* being an obsolescent de-
notation of possession as in "J. Smith
his book".

140. *riding-rods*] switches used by
riders.

142. *ear*] Lovers once wore flowers
behind the ear (Steevens, citing Bur-
ton's *Anatomy of Melancholy*).

*rose*] On 6d., 3d., 1½d., ¾d. coins a
rose was placed behind the queen's
ear, to avoid confusion with 4d., 2d.,
1d., ½d. (Theobald).

143. *three-farthings*] Cf. Introduction,
p. xlv.

144. *to his*] in addition to his.

*all this land*] Often thought = "all
this land that is in question" (I. John).
But Faulconbridge dichotomizes
Richard I and Sir Robert, their lands,
their shapes; his point here is that he
rejects Sir Robert's shape even if it
brings *Richard's* land (all this land =
England).

145. *from off*] Shakespeare alters the
common "Would I might never stir
from this place!" His new preposition
means "stir from off this place (to
another)", and "stir, (after I have

moved) from off this place" (this alternative Shakespeare adds to help his
puns: cf. *stir*, l. 147, notes).

146. *I would*] For extra-metr. *I
would* cf. II. i. 292; for the contracted
form cf. II. i. 385, etc.

147. *It*] In l. 146 *it* stands for *shape*
and *land* (l. 144), in l. 147 primarily for
*shape*. Cf. l. 147, notes.

*Sir Knob*] "a pet name for 'Robert'"
(Smith, comparing the surname
Nobbs). *Nob* probably also meant *head*
(Capell); cf. T. Harman, *Caueat . . . for
Commen Cursetors* (ed. 1567): "Nab. a
head. Nabchet. a hat or cap" (slang
index, sig. G₂ᵛ). *Knob* and *nob* were
alternative spellings, whence a further
meaning: cf. next note.

*in any case*] "by any means", or "in
any state". But this is also the climax of
a series of indecent puns. For *shape*
(l. 144) cf. *O.E.D.*, shape, 16, *Tim.*, II.
ii. 113-21; for *stir* (l. 145) cf. I. i. 172,
below, *Per.*, IV. ii. 159; for *foot* (l. 146)
cf. I. i. 182, below, *H 5*, III. iv. 54-64,
*LLL.*, V. ii. 671-3; for *case* (l. 147) cf. E.
Partridge, *Shakespeare's Bawdy* (1947),
p. 84, *Wiv.*, IV. i. 60-82; for *eel-skin*
with *case* and *shape* cf. *2 H 4*, III. ii. 354-
62. *Sir Knob* (l. 147) also belongs to this
context, and probably *riding-rods* (l.
140) too (cf. *O.E.D.*, ride, 3).

Bequeath thy land to him and follow me?
I am a soldier and now bound to France.                    150
*Bast.* Brother, take you my land, I'll take my chance.
Your face hath got five hundred pound a year,
Yet sell your face for five pence and 'tis dear.
Madam, I'll follow you unto the death.
*Elea.* Nay, I would have you go before me thither.        155
*Bast.* Our country manners give our betters way.
*K. John.* What is thy name?
*Bast.* Philip, my liege, so is my name begun;
Philip, good old Sir Robert's wive's eldest son.
*K. John.* From henceforth bear his name whose form thou
bearest:                                                   160
Kneel thou down Philip, but rise more great,
Arise Sir Richard, and Plantagenet.
*Bast.* Brother by th' mother's side, give me your hand:
My father gave me honour, yours gave land.
Now blessed be the hour, by night or day,                  165
When I was got, Sir Robert was away!
*Elea.* The very spirit of Plantagenet!
I am thy grandam, Richard; call me so.

---

152. *pound*] F1; *pounds* Steevens.      159. *wive's*] F1 (*wiues*); *Wife's* Rowe.
*eldest*] F1; *eld'st* Dyce ii.      160.] One line Pope; two lines F1 (ending *name/* . . .
*bearest:/*).      *bearest*] F1; *bear'st* Pope.      161. *rise*] F1; *rise up* Pope; *arise*
Variorum 1773.      162.] F1; [knighting him. Capell.      168. *grandam, Richard;*]
As Capell; *grandame* Richard, F1; *grandam;* Richard, Pope.

149. *Bequeath*] Formally assign, hand over.

152. *face*] Cf. l. 93.

153. *Yet . . . dear.*] "Because a groat (cf. l. 94) was worth 4*d.*" (Wilson).

154–6. *Madam . . . way.*] "Madam, I'll serve (= *follow*) you to the best of my ability (= *unto the death*)." Eleanor in a quibble prefers him to precede her, i.e. "on the road to death" (Deighton). Was the point that Faulconbridge says he'll follow, without stirring (viz. he'll serve—without kneeling)? As squires went *before* their masters, Eleanor means that he is not yet properly her squire. Cf. Tilley, p. 524; and III. ii. 26, IV. ii. 169, v. vi. 1–5, notes, for Faulconbridge's independent slowness.

156. *manners*] Cf. IV. iii. 28–33.

162. *Richard*] Cf. I. i. 168, 178, 185, IV. iii. 41, v. iii. 12.

163. *Brother . . . hand*] i.e. "In so far as we have one mother we are equals (but not otherwise)". Cf. III. i. 118, note.

165. *hour*] H. Kökeritz has shown that *hour* and *whore* were homophones [*R.E.S.*, XIX (1943), p. 358]. Cf. *Err.*, IV. ii. 53–62, *2 H 6*, II. i. 179. If the pun is thought too violent, cf. *Ham.*, v. ii. 64.

168. *grandam*] F1 *grandame* does not show whether the second syllable is long or short, but "Grandams" in *T.R.* (I. i. 293) supports the favourite reading.

*Bast.* Madam, by chance but not by truth; what though?

     Something about, a little from the right,           170

       In at the window, or else o'er the hatch:

     Who dares not stir by day must walk by night,

       And have is have, however men do catch.

     Near or far off, well won is still well shot,

     And I am I, howe'er I was begot.              175

*K. John.* Go, Faulconbridge: now hast thou thy desire;

     A landless knight makes thee a landed squire.

     Come, madam, and come, Richard, we must speed

     For France, for France, for it is more than need.

*Bast.* Brother, adieu: good fortune come to thee!      180

     For thou wast got i' th' way of honesty.

                                     *[Exeunt all but Bastard.*

170. *about,*] F4; *about* F1.

169. *truth*] = honesty = honourable conduct.

*though*] then. Cf. *AYL.,* III. iii. 53, *H 5,* II. i. 9.

170–5. *Something . . . begot*] "The proverbial sayings which follow are characteristic of the Bastard's rusticity of breeding" (Wright, comparing *Cor.,* I. i. 211). But the first purpose is indelicate innuendo. Note the climax: absence of verbs in ll. 169–71, then the highly charged *stir, walk, have, catch, shot.*

170. *Something about*] A little indirectly, or irregularly.

*from the right*] "Suggesting the 'bar sinister' " (Wilson).

171. *In . . . hatch*] Proverbial expressions meaning to be born out of wedlock [Steevens, comparing Middleton's *Famelie of Love* (1608): "Woe worth the time that euer I gaue sucke to a Child that came in at the window" (sigs. F₄, I₂); *Northward Hoe* (Dekker & Webster): "kindred that comes in o'er the hatch" (I. i.); etc.].

*o'er the hatch*] over the lower part of a door that opened in two parts.

172. *Who . . . night*] Shakespeare combines three themes: (a) "walking" in love-poetry, as in Venus's line

"Rome thou abroad for I intend to range" [R. Wilson, *Coblers Prophesie* (1594), sig. Eᵛ]; (b) the play on *stir* (cf. I. i. 147, note); (c) walking by night, which was thought suspicious—*night-walker* was slang for *thief.*—The verb *to walk* = to be in motion (cf. IV. ii. 128).—Furness took this line to refer to Faulconbridge, not to Richard.

173. *have*] Idiomatic, as in *1 H 4,* III. iii. 144; "to have is to have" recurs in *AYL.,* v. i. 45.

*catch*] take hold of suddenly.

174. *Near . . . shot*] In *The Institucion of a Gentleman* (1568) occurs a proverb "He sheteth like a gentleman faire & fur of", and "welshot" = the formula of appreciation of good marksmanship (sig. D₈). Perhaps Faulconbridge ironically gives social approbation to his father's "shooting" (Partridge, *Shakespeare's Bawdy,* p. 187, noted that shooting often has a sexual subaudition in Shakespeare, as in *LLL.,* IV. i. 121–43).

177. *knight . . . squire*] Cf. I. i. 54, 137, notes. The Bastard, not John ("John Lackland"), is the knight.

180–1. *good . . . honesty*] "Alluding to the proverb, that 'bastards are born lucky' " (Collier).

181–2. *honesty . . . honour*] Shake-

A foot of honour better than I was,
But many a many foot of land the worse.
Well, now can I make any Joan a lady.                    184
"Good den, Sir Richard!"—"God-a-mercy, fellow!"—
And if his name be George, I'll call him Peter;
For new-made honour doth forget men's names:
'Tis too respective and too sociable
For your conversion. Now your traveller,
He and his toothpick at my worship's mess,                190

182.] F1; *Scene* III. Pope; II. Capell.        *A*] Rowe; Bast. *A* F1.        187. *new-made*]
Pope; no hyphen F1.        189. *conversion.*] Capell; *conuersion*, F1; *conversing*
Pope.

speare preserves the distinction between the middle-class and the aristocratic virtues.

182.] Wilson thought that the F1
speech heading "was added at the time
of the second revision" (cf. Introduction, p. xxxvi). But a new heading was
not uncommonly added with a new
form of speech (aside, soliloquy, quotation).

*foot*] footing, status, degree; for the
pun cf. I. i. 147, note.

182–3. *foot . . . foot*] The juxtaposition of feet was a common trope, de-
riving from the Bible. Cf. II. i. 144,
note, and *Ado*, II. iii. 67.

183. *many a many*] "A many" was
often used where we use "many a";
*many a many* is unique here in Shakespeare, typical of Faulconbridge's
loose language.

*foot of land*] A set phrase long before
Shakespeare, used in *Cuer du Lyon*
(1528): "He shall not haue a fote of
londe / Neuer more but of my honde"
(sig. G₄).

184. *Joan*] "A generic name for a
female rustic" (*O.E.D.*). But often
Joan = whore, which may be Shakespeare's thought, as in *LLL.*, III. i. 215.
In B. Googe's translation of Palin-
genius's *Zodiake of Life* (1576) "Joan"
stands for "scortum" (sig. E₄ᵛ); cf.
B. & F.'s *Sea Voyage* (ed. 1647): "when
I am drunk, / Joane is a Lady to me,
and I shall / Lay about me like a
Lord" etc. (sig. 5Cᵛ).

185. *Good den*] Common abbreviation of "God give ye good even".

*God-a-mercy*] God reward you; "response to a respectful salutation or a
wish, usu. expressed by an inferior"
(On.).

187–9. *For . . . conversion*] "an ellipse
. . . *remembering* (not forgetting) men's
names implies too much regard"
(Ridley).

188. *respective*] respectful.

189. *conversion*] Could mean "con-
verse (= conversation)" (Halliwell).
We must choose whether to put a stop
after l. 188, or after *conversion* (=
change). But Shakespeare, punctuat-
ing lightly, probably intended both
meanings.

*traveller*] Travellers carried round
the news. Johnson compared *All's W.*:
"A good traveller is something at the
latter end of a dinner" (II. v. 31).

190. *toothpick*] The affectation of
travellers long before Shakespeare.
Steevens quoted one of Gascoigne's
poems ridiculing it.

*my . . . mess*] "at that part of the table
where I, as a *knight*, shall be placed . . .
'Your *worship*' was the regular address
to a knight or esquire" (Malone). "A
mess was properly a party of four . . . at
great dinners the parties were always
arranged in fours" (Wright).—It is
just possible that F1 *tooth-picke at*
should be *tooth-pick eat*, though the
absence of a verb is typical of Faulconbridge's impulsive thought.

And when my knightly stomach is suffic'd,
Why then I suck my teeth and catechize
My picked man of countries: "My dear sir,"—
Thus, leaning on mine elbow, I begin,
"I shall beseech you,"—that is Question now;                    195
And then comes Answer like an Absey book:
"O sir," says Answer, "at your best command;
At your employment; at your service, sir:"
"No, sir," says Question, "I, sweet sir, at yours:"
And so, ere Answer knows what Question would,                    200
Saving in dialogue of compliment,
And talking of the Alps and Apennines,
The Pyrenean and the river Po,
It draws toward supper in conclusion so.
But this is worshipful society,                    205
And fits the mounting spirit like myself;
For he is but a bastard to the time
That doth not smack of observation;

193. *picked*] F1; *piked* Pope; *picqued* Theobald.        *man*] F1; *man,* Heath (*Revisal*, p. 223).        196. *Absey book*] F1; *A B C-book* Pope.        201. *Saving*] F1; *Serving* Warburton conj.        203. *Pyrenean*] *Perennean* F1.        208–9. *smack . . . smoke*] Pope; *smoake . . . smacke* F1; *smack . . . smack* Theobald.

193. *picked*] = (*a*) dandified (cf. *LLL.*, v. i. 14); (*b*) who has picked his teeth; (*c*) select (because a traveller).

195–200. *Question . . . Answer*] In 16th-century children's manuals, e.g. catechisms, ABC books, instruction was often given in dialogues between Question and Answer. Faulconbridge is a mere child in travelling.

196. *Absey book*] a primer, introductory book.

200. *ere . . . would*] So Sir J. Davies, on meeting a traveller: "so neyther of vs vnderstanding eyther / We part as wise as when we came together" [*Epigrammes* (*c.* 1595), sig. C].

201. *dialogue of compliment*] Shakespeare ridicules excessive formality. The epigram writers soon followed him. Cf. *AYL.*, II. v. 26: "that they call compliment is like the encounter of two dog-apes" (Wright), *Ham.*, v. ii. 81–190 (Wilson), *LLL.*, I. i. 167.

202–3. *Alps . . . Pyrenean*] See Introduction, p. xlvii.

205. *worshipful society*] In the *De Officiis* Cicero, discussing ambition (Faulconbridge's theme here), says that it leads to "contentio, ut difficillimum sit servare 'sanctam societatem' " (Bk 1, cap. 8). Faulconbridge's *worshipful* is sarcastic (cf. I. i. 190, note); but Shakespeare may have recalled a popular classic.

206. *mounting spirit*] The cliché was "mounting mind": cf. *LLL.*, IV. i. 4. *T.R.* reverted to this (I. i. 261).

207. *but . . . time*] no true child of the age (Belden).

208. *observation*] "obsequiousness" is a secondary sense, as in *Ham.*, III. i. 163 "observed of all observers" (Wright).

208–9. *smack . . . smoke*] The F1 transposition shows that these forms were not distinct; cf. II. i. 139. In Greene's *Notable Discouery* (1591)

And so am I, whether I smoke or no.
And not alone in habit and device,                              210
Exterior form, outward accoutrement,
But from the inward motion to deliver
Sweet, sweet, sweet poison for the age's tooth:
Which, though I will not practise to deceive,
Yet, to avoid deceit, I mean to learn;                          215
For it shall strew the footsteps of my rising.
But who comes in such haste in riding-robes?
What woman-post is this? hath she no husband
That will take pains to blow a horn before her?

*Enter* LADY FAULCONBRIDGE *and* JAMES GURNEY.

212. *to*] F1; *too* Hanmer.     220. S.D.] Capell; after l. 221 F1; after *mother* l. 220
Staunton.

*smack* and *smoke* were used indifferent-
ly, *passim*, signifying "to see through,
be suspicious about". This slang sense
is present in l. 209, after *observation*.
Another possibility for l. 209 is
"whether I smoke (tobacco) or not".
Puritans condemned tobacco as im-
moral ("bastard to the time"), and
Faulconbridge glories in irrelevance;
but this would be an early use of intransitive "to smoke".

210–16. *And . . . rising.*] Shakespeare
laughs at moralists who called extravagant apparel and hypocrisy the twin
vices of travellers. Cf. W. R., *The English Ape, the Italian Imitation, the Foote-
steppes of Fraunce* (1588): "the cunning
conuey of his imitation in inwarde disposition, and externall habite . . . to
follow the footsteps of other Nations"
(sig. Aᵛ); "Ambition like vnto stronge
poyson" (sig. Bᵛ).

210–11. *habit . . . accoutrement*] "He
refers . . . to the knightly 'accoutrement' he will wear, of which the
'device' with its bar sinister will be a
prominent feature" (Wilson).

212. *motion*] inclination, impulse.

213. *sweet poison*] A favourite phrase
for flattery. Cf. H. Swinburne, *op. cit.*:
"flatteries . . . with whose sweete poison

and pleasant sting manie men are so
charmed" (sig. 2D₄ᵛ); Marlowe,
*Ovid's Elegies*: "Let thy tongue flatter
while thy mind harm works :/ Under
sweet honey deadly poison lurks"
(I. viii).

*tooth*] appetite.

216. *For . . . rising*] "as I rise flattery
will be strewn before me like flowers
before one making a progress" (I.
John). Or he may refer to the rushes
strewing the presence-chamber of a
king, and the stage (C. Porter).

217–20. *But . . . mother.*] The usual
formula to describe an entering person
in pre-Shakespearean drama. Cf.
Udall's *Roister Doister*: "But who commeth forth yond . . . ?", "But what two
men are yonde . . . ?" (M.S.R., ll. 255,
1342).

219. *take . . . horn*] In cuckold stories
the husband who "blows the horn"
proclaims his own misfortune: cf.
Chapman, *All Fools*, v. ii. 180, Middleton, *Famelie of Love* (1608), sig. H₄ᵛ.
With *take pains* cf. I. i. 78, 121. Read:
"Has she no husband who will proclaim her a loose woman (i.e. must she
do so herself by gadding about)?" The
*post* (never a woman) was always *in
haste*, therefore *blew the post-horn*.

O me! 'tis my mother.—How now, good lady?          220
What brings you here to court so hastily?
*Lady F.*  Where is that slave, thy brother? where is he,
That holds in chase mine honour up and down?
*Bast.*  My brother Robert? old Sir Robert's son?
Colbrand the giant, that same mighty man?          225
Is it Sir Robert's son that you seek so?
*Lady F.*  Sir Robert's son! Ay, thou unreverend boy—
Sir Robert's son?—why scorn'st thou at Sir Robert?
He is Sir Robert's son, and so art thou.
*Bast.*  James Gurney, wilt thou give us leave awhile?          230
*Gur.*  Good leave, good Philip.
*Bast.*                    Philip?—sparrow!—James,
There's toys abroad: anon I'll tell thee more.
                                        [*Exit Gurney.*
Madam, I was not old Sir Robert's son:

220. *'tis*] F1; *it is* Pope, edd.          222.] F1; *Scene* IV. Pope.          231. *Philip?—*
*sparrow!—*] Upton; Philip, *sparrow*, F1.          232. S.D. Gurney.] Iames. F1.

220. *'tis*] Edd. have conspired to
ignore the facetiousness of Faulconbridge's mincing *'tis.*
    223. *holds in chase*] pursues; cf. *Cor.*,
i. vi. 19 (Furness).
    225. *Colbrand*] In the old romances
of Guy of Warwick, Colbrand is Guy's
last and doughtiest opponent. Shakespeare might have looked on Guy
as his own ancestor, through the
Ardens and Beauchamps: cf. i. i. 232,
note.
    231. *Good . . . Philip*] "Good leave" =
(a) "I give you willing *permission*" [as
in R. W.'s *Three Ladies of London* (1584),
sig. C₃]; (b) "What a courteous *dis-*
*missal!*" (veiled). The formula "Good
. . . , good . . ." was used with equals
and inferiors, as in "Good words, good
brother!" Furness thought Gurney a
friend (he is usually thought a servant).
His familiarity and Lady Faulconbridge's impulsiveness sketch in the
two major qualities Faulconbridge
derived from his background.
    *Philip? — sparrow! —*]    "Mere

Philip", exclaims Faulconbridge "is a
name good enough for a sparrow!" He
is now *Sir Richard*. Philip was a favourite name for (tame) sparrows. Skel-
ton's elegy for *Philip Sparowe*, Gascoigne's *Praise of Philip Sparrow* (written for a hen-sparrow), are well-
known.
    232. *There's toys abroad*] Trifling
gifts (i.e. knighthoods) are being
handed out. Some take *toys* = "rumours, whims", which would suit
A. Harbage's thesis that *Guy Earl of
Warwick* (1661) ("by B. J.") contains
an early satire of Shakespeare. [See
*Shakespeare Association Bulletin*, xvi
(1941), pp. 42–9.] Guy's servant, the
clown Philip Sparrow, may skit
Shakespeare in a number of ways,
even declares "I was born . . . at *Strat-*
*ford* upon *Aven* in *Warwickshire*" (sig.
E₂ᵛ). It is curious that Shakespeare
drags in the Guy story (l. 225), then
recalls P. Sparrow (l. 231), whom B. J.
first associated with Guy, adding
"There's *rumours* abroad".

Sir Robert might have ate his part in me
Upon Good Friday and ne'er broke his fast:                235
Sir Robert could do—well, marry, to confess—
Could ... get me? Sir Robert could not do it.
We know his handiwork: therefore, good mother,
To whom am I beholding for these limbs?
Sir Robert never holp to make this leg.                   240
*Lady F.* Hast thou conspired with thy brother too,
That for thine own gain shouldst defend mine honour?
What means this scorn, thou most untoward knave?
*Bast.* Knight, knight, good mother, Basilisco-like:

236. *do ... confess—*] As Alexander (*do: well—marry, to confess—*); *doe well, marrie to confesse* F1; *do well; Marry, to confess,* Capell, edd.    237. *Could ... me?*] This ed.; *Could get me* F1; *Could he get me?* Pope, edd.

234-5. *Sir ... fast*] Steevens compared Heywood's *Proverbs* (1564): "he may his parte on good fridaie eate, And fast never the wurs, for ought he shall geate."

236-7. *Sir ... it.*] Here *do* = "copulate", as in *Tim.,* IV. i. 8, *All's W.,* II. iii. 245 (see Schmidt, do, 5). Read: "Sir R. could do—well, at any rate he could marry; to confess the truth he could (*interrupting himself*)—beget me? He could not do it!" Edd. generally take *marrie* as exclamation; Wilson paraphrased *marrie to confesse* as "though I says it, as shouldn't". Our textual surgery is not drastic, since Faulconbridge habitually interrupts himself (cf. I. i. 191, II. i. 571), and breaks were not always indicated in the old texts.

237. *Could*] Occurring three times in two lines, this word might here be a compositor's repetition. "But" would read smoothly in its place.

238. *handiwork*] Cf. I. i. 267, note. Faulconbridge's irreverence = Elizabethan slang for begetting children ("fair work", "good workmanship", cf. *Wint.,* III. iii. 75). In the Bible the earth is often called the work of God's hands.

239. *beholding*] beholden, indebted.

240. *Sir ... leg.*] A *leg* was an obei-

sance. But after *handiwork, limbs,* Faulconbridge also means "Sir R. never helped to beget this leg." Cf. H. Swinburne, *op. cit.,* who writes of "fathers" who were not "any way priuie to the begetting either of a leg or an arm, no not somuch as of the litlefinger" of their wives' children (sig. Z); J. Gough, *Strange Discovery* (1640): "to father a child, of which I did not beget so much as the least finger or the least toe" (sig. D₄ᵛ). Perhaps Shakespeare told the actor to make a mock-obeisance, slapping his leg (*this leg*), to imply that Sir R.'s son would bow humbly, for the words contradict the sense: "Sir R. never helped to make me, *high-spirited as I am.*" In *T.R.* Faulconbridge asks the question "on knees" (I. i. 338); cf. *John,* I. i. 82.

*holp*] helped. The older form.

243. *untoward*] unmannerly.

244. *Basilisco-like.*] Theobald spotted the point in *Soliman and Perseda,* a play of this time: "*Pist[on].* I, the aforesaid *Basilisco—* | *Bas[ilisco].* I, the aforesaid *Basilisco—*Knight, goodfellow, Knight, Knight— | *Pist.* Knaue, goodfellow, Knaue, Knaue—" (Kyd, p. 173). Here the bragging knight Basilisco knuckles under to the servant Piston—Faulconbridge laughs at himself in the allusion. Cf. II. i. 75, note.

What! I am dubb'd! I have it on my shoulder.                    245
But, mother, I am not Sir Robert's son:
I have disclaim'd Sir Robert and my land;
Legitimation, name and all is gone.
Then, good my mother, let me know my father;
Some proper man, I hope: who was it, mother?                    250
*Lady F.* Hast thou denied thyself a Faulconbridge?
*Bast.* As faithfully as I deny the devil.
*Lady F.* King Richard Cœur-de-lion was thy father:
By long and vehement suit I was seduc'd
To make room for him in my husband's bed.                    255
Heaven, lay not my transgression to my charge
That art the issue of my dear offence,
Which was so strongly urg'd past my defence!
*Bast.* Now, by this light, were I to get again,
Madam, I would not wish a better father.                    260
Some sins do bear their privilege on earth,

---

247. *Robert . . . land;*] Theobald; Robert . . . *land*, F1; *Robert; . . . land*, Fleay.
256. *Heaven,*] As Knight (*Heaven!*); *Heauen* F1.    *to my*] F1; *to thy* Staunton conj.
257. *That*] F1; *Thou* F4.

245. *dubb'd*] Used half a dozen times in Shakespeare, often facetiously, because old-fashioned: "that terme dubbing was the old terme in this poynt, and not creating" (Segar, *op. cit.*, sig. Q₃).

*I have it*] Facetious twist of an idiom which meant "I have been (mortally) struck", as in *Rom.*, III. i. 113, *A Larum for London* (1602): "See Captaine, now I haue it on my brest, / The Honourable cognisance of death" (sig. F₄ᵛ).

247. *disclaim'd*] " 'Disclaim' can hardly mean both *disavow* and *renounce;* here it seems to apply to Sir Robert alone" (Furness). But loose grammar was natural to Faulconbridge: cf. I. i. 190, note.

252. *As . . . devil*] Furness detected an echo from the Catechism: "renounce the devil and all his works". The repeated *deny* Delius took as = "disavow" (l. 251) and "abjure" (l. 252); Schmidt took both = "disavow".

256–7. *Heaven, . . . offence*] For

Heaven's sake, lay not (thou) my transgression to my charge that art the issue of it. The reply of Faulconbridge immediately deprecates any intention of upbraiding his mother (Knight). Shakespeare often uses "O heaven!", "Heavens!"; in *Per.*, I. i. 109 occurs "Heaven! that I had thy head!"—we need not boggle at the exclamation. —Carter compared *Acts*, vii. 60: "Lorde, lay not this sinne to their charge" (cf. also *Deuteronomy*, xxi. 8, 2 *Timothy*, iv. 16). So *A Larum for London* (1602): "The bloud that I haue spilt . . . / Heauen lay not to my charge" (sig. G). But Knight must be right.

258. *urg'd . . . defence*] importuned, beyond my power to forbid it; forced through my defences.

259. *by . . . light*] A common oath. But *by night or day* (I. i. 165) is resumed as well, suggesting "If I had to be got again by this day-light".

261. *Some . . . earth*] Alluding to the

And so doth yours: your fault was not your folly.
Needs must you lay your heart at his dispose,
Subjected tribute to commanding love,
Against whose fury and unmatched force                         265
The aweless lion could not wage the fight,
Nor keep his princely heart from Richard's hand.
He that perforce robs lions of their hearts
May easily win a woman's. Ay, my mother,
With all my heart I thank thee for my father!               270
Who lives and dares but say thou didst not well
When I was got, I'll send his soul to hell.
Come, lady, I will show thee to my kin;
   And they shall say, when Richard me begot,
If thou hadst said him nay, it had been sin;                 275
   Who says it was, he lies: I say 'twas not!            [*Exeunt.*

Roman Catholic doctrine of venial sin? In a similar context A. C. wrote: "But he that could command thee, made thee sin: / Yet that is no priuiledge, no sheeld to thee" [*Beawtie Dishonoured* (1593), sig. Eᵛ].

262. *fault . . . folly*] The *fault* and *folly* of a lapse such as Lady Faulconbridge's were conventionally juxtaposed: cf. *The Cobler of Caunterburie* (1590), sig. C₃, *Brittons Bowre of Delights* (1591), sig. E₃, R. W.'s *Tancred and Gismund* (1591), sig. E₃.

263. *dispose*] disposal.

264. *Subjected*] *The Book of Common Prayer*, following various biblical verses, enunciated "Let wiues be subiect to their owne husbands" (in "Of Matrimonie"); and Shakespeare quibbles etymologically.

266. *lion*] Various accounts of Richard's nickname were current. The favourite one describes him en-

countering a lion unarmed, thrusting his hand into the lion's mouth, and plucking out his heart and lungs.

267. *hand*] Cf. 1. i. 53, 238.

270. *heart*] After the joke about the exchange of hearts, Faulconbridge may now intend a quibble: "*I*, my dear mother, *I* thank thee *on behalf of* my father with the tender of all *my* heart (since he owed you a heart)".

271–6. *lives . . . lies*] Cf. III. i. 264, note.

276. *not*] The F1 reading has been called lame. But *not* was the unstressed form of *naught*, these words being interchangeable. Shakespeare wrote *not* for the rhyme's sake, but *naught* ( ="wickedness", or specifically "a sexual lapse") seems typical of Faulconbridge, and the actor would linger on the word. Cf. *Meas.*: "this house, if it be not a bawd's house . . . is a naughty house" (II. i. 77–9).

# ACT II

## SCENE I.—[*France. Before Angiers.*]

*Enter, on one side, the Archduke of Austria, and Forces; on the other,*
PHILIP, *King of France, and Forces,* LEWIS, CONSTANCE, ARTHUR,
*and Attendants.*

*Lew.* Before Angiers well met, brave Austria.
*K. Phi.* Arthur, that great forerunner of thy blood,
    Richard, that robb'd the lion of his heart
    And fought the holy wars in Palestine,
    By this brave duke came early to his grave:          5
    And for amends to his posterity
    At our importance hither is he come,
    To spread his colours, boy, in thy behalf,
    And to rebuke the usurpation
    Of thy unnatural uncle, English John:          10
    Embrace him, love him, give him welcome hither.
*Arth.* God shall forgive you Cœur-de-lion's death
    The rather that you give his offspring life,

### ACT II

#### Scene 1

*Act* II *Scene* I.] Rowe iii; Scaena Secunda. F1 ; *Act* I *Scene* III. Donovan.    S.D.]
As Capell; Enter before Angiers, Philip King of France, Lewis, Daulphin,
Austria, Constance, Arthur. F1.    1. Lew.] Lewis. F1 ; K. Phi. Theobald conj.
2. K. Phi.] This ed.; speech contd. F1.

Angiers] Angers. Holinshed repeatedly mentions Angiers (160, ii;
170, i; etc.), but Acts II and III really
expand on the siege of Mirabeau
(Hol., 164, ii).

2. K. Phi.] Cf. Introduction, p. xxxiv.

*forerunner*] Cf. ll. 6, 13, 177, notes,
Introduction, p. l. In Marlowe's
*Faustus* (ed. 1616) the pope talks of
"Pope *Alexander* our Progenitour"
(sig. D₈).

5. *By . . . grave*] For the identification
of Limoges and Austria cf. Introduction, p. xxi.

7. *importance*] entreaty, importun-
ity.

8. *colours*] military ensigns.

13. *offspring*] Arthur means not himself, but the whole of Richard's family
collectively, as is shown by *their* in l. 14
(Delius). Or does *their* refer to Richard
and Arthur? Shakespeare follows the

Shadowing their right under your wings of war:
I give you welcome with a powerless hand,                    15
But with a heart full of unstained love:
Welcome before the gates of Angiers, duke.

*Lew.* Ah, noble boy, who would not do thee right?

*Aust.* Upon thy cheek lay I this zealous kiss,
As seal to this indenture of my love:                        20
That to my home I will no more return,
Till Angiers and the right thou hast in France,
Together with that pale, that white-fac'd shore,
Whose foot spurns back the ocean's roaring tides
And coops from other lands her islanders,                    25
Even till that England, hedg'd in with the main,
That water-walled bulwark, still secure
And confident from foreign purposes,
Even till that utmost corner of the west
Salute thee for her king; till then, fair boy,               30

18. Lew.] Lewis. F1; K. Phi. Theobald conj.     *Ah*] Fleay conj.; *A* F1.

language of official documents "in
which kings are held to be *descended*
from their predecessors. So even
Henry VII. repeatedly speaks of 'our
royal progenitor, King Edward the
Fourth' " (Moberly).

14. *Shadowing . . . war*] *Shadowing* =
sheltering. Shakespeare uses a favourite image of the Psalmist ["hide me
under the shadow of thy wings" (*Psalms*,
xvii. 8) which fuses with *wings of war*
(= flanks of an army)].

16. *unstained*] Cf. Introduction, p.
lxii; iv. ii. 6. He means "no longer
stained with hatred as before".

18. *Ah,*] The exclamation "Ah!",
often printed "A" in old texts, is appropriate since Arthur is addressed.
So *T.R.*: "Ah boy, thy yeares I see are
farre too greene" (i. iv. 196).

*do thee right*] treat thee right, take thy
part.

19. *zealous*] Zeal usually = religious
fervour in *John*.

20. *seal*] Wilson suspected a quibble
on *zealous*, comparing ii. i. 477-9.

*indenture*] a (sealed) agreement.
After *cheek* and *kiss* there is a quibble

in *indenture* (< Latin *dentem*, a tooth).

23. *pale*] "*England* is supposed to be
called *Albion* from the *white rocks* facing
*France*" (Johnson); *pale* is in apposition
to both *white-fac'd* and *shore*, being a
quibble on the sense "an enclosed
place" (resumed by *water-walled*, l. 27,
etc.).

23-9. *that . . . west*] Patriotic descrip-
tions of invincible England became
popular in the Armada period: cf. *R 2*,
ii. i. 40-63, Greene's *Bacon and Bungay*
(1594), sig. Cᵛ, Peele's *Alcazar* (1594),
sigs. C₄ᵛ, D. *John* makes dramatic
capital out of the convention (the
French nearly conquer England in
Act v).

25. *coops*] encloses for protection.

26. *hedg'd*] Halliwell compared
Greene's *Spanish Masquerado* (1589):
"reposing our selues in that our owne
strength, for that wee were hedged in
with the sea" (sig. B₄); so A. Andreson,
*Sermon* (1581): God has "set *a Hedge of
defence* rounde aboute" England (sig.
C₂ᵛ). Armada common-place.

29. *utmost . . . west*] Cf. v. vii. 116,
note.

Will I not think of home, but follow arms.
*Const.*  O, take his mother's thanks, a widow's thanks,
        Till your strong hand shall help to give him strength
        To make a more requital to your love!
*Aust.*  The peace of heaven is theirs that lift their swords      35
        In such a just and charitable war.
*K. Phi.*  Well then, to work; our cannon shall be bent
        Against the brows of this resisting town.
        Call for our chiefest men of discipline,
        To cull the plots of best advantages:                      40
        We'll lay before this town our royal bones,
        Wade to the market-place in Frenchmen's blood,
        But we will make it subject to this boy.
*Const.*  Stay for an answer to your embassy,
        Lest unadvis'd you stain your swords with blood:           45
        My Lord Chatillon may from England bring
        That right in peace which here we urge in war,
        And then we shall repent each drop of blood
        That hot rash haste so indirectly shed.

*Enter* CHATILLON.

*K. Phi.*  A wonder, lady! lo, upon thy wish,                     50
        Our messenger Chatillon is arriv'd!
        What England says, say briefly, gentle lord;
        We coldly pause for thee; Chatillon, speak.

37, 50. K. Phi.] King. F1.      37. *then, to work;*] Theobald; *then to worke* F1.
49. *indirectly*] F1; *indiscreetly* Collier MS.

34. *more*] greater.
37. *bent*] aimed, directed. "The terms of archery were applied to other weapons than the bow" (Wright). Semantic contamination may have been caused by the phrase "to be bent to" = "to be intent on" (cf. II. i. 422).
39. *discipline*] From "instruction, learning" this word acquired the technical meaning "military training, or experience".
40. *cull . . . advantages*] choose the places (plots of ground) with most advantages (for the cannon).
42. *Wade . . . blood*] A common

image. Cf. *The First Part of Ieronimo* (1605): "Ide wade up to the knees in bloud, / Ide make a bridge of Spanish carkases, / To single thee out of the gasping armye" (Kyd, p. 310).
43. *But*] Unless.
49. *indirectly*] Hot haste is usually direct; *indirect* here means "round about, out of course", and refers to the motives (*indirectly* or wrongly assessing John) which dictate haste.
53. *coldly*] dispassionately. After *hot* (1. 49), Shakespeare already points to the hypocrisy of France, beneath whose hot zeal cold calculation presides.

*Chat.* Then turn your forces from this paltry siege
    And stir them up against a mightier task.          55
    England, impatient of your just demands,
    Hath put himself in arms: the adverse winds,
    Whose leisure I have stay'd, have given him time
    To land his legions all as soon as I;
    His marches are expedient to this town,          60
    His forces strong, his soldiers confident.
    With him along is come the mother-queen,
    An Ate, stirring him to blood and strife;
    With her her niece, the Lady Blanche of Spain;
    With them a bastard of the king's deceas'd,          65
    And all th'unsettled humours of the land;
    Rash, inconsiderate, fiery voluntaries,
    With ladies' faces and fierce dragons' spleens,
    Have sold their fortunes at their native homes,

63. *Ate*] Rowe; *Ace* F 1.    65. *king's*] As F 1; *King* F 2.    65–6. *deceas'd, . . . land;*]
Pope; *deceast, . . . Land,* F 1; *deceas'd: . . . land,*—Capell.

55. *stir . . . against*] animate them in
preparation for.

56. *just demands*] In the "sawcie
speech of proud Pandulph the popes
lewd legat, to king Iohn", a similar
context, we read: "I would aduise you
. . . to obeie the popes iust demands"
(Hol., 177, i).

60. *expedient*] expeditious, hasting.

63. *Ate*] Rowe's emendation supposes the common *t : c* misreading.
Ate was familiar in Elizabethan
drama, as is shown by "More Ates,
more Ates! stir them on! stir them on!"
(*LLL.*, v. ii. 692–3). Perhaps the derivative *Atin* in *Faerie Queene* influenced
Shakespeare: "For all in *blood* and
spoile is his delight. / His am I Atin, his
in wrong and right, / . . . And *stirre* him
*up* to *strife* and cruell fight" (Bk II, c. iv,
st. 42).

64. *niece*] grand-daughter, a common meaning at this time, though the
modern one was also in use (cf. II. i.
424). In his will Shakespeare referred
to his grand-daughter as "my Neece
Elizabeth Hall".

65. *of the king's*] Double genitive.

Cf. *T.R.*: "Next them a Bastard of the
Kings deceast" (I. ii. 69).

66–75. *And . . . Christendom*] Upton
and Malone thought this an allusion
to the Cadiz expedition of 1596; Wilson noted that "the suggestion might
equally well have come from the
French campaigning of 1591 under
Essex and Sir Roger Williams". But
topicality is not necessary.

66. *unsettled humours*] "restless, dis-
satisfied men" (Wilson). The *land* is
envisaged as a body (cf. IV. ii. 243–8,
v. i. 5–16), the humours being the four
chief fluids which were thought to determine its qualities; *unsettled humours*
may = fluids of choler.

67. *inconsiderate*] not considering
themselves, reckless.

*voluntaries*] volunteers.

68. *spleens*] The spleen was the seat
of passions and emotions in the old
physiology. Here, as often, it simply
means "fiery temper". Cf. *R 3*, v. iii.
351.

69. *native homes*] A set phrase [as in
W. Rankins's *English Ape* (1588), sig.
A₂ᵛ; G. Gerbier D'Ouvilly's *False*

Bearing their birthrights proudly on their backs,          70
To make a hazard of new fortunes here:
In brief, a braver choice of dauntless spirits
Than now the English bottoms have waft o'er
Did never float upon the swelling tide,                     74
To do offence and scathe in Christendom.    [*Drum beats.*
The interruption of their churlish drums
Cuts off more circumstance: they are at hand,
To parley or to fight; therefore prepare.
*K. Phi.* How much unlook'd for is this expedition!
*Aust.* By how much unexpected, by so much              80
We must awake endeavour for defence,
For courage mounteth with occasion:
Let them be welcome then; we are prepar'd.


*Enter* KING JOHN, ELEANOR, BLANCHE, *the* BASTARD, *Lords,*
*and Forces.*


*K. John.* Peace be to France, if France in peace permit
Our just and lineal entrance to our own;                    85
If not, bleed France, and peace ascend to heaven,
Whiles we, God's wrathful agent, do correct
Their proud contempt that beats His peace to heaven.

75. S.D.] After l. 77 F1.      77–8. *hand, . . . fight;*] Capell; *hand, . . . fight*, F1;
*hand. . . .fight*, Pope.     79. K. Phi.] Kin. F1.      81. *awake*] F1; *awake*, Rowe.
84.] F1; *Scene* II. Pope.      84. S.D.] Enter K. of England, Bastard, Queene,
Blanch, Pembroke, and others. F1.      88. *beats*] F1; *beat* Hanmer.

*Favourite Disgrac't* (1657), sig. D₂ᵛ],
meaning "native land(s)".

   70. *Bearing . . . backs*] Johnson compared *H 8*, I. i. 83–4; Tilley (p. 392)
called this the proverb "He wears a
whole Lordship on his back."

   73. *bottoms*] ships.

   *waft*] Past tenses and participles of
verbs ending in "t" often retained the
present form unaltered; cf. *heat* (IV. i.
61), and Abbott, sect. 342.

   75. *scathe in Christendom*] In *Soliman
and Perseda* (cf. I. i. 244, note) these
words also go together: "Till it haue
prickt the hart of Christendome. /
Which now that paltrie Iland keeps
from scath" (I. v. 16–17); "What mil-

lions of men, opprest with ruine and
scath, / The Turkish armies did oer-
throw in Christendome" (III. v. 5–6).

   76. *churlish*] inferior, miserable; cf.
III. i. 229, *Ven.*, l. 107.

   77. *circumstance*] detailed discourse.

   77–8. *hand, . . . fight;*] On the stage
the flow of phrase can ignore the need
of a semi-colon.

   79. *unlook'd for*] See Introduction,
p. xii.

   82. *occasion*] emergency (Wilson).
Tilley (p. 122) called this the proverb
"Great Courage is in greatest dangers
tried."

   85. *lineal*] due by right of descent;
cf. V. vii. 102.

*K. Phi.*  Peace be to England, if that war return
    From France to England, there to live in peace.    90
    England we love; and for that England's sake
    With burden of our armour here we sweat.
    This toil of ours should be a work of thine;
    But thou from *l*oving England art so far,
    That thou hast underwrought his lawful king,    95
    Cut off the sequence of posterity,
    Outfaced infant state, and done a rape
    Upon the maiden virtue of the crown.
    Look here upon thy brother Geoffrey's face;
    These eyes, these brows, were moulded out of his:    100
    This little abstract doth contain that large
    Which died in Geoffrey: and the hand of time
    Shall draw this brief into as huge a volume.
    That Geoffrey was thy elder brother born,
    And this his son; England was Geoffrey's right,    105
    And this is Geoffrey's; in the name of God
    How comes it then that thou art call'd a king,

95. *his*] F1; *its* Rowe.    105. *right,*] F1; *right,* [he points to Angiers Wilson. 106. *this*] F1; *his* J. M. Mason [*Comments* (1785), p. 154].    *Geoffrey's;*] As Rowe; Geffreyes F1; *Geffrey's* [points to *Arthur*] Sisson.    *God*] Pope; *God:* F1.

89–90. *Peace . . . peace.*] "Perhaps Philip points at the English army (war) as he speaks" (Moberly). This is the type of inconsistency Jonson ridiculed with Shakespeare's "Caesar did never wrong, but with just cause."

91. *England's*] Arthur's. Philip insists Arthur is rightful king by linking the two Englands of l. 91 with *that*, as if they were one.

93. *toil . . . work*] Philip has to *toil* because contending with John and Angiers; John, if loyal to Arthur, would only have had to *work* against Angiers.

95. *underwrought*] "underworked, undermined" (Steevens).

*his*] its. The old possessive.

97. *Outfaced*] Intimidated, defied; as in v. i. 49.

*state*] rank, majesty.

101. *abstract*] "epitome (of something greater), compendium (of many qualities)" (On.). So *Ant.*, i. iv. 9.

103. *draw*] write out, compose.

*brief*] "short note, or description" (Malone).

106. *And . . . Geoffrey's;*] This right is Geoffrey's (C. Porter); "'this' means the city of Angiers . . . King Philip points to it as he speaks" (Wilson). If *this* resumes l. 105 *this*, Philip's two points may be "And this is (Arthur, who is) Geoffrey's (heir)."

*God*] Knight supported the F1 colon, since "Philip makes a solemn asseveration that this (Arthur) is Geffrey's son and successor . . . in the name of God; asserting the principle of legitimacy, by divine ordinance". We think *in the name of God* goes with l. 106 *and* l. 107, the colon being *connective*. Perhaps Shakespeare thought of the usual opening of wills, as in "In the name of god Amen I William Shackspeare . . ."

107. *How . . . king*] Cf. *Faustus:*

When living blood doth in these temples beat,
Which owe the crown that thou o'ermasterest?
*K. John.* From whom hast thou this great commission, France,
To draw my answer from thy articles?                    111
*K. Phi.* From that supernal judge that stirs good thoughts
In any beast of strong authority
To look into the blots and stains of right.
That judge hath made me guardian to this boy:          115
Under whose warrant I impeach thy wrong
And by whose help I mean to chastise it.
*K. John.* Alack, thou dost usurp authority.
*K. Phi.* Excuse it is to beat usurping down.
*Elea.* Who is it thou dost call usurper, France?        120
*Const.* Let me make answer: thy usurping son.
*Elea.* Out, insolent! thy bastard shall be king,
That thou mayst be a queen, and check the world!
*Const.* My bed was ever to thy son as true
As thine was to thy husband; and this boy              125

109. *owe*] F1; *own* Pope.    110. *France*] F1; om. Rowe.    111. *from*] F1; *to*
Pope.    113. *beast*] F1; *breast* F2, edd.    113–14. *authority . . . right.*] Pope;
*authoritie, . . . right,* F1; *authority; . . . right,* Fleay.    119. *Excuse it is*] F1; *Excuse
it, 'tis* Rowe iii; *Excuse; it is* Malone.    120, 122, 132, 159. Elea.] Queen. F1.

"How comes it then that thou art out
of hell?" (I.iii).

109. *owe*] own.
*o'ermasterest*] make yourself master of
(*O.E.D.*, overmaster).

111. *draw*] extract, demand.
*articles*] Each of the distinct charges
of an accusation (*O.E.D.*).

112. *supernal*] celestial.

113. *beast*] A conceit is required to
exaggerate John's inhumanity, and
*beast* is as effective as in *Caes.*: "O
judgment! thou art fled to brutish
beasts, / And men have lost their
reason" (III.ii. 110–11).

114. *blots*] blemishes.

115. *guardian*] "Constance . . .
doubting the suertie of hir sonne, committed him to the trust of the French
king, who receiuing him into his tuition, promised to defend him . . ."
(Hol., 158, i, ii).

119. *is*] Malone's punctuation,

favourite for a century, assumes an
absolute use of the verb *excuse* which
P. Simpson found un-English (*N. &
Q.*, 3 Mar. 1900). Simpson defended
F1 as meaning "It is sufficient excuse
for my usurpation of authority that I
am fighting against usurpation."

123. *queen . . . check*] Staunton saw an
allusion to chess.—Shakespeare follows Holinshed closely: "Elianor . . .
was sore against hir nephue Arthur,
rather mooued thereto by enuie conceiued against his mother . . . she saw
if he were king, how his mother Constance would looke to beare most rule
within the realme" (158, i).

124–5. *My . . . husband*] "Constance
alludes to Elinor's infidelity to her
husband Lewis the Seventh, when they
were in the Holy Land; on account of
which he was divorced from her. She
afterwards (1151) married our King
Henry II" (Malone).

Liker in feature to his father Geoffrey
Than thou and John in manners; being as like
As rain to water, or devil to his dam.
My boy a bastard! By my soul, I think
His father never was so true begot:                    130
It cannot be and if thou wert his mother.

*Elea.*  There's a good mother, boy, that blots thy father.
*Const.*  There's a good grandam, boy, that would blot thee.
*Aust.*  Peace!
*Bast.*          Hear the crier!
*Aust.*                    What the devil art thou?
*Bast.*  One that will play the devil, sir, with you,    135
And a may catch your hide and you alone:
You are the hare of whom the proverb goes,
Whose valour plucks dead lions by the beard.
I'll smoke your skin-coat, and I catch you right;
Sirrah, look to't; i' faith I will, i' faith.         140

---

127. *John in manners;*] Roderick; Iohn, *in manners* F1.       133.] One line Pope; two lines F1 (ending *boy/ . . . thee./*).       *grandam*] F1 (*grandame*).       140. *i' faith I*] As F1; *i'faith, I* Theobald.

---

132. *blots*] calumniates.

134. *Peace!*] Austria's ineffective exclamation is characteristic: cf. II. i. 293, III. i. 38, also his pious thought about "the peace of heaven" (II. i. 35).
*crier*] "Alluding to the usual proclamation for *silence*, made by criers in courts of justice" (Malone).

135. *devil*] Cf. Introduction, p. xxii. "To play the devil", a phrase first recorded in the 16th century in *O.E.D.*, is one of the references to the older drama which Shakespeare has concentrated round Faulconbridge (Introduction, p. lxxi).

136. *hide*] The lion-skin seems to have been Shakespeare's embellishment of the Cœur-de-lion story (Introduction, p. xxiii). *MND.* also calls for this property (v. i. 129), and belongs to the same years.

137. *the proverb*] "The proverb alluded to is, 'Mortuo leoni et lepores insultant.'" (in the *Adagia* of Erasmus) (Malone). Steevens (cf. Introduction,

p. xliv) noted the close resemblance to *The Spanish Tragedy*. Nashe, in 1592, needing a quotation for a similar situation, remembered Kyd, not Shakespeare: "Out vppon thee for an arrant dog-killer, strike a man when he is dead? *So Hares may pull dead Lions by the beards. Memorandum:* I borrowed this sentence out of a Play" (Nashe, I, 271).

138. *plucks . . . beard*] From Alciatus: "sic cassi luce leonis / Conuellunt barbam vel timidi lepores" (*Emblemata, v.* "Cum laruis non luctandum."). To *beard* a man was an outrage compelling a challenge.

139. *smoke*] Cf. I. i. 208–9, note. The two meanings are (*a*) I'll give you a thrashing (Wright); (*b*) I'll smoke (disinfect) your lion-skin (Delius). Wilson also proposed "a glance at the smoke caused by branding the skins of sheep or cattle".
*skin-coat*] skin. A common word in "thrashing" contexts.

140. *i'faith . . . i'faith!*] So in W.

*Blanche.* O, well did he become that lion's robe
    That did disrobe the lion of that robe!
*Bast.* It lies as sightly on the back of him
    As great Alcides' shoes upon an ass:
    But, ass, I'll take that burthen from your back,    145
    Or lay on that shall make your shoulders crack.
*Aust.* What cracker is this same that deafs our ears
    With this abundance of superfluous breath?
*K. Phi.* Lewis, determine what we shall do straight.
*Lew.* Women and fools, break off your conference.    150
*K. Phi.* King John, this is the very sum of all:
    England and Ireland, Anjou, Touraine, Maine,

144. *shoes*] F1 (*shooes*); *shews* Theobald.    149. K. Phi. *Lewis, determine*] As Capell; *King Lewis, determine* F1; *King Philip, determine* Theobald; *King,—Lewis, determine* Malone conj.    150. Lew.] F1; *K. Philip.* Theobald.    151. K. Phi.] This ed.; speech contd. F1.    152. *Anjou*] Theobald; *Angiers* F1.

Haughton's *English-men for my Money* (1616): "Ile haue my will ynfayth, y'fayth I will" (sig. I^v).

141–3. *O . . . him*] After the emphasis on *robbing* lions (I. i. 268, II. i. 3) we suspect an intended *rob/robe* quibble. If we may postulate a lost line, the *lion/ lies on* echo may have had more point. Faulconbridge might have begun: "I'll robe him, and make better lie on's back: It lies as sightly . . ." [I'll robe him, i.e. rob, i.e. disrobe; and make (*a*) something better lie on his back, i.e. a beating; (*b*) better lions back away; (*c*) a better man than he lie on his back.]

144. *shoes*] *shows* and *shoes* were homophones (Fleay), and both meanings are present. The two words could be spelt the same (Maxwell: *N. & Q.*, 18 Feb. 1950). Steevens showed that comparison with the *shoes* of Hercules was proverbial (Tilley, p. 600, quoted many examples, one from Gosson, 1579: "toyles too draw the Lyons skin vpon Aesops Asse. Hercules shoes on a childes feete"). And *shows* makes sense too: "As great A. appears vpon an ass". Segar mentions that one order of knighthood had a rule that knights "should not bee seen mounted vppon any Mule, or other vnseemelie Hack-

ney" (*op. cit.*, sig. S₃^v). Theobald's "*Alcides'* shews", thirdly, refers us to (*a*) the lion-skin of Hercules; (*b*) the fable of the ass in the lion-skin.

146. *lay on*] "lay on (load)" = thrash soundly. The first sense is "lay on (a load of) blows", but a technical *burthen* (l. 145) is also implied. When a knight was dishonoured "the burthen shall rest vpon him" (Segar, *op. cit.*, sig. B₂), i.e. he has to challenge. Faulconbridge insinuates that Austria will carry any burthen rather than challenge. The *T.R.* makes Faulconbridge challenge Austria and Austria basely evade the issue (I. v. 15–56).

147. *cracker*] braggart.

149–51. K. Phi. . . . K. Phi.] See Introduction, p.xxx iv.

151–5. *King . . . France.*] In 1202 King Philip "commanded king Iohn with no small arrogancie . . . to restore vnto his nephue . . . all those lands now in his possession on that side the sea, which king Iohn earnestlie denied to doo" (Hol., 164, i).

152. *Anjou*] Cf. II. i. 487. Wilson, intent on belittling Shakespeare's historical knowledge, claimed that "Shakespeare imagines Anjou and Angiers to be the same", which is unfair. Probably a printing-house error.

In right of Arthur do I claim of thee.
Wilt thou resign them and lay down thy arms?
*K. John.*  My life as soon: I do defy thee, France.        155
Arthur of Britain, yield thee to my hand;
And out of my dear love I'll give thee more
Than e'er the coward hand of France can win:
Submit thee, boy.
*Elea.*                    Come to thy grandam, child.
*Const.*  Do, child, go to it grandam, child;              160
Give grandam kingdom, and it grandam will
Give it a plum, a cherry, and a fig:
There's a good grandam.
*Arth.*                    Good my mother, peace!
I would that I were low laid in my grave:
I am not worth this coil that's made for me.             165
*Elea.*  His mother shames him so, poor boy, he weeps.
*Const.*  Now shame upon you, whe'r she does or no!
His grandam's wrongs, and not his mother's shames,
Draws those heaven-moving pearls from his poor eyes,
Which heaven shall take in nature of a fee;             170
Ay, with these crystal beads heaven shall be brib'd

---

156. *Britain*] F1 (*Britaine* throughout); *Bretagne* Hanmer (throughout).
160. *Do, child,*] F1; *Do, go, child, go;* Capell.      160–1. *it . . . it*] F1 (*yt . . . it*);
*it' . . . it'* Johnson.       166. Elea.] Qu. Mo. F1.       167. *whe'r*] F1 (*where*);
*whether* Johnson.       169. *Draws*] F1; *Draw* Capell.

156–9. *Arthur . . . boy.*] So M. Paris
described John's words to Arthur
(when Arthur was captured): "coepit
eum [Arturum] Rex blandis alloqui
verbis, & multos honores promittere,
exhortans vt a Rege Francorum rece-
deret, & sibi vt Domino & auunculo
fideliter adhaereret" (p. 278).

156. *Britain*] Brittany.

160–2. *it . . . it*] Here *it* = (*a*) the
early possessive (later "its"), as in *Lr.*,
I. iv. 239; (*b*) baby language (hence
contemptuous, of older persons, as in
*LLL.*, v. ii. 338).

162. *Give . . . fig:*] In Heywood's *If
You Know Not Me* (1605), a boy is
caioled "Come tell me what letters
thou carryedst her, / Ile giue thee figgs
and suger plummes" (sig. D₂ᵛ). Per-

haps Shakespeare does not mean fresh
fruit either.—*Give . . . a fig* also alludes
to the cant "to give the fig", as in
*2 H 6*, II. iii. 68, *H 5*, III. vi. 62, etc.

164. *low laid*] Quibbling on "lay
low" = kill.

165. *coil*] uproar, commotion.

167. *whe'r*] Cf. I. i. 75, note.

171. *crystal*] Though "crystal tears"
was a poetic cliché in 1590, the adjective is appropriate since in the Elizabethan world-picture heaven was
"crystalline" (therefore the more likely to be so bribed?).

*beads*] "There is here an implied reference to *prayers* as one of the meanings of the word *beads*" (J. Hunter).
This meaning implied the rosary
(*O.E.D.*, bead, 1b); cf. III. i. 35, note.

To do him justice and revenge on you.
*Elea.* Thou monstrous slanderer of heaven and earth!
*Const.* Thou monstrous injurer of heaven and earth!
    Call not me slanderer; thou and thine usurp       175
    The dominations, royalties and rights
    Of this oppressed boy: this is thy eldest son's son,
    Infortunate in nothing but in thee:
    Thy sins are visited in this poor child;
    The canon of the law is laid on him,        180
    Being but the second generation
    Removed from thy sin-conceiving womb.
*K. John.* Bedlam, have done.
*Const.*             I have but this to say,
    That he is not only plagued for her sin,
    But God hath made her sin and her the plague    185
    On this removed issue, plagued for her
    And with her plague; her sin his injury,

---

177. *boy: this is*] As F1; *boy:* Ritson; *boy, this* Vaughan.    *eldest*] F1; *eld'st*
Capell.    183. *Bedlam*] F1; *Beldam* Ritson.    184. *he is*] F1; *he's* Johnson.
185, 187. *sin*] F1; *son* Spence (*N. & Q.*, 27 Jan. 1894).    186. *her*] F1 (*her,*);
*her;* Capell.    187. *her plague; her sin*] Roby (*ap.* Cambridge); *her plague her
sinne:* F1; *her.—Plague her sin;* Johnson; *her plague, her sin;* Malone.

---

Craig (*ap.* I. John) suggested an allusion to Indians being bribed with
beads.
  176. *dominations*] dominions.
  177. *eldest . . . son*] Not "the son of
your eldest son", but "your eldest
grand-son". The form, as in *R 2*, II. i.
105, is biblical (cf. *Deuteronomy*, vi. 2:
"thou, and thy sonne, and thy sonnes
sonne"). Edd. have said that here
Shakespeare makes Arthur the son of
Richard I, and compared II. i. 2, 6, 13.
Shakespeare may have intended this
genealogy (cf. Introduction, p. l),
though Richard was not Eleanor's
eldest son.
  179. *visited*] punished (biblical).
  180. *The . . . law*] *canon* = law or
decree of the Church; *law* = the system of divine commands contained in
Holy Scripture (On.). Constance
alludes to *Exodus*, xx. 5, a canon much
quoted in the Bible. Shakespeare here

remembers Holinshed's Life of Henry
III: "neither shall the child (as the
scripture teacheth vs) beare the iniquitie of his father . . ." (p. 197).
  182. *sin - conceiving*] Shakespeare
turns the Psalmist's "in sin hath my
mother conceived me" (li. 5) (Noble)
to imply that anything conceived by
Eleanor must be sinful.
  183. *Bedlam*] Lunatic.
  184. *plagued . . . sin*] That plagues
punish sin was the watch-word of
preachers in plague-infested London.
The idea, biblical ultimately, helped
to give *plague* the new meaning of
"punishment", as here.
  185–90. *But . . . her!*] Following the
*sin* of ll. 182, 184, *sin* in ll. 185, 187, 188
= moral sin and the person of John
(sin-conceived) [Johnson]. The sense
of these intentionally obscure lines is
that Arthur is punished for Eleanor's
sins and by her person.

Her injury the beadle to her sin,
All punish'd in the person of this child,
And all for her; a plague upon her!                                190
*Elea.* Thou unadvised scold, I can produce
A will that bars the title of thy son.
*Const.* Ay, who doubts that? a will! a wicked will;
A woman's will; a cank'red grandam's will!
*K. Phi.* Peace, lady! pause, or be more temperate:        195
It ill beseems this presence to cry aim
To these ill-tuned repetitions.
Some trumpet summon hither to the walls
These men of Angiers: let us hear them speak
Whose title they admit, Arthur's or John's.                      200

*Trumpet sounds. Enter* HUBERT *upon the walls.*

*Hub.* Who is it that hath warn'd us to the walls?
*K. Phi.* 'Tis France, for England.
*K. John.*                              England, for itself.

197. *ill-tuned*] F1; no hyphen F2, edd.      201.] F1; *Scene* III. Pope.      201. S.D.]
This ed.; Trumpet sounds./Enter a Citizen vpon the walles. F1; Trumpets . . .
ed. 1760; Trumpets . . . citizens . . . Variorum 1773.      Hub.] This ed.;
Cit. F1 (throughout to l. 281); *1* Cit. Variorum 1773, edd.

188. *injury*] taunts, reviling.
  *beadle*] whipper. The beadle, or par-
ish officer, had to whip petty offenders.
Read: "Eleanor's injurious tongue
like a beadle whips John (into a fury
against Arthur)".
  191. *scold*] railer, quarreller.
  192. *A will*] Richard I, before dying,
"ordeined his testament . . . Vnto his
brother Iohn he assigned the crowne
of England . . ." (Hol., pp. 155–6).
Shakespeare belittles the will (ll. 193–
4) to make John seem a usurper (cf. I.
i. 40, note).
  *bars*] A bar was an objection that
could arrest entirely an action at law
(On.).
  194. *A woman's will*] Women in 1590
were not allowed to make wills for
their lands, tenements, etc., if married,
as the husband's influence was feared
[H. Swinburne, *Briefe Treatise of Testaments* (1590), sig. H₂]. A "woman's

will" was proverbially an influenced
will: Constance (reversing the process
to emphasize Eleanor's domination)
suggests that Richard's will was influenced by a woman. Cf. Chapman's
*All Fools*, III. i. 230–5.
  196. *cry aim*] to encourage archers
when shooting, hence "to applaud, encourage".
  197. *repetitions*] recitals.
  198. *trumpet*] trumpeter.
  201. Hubert] See Introduction, p.
xxxvi.
  *warn'd*] summoned.
  202. *'Tis . . . itself.*] "It is the king of
France for the king of England" says
Philip. John's three words imply that
the real England needs no spokesman,
that he therefore is the true king. This
quibble on the identity of king and
country (as in II. i. 91, 365, IV. iii. 142
*sqq.*) drives home the moral of the history.

You men of Angiers, and my loving subjects—
*K. Phi.* You loving men of Angiers, Arthur's subjects,
  Our trumpet call'd you to this gentle parle—  205
*K. John.* For our advantage; therefore hear us first.
  These flags of France, that are advanced here
  Before the eye and prospect of your town,
  Have hither march'd to your endamagement.
  The cannons have their bowels full of wrath,  210
  And ready mounted are they to spit forth
  Their iron indignation 'gainst your walls:
  All preparation for a bloody siege
  And merciless proceeding by these French
  Comforts your city's eyes, your winking gates;  215
  And but for our approach those sleeping stones,
  That as a waist doth girdle you about,
  By the compulsion of their ordinance
  By this time from their fixed beds of lime
  Had been dishabited, and wide havoc made  220
  For bloody power to rush upon your peace.
  But on the sight of us your lawful king,

---

215. *Comforts*] *Comfort* F1; *Confront* Rowe; *Come 'fore* Collier MS.        *your*] F3;
*yours* F1.      217. *doth*] F1; *do* Rowe.

205. *parle*] parley, conference.
207–34. *These . . . walls.*] For the imagery cf. Introduction, p. lxii. Shakespeare reverses the "siege" convention of love-poetry, in which the lady is a fortress to be stormed, threatening the city as a woman.
207. *flags*] An anachronism. Flags were not known till the 15th century (cf. *O.E.D.*).
*advanced*] raised. So *Tp.*, I. ii. 405, *R 3*, I. ii. 40.
210–12. *The . . . walls:*] So Greene's *Alphonsus, King of Aragon* (1599): "the roaring cannon shot / Spit forth the venome of their fiered panch" (*sig.* G₄).
210. *bowels*] The bowels were thought the seat of pity and compassion.
215. *Comforts*] F1 was rejected since irony was said to be out of place. As

John's speech is full of innuendo, of over- and under-statement, the *winking* of this very line being playful, as though the gates are no stronger than eyelids, we return to F1. With Capell we transfer the "s" of *yours* to *Comfort(s)*.
*winking*] closing; thus both eyes could wink at once.
217. *waist*] girdle, or garment for the waist.
*doth*] Singular, attracted by *waist*.
220. *dishabited*] dislodged; stripped. Shakespeare's coinage.
*wide havoc*] a wide breach with stones tumbling in confusion.
221. *bloody*] blood-smeared; fierce, passionate (cf. I. i. 17). Chastity (= Right), i.e. cold stones sleeping in their beds, attacked by passionate *power* mirrors the scheme of the play— the zestful vitality of Wrong fighting the sickly coldness of Right.

Who painfully with much expedient march
Have brought a countercheck before your gates,
To save unscratch'd your city's threat'ned cheeks,          225
Behold, the French amaz'd vouchsafe a parle;
And now, instead of bullets wrapp'd in fire,
To make a shaking fever in your walls,
They shoot but calm words folded up in smoke,
To make a faithless error in your ears:                    230
Which trust accordingly, kind citizens,
And let us in, your king, whose labour'd spirits
Forwearied in this action of swift speed
Craves harbourage within your city walls.

*K. Phi.* When I have said, make answer to us both.        235
Lo, in this right hand, whose protection
Is most divinely vow'd upon the right
Of him it holds, stands young Plantagenet,
Son to the elder brother of this man,
And king o'er him and all that he enjoys:                  240
For this down-trodden equity we tread
In warlike march these greens before your town,
Being no further enemy to you
Than the constraint of hospitable zeal
In the relief of this oppressed child                      245

---

232. *in, your king,*] Ed. 1735; *in. Your King,* F1 ; *in, your king;* Capell.     234.
*Craves*] F1 ; *Crave* Pope.     243. *further*] F1 ; *farther* Collier.

223. *expedient*] speedy.
227. *bullets*] cannon-balls.
*wrapp'd in fire*] So *The Spanish Tragedy*: "violence . . . / Wrapt in a ball of fire" (Kyd, p. 60); T. Andrewe, *Unmasking of a Feminine Machiauell* (1604): "bullets in fire wrapt round, / Circled in smoke" (sig. D4); B. & F.'s *Maid in the Mill* (ed. 1647): "a bullet / Wrapt in a cloud of fire" (p. 2).
228. *To . . . walls,*] For the reverse image cf. *this wall of flesh* (III. ii. 30).
229. *smoke*] The idiom may be illustrated from *The Contre-Guyse* (1589): "A pitifull case, that they should take the shadow for the substance, smoke for fire, the visage and lies, for truth . . ." (sig. Eᵛ). Malone compared *Lucr.*,

1027: "This helpless smoke of words doth me no right."
233. *Forwearied*] Tired out.
235. *said*] finished speaking, spoken my mind.
236. *in . . . hand*] "Compare Richard III, IV. i. 2: 'Led in the hand of her kind aunt of Gloucester.' And Genesis xxi. 18" (Wright). Or Shakespeare may follow M. Paris: "Constantia . . . tradidit ei [Regi Francorum] Arturum memoratum, quem Rex continuo misit Parisios . . . & accepit in manu sua ciuitates omnes & castella, quae Arturi erant" (p. 263).
241–2. *tread . . . march*] The common expression was "to tread a march".

Religiously provokes. Be pleased then
To pay that duty which you truly owe
To him that owes it, namely this young prince:
And then our arms, like to a muzzled bear,
Save in aspect, hath all offence seal'd up;                    250
Our cannons' malice vainly shall be spent
Against th' invulnerable clouds of heaven;
And with a blessed and unvex'd retire,
With unhack'd swords and helmets all unbruis'd,
We will bear home that lusty blood again                    255
Which here we came to spout against your town,
And leave your children, wives and you in peace.
But if you fondly pass our proffer'd offer,
'Tis not the roundure of your old-fac'd walls
Can hide you from our messengers of war,                    260
Though all these English and their discipline
Were harbour'd in their rude circumference.
Then tell us, shall your city call us lord,
In that behalf which we have challeng'd it?
Or shall we give the signal to our rage                    265

---

248. *owes*] F1; *owns* Pope.     250. *hath*] F1; *have* Hanmer.     259. *roundure*]
Capell; *rounder* F1.

---

248. *owes*] owns.
251. *malice*] power to harm.
253. *unvex'd*] unmolested.
254. *helmets . . . unbruis'd*] So Spenser:
"And helmes unbruzed wexen daylie
browne" [*Shepheardes Calender* (October)]; Chapman: "my helmet yet unbruis'd" (*All Fools*, v. i. 15); T. Andrewe: "broken Pikes, bruz'd Helmets, batterd shields" (*op. cit.*, sig. E).
258. *proffer'd*] Proffer could mean
"attempt" (*O.E.D.*, proffer, 3), but
here only the empty jingle of the old
alliterative drama may be intended, as
in *Tom Tyler*: "I never did proffer you
such an offer" (ed. 1661, sig. C₂), to
score off this inflated speech.
259. *roundure*] So Sonnet xxi.—The
experts on fortification advised against
sharp angles in walls, because hard to
defend. Angiers, with circular walls,
would not be easily stormed. [See Paul

Ive, *Practise of Fortification* (1589), p. 7.]
*old-fac'd*] Not only the walls, but the
faces (outer layers of stone) were old.
Walls were often built with vertical
scarp, so as to lean inwards, and tend-
ed to *shoot* (crumble): *old-fac'd walls*
were therefore well-built.
260. *messengers of war*] i.e. cannon-
balls. Shakespeare may have had in
mind the biblical cliché "messengers
of death"—as in "The wrath of a King
(is as) messengers of death" (*Proverbs*,
xvi. 14).
261. *discipline*] See II. i. 39, note.
263. *call us lord*] Arthur, it is implied,
has done homage to Philip. Cf. II. i.
115, note, and Hol., 160, ii.
264. *In . . . which*] On behalf of him
for whom.
265. *signal . . . rage*] Philip is so inhuman that he controls even his rage
(uncontrolledness); cf. II. i. 53, note.

And stalk in blood to our possession?

*Hub.*  In brief, we are the king of England's subjects:
    For him, and in his right, we hold this town.

*K. John.*  Acknowledge then the king, and let me in.

*Hub.*  That can we not; but he that proves the king,    270
    To him will we prove loyal: till that time
    Have we ramm'd up our gates against the world.

*K. John.*  Doth not the crown of England prove the king?
    And if not that, I bring you witnesses,
    Twice fifteen thousand hearts of England's breed—  275

*Bast.*  Bastards and else.

*K. John.*  To verify our title with their lives.

*K. Phi.*  As many and as well-born bloods as those—

*Bast.*  Some bastards too.

*K. Phi.*  Stand in his face to contradict his claim.    280

*Hub.*  Till you compound whose right is worthiest,
    We for the worthiest hold the right from both.

*K. John.*  Then God forgive the sin of all those souls
    That to their everlasting residence,
    Before the dew of evening fall, shall fleet,    285
    In dreadful trial of our kingdom's king!

*K. Phi.*  Amen, amen! Mount, chevaliers! to arms!

*Bast.*  Saint George, that swindg'd the dragon, and e'er since

---

276, 279.] F1; Aside. Pope.    282.] F1; [Exeunt Citizens. Donovan.    288–9.
*Saint . . . door,*] Pope; two lines F1 (ending *Dragon,/ . . . dore/*).

---

266. *stalk*] Less specific than to-day, *stalk* could mean simply walk: but the modern sense is present here, suggesting Philip's haughtiness.

270. *he*] Classed as a noun absolute by Abbott, who compared *H 5*, IV. iii. 35, *R 3*, III. ii. 58, adding "These three examples might, however, come under the head of construction changed [through change of thought]" (p. 304).

273. *crown of England*] Cf. I. i. 40. C. K. Davis compared a statute of Henry VII: "If there be a king regnant in possession of the crown, though he be but *rex de facto* and not *de jure*, yet he is *seignior le roy*; and if another hath right, if he be out of possession, he is not within the meaning of the statute"

[*Law in Shakespeare* (1884), p. 150].

276. *Bastards and else*] "bastards and otherwise" (Smith); "Bastards and such-like" (Schmidt, On.). Surely the words mean both.

278. *bloods*] men of mettle, spirit; men of good stock or family.

281. *compound*] agree, settle.

285. *fleet*] (flit) pass away, vanish; cf. the cliché "his fleeting soul".

287. *Amen, amen!*] Philip is impatient to have been preceded in a pious thought.

288–9. *Saint . . . door*] Tilley (p. 581) quoted the proverb: "Like Saint George, who is ever on horseback yet never rides."

288. *swindg'd*] thrashed.

Sits on's horse-back at mine hostess' door,          289
Teach us some fence! [*To Aust.*] Sirrah, were I at home,
At your den, sirrah, with your lioness,
I would set an ox-head to your lion's hide,
And make a monster of you.
*Aust.*                            Peace! no more.
*Bast.* O, tremble: for you hear the lion roar!
*K. John.* Up higher to the plain; where we'll set forth    295
In best appointment all our regiments.
*Bast.* Speed then, to take advantage of the field.
*K. Phi.* It shall be so; and at the other hill
Command the rest to stand. God and our right!
          [*Exeunt, severally, the English and French Kings, etc.*

*Here, after excursions, enter the Herald of France,
          with Trumpeters, to the gates.*

*F. Her.* You men of Angiers, open wide your gates,       300
And let young Arthur, Duke of Britain, in,

289. *on's*] F1; *on his* Pope.   290. S.D.] Rowe iii; om. F1.   292. *I would*] F1;
*I'd* Pope.   299. S.D.] Dyce; Exeunt F1.   300.] F1; *Scene* IV. Pope; II.
Capell; *Act* II *Scene* I. Fleay.   300. S.D.] Heere after excursions, Enter the
Herald of France with Trumpets to the gates. F1.   301. *Britain*] As F1;
Bretagne Rowe iii.

289. *on's*] "The abbreviation is almost certainly due to the extra long
line . . . which the compositor could
only just crowd into the available
space" (Wilson). Since *on's* staggers
the rhythm in the manner of gallop-
ing, possibility of corruption should
not outweigh an acceptable reading.
    *hostess'*] Why not *host's* (apart from
metre)? Perhaps to imply a viler
domestication. In John's reign there
were no inn-signs; in Elizabeth's St
George was popular on them (Halliwell).
    290. *fence*] swordsmanship (cf. *Ado*,
v. i. 75); defence (cf. *3 H 6*, IV. i. 44).
    291. *lioness*] A double insult. Apart
from the horn-joke, Faulconbridge
calls Austria's duchess a *lioness* [slang
for *whore*: cf. Sir J. Davies, *Epigrammes*
(*c.* 1595), "In Faustem" (16); Sir J.

Harington, *Letters and Epigrams*, ed.
McClure, p. 175; Jonson, *Alchemist*
(IV.iii.49)].
    294. *lion*] The reincarnation of
Cœur-de-lion in Faulconbridge is
brought out in *the lion* (cf. Introduction
p. lxx).
    296. *regiments*] In the modern sense,
"a definite unit of an army", which
*O.E.D.* first records in the 16th century.
    297. *advantage*] Cf. II. i. 40, note.
    299. *God . . . right!*] An English royal
motto in Shakespeare's time, given to
France, perhaps, to underline his
claim that he fights for England.
    300. S.D. Trumpeters] See II. i. 198,
note.
    301. *Duke of Britain*] Cf. II. i. 551
(John promises to make Arthur Duke
of Brittany), II. i. 156 (he addresses him

Who by the hand of France this day hath made
Much work for tears in many an English mother,
Whose sons lie scatter'd on the bleeding ground:
Many a widow's husband grovelling lies,                 305
Coldly embracing the discolour'd earth;
And victory, with little loss, doth play
Upon the dancing banners of the French,
Who are at hand, triumphantly display'd,
To enter conquerors, and to proclaim                    310
Arthur of Britain England's king, and yours.

*Enter English Herald, with Trumpeter.*

*E. Her.*  Rejoice, you men of Angiers, ring your bells;
King John, your king and England's, doth approach,
Commander of this hot malicious day.
Their armours, that march'd hence so silver-bright,   315
Hither return all gilt with Frenchmen's blood;
There stuck no plume in any English crest
That is removed by a staff of France;
Our colours do return in those same hands
That did display them when we first march'd forth;   320
And, like a jolly troop of huntsmen, come

309. *Who . . . display'd*] F1; *Triumphantly display'd; who are at hand,* Keightley.
312. S.D. Trumpeter.] F1 (Trumpet.); trumpets. Hanmer.

as "Arthur of Britain"). Arthur in-
herited Brittany from Constance, and
was already its duke at this time (Hol.).
Shakespeare seems to think that (a)
Arthur was "of Britain" (II. i. 156,
311), because born there; (b) Arthur
had been wrongly made duke by his
adopted lord, France; (c) John, not
recognizing France's creation, promises the dukedom himself (II. i. 551).
Or perhaps Shakespeare followed
Holinshed (161, ii) at II. i. 551 and
failed to notice that John did not *create*
Arthur Duke of Brittany, but merely
received homage for Brittany.

305. *grovelling*] prone, lying on his
belly.

306. *embracing*] "they that were
brought vp in skarlet, embrace

the dongue" (*Lamentations*, iv. 5).

309. *display'd*] Furness suggested the
(pre-Shakespearean) military sense
("deployed, spread out in an extended
line"). Others refer *triumphantly display'd* to *banners*.

312. *Rejoice . . . Angiers*] This and the
last speech resemble that opening
*Tamburlaine*, Pt 1, IV. i: "Awake, ye
men of Memphis!"

315–16. *silver-bright . . . gilt*] Gold was
thought of as red, as well as yellow.
Johnson compared *Mac.* ["His silver
skin lac'd with his golden blood" (II.
iii. 119); "I'll gild the faces of the
grooms withal; / For it must seem their
guilt" (II. ii. 57–8)].

318. *staff*] spear (literally "shaft of a
spear", implying *accidental* removal).

Our lusty English, all with purpled hands,
Dyed in the dying slaughter of their foes:
Open your gates and give the victors way.
*Hub.* Heralds, from off our towers we might behold,    325
From first to last, the onset and retire
Of both your armies; whose equality
By our best eyes cannot be censured:
Blood hath bought blood and blows have answer'd
    blows;
Strength match'd with strength, and power confronted
    power:    330
Both are alike, and both alike we like.
One must prove greatest: while they weigh so even
We hold our town for neither, yet for both.

*Re-enter, on one side,* KING JOHN, ELEANOR, BLANCHE, *the*
BASTARD, *Lords and Forces; on the other,* KING PHILIP, LEWIS,
AUSTRIA, *and Forces.*

*K. John.* France, hast thou yet more blood to cast away?
    Say, shall the current of our right roam on?    335

323. *Dyed*] F1; *Stain'd* Pope.    325. Hub.] Hubert. F1; Citi. Rowe.    334.]
F1; *Scene* V. Pope.    334. S.D.] Dyce; Enter the two Kings with their powers,
at seuerall doores. F1.    335. *roam*] F1; *runne* F2, edd.

322. *lusty*] vigorous; the sense
"merry" is also present (cf. I. i. 108)
after *jolly*.

323. *Dyed*] It was "one of the savage
practices of the chase, for all to stain
their hands in the blood of the deer"
(Johnson). *Caes.*, III. i. 205 was compared, but modern edd., for want of
other allusions to the practice, thought
it figmentary. But cf. *The Brazen Age*:
"al our bore-speares stain'd / And gory
hands lau'd in his reeking bloud"
(Heywood, III, 194); W. Cavendish,
*The Varietie* (1649): "those were the
dayes . . . such brave jeasts, at the
death of a Stag, and Buck, to throw
blood up and downe, upon folkes
faces" (sig. C₁₂ᵛ) (this might explain
*jolly*, l. 321).

325. Hub.] F1 here first introduces
Hubert (cf. Introduction, p. xxxvi).

Wilson thought that Shakespeare
decided at this stage to merge Hubert
and the citizen, which would indicate
how far he thought ahead.

328. *censured*] "estimated" (usual
gloss). But, as Malone noted, their *in-
equality* cannot be estimated. Perhaps
an early use of the modern sense: their
equality allows of no adverse opinion,
no flaw can be found in it.

329. *Blood . . . blood*] Cf. I. i. 19. Tilley (p. 55) referred to the "Blood will
have blood" proverb, which goes back
to *Genesis*, ix. 6.

335. *roam*] Ridley, comparing *Ham.*,
I. iii. 109, wondered whether "instead
of putting both readings down to error
we should not be wiser to accept the
word in both places, even at the cost of
an addition to O.E.D." Malone compared "the *wandering* brooks" (*Tp.*, IV.

Whose passage, vex'd with thy impediment,
Shall leave his native channel and o'erswell,
With course disturb'd, even thy confining shores,
Unless thou let his silver water keep
A peaceful progress to the ocean.                                    340

*K. Phi.*  England, thou hast not sav'd one drop of blood,
In this hot trial, more than we of France;
Rather, lost more. And by this hand I swear,
That sways the earth this climate overlooks,
Before we will lay down our just-borne arms,                         345
We'll put thee down 'gainst whom these arms we bear,
Or add a royal number to the dead,
Gracing the scroll that tells of this war's loss
With slaughter coupled to the name of kings.

*Bast.*  Ha, majesty! how high thy glory towers                      350
When the rich blood of kings is set on fire!
O, now doth death line his dead chaps with steel;
The swords of soldiers are his teeth, his fangs;
And now he feasts, mousing the flesh of men,

---

345. *down*] F 1 ; *by* Pope.        354. *mousing*] F 1 ; *mouthing* Pope.

i. 128). Dyce pleaded for *run* on account of the "repetition" in v. iv. 56. Tilley (p. 637) quoted the proverb "The Stream (current, tide) stopped swells the higher."

337. *o'erswell*] The image of overflowing water to express *rebellion* was conventional. The *confining shores* may be the boundaries inside France between John's lands and Philip's. Holinshed told Shakespeare that John did homage for his French lands: Shakespeare may have in mind a vassal's rebellion.

339. *silver water*] An army marching in armour must have sparkled at a distance like a river: cf. *R 2*, III. ii. 106–11 ("silver rivers . . . hard bright steel").

343. *this hand*] Arthur's hand, held up by Philip (Furness); his own hand (Wilson, taking *climate* = France).

344. *climate*] portion of the sky. I. John quoted Cotgrave: "*Climat:* a clime, or *climate;* a division in the skie, or portion of the world".

346. *put . . . down*] subdue, overthrow.

347. *a royal number*] "a royal item in the list [of dead]" (Smith).

348. *scroll*] In *H 5* a herald brings a *note* which contains "the number of the slaughter'd French" (IV. viii. 79), and Shakespeare thinks of the same afterbattle procedure here.

349. *With . . . kings.*] With a royal name in the list of the dead.

350. *glory*] vaunting, boastful spirit. *towers*] soars. A hawking term (cf. v. ii. 149).

351–3. *set . . . fangs;*] *chaps* = jaws; *fangs* = teeth, tusks. The image is ultimately biblical: "the children of men, that are set on fyre: whose teeth (are) speares and arrowes, and their tongue a sharpe sworde" (*Psalms*, lvii. 4; cf. *Proverbs*, xxx. 14; *Revelation*, i. 16, ii. 16, xix. 15, etc.)

354. *feasts*] Tilley (p. 704) quoted the proverb "War is death's feast." This follows the biblical common-

In undetermin'd differences of kings.                    355
Why stand these royal fronts amazed thus?
Cry "havoc!" kings; back to the stained field,
You equal potents, fiery kindled spirits!
Then let confusion of one part confirm
The other's peace; till then, blows, blood, and death! 360
*K. John.* Whose party do the townsmen yet admit?
*K. Phi.* Speak, citizens, for England; who's your king?
*Hub.* The king of England, when we know the king.
*K. Phi.* Know him in us, that here hold up his right.
*K. John.* In us, that are our own great deputy,                    365
And bear possession of our person here,
Lord of our presence, Angiers, and of you.
*Hub.* A greater power than we denies all this;
And till it be undoubted, we do lock

358. *potents*] F1; *potent* Collier ii.    *fiery kindled*] F1; *fire-ykindled* Collier ii (MS).
363, 416, 423, 480. Hub.] F1; Citi. Rowe.    368. Hub.] This ed.; Fra. F1;
Citi. Rowe.    *we*] F1; *ye* Warburton conj.

place: "death devoureth them" (*Psalms*, xlix. 14, etc.).

*mousing*] tearing, as a cat tears a mouse, as in *MND.*, v. i. 276.

355. *In . . . kings.*] "making no difference between the flesh of kings and that of common men" (Wilson). We would read "In the unsettled disputes of kings", or "In the unresolved inequalities of kings" (connecting with ii. i. 327–8, 358; iii. i. 164).

356. *fronts*] foreheads, (hence) faces.

357. *havoc*] The cry *havoc!* was the signal for indiscriminate slaughter. Edd. compare *Caes.*: "with a monarch's voice / Cry 'Havoc!' and let slip the dogs of war" (iii. i. 272–3). Furness thought that "to 'cry havoc' was the prerogative of the Monarch".

358. *potents*] potentates. An early use of the substantive—unique in Shakespeare. Possibly we should read *potent*.

359. *confusion*] defeat.

*part*] party. The legal jargon "on the one part . . . on the other part" brought a dual meaning to this word (= one of two parties) as here and in v. vi. 2.

361. *yet*] "as yet, in the present state of affairs" (Wright).

364. *hold . . . right*] "uphold his rightful claim"; or "hold up his right hand" (cf. ii. i. 236–8).

365. *our . . . deputy*] Cf. ii. i. 202, note. John suggests: The king of England does not need a deputy.

366. *And . . . here*] Wilson takes this line, and *Lord of our presence* in the next, to imply feudal supremacy. Arthur does not bear possession of his person, is not lord of his presence (for this phrase cf. i. i. 137, ii. i. 377).

368. Hub.] Cf. Introduction, p. xxxiv.

*power*] "Tollet thought that *a greater power* might mean the Lord of Hosts . . . but, surely, the *greater power* is their *fears*" (Deighton). As kings have just been called deputies (l. 365; cf. iii. i. 62), an Elizabethan would have thought a claim like Tollet, though *fears* have a claim too.

369. *undoubted*] As *doubt* = (*a*) uncertainty; (*b*) fear, *undoubted* in a "fear" and "certainty" context = put beyond doubt (with both meanings).

Our former scruple in our strong-barr'd gates:          370
Kings of our fear, until our fears, resolv'd,
Be by some certain king purg'd and depos'd.
*Bast.* By heaven, these scroyles of Angiers flout you, kings,
And stand securely on their battlements,
As in a theatre, whence they gape and point          375
At your industrious scenes and acts of death.
Your royal presences be rul'd by me:
Do like the mutines of Jerusalem,
Be friends awhile and both conjointly bend
Your sharpest deeds of malice on this town.          380
By east and west let France and England mount
Their battering cannon charged to the mouths,
Till their soul-fearing clamours have brawl'd down

371. *Kings*] F1; *King'd* Tyrwhitt, edd.        *fear*] F1; *fears* Theobald.        377.
*Your*] F1; *You* Rowe.        381. *mount*] *mount.* F1.

371–2. *Kings of . . . by*] Tyrwhitt's
reading is ingenious but unnecessary.
Cf. Abbott: "*by* is used of external
agencies, *of* is used of internal motives,
thus: 'Comest thou hither by chance,
or *of* devotion?' (*2 H 6*, II. i. 88), 'The
king *of* his own royal disposition.'
(*R 3*, I. iii. 63)" (p. 111). Read: "We
must be our own kings on account of
our fear, until all our fears (and thus
our kingship, which follows from our
fears) be deposed." Staunton thought
that *strong-barr'd gates* are the *Kings*.
Malone compared *Lucr.*, l. 659, *Lr.*,
IV. iii. 15–17.

373. *scroyles*] scabby scoundrels.

375. *gape*] In pre-Shakespearean
drama the audience was often ridiculed for *gaping*, and Shakespeare
adapts the joke. Cf. R. W.'s *Three
Ladies of London* (1584): "But yonder is
a fellow that gapes to bite me or els to
eate that which I sing. / Why thou art
a foole canst not thou keepe thy mouth
strait together?" (sig. D₂ᵛ).

376. *industrious*] your laborious *in-
dustry* of war (Steevens, comparing
*Mac.*, v. iv. 17); "clever, ingenious"
(On.). Comparison of the business of
actors and the idleness of spectators

was common in the old drama.
*scenes and acts*] acting, performance.
This untechnical quibble was common, as in the old *King Leir* (1605):
"When will this Scene of sadnesse haue
an end, / And pleasant acts insue, to
moue delight?" (sig. E₂).

377. *presences*] "persons" (On.); cf.
I. i. 137, II. i. 367, also the idiom "in the
presence" (viz. royal presence).

378. *mutines of Jerusalem*] mutineers
of Jerusalem. In the civil war of Jerusalem the factions united to fight the
Romans. The story was well known
*c.* 1590: Strange's company had an old
play *Jerusalem* in 1592 (Greg, *Henslowe's Diary*, i, 13, 14); in 1584 and
1591 a play on this subject was acted at
Coventry, sixteen miles from Stratford
(Harris, *N. & Q.*, 8 Aug. 1931).

382. *Their . . . mouths*] *battering cannon*
= the great cannon. These, "filde
with peeces of yron, or of some other
Mettall, or with stones or chaynes, for
these thinges worke a marueilous
effect", could be used to clear breaches
or walls [W. Garrard, *Arte of Warre*
(1591), p. 288]. Here *charged* = filled;
*mouths* is technical.

383. *soul-fearing*] soul-frightening.

The flinty ribs of this contemptuous city:
I'd play incessantly upon these jades,                385
Even till unfenced desolation
Leave them as naked as the vulgar air.
That done, dissever your united strengths,
And part your mingled colours once again;
Turn face to face and bloody point to point;         390
Then, in a moment, fortune shall cull forth
Out of one side her happy minion,
To whom in favour she shall give the day,
And kiss him with a glorious victory.
How like you this wild counsel, mighty states?       395
Smacks it not something of the policy?

*K. John.* Now, by the sky that hangs above our heads,
I like it well. France, shall we knit our powers
And lay this Angiers even with the ground;
Then after fight who shall be king of it?            400

*Bast.* And if thou hast the mettle of a king,
Being wrong'd as we are by this peevish town,
Turn thou the mouth of thy artillery,
As we will ours, against these saucy walls;
And when that we have dash'd them to the ground,     405
Why then defy each other, and pell-mell
Make work upon ourselves, for heaven or hell.

---

Shakespeare's coinage makes sense, but the emendation "soul-searing" is tempting.

*brawl'd down*] beaten down with clamour.

385. *play . . . upon*] fire at, play the guns upon (technical); play with, mock (resuming l. 373); cf. *Per.*, I. i. 84.

*jades*] a word of contempt for women, (hence) sorry creatures.

387. *vulgar*] common.

392. *minion*] darling.

395. *states*] persons of rank.

396. *the policy*] Machiavellian statesmanship, low cunning. Abbott (sect. 92) shows that *the* could "denote notoriety", as in "I am alone the villain of the earth" (*Ant.*, IV. vi. 30). Faulconbridge delights naively in *policy* because it does not come naturally to him.

401. *mettle*] = substance, material (cf. *Lr.*, I. i. 71); spirit, courage (cf. *Oth.*, IV. ii. 207); material from which arms are made, (hence) sword. F1 spells "metal" *mettle* in v. ii. 16, below.

406. *pell-mell*] in disorderly manner, hand to hand, with broken ranks. Furness compared *R 3*, v. iii. 313–14.

407. *Make . . . hell*] Make work for heaven or hell amongst ourselves, being killed; set upon each other on behalf of heaven or hell (as we wish to invoke them). The French side in *John* claim the sanction of heaven throughout, and John's side that of hell. Furness noted that Shakespeare uses *make work* as in II. i. 303, and *Cor.*: "what work he makes / Amongst your cloven army" (I. iv. 20–1).

*K. Phi.* Let it be so. Say, where will you assault?

*K. John.* We from the west will send destruction
    Into this city's bosom.    410

*Aust.* I from the north.

*K. Phi.*              Our thunder from the south
    Shall rain their drift of bullets on this town.

*Bast.* [*Aside.*] O prudent discipline! From north to south
    Austria and France shoot in each other's mouth:
    I'll stir them to it.—Come, away, away!    415

*Hub.* Hear us, great kings: vouchsafe awhile to stay,
    And I shall show you peace and fair-fac'd league;
    Win you this city without stroke or wound;
    Rescue those breathing lives to die in beds,
    That here come sacrifices for the field:    420
    Persever not, but hear me, mighty kings!

*K. John.* Speak on, with favour; we are bent to hear.

*Hub.* That daughter there of Spain, the Lady Blanche,
    Is near to England: look upon the years
    Of Lewis the Dolphin and that lovely maid:    425
    If lusty love should go in quest of beauty,
    Where should he find it fairer than in Blanche?
    If zealous love should go in search of virtue,
    Where should he find it purer than in Blanche?
    If love ambitious sought a match of birth,    430
    Whose veins bound richer blood than Lady Blanche?
    Such as she is, in beauty, virtue, birth,
    Is the young Dolphin every way complete:
    If not complete of, say he is not she;

---

411. *thunder*] F1 ; *thunders* Capell conj.    413. S.D.] Capell; om. F1.    422. *on, with favour ;*] Theobald; *on with fauour,* F1 ; *on ; with Favour* Rowe.    424. *near*] F1 ; *niece* Collier MS.    434. *complete of*] F1 ; *completed* Sisson.    *of,*] F1 ; *oh!* Hanmer; *so,* B. G. Kinnear [*Cruces Sh.* (1883), p. 192]; *I* Kittredge; *all* Wilson conj.

411. *thunder*] cannon.

412. *drift*] shower. A "rain" of cannon-balls was a familiar conceit.

414. *mouth*] The mouths of the men and of the cannon.

422. *bent*] inclined, willing.

424. *near*] near, dear (relation) to John. A common idiom. Blanche was John's *niece*, but emendation is unjustified.

425. *Dolphin*] Dauphin.

426. *lusty*] full of healthy vigour *or* sexual desire.

428. *zealous*] pious.

431. *bound*] enclose (cf. l. 442, below).

433. *complete*] perfect.

434. *of*] "*thereof*, or *therein*" (Rolfe). Fleay compared *Fair Em*: "But father, are you assured of the wordes he spake

And she again wants nothing, to name want,          435
If want it be not that she is not he:
He is the half part of a blessed man,
Left to be finished by such as she;
And she a fair divided excellence,
Whose fulness of perfection lies in him.            440
O, two such silver currents, when they join,
Do glorify the banks that bound them in;
And two such shores, to two such streams made one,
Two such controlling bounds shall you be, kings,
To these two princes, if you marry them.            445
This union shall do more than battery can
To our fast-closed gates; for at this match,
With swifter spleen than powder can enforce,
The mouth of passage shall we fling wide ope,
And give you entrance: but without this match       450
The sea enraged is not half so deaf,
Lions more confident, mountains and rocks

---

438. *as she*] F1; *a She* Thirlby conj. (*ap.* Theobald).          447. *fast-closed*] Theobald;
no hyphen F1.          448. *spleen*] F1; *speed* Pope.

were concerning *Manuile*?" (M.S.R.,
sig. E₂ᵛ); Marston's *Antonio and Mellida*
(1602): "Ile . . . suruey . . . my seruants; & he that hath the best parts of,
Ile pricke him downe for my husband"
(sig. I₄ᵛ). F1 is idiomatic, though *oh*
was often printed *of* [S. Rowley's
*When You See Me* (1605), sig. I₄; Glapthorne's *Ladies Priviledge* (1640), sig.
E₃; etc.].

434–40. *If . . . him.*] C. Wordsworth
thought these lines so unworthy of
Shakespeare that they could not be
his.—As often, Shakespeare uses the
nice balance of formal poetry to point
to human formalities.

435. *wants*] lacks (after *not complete*,
l. 434); desires (after *go in quest, go in
search* etc., ll. 426–30).

436. *If . . . that*] Unless it be a want
that.

438. *finished*] Cf. *fast-closed* (l. 447),
*enraged* (l. 451). These falsely stressed
participles with the colourless verbs
and auxiliaries of the speech, and the

balance of pictures (ll. 451–5), all reinforce the formal effect.

440. *perfection*] In the doctrine of
courtly love, human perfection was
impossible without love.

441. *currents*] Similar order-disorder
pictures occur in II. i. 335, v. i. 12,
v. iv. 53, v. vii. 38. The "marriage =
two joining streams" image was in
great vogue (boosted by Spenser).

447. *match*] Johnson noticed the
pun.

448. *spleen*] Cf. v. vii. 50.

449. *mouth*] gates; in II. i. 215 likened
to eye-lids. Appropriate for *double*
gates. Cf. *R 2*: "Doubly portcullis'd
with my teeth and lips" (I. iii. 167).

451–4. *The . . . peremptory*] Note the
antithesis: *half so, more, more, half so*, as
in III. iii. 11–12.

451. *sea . . . deaf*] Cf. *R 2*, I. i. 19.
Proverbial.

452–3. *mountains . . . motion*] The
"moving mountains" image is popular
in the Bible (cf. note to III. iii. 39).

More free from motion, no, not death himself
In mortal fury half so peremptory,
As we to keep this city.

*Bast.*                                    Here's a stay                          455
That shakes the rotten carcass of old death
Out of his rags! Here's a large mouth indeed,
That spits forth death and mountains, rocks and seas,
Talks as familiarly of roaring lions
As maids of thirteen do of puppy-dogs!                                          460
What cannoneer begot this lusty blood?
He speaks plain cannon, fire, and smoke, and bounce;
He gives the bastinado with his tongue;
Our ears are cudgell'd; not a word of his
But buffets better than a fist of France.                                       465

---

455.] F1; [The *Kings*, &c., talk apart. Collier iii.        *stay*] F1; '*Stay!*' Kittredge.
462. *cannon, fire*,] Capell; *Cannon fire*, F1.

454. *peremptory*] determined.

455. *stay*] Much discussed. After
l. 416 (*stay* = pause) it means "interruption"; but it = "check" too. "The
B. refers to the sudden check in a manage, which shakes the rider (Death)
from his seat [on his horse]" (Wilson).

456–7. *That . . . rags!*] Cf. *Cor.*:
"Hence, rotten thing! or I shall shake
thy bones / Out of thy garments" (III.
i. 178–9).

457–61. *Here's . . . blood?*] "I haue
tearmes (if I be vext) laid in steepe in
*Aquafortis*, & Gunpowder, that shall
rattle through the Skyes, and make an
Earthquake in a Pesants eares" wrote
Nashe in 1592 (I, 195). Martin Marprelate and Nashe introduced "gunpowder terms" in 1588–9. Steevens
noted the parallel in *Thomas Stukeley*
(1605): "Why heers a gallant, heers a
king indeed, / He speaks all Mars tut
let me follow such a / Lad as this: This
is pure fire. / . . . He brings a breath
that sets our sailes on fire, / Why now
I see we shall haue cuffs indeed" (sig.
K₂ᵛ).

460. *puppy-dogs*] The last word in
foolishness for Shakespeare; as in *H 5*:
"no more directions in the true discip-

lines of the wars, look you, of the
Roman disciplines, than is a puppy-
dog" (III. ii. 78–81).

461. *What . . . blood?*] Cf. I. i. 108;
*blood* quibbles on the sense "man of
fire, mettle".

462. *He . . . bounce;*] He plainly
speaks the language of cannon, fire,
etc. To "speak fire and smoke" may
have been an idiom; cf. Mrs Cent-
livre's *Basset-Table*: "the Sea Captain
. . . can entertain one with nothing but
Fire and Smoke" [*Works* (1761), I,
205]. "Bounce" was Elizabethan for
modern "bang".

*speaks . . . cannon*] Cf. *Ado*: "She
speaks poniards" (II. i. 257); *H 5*: "I
speak to thee plain soldier" (v. ii. 155)
(Smith).

463. *bastinado*] cudgel (hence) cud-
gelling. Cf. *Arden of Feversham* (1592):
"Zounds I hate them as I hate a toade,/
That cary a muscado in their tongue./
And scarce a hurting weapon in their
hand" (sig. F₂). Here *muscado* is a
nonce-word (*O.E.D.*), which suggests unintelligent imitation.

465. *But . . . France*] The *buffeting* of
*fists* was a cliché, common in the Bible,
etc. In the old romances duels of
strength were sometimes tried in buf-

Zounds! I was never so bethump'd with words
Since I first call'd my brother's father dad.
*Elea.* Son, list to this conjunction, make this match;
Give with our niece a dowry large enough:
For by this knot thou shalt so surely tie                470
Thy now unsur'd assurance to the crown,
That yon green boy shall have no sun to ripe
The bloom that promiseth a mighty fruit.
I see a yielding in the looks of France;                474
Mark, how they whisper: urge them while their souls
Are capable of this ambition,
Lest zeal, now melted by the windy breath
Of soft petitions, pity and remorse,
Cool and congeal again to what it was.
*Hub.* Why answer not the double majesties                480
This friendly treaty of our threat'ned town?

468. Elea.] Old Qu. F1.        468–79.] F1; Aside. Capell.

fets; Richard I killed Austria's son in one of these. Buffets were aimed at the head ("our *ears* are cudgell'd"), each party having to stand still in turn.

466. *Zounds!*] = "(God's)wounds!" Apparently thought profane and excised in many prompt-books after the Act of Abuses, 1606.

467. *dad*] Perhaps playing on the dialectal (northern) verb "to dad" (= to beat, thump), which was pre-Shakespearean; cf. Introduction, p. xxv, where the existence of northern Faulconbridges, prototypes of those in *John*, is suggested.

468. *list*] listen.

470–3. *For . . . fruit.*] John had high hopes of this marriage, says Holinshed, and "supposed that by his affinitie, and resignation of his right to those places, the peace now made would haue continued for euer" (161, ii).

470–1. *surely . . . assurance*] Cf. II. i. 534–5 ("assur'd . . . assur'd"); *assurance* = certainty, security; legal settlement of property; betrothal.

472. *green*] youthful, inexperienced (cf. III. iii. 145).

473. *The . . . fruit.*] Cf. *Soliman and*

*Perseda* for this common thought: "*Sol.* The Prince of Cipris to is likewise slaine. / *Erast.* Faire blossome, likely to haue proued good fruite" (Kyd, p. 206). That kingship = fruition had been established by Marlowe's great line "The sweet fruition of an earthly crown" (*Tamburlaine*, Pt I, II. vii).

477–9. *Lest . . . was.*] Lest Philip's zeal to help Arthur, melted by Hubert's petitions for pity for Angiers, cool and harden against you as before. Johnson thought the image unjust, because *zeal* is usually seen as a flame. Steevens took zeal = metal in a state of fusion, and Wilson = wax ["accompanied, too, with the inevitable quibble (zeal-seal), cf. note 2. 1. 19–20"]. But Shakespeare has already emphasized the *coldness* (cf. II. i. 53, note) and fake *zeal* (II. i. 19, 244, 428, etc.) of the French side, and the "icy zeal" envisaged may be a significant paradox. Cf. III. i. 31, note.

478. *pity and remorse*] A stock phrase; *remorse* usually = "pity" at this time (cf. IV. iii. 50).

481. *treaty*] negotiation, propos al.

*K. Phi.*  Speak England first, that hath been forward first
　　To speak unto this city: what say you?
*K. John.*  If that the Dolphin there, thy princely son,
　　Can in this book of beauty read "I love",　　　　　　485
　　Her dowry shall weigh equal with a queen:
　　For Anjou, and fair Touraine, Maine, Poictiers,
　　And all that we upon this side the sea—
　　Except this city now by us besieg'd—
　　Find liable to our crown and dignity,　　　　　　490
　　Shall gild her bridal bed, and make her rich
　　In titles, honours and promotions,
　　As she in beauty, education, blood,
　　Holds hand with any princess of the world.
*K. Phi.*  What say'st thou, boy? look in the lady's face.　495
*Lew.*  I do, my lord; and in her eye I find
　　A wonder, or a wondrous miracle,
　　The shadow of myself form'd in her eye;
　　Which, being but the shadow of your son,
　　Becomes a sun and makes your son a shadow:　　　500
　　I do protest I never lov'd myself

---

482. *first, that*] *sir st, that* F1.　486. *queen*] F1; *queen's* Keightley.　487. *Anjou*] Theobald; Angiers F1.　494. *hand*] F1; *hands* F2.

482. *forward*] Glancing at John's forwardness in II. i. 202–6?

485. *Can . . . love*",] "The book is Lily's Grammar '*amo*, I love'; the beauty is Blanch" [T. W. Baldwin: *William Shakspere's Small Latine* (1944), I, 569]. Lily used *amo* as paradigm. The *book* may be Blanche's face or eyes: cf. *Mac.*, I. v. 63; *LLL.*, I. i. 72–87, IV. iii. 302–4; *Rom.*, I. iii. 87: "This precious book of love" (i.e. Paris).

486. *queen*] i.e. queen's.

487. *Anjou*] Cf. II. i. 152, note.

489. *Except . . . besieg'd*] Shakespeare follows Holinshed: "Iohn . . . resigned his title to . . . all those townes which the French king had by warre taken from him, the citie of Angiers onelie excepted" (161, i).

490. *liable*] subject.

493. *education*] Cf. II. i. 426–32; *education* (= breeding, upbringing) corresponds to *virtue*. But in the progress-

ive aristocratic circle to which Shakespeare probably belonged learning (= *education*) was now thought necessary in a lady.

494. *Holds . . . with*] Is equal to.

496. *in her eye*] For this popular conceit cf. *Ven.*, l. 119, and IV. i. 64, note.

498. *shadow*] reflected image. In l. 499 a pun on the modern sense, in l. 500 only the modern sense.

500. *sun*] The hackneyed mistress-sun image emphasizes the formality of the wooing.

501. *lov'd myself*] In "courtly love", the lover loves himself, i.e. his good qualities, in his lady, beholding himself (cf. l. 502) abstractly in her. So Chapman said of Beauty that it is doomed unless it loves: "Enamourd (like good selfe-loue) with her owne,/ Seene in another, then tis heauen alone" [*Ouids Banquet of Sence* (1595), st. 51].

Till now infixed I beheld myself
Drawn in the flattering table of her eye.

                       *[Whispers with Blanche.*

*Bast.* [*Aside.*] Drawn in the flattering table of her eye!
    Hang'd in the frowning wrinkle of her brow!    505
And quarter'd in her heart! he doth espy
    Himself love's traitor: this is pity now,
That, hang'd and drawn and quarter'd, there should be
In such a love so vile a lout as he!

*Blanche* [*to Lew.*] My uncle's will in this respect is mine:   510
If he see aught in you that makes him like,
That any thing he sees, which moves his liking,
I can with ease translate it to my will;
Or if you will, to speak more properly,
I will enforce it eas'ly to my love.          515
Further I will not flatter you, my lord,
That all I see in you is worthy love,
Than this: that nothing do I see in you,
Though churlish thoughts themselves should be your
    judge,

504. S.D.] Dyce; om. F1.    510. S.D.] Capell; om. F1.    510. *mine :*] Capell;
*mine*, F1; *mine.* F3.    512. *any thing*] F1; *anything* Knight.    516. *Further*] F1;
*Farther* Collier.

503. *table*] board, surface, on which
a picture is painted.

S.D. Whispers] As an aside follows,
we need not assume that *only* Lewis
and Blanche whisper, merely that
their being placed together is essential.

504. *Drawn*] Quibbling on the sense
"disembowelled", as in *Meas.*,ii. i. 221,
*Ado.* iii. ii. 22. Traitors to the realm
were hanged, drawn and quartered.

506. *quarter'd*] Quibbling on the
sense "lodged in, having quarters in",
the cliché that the lover's heart is
locked up in his mistress's bosom.

509. *love*] passion of love; loved
person.

*so . . . he!*] Lewis's cold-blooded formality rouses Faulconbridge (cf. also
Appendix B, p. 167). Furness noted
that the poetic style ridiculed (ll. 496–
503) resembles Shakespeare's own
sonnets (especially no. 24).

510. *in . . . respect*] Edd. adopting the
F1 stop presumably read: "My uncle's
will governs mine completely in this
matter." But *respect* = particular
(*O.E.D.*, 8b), and the possibility of the
opposite sense can be left open with a
colon ("My uncle's will governs mine
(only) in this particular: Supposing he
sees aught etc."): so that l. 513 surprises more.

512. *any*] adjectival: "That thing,
whatsoever it may be". Blanche is
vague to cover the remotest possibilities.

513. *translate . . . will*] transform it so
as to suit my *wishes* too (though it may
really jar with them); *or* carry it across
(from his *liking*) to my *good-will*.

514. *properly*] accurately (as in
*AYL.*, i. i. 8); beseemingly.

517. *all*] Cf. *any*, l. 512.

519. *churlish*] niggardly, miserly.

That I can find should merit any hate.                                        520

*K. John.* What say these young ones? What say you, my
    niece?

*Blanche.* That she is bound in honour still to do
    What you in wisdom still vouchsafe to say.

*K. John.* Speak then, prince Dolphin: can you love this
    lady?

*Lew.* Nay, ask me if I can refrain from love;                                525
    For I do love her most unfeignedly.

*K. John.* Then do I give Volquessen, Touraine, Maine,
    Poictiers, and Anjou, these five provinces,
    With her to thee; and this addition more,
    Full thirty thousand marks of English coin.                          530
    Philip of France, if thou be pleas'd withal,
    Command thy son and daughter to join hands.

*K. Phi.* It likes us well; young princes, close your hands.

*Aust.* And your lips too; for I am well assur'd
    That I did so when I was first assur'd.                              535

*K. Phi.* Now, citizens of Angiers, ope your gates,
    Let in that amity which you have made;
    For at Saint Mary's chapel presently
    The rites of marriage shall be solemniz'd.
    Is not the Lady Constance in this troop?                             540

---

521. *young ones*] Rowe; hyphened F1.    523. *still*] F1; *will* Pope; *shall* Capell
conj.    535. *assur'd*] F1; *affied* Walker.

522–3. *still*] always.

527. *Volquessen*] "now called *the Vexin*; in Latin, *Pagus Velocassinus*" (Steevens); i.e. Rouen and district.

528. *Poictiers . . . provinces,*] One o the two lines in *John* identical in *T.R.* (cf. v. iv. 42, note). Malone compared "Then I demaund *Volquesson, Torain, Main,* / *Poiters* and *Aniou,* these fiue Prouinces" (*T.R.,* i. iv. 158–9).

529. *addition*] Could mean *title,* and there is a quibble after ll. 527–8.

530. *Full . . . marks*] So Holinshed: "thirtie thousand markes in siluer, as in respect of dowrie assigned to his said neece" (161, i). The mark = 13s. 4d. The five provinces are Shakespeare's invention—John gave far less —to underline John's impulsiveness.

533–4. *close . . . too;*] Rolfe compared *Tw.N.*: "A contract of eternal bond of love, / Confirm'd by mutual joinder of your hands, / Attested by the holy close of lips" (v. i. 160–2). Some thought only the joining of hands legally necessary in troth-plighting, others included a kiss. Middleton (*Mad World,* 1608) says "What ist a match, if't be clap hands & lips" (sig. G₃ᵛ). It seems that Austria only kissed because he thought it legally necessary!

535. *assur'd*] betrothed.

538. *Saint Mary's*] Halliwell identified this with "the church of Ronceray". But it must have been a safe guess that any Roman Catholic city would have a St Mary's chapel.

I know she is not, for this match made up
Her presence would have interrupted much:
Where is she and her son? tell me, who knows.

*Lew.* She is sad and passionate at your highness' tent.

*K. Phi.* And, by my faith, this league that we have made　545
Will give her sadness very little cure.
Brother of England, how may we content
This widow lady? In her right we came;
Which we, God knows, have turn'd another way,
To our own vantage.

*K. John.*　　　　　We will heal up all;　　　　　550
For we'll create young Arthur Duke of Britain
And Earl of Richmond; and this rich fair town
We make him lord of. Call the Lady Constance;
Some speedy messenger bid her repair
To our solemnity: I trust we shall,　　　　　555
If not fill up the measure of her will,
Yet in some measure satisfy her so
That we shall stop her exclamation.
Go we, as well as haste will suffer us,
To this unlook'd for, unprepared pomp.　　　　　560
　　　　　　　[*Exeunt all but the Bastard.*

*Bast.* Mad world! mad kings! mad composition!

543. *son?...knows.*] Steevens; *sonne,...knowes?* F1.　544. *She is*] F1; *She's* Pope.
560. S.D.] Rowe; Exeunt. F1.　561.] F1; *Scene* VI. Pope.

544. *passionate*] full of violent feelings, very sorrowful. I. John compared *Arden of Feversham*: "How now, Alice? what, sad and *passionate?*" (sig. E₄); cf. notes to II. i. 463, III. i. 126.

551. *Duke*] Cf. II. i. 301, note. Holinshed says that Arthur did homage to John for Brittany and Richmond (p. 161, ii); Shakespeare added Angiers (cf. II. i. 489, note). This is interesting, since some early sources called Geoffrey "Count of Angiers" (Arthur's title to Brittany came from Constance). Shakespeare may here think of Angiers as Arthur's patrimony.

556–7. *measure...measure*] A variation of the "Measure for measure" proverb (Tilley, p. 452), for which cf.

3 H 6, II. vi. 55, *Meas.*, title and v. i. 412.

558. *stop*] stop up (or, put a stop to) her loud complaints; cf. III. iii. 32.

560. *pomp*] ceremony, pageant.

S.D.] "F. 'Exeunt' The absence of 'manet Bastard' suggests that the Bastard's speech may have been an afterthought. T.R. contains nothing corresponding to it" (Wilson).—For *T.R.* echoes of the soliloquy cf. Introduction, p. xlii.

561. *Mad world!*] A common exclamation (cf. Middleton's *A Mad World, My Masters*). The state of the world was used by other dramatists to introduce an analysis of the situation, e.g. by Greene in *James the Fourth*: "And. Go, and the rot consume thee? Oh

John, to stop Arthur's title in the whole,
Hath willingly departed with a part:
And France, whose armour conscience buckled on,
Whom zeal and charity brought to the field          565
As God's own soldier, rounded in the ear
With that same purpose-changer, that sly divel,
That broker, that still breaks the pate of faith,
That daily break-vow, he that wins of all,
Of kings, of beggars, old men, young men, maids,    570
Who, having no external thing to lose
But the word "maid", cheats the poor maid of that,
That smooth-fac'd gentleman, tickling commodity,
Commodity, the bias of the world,
The world, who of itself is peised well,             575

what a trim world is this? My maister
lius by cousoning the king, _I_ by fllatter-
ing him: _Slipper_ my fellow by stealing
. . ." (ed. 1598, sig. G₃).

562. _stop . . . whole_] _stop_ = bar, pre-
clude (legal). Shakespeare may quibble on "stop a hole" (cf. _Ham._, v. i. 236,
_1 H 4_, iv. i. 71), following l. 558
(= stop her _mouth_): viz. "to stop the
hole (Arthur's _title_ or claim) through
which he might lose his lands".

563. _departed with_] given up.

566. _God's . . . soldier_] I. John compared Siward's last words about his
dead son: "Why then, God's soldier be
he!" (_Mac._, v. vii. 76).

_rounded_] whispered.

567. _With_] By.

_divel_] Variant of "devil": cf. iv. iii.
95, 100, v. iv. 4.

568. _broker_] "_pimp_ or _procuress_"
[Malone, comparing the same quibble
in _Ham._, "Do not believe his vows, for
they are brokers" (i. iii. 127)].

569. _wins of_] wins something from.

571. _Who, having_] "the relative 'who'
appears to refer to 'maids', especially
when taken with the following parenthesis, but actually is connected with
'cheats' and so points back to 'Commodity'" [D. A. Traversi, _Approach to
Shakespeare_ (1938), p. 28]. Malone
took _Who having_ as the "absolute case,

in the sense of '_they_ having'", comparing _Wint._, v. iii. 149–51. Abbott
(sect. 399) classified as "Ellipsis of
Nominative", presumably reading
"Who, (they) having—".

573. _smooth-fac'd_] bland, deceitful.

_tickling_] Also = flattering.

_commodity_] self-interest, gain. The
harangue follows the moralities' de-
nunciations of lucre, like that in
Lyly's _Midas_ (_c._ 1589), Act i, Sc. i.

574. _bias . . . world_] The bias was the
lead weight on one side of bowls which
caused the swerving motion. Chapman
imitated this passage, also with an
_astronomical image_: "Now is it true,
earth moves, and heaven stands still;/
. . . The too huge bias of the world hath
sway'd / Her back-part upwards, and
with that she braves / This hemi-
sphere" (_Bussy D'Ambois_, v. i. 161–5).
Like Chapman, Shakespeare refers to
the heliocentric system (_world_ =
earth); an early allusion, but Prof.
Hotson has proved Shakespeare's connections with the main English champion of Copernicus [cf. _I, William
Shakespeare_ (1937), chap. 6].

575–6. _peised . . . even_] Cf. F. Sabie's
_Adams Complaint_ (1596): "For thee he
fram'd earths euen-peysed globe,/
Hanging it in the aire to humaine
woonder:" (sig. Bᵛ).

Made to run even upon even ground,
Till this advantage, this vile drawing bias,
This sway of motion, this commodity,
Makes it take head from all indifferency,
From all direction, purpose, course, intent:          580
And this same bias, this commodity,
This bawd, this broker, this all-changing word,
Clapp'd on the outward eye of fickle France,
Hath drawn him from his own determin'd aid,
From a resolv'd and honourable war,          585
To a most base and vile-concluded peace.
And why rail I on this commodity?
But for because he hath not woo'd me yet:
Not that I have the power to clutch my hand,
When his fair angels would salute my palm;          590
But for my hand, as unattempted yet,
Like a poor beggar, raileth on the rich.
Well, whiles I am a beggar, I will rail
And say there is no sin but to be rich;

577. *vile drawing*] F1; hyphened Pope.      582. *all-changing word*] Pope; *all-changing-word* F1.      584. *own determin'd*] F1; hyphened Capell.      *aid*] F1; *end* Maxwell conj. (*N. & Q.*, 18 Feb. 1950).

578. *sway*] management, control (On.). Probably also = "that which sways" (cf. l. 574, note).

579. *take head*] rush away.

*indifferency*] impartiality. Tillyard [*Shakespeare's History Plays* (1944), p. 219] compared the Degree speech in *Troil.*: "The heavens themselves, the planets, and this centre / Observe degree, priority, and place, / Insisture, course, proportion, season, form" (I. iii. 85–7). This (cf. l. 574, note) is an *astronomical* parallel.

583. *Clapp'd . . . eye*] "suddenly presented to the eye" (Smith, comparing III. i. 161); "France is now the bowl, 'drawn' aside by the bias, and 'eye' is used in the double sense of (i) eyeball . . . (ii) the hole in the bowl in which the lead for the bias was inserted (Staunton). 'Clapped in' = stuck in; 'outward eye' = the worldly or physical eye, as distinct from the

'inward eye' of conscience" (Wilson).

586. *base and vile*] *base and vile* was a common cliché. This comment on the *composition* (l. 561) is Shakespeare's, but echoes M. Paris's condemnation of Magna Carta, which he (more than once) called "compositio vilis et turpis" (p. 357, etc.).

588. *for because*] = because.

589. *clutch*] close (refusing the gift). The *clenched fist* balances the *palm*, symbol of peace.

590–2. *angels . . . salute . . . raileth*] "Our gold is either old or new . . . we have yet remaining, the *riall*, the George noble, the Henry *riall*, the salut, the angell" [Holinshed, quoted by W. Rushton, *Shakespeare Illustrated* (1867), I, 15].—Shakespeare may quibble on angel–salute–rail (riall) (Furness).

591. *unattempted*] unassailed, untempted.

And being rich, my virtue then shall be          595
To say there is no vice but beggary.
Since kings break faith upon commodity,
Gain, be my lord, for I will worship thee!          [*Exit.*


SCENE II.—[*The French King's Pavilion.*] [Act III, Sc. i]

*Enter* CONSTANCE, ARTHUR, *and* SALISBURY.

*Const.* Gone to be married! gone to swear a peace!
False blood to false blood join'd! gone to be friends!
Shall Lewis have Blanche, and Blanche those provinces?
It is not so; thou hast misspoke, misheard;
Be well advis'd, tell o'er thy tale again.          5
It cannot be; thou dost but say 'tis so.
I trust I may not trust thee, for thy word
Is but the vain breath of a common man;
Believe me, I do not believe thee, man:
I have a king's oath to the contrary.          10
Thou shalt be punish'd for thus frighting me,
For I am sick and capable of fears,
Oppress'd with wrongs and therefore full of fears,
A widow, husbandless, subject to fears,

---

*Scene II*

*Act* II *Scene* II.] White; Actus Secundus F1; *Scene* VII. Pope; *Act* III *Scene* I. Theobald, edd.          The . . . Pavilion.] Theobald; om. F1.          7. *I trust*] F1; *I think* Pope.

596. *vice*] Possibly giancing at the *vice*-like *clutch* of the *hand* that is *beggary* (ll. 589–92), which a gesture could convey.

597. *upon*] on account of.

*Scene II*

*Scene* II] Cf. Introduction, p. xxxvii.
Pavilion] For tents on the stage cf. Chambers, *Elizabethan Stage*, III, 53, 106.

2. *blood . . . blood*] Resuming I. i. 19, II. i. 329.

12. *For . . . sick*] "This point of phy-

sical disturbance is rarely omitted by Shakspeare in the development of insanity" [J. C. Bucknill, *Mad Folk of Shakespeare* (1867), p. 276].

12–15. *fears*] Furness noted similar antistrophe in *Mer. V.*, v. i. 193–7.

14. *husbandless*] Constance was Geoffrey's widow, but married at this time to her third husband. Shakespeare suppressed the later husbands (cf. Introduction, p. lxiv), which may explain his afterthought that a widow is not necessarily husbandless.

*subject to*] Cf. I. i. 264, note.

A woman, naturally born to fears;                                15
And though thou now confess thou didst but jest
With my vex'd spirits I cannot take a truce,
But they will quake and tremble all this day.
What dost thou mean by shaking of thy head?
Why dost thou look so sadly on my son?                          20
What means that hand upon that breast of thine?
Why holds thine eye that lamentable rheum,
Like a proud river peering o'er his bounds?
Be these sad signs confirmers of thy words?
Then speak again; not all thy former tale,                      25
But this one word, whether thy tale be true.

*Sal.* As true as I believe you think them false
That give you cause to prove my saying true.

*Const.* O, if thou teach me to believe this sorrow,
Teach thou this sorrow how to make me die,                      30
And let belief and life encounter so
As doth the fury of two desperate men
Which in the very meeting fall, and die.
Lewis marry Blanche! O boy, then where art thou?
France friend with England, what becomes of me?                35
Fellow, be gone: I cannot brook thy sight.
This news hath made thee a most ugly man.

---

15. *born*] F1 (*borne*).    16–17. *jest . . . spirits*] This ed.; *iest . . . spirits*, F1; *jest, . . . Spirits* Rowe, edd.    17. *spirits*] F1; *sprites* Fleay.    24. *signs*] F1; *sighs* Warburton.

15. *born*] Punning on "borne" (= carried).

16. *jest*] For Shakespeare's puns on jest-just (joust), cf. *Err.*, II. ii. 8, *R 2*, I. iii. 95, *Troil.*, I. ii. 221; *take a truce* (= make peace) of l. 17 supports the quibble, which plays on two ways of not being in earnest.

17. *spirits*] The F1 comma is not disjunctive, but connective: yet to take *With my vex'd spirits* with either the preceding or the following clause spoils the jest, for it goes with both.

22. *Why . . . rheum,*] Why does thy eye contain those sorrowful tears.

23. *Like . . . bounds?*] The "disorder image" (cf. II. i. 337, note) emphasizes

Arthur's unnatural situation. With rivers, seas, etc., *proud* = swollen, in flood.

26. *one word*] To say in one word = to make a simple statement. The *one word* Constance wants is "The tale is (not) true."

27. *you*] "Notice Salisbury's use of the deferential 'you,' while Constance uniformly addresses him with 'thou'" (Furness).

32. *fury*] The traditional Furor of emblematists. Cf. W. Lightfoote's *Complaint of England* (1587): "the picture of *Furie*, who is painted with a sword in his hand, and . . . desperatly rusheth vpon a iauelin, slayeng him-selfe" (sig. H₂).

*Sal.* What other harm have I, good lady, done,
    But spoke the harm that is by others done?
*Const.* Which harm within itself so heinous is         40
    As it makes harmful all that speak of it.
*Arth.* I do beseech you, madam, be content.
*Const.* If thou, that bid'st me be content, wert grim,
    Ugly, and sland'rous to thy mother's womb,
    Full of unpleasing blots and sightless stains,      45
    Lame, foolish, crooked, swart, prodigious,
    Patch'd with foul moles and eye-offending marks,
    I would not care, I then would be content,
    For then I should not love thee: no, nor thou
    Become thy great birth, nor deserve a crown.     50
    But thou art fair, and at thy birth, dear boy,
    Nature and fortune join'd to make thee great:
    Of nature's gifts thou mayst with lilies boast

42. *be content*] be calm, quiet (cf. *R 2*, v. ii. 82).

43–8. *If . . . content*] Cf. *Ven.*, ll. 133–8.

44. *sland'rous*] "that is a disgrace or reproach" (On., comparing *Lucr.*, l. 1001).

45. *blots*] stains.

*sightless*] unsightly.

46. *swart*] swarthy, dark.

*prodigious*] "*portentous*, so deformed as to be taken for a *foretoken of evil*" (Johnson).

47. *Patch'd*] Cf. iv. ii. 32–4. Shakespeare seems to have looked on patches as signs of deficiency, not of carefulness.

*eye-offending*] For the imagery of this important speech cf. Introduction, pp. lxi–lxiii.

50. *deserve*] A fair body (reflecting a fair mind) was thought a recommendation for high office. Tilley (p. 198) quoted the proverb "A fair Face must have good conditions."

51–2. *But . . . great:*] See Introduction, p. xliv. S. Daniel's *Complaint of Rosamond* (1592) is close to Shakespeare: "The blood I staind was good and of the best, / My birth had honor,

and my beautie fame: / Nature and Fortune ioyn'd to make me blest,/ Had I had grace t'haue knowne to vse the same:" (sig. H₄ᵛ). Repeated, beside l. 52, is the collocation of beauty-birth, Nature-Fortune; the lament that these advantages have been lost; the adultery context.

52. *Nature and fortune*] The gifts of Nature and Fortune were often compared in the pre-Shakespearean love-novel. Shakespeare's best summary is in *AYL.*: "Fortune reigns in gifts of the world, not in the lineaments of Nature" (i. ii. 45–6).

53–4. *lilies . . . rose*] The imagery of female beauty is applied to Arthur partly because his *stains* (ll. 43–7, above) = fortune's *adultery* (ll. 56–61) (cf. Introduction, p. lxiii); the feminine beauty of Adonis is similarly described (*Ven.*, 8–12). Miss Porter thought that the rose of England and lily of France were implied, blended in the boy born of both races and heir in both lands. Furness disagreed, since the lily-rose comparison was common, also "one other objection . . . the rose was not adopted as the national emblem until after the Wars of the Roses."

And with the half-blown rose. But fortune, O,
She is corrupted, chang'd and won from thee;    55
Sh' adulterates hourly with thine uncle John,
And with her golden hand hath pluck'd on France
To tread down fair respect of sovereignty,
And made his majesty the bawd to theirs.
France is a bawd to fortune and King John,    60
That strumpet fortune, that usurping John!
Tell me, thou fellow, is not France forsworn?
Envenom him with words, or get thee gone,
And leave those woes alone which I alone
Am bound to underbear!
*Sal.*                Pardon me, madam,    65
I may not go without you to the kings.
*Const.* Thou mayst, thou shalt; I will not go with thee:
I will instruct my sorrows to be proud,
For grief is proud an't makes his owner stoop.
To me and to the state of my great grief    70

---

68. *sorrows*] F1; *Sorrow* Rowe ii.      69. *an't*] Anon. *ap.* Cambridge; *and* F1.
*his*] F1; *its* Variorum 1821.

54. *half-blown*] half-blossomed.
56. *adulterates*] The idea may derive from the whore of Babylon in *Revelation*: "With whom the kings of the earth haue committed fornication" (xvii. 2).
57. *golden hand*] The *golden hand* of *Fortune* recurs in Peele's *Descensus Astraeae* (Oct. 1591) (ed. Bullen, I, 362). Cf. Introduction, p. xlv; I. i. 267, note.
58. *tread down*] The treading down of enemies and opposition is a biblical image, common also in Shakespeare.
63. *Envenom*] Poison, destroy (Schmidt); vituperate (Wilson).—Perhaps Shakespeare had in mind the Psalmist's notion that lies are as venomous as the poison of a serpent, and intended "Tell your *lies* to (Envenom) him, or at any rate leave me."
65. *underbear*] endure; imitated in Chapman's *Alphonsus*, IV. i. 183.
68–74. *I . . . it.*] Shakespeare depicts Constance bowed down by the pride

which Grief is said to possess, and "actuated by this very pride . . . exacting the same kind of obeisance from others" (Malone). Cf. T. White's *Sermon* (1589): "for the *Affliction of an houre wil make the prowdest stoope and sit vpon the grounde, and forget all former felicitie.* Sirac. 11. 27" (sig. E4v). Or should we read *prov'd . . . prov'd* (ll. 68–9), resuming ll. 28–30? The ideas of *teaching* (*instructing*) Constance's *sorrow(s)* [and of *proving* sorrow(s)] repeat, and *prov'd* was often spelt *proud*. The sense would be: "I will instruct my sorrows to be *tested*; for grief is *experienced* (suffered, i.e. proved to exist) if it makes its owner stoop (to this course of proving it)."
69. *an't*] Often spelt "and". Cf. *Ham.*, IV. vi. 8 (Q2); *Knacke to Know an Honest Man* (1596): "And shal please your honors" (sig. B2).
70. *state*] high rank, majesty; seat of state, throne.

Let kings assemble; for my grief's so great
That no supporter but the huge firm earth
Can hold it up: here I and sorrows sit;
Here is my throne, bid kings come bow to it.
          [*Throws herself on the ground. Exit Salisbury.*

72. *earth*] F1; *earth* [throwing herself upon it. Capell.          73. *sorrows*] F1; *sorrow*
Pope.          74. S.D.] This ed.; om. F1; [Sits down on the Floor. Theobald.

71–3. *for . . . up:*] *sorrows* (l. 68),
*grief* (ll. 69, 70, 71), *sorrow* (l. 73), all
resume the *woes* of l. 64, which *adulter-
ate* with Constance as Fortune with
John. The dualism is now extended: behind the picture in ll. 71–3
we must see the emblem of Fortune
standing on the rolling earth.

74. S.D.] Cf. Introduction, p. xxxix.
In *MND.* at the end of Act III, F1
prints "They sleepe all the Act" (i.e.
all the *act-interval*): so Constance (and
Arthur?) remain on-stage during this
interval.

# ACT III

## SCENE I.—[*The French King's Pavilion.*]

CONSTANCE *and* ARTHUR, *seated. Enter* KING JOHN, KING
PHILIP, LEWIS, BLANCHE, ELEANOR, *the* BASTARD, AUSTRIA,
SALISBURY, *and Attendants.*

*K. Phi.* 'Tis true, fair daughter; and this blessed day      [75]
Ever in France shall be kept festival:
To solemnize this day the glorious sun
Stays in his course and plays the alchemist,
Turning with splendour of his precious eye      5 [79]
The meagre cloddy earth to glittering gold:
The yearly course that brings this day about
Shall never see it but a holy day.
*Const.* A wicked day, and not a holy day!      [*Rising*

ACT III

*Scene* 1

*Act* III *Scene* I.] F1 (Actus Tertius, Scaena prima.); scene contd. Theobald,
edd.; *Act* III *Scene* II. Hanmer.      The . . . Pavilion.] As Theobald; om. F1.
S.D.] This ed.; Enter King Iohn, France, Dolphin, Blanch, Elianor, Philip,
Austria, Constance. F1; King *John*, King *Philip*, discovered on a Throne, . . . Bell.
8, 9. *holy day*] F1; *holiday* ed. 1753.      9. S.D.] Theobald; om. F1.

*Act* III *Scene* 1] For the division cf.
Introduction, p. xxxvii.
  1. '*Tis true*] Resuming II. ii. 26?
  1–2. *this . . .festival:*] Cf. R. W.'s
*Three Lordes and Three Ladies of London*
(1590): "By my consent one day shal
serue vs all,/ Which shall be kept for
euer festiuall" (sig. H₂).
  3–4. *To . . . course*] Carter compared
*Joshua*, x. 12–4: "Sunne, staye thou
in Gibeon," etc.
  3. *the glorious sun*] A favourite cliché
of Shakespeare and contemporaries
(cf. *LLL.*, I. i. 84; *Tw.N.*, IV. iii. 1;
*2 H 6*, III. i. 353); *glorious* was a richer
word than now.

  4. *plays the alchemist*] So Sonnet 33
(Malone).
  5–6. *Turning . . . gold:*] An old min-
eralogical theory, as in Peele's *Descensus Astraeae* (1591): "in Tellus' veins
the parching sun / Doth gold and glittering minerals create" (ed. Bullen,
I, 367).
  5. *precious eye*] The sun as eye was a
common-place image.
  6. *meagre*] barren.
  8. *holy day*] "Holy day" and "holiday" were not yet distinct.
  9, etc. *day*] With this repetition of
*day* cf. *Zephaniah*, i. 15, 16 and Constance's style throughout.

59

What hath this day deserv'd? what hath it done, 10 [84]
That it in golden letters should be set
Among the high tides in the calendar?
Nay, rather turn this day out of the week,
This day of shame, oppression, perjury.
Or, if it must stand still, let wives with child      15 [89]
Pray that their burthens may not fall this day,
Lest that their hopes prodigiously be cross'd:
But on this day let seamen fear no wrack;
No bargains break that are not this day made;
This day, all things begun come to ill end,         20 [94]
Yea, faith itself to hollow falsehood change!

*K. Phi.*  By heaven, lady, you shall have no cause
To curse the fair proceedings of this day:
Have I not pawn'd to you my majesty?

*Const.*  You have beguil'd me with a counterfeit     25 [99]
Resembling majesty, which, being touch'd and tried,

18. *But on this day*] Dyce; *But* (*on this day*) F1.     26. *being*] F1; om. Pope.

12. *high tides*] festival days (usual gloss). Malone suggested that they are the high tides of the sea, "marked in every almanack", withdrawing the note when criticized that in this sense they are wicked, not holy. Deighton thought the Golden Number might be referred to. (N.B. The Golden Number is explained in one old calendar as written "with letters of gold, right at that day whereon the Moone changed"; Furness thought that *golden letters* (l. 11) meant "red letters", comparing *LLL.*, v. ii. 44: cf. our note to II. i. 316.) The "tides of the sea" sense recurs in l. 18, and must be present. Read: "How has this day deserved to be set with golden letters with the (holy) festivals *and likewise with the* (*wicked*) *tides* (even these latter being too good company for it)? Nay—".

13–14. *Nay, . . . perjury*] Following *Job.*, iii. 3, v. 6 (Upton).

15–17. *Or, . . . cross'd:*] Following *Matthew*, xxiv. 19 (Deighton).

15. *wives*] women, the older sense.

17. *prodigiously*] "(?) by monstrous births" (On.); "by the production

of a prodigy, a monster" (Steevens).

18. *But*] Except. The transition from *wives with child* to *seamen* may be due to the Litany, where they were prayed for together.

19. *No . . . break*] "In the ancient almanacks . . . days supposed to be favourable or unfavourable to bargains, are distinguished" (Steevens); *bargains* = agreements.

20. *This . . . end*] Alluding to the proverb "An ill Beginning has an ill ending" (Tilley, p. 41).

23. *fair*] favourable, fortunate; equitable, honest.

25. *counterfeit*] "a false coin. A *counterfeit* formerly signified also a portrait.—A representation of the king being usually impressed on his coin, the word seems to be here used equivocally" (Malone).

26. *touch'd and tried*] "tested by being rubbed on a touchstone . . . the trained eye could tell the fineness of gold rubbed on it by the character of the streak left" (I. John). Shakespeare at times used *touch'd* alone in this sense; possibly *and tried* was added by the

Proves valueless: you are forsworn, forsworn!
You came in arms to spill mine enemies' blood,
But now in arms you strengthen it with yours.
The grappling vigour and rough frown of war    30 [104]
Is cold in amity, and painted peace,
And our oppression hath made up this league.
Arm, arm, you heavens, against these perjur'd kings!
A widow cries; be husband to me, heavens!
Let not the hours of this ungodly day    35 [109]
Wear out the day's in peace; but, ere sunset,
Set armed discord 'twixt these perjur'd kings!
Hear me, O, hear me!

*Aust.*                          Lady Constance, peace!
*Const.* War! war! no peace! peace is to me a war.
O Limoges! O Austria! thou dost shame    40 [114]
That bloody spoil: thou slave, thou wretch, thou
    coward!

31. *cold*] F1; *cool'd* Hanmer.    *in amity*] F1; *inamity* Crowdown (*N. & Q.*, 16 Dec.
1871).    *amity,*] F1; *amity* Pope.    36. *day's*] F1 (*daies*); *day* Theobald, edd.

compositor unconsciously completing a familiar phrase.

28–9. *in arms . . . in arms*] "*You came in war to destroy my enemies*, but *now you strengthen them* in embraces" (Johnson). Perhaps the quartering of the arms of England and France in the marriage of Blanche and Lewis is also meant. Cf. II. i. 345–6.

28. *spill*] shed; destroy, kill (as in *Ham.*, IV. v. 20, *Lr.*, III. ii. 8).

31. *cold*] The metaphor has been called inconsistent, but is so no more than II. i. 479 (see note).

*painted peace*] "feigned, unreal peace"; or perhaps "patched up peace"; in apposition to *amity* and to *oppression*.

32. *our*] The only (and very slight) evidence that Arthur is present in this scene (cf. Introduction, p. xxxix).

33. *perjur'd kings*] Cf. Appendix B, p. 169.

34. *A . . . heavens!*] Many biblical passages where *heaven* is the *husband* of *widows* were compared by Carter, e.g.: "Thou . . . shalt not remember the re-

proch of thy widowhood. . . . Hee that made thee is thine husband" (*Isaiah*, liv. 4–5).

35–6. *Let . . . peace;*] In R.C. Latin religious verse "hora" was often used with a quibbling sense (= hour; prayer), and here *hours* may mean prayers (cf. *O.E.D.*, hour, 5), viz. "Let not my prayers on this ungodly day see the hours of the day come to a peaceful conclusion." The Roman Catholic views of John's enemies are clear (cf. III. i. 62 ff.; II. i. 171, note), and F1 makes sense.

36–7. *ere . . . kings!*] Adapted from *Ephesians*, iv. 26? ("let not the sunne go downe vpon your wrath").

39. *peace . . . war.*] So in B. and F.'s *Laws of Candy* (ed. 1647): "I found no difference 'twixt War and Peace / For War was peace to me, and Peace was war" (sig. 3G₂ᵛ).

40. *Limoges . . . Austria*] Cf. Introduction, p. xxi.

41. *spoil*] Cœur-de-lion's lion's-skin. Following Ovid's *spolium leonis* (*Metam.*, ix. 113).

Thou little valiant, great in villainy!
Thou ever strong upon the stronger side!
Thou fortune's champion, that dost never fight
But when her humorous ladyship is by            45 [119]
To teach thee safety! thou art perjur'd too,
And sooth'st up greatness. What a fool art thou,
A ramping fool, to brag, and stamp, and swear
Upon my party! Thou cold-blooded slave,
Hast thou not spoke like thunder on my side,    50 [124]
Been sworn my soldier, bidding me depend
Upon thy stars, thy fortune and thy strength,
And dost thou now fall over to my foes?
Thou wear a lion's hide! doff it for shame,
And hang a calve's-skin on those recreant limbs. 55 [129]
*Aust.* O, that a man should speak those words to me!
*Bast.* And hang a calve's-skin on those recreant limbs.
*Aust.* Thou dar'st not say so, villain, for thy life.
*Bast.* And hang a calve's-skin on those recreant limbs.
*K. John.* We like not this; thou dost forget thyself.    60 [134]

*Enter* PANDULPH.

*K. Phi.* Here comes the holy legate of the pope.
*Pand.* Hail, you anointed deputies of heaven!

49. *cold-blooded*] F4; no hyphen F1.
*skin* throughout); *ralf's-skin* Capell, edd.
61. S.D.] F1; ... attended. Capell.

55. *calve's-skin*] F1 (*Calues skin* or *Calues-skin*
61.] F1; *Scene* II. Pope; III. Hanmer.

43. *strong upon*] "determined, resolute (to side with the stronger)"; or "strong, *because* on the stronger side".
45. *humorous*] capricious.
47. *sooth'st up*] flatterest; *up* is emphatic.
48. *ramping*] "'Ramping' is suggested by the lion's skin which Austria wears, and is a proper epithet of the lion, in the sense tearing, pawing. So in 3 Henry VI, v. 2. 13" (Wright). Furness interpreted "rushing wildly about".
53. *fall over*] revolt.
55. *calve's-skin*] "When fools were kept for diversion in great families, they were distinguished by a calf's-

skin coat ... that they might be known for fools" (Hawkins, *ap.* Furness). Ritson thought Austria's cowardice not his foolishness is jeered at, for *calf* = meek fellow was pre-Shakespearean. Both meanings were probably intended.
56. *O ... me!*] Dyce compared Sidney's *Arcadia* (1590): "O God (cried out *Pyrocles*) that thou wert a man that usest these wordes unto me" (p. 486).
62. *anointed deputies*] Reminding the kings of their place in the religious scheme of the world.
62–72. *Hail, ... thee.*] A speech very similar in *John* and *T.R.* Pandulph's reference to Langton comes from

To thee, King John, my holy errand is.
I Pandulph, of fair Milan cardinal,
And from Pope Innocent the legate here,　　　65 [139]
Do in his name religiously demand
Why thou against the church, our holy mother,
So wilfully dost spurn; and force perforce
Keep Stephen Langton, chosen archbishop
Of Canterbury, from that holy see:　　　　　70 [144]
This, in our foresaid holy father's name,
Pope Innocent, I do demand of thee.

*K. John.* What earthy name to interrogatories
　　Can taste the free breath of a sacred king?
　　Thou canst not, cardinal, devise a name　　75 [149]
　　So slight, unworthy and ridiculous,
　　To charge me to an answer, as the pope.
　　Tell him this tale; and from the mouth of England
　　Add thus much more, that no Italian priest
　　Shall tithe or toll in our dominions;　　　80 [154]
　　But as we, under God, are supreme head,
　　So under Him that great supremacy,

---

73. *earthy*] F1; *earthly* Pope.　　74. *taste*] F1; *tax* Rowe iii; *task* Theobald.
81. *God*] Collier MS.; *heauen* F1.

---

Foxe, but the words of the reference from (a different context in) Holinshed. (Cf. Introduction, pp. xiii, xx.)

63–71. *holy*] Cf. *noble*, v. ii. 40–3, *honourable* in *Caes.*, iii. ii. 88, *sqq.* The "holy father Pope, holy mother Church" jargon was detested by Protestants.

64. *cardinal*] The Cardinal Pandulf with whom the legate Pandulph in *John* was confused by Shakespeare and some earlier writers (Introduction, p. xxv) was not cardinal of Milan.

65. *Innocent*] Innocent III, the great upholder of papal authority.

68. *force perforce*] by compulsion; so *2 H 6*, i. i. 259.

69. *Stephen Langton*] Cf. Appendix A, p. 155.

73–4. *What . . . king?*] Cf. ii. i. 110-12.

73. *earthy*] John compares the dis-

parity between kings and others through the elements air (= *breath*) and earth; "earthly" and "earthy" were not sharply distinct as now.

*name to interrogatories*] title or claim to demand answers as from interrogatories. An accused person or witness had to answer interrogatories (questions formally put) as upon oath; cf. *All's W.*, iv. iii. 198, *sqq.*, *Mer.V.*, v. i. 298.

74. *taste*] put to the proof, try, test (*O.E.D.* taste, 2), as (quibblingly) in *Troil.*: "Praise us as we are tasted, allow us as we prove" (iii. ii. 97), *Tw.N.*, iii. i. 89, iii. iv. 270, etc.; *task* is no improvement.

*breath*] "speech" (Malone); or perhaps "life".

81. *God*] Cf. Introduction, p. xxxiii n. In *T.R.* John says "I raigne next vnder God, supreame head" (i. v. 80).

Where we do reign, we will alone uphold
Without th' assistance of a mortal hand:
So tell the pope, all reverence set apart          85 [159]
To him and his usurp'd authority.

*K. Phi.* Brother of England, you blaspheme in this.

*K. John.* Though you and all the kings of Christendom
Are led so grossly by this meddling priest,
Dreading the curse that money may buy out;     90 [164]
And by the merit of vild gold, dross, dust,
Purchase corrupted pardon of a man,
Who in that sale sells pardon from himself;
Though you and all the rest so grossly led
This juggling witchcraft with revenue cherish,   95 [169]
Yet I alone, alone do me oppose
Against the pope, and count his friends my foes.

*Pand.* Then, by the lawful power that I have,
Thou shalt stand curs'd and excommunicate:
And blessed shall he be that doth revolt          100 [174]
From his allegiance to an heretic;
And meritorious shall that hand be call'd,

---

91. *by*] F1; *buy* Warburton (press-corrected).

---

86. *usurp'd authority*] Cf. II. i. 118.—
In Protestant England the "usurped
power" of the pope became a watch-
word. In Bale's *King Iohan* "Usurped
Power" is a character; Foxe often used
the phrase (cf. Introduction, p. xv);
"usurped authority" was almost
equally common.

87. *Brother of England*] Common
form of address between kings in the
old drama.

89. *grossly*] "stupidly"; or perhaps
"materially, opposed to spiritually"
as in *Mer. V.*, v. i. 65, *Tw.N.*, v. i.
247.

91. *merit*] Alluding to the doctrine of
merit. Whereas the Protestants expected "through thonelie merittes of
Jesus Christe . . . to be made partaker
of lyfe everlastinge'' (Shakespeare's
will), Roman Catholics held that for-
giveness of sins is impossible unless
man himself "satisfy", "which they

for money sake haue inuented,
in steede of the bloodsheeding of
Iesus Christ" (Protestant pamphlet,
1588).

*gold, dross*] The thought that "gold
is dross" was common.

93. *from himself*] "i.e. not from God.
Some take it as 'sells away his own
pardon.'" (Wilson).

95. *juggling witchcraft . . . revenue*] Cf.
Introduction, p. xv; *juggling* = trick-
ing.

100–1. *And . . . heretic*] Tilley (p. 200)
quoted the proverb "No Faith with
heretics." Protestants hated this Roman Catholic doctrine.

102. *meritorious*] In the trials of the
intending assassins of the Queen in the
1580's the "merit" (cf. l. 91, note) of
the murder became notorious. Shakespeare's cousin Edward Arden was
executed for such attempted regicide
in 1583.

Canonized and worshipp'd as a saint,
That takes away by any secret course
Thy hateful life.

*Const.*                    O, lawful let it be          105 [179]
That I have room with Rome to curse awhile!
Good father cardinal, cry thou amen
To my keen curses; for without my wrong
There is no tongue hath power to curse him right.

*Pand.* There's law and warrant, lady, for my curse. 110 [184]

*Const.* And for mine too: when law can do no right
Let it be lawful that law bar no wrong!
Law cannot give my child his kingdom here,
For he that holds his kingdom holds the law;
Therefore, since law itself is perfect wrong,    115 [189]
How can the law forbid my tongue to curse?

*Pana.* Philip of France, on peril of a curse,
Let go the hand of that arch-heretic;
And raise the power of France upon his head,
Unless he do submit himself to Rome.            120 [194]

*Elea.* Look'st thou pale, France? do not let go thy hand.

---

106. *room*] F1; *leave* Pope.    111. *too: . . . right*] *too, . . . right.* F1.

---

103. *Canonized*] For the accent cf.
III. iii. 52, *Ham.*, I. iv. 47. Canonization
was promised to the murderers of
Elizabeth, not of John (Furness). In
1590 an audience would think first of
Jaques Clement, the murderer of
Henry III, whose proposed canonization was causing great indignation:
cf. Introduction, p. xlvi.

106. *room with Rome*] Cf. *Caes.*, I. ii.
155. Two pronunciations of "Rome"
were current, a variant ru:m (=
room) as well as ro:m. The obvious
pun was pre-Shakespearean, as in W.
Lightfoote's *Complaint of England*
(1587): "But roome now, els shall we
bring all *Rome* on our back" (sig. G₂).

107-8. *Good . . . curses;*] Noble suggested a reference to the Commination
Service (which was compulsory four
times a year). The minister recited the
curses and the people had to answer
"Amen" (cf. *Deuteronomy*, xxvii. 14–

26). N.B. Constance reverses the role
of the priest.

111–16. *when . . . curse?*] Noble compared *Romans*, iii. 19, iv. 15, vii. 6–7.

112. *bar*] Cf. II. i. 192, note.

113. *here*] Cf. IV. ii. 89, note.

115–16. *law . . . law*] M. Joseph
detected equivocation: "Constance
argues as if the law of England, mis-
held by John and by him made perfect
wrong, is identical with the law of
God forbidding individuals to curse"
[*Shakespeare's Use of the Arts of Language*
(1949), p. 231].

118. *hand*] The holding of hands was
a sign of courtesy and affection between equals. Its significance here has
been prepared for: cf. I. i. 163, note,
II. i. 494, 532, 533. Cf. also *Proverbs*:
"(Thogh) hand (ioyne) in hand, the
wicked shal not be vnpunished" (xi.
21).

119. *head*] = head; army (Wilson).

*Const.* Look to that, devil, lest that France repent,
     And by disjoining hands, hell lose a soul.
*Aust.* King Philip, listen to the cardinal.
*Bast.* And hang a calve's-skin on his recreant limbs. 125 [199]
*Aust.* Well, ruffian, I must pocket up these wrongs,
     Because—
*Bast.*          Your breeches best may carry them.
*K. John.* Philip, what say'st thou to the cardinal?
*Const.* What should he say, but as the cardinal?
*Lew.* Bethink you, father; for the difference     130 [204]
     Is purchase of a heavy curse from Rome,
     Or the light loss of England for a friend:
     Forgo the easier.
*Blanche.*          That's the curse of Rome.
*Const.* O Lewis, stand fast! the devil tempts thee here
     In likeness of a new untrimmed bride.       135 [209]
*Blanche.* The Lady Constance speaks not from her faith,
     But from her need.
*Const.*          O, if thou grant my need,
     Which only lives but by the death of faith,
     That need must needs infer this principle,

---

122. *that*] F1; *it* Maxwell (*N. & Q.*, 18 Feb. 1950).      135. *untrimmed*] F1; *and trimmed* Theobald; *uptrimmèd* Dyce.

---

122. *that*] "The normal expression before a clause beginning 'that' or 'lest' is 'look to it,'" (Maxwell, postulating "it", spelt "yt").

125. *calve's-skin*] The jibe may be resumed in contempt of Austria's support of the pope. After the Bull of Excommunication the pope was nicknamed the "bull" of Rome, and his supporters his "calves"—an idiom still popular in 1590.

126–7. *Well . . . them.*] Did Austria wear breeches with extra-large pockets? Steevens compared *King Leir* (1605): "Well, I haue a payre of slops for the nonce, / Will hold all your mocks" (sig. G₃). Cf. also *Arden of Feversham* (1592): "But rather then I pocket vp this wrong. / *Francklin.* What will you doo sir? / *Mos.* Reuenge it on the proudest of you both:" (sig. B₃).

"Pocket up" had only recently acquired the sense "put up with".

135. *untrimmed*] "unbedded" (Ridley). This slang sense of *trim* was once common (cf. *Tit.*, v. i. 92–9). The allusion to the temptation of St Anthony (St Dunstan) supports it (noted by Z. Grey. The devil tempted Anthony as a naked woman). Some take *untrimmed* = "with hair hanging loose in the fashion of a bride". Malone compared *Rom.*: "Go waken Juliet, go and trim her up" (IV. iv. 25).

136–7. *speaks . . . need.*] "says not what she thinks but what suits her purpose" (Wilson).

137–42. *O . . . down!*] "Here 'need' = her distress, and 'faith' = the promise of France. The image of the last two lines reminds us of *Rich. II*, 4. 1. 181–99" (Wilson).

That faith would live again by death of need.   140 [214]
O then tread down my need, and faith mounts up:
Keep my need up, and faith is trodden down!
*K. John.* The king is mov'd, and answers not to this.
*Const.* O, be remov'd from him, and answer well!
*Aust.* Do so, King Philip; hang no more in doubt.   145 [219]
*Bast.* Hang nothing but a calve's-skin, most sweet lout.
*K. Phi.* I am perplex'd, and know not what to say.
*Pand.* What canst thou say but will perplex thee more,
        If thou stand excommunicate and curs'd?
*K. Phi.* Good reverend father, make my person yours,
        And tell me how you would bestow yourself.   151 [225]
        This royal hand and mine are newly knit,
        And the conjunction of our inward souls—
        Married in league, coupled and link'd together
        With all religious strength of sacred vows;   155 [229]
        The latest breath that gave the sound of words—
        Was deep-sworn faith, peace, amity, true love
        Between our kingdoms and our royal selves.
        And even before this truce, but new before,
        No longer than we well could wash our hands   160 [234]
        To clap this royal bargain up of peace,
        Heaven knows, they were besmear'd and overstain'd
        With slaughter's pencil, where revenge did paint
        The fearful difference of incensed kings:

---

153–6. *souls— . . . vows; . . . words—*] This ed; *soules . . . vowes, . . . words* F1;
*soules . . . vowes : . . . words* F2.

---

141. *tread down*] Cf. II. ii. 58.

144. *O . . . well*] Perhaps a chess-allusion (cf. II. i. 123), i.e. to the danger when kings are near one another; *remove* = our "move", *answer* = make a counter-move.

150. *make . . . yours*] put yourself in my place (Wilson).

153–5. *And . . . vows;*] "It seems doubtful whether the construction here is, 'the conjunction of our souls *is* married in league,' the words 'coupled . . . vows' being an amplification o 'married in league'; or, 'the conjunction of our souls *being* married in league' is 'coupled,' etc. In either case

there is tautology" (Deighton). We prefer a parenthesis (ll. 154–6), with l. 156 an amplification of *vows* (l. 155).

154. *coupled*] = both *Married* and *link'd*: cf. III. iii. 17–19, note.

159. *even before*] just before.
*new before*] recently, lately before.

161. *clap . . . up*] "clap hands and a bargain" (*H 5*, V. ii. 134) was proverbial since a hand-shake sealed a bargain; *clap up* = settle hastily (On. compared *Shr.*, II. i. 319).

163. *pencil*] a (thick) paint-brush.

164. *difference*] disagreement; cf. II. i. 355.

And shall these hands, so lately purg'd of blood, 165 [239]
So newly join'd in love, so strong in both,
Unyoke this seizure and this kind regreet?
Play fast and loose with faith? so jest with heaven,
Make such unconstant children of ourselves,
As now again to snatch our palm from palm,    170 [244]
Unswear faith sworn, and on the marriage-bed
Of smiling peace to march a bloody host,
And make a riot on the gentle brow
Of true sincerity? O, holy sir,
My reverend father, let it not be so!           175 [249]
Out of your grace, devise, ordain, impose
Some gentle order, and then we shall be blest
To do your pleasure and continue friends.
*Pand.* All form is formless, order orderless,
Save what is opposite to England's love.       180 [254]
Therefore to arms! be champion of our church,
Or let the church, our mother, breathe her curse,
A mother's curse, on her revolting son.
France, thou mayst hold a serpent by the tongue,

166. *strong in both*] Both "love so strong in both parties" and "hands (i.e. kings) so strong in blood (i.e. enmity) and love" have been proposed.

167. *seizure*] clasp, grasp.

*regreet*] "A(return of a) salutation or greeting" (*O.E.D.*).

168. *Play . . . loose*] i.e. cheat; *fast and loose* was a cheating game in which a leather belt was folded up, the victim having to thrust a skewer through the middle. The belt was "fast" or "loose" at the wish of the holder, who had only to move the ends to change the middle (Furness). Cf. *Ant.*, IV. x. 41, *LLL.*, I. ii. 164.

169. *children*] i.e. children of the Church.

170. *palm*] i.e. the symbol of peace.

173. *brow*] forehead. The brow reflected character to the Elizabethans (cf. v. ii. 176), so that *gentle brow* = gentleness. Read: "do an outrage to

the person of our gentle bride (i.e. *true sincerity*)".

174. *true sincerity*] Theologians had made "the true sincerity of Christianity" a cliché.

176-7. *devise . . . order*] Pseudo-legal jargon, as in royal proclamations, where it was a set formula, after the statement of a grievance, that "some present (or good, or fair) order be ordained (or devised, or imposed etc.)", with the usual multiplication of terms; *order* = suitable measures.

179. *form . . . order*] Synonyms (cf. IV. ii. 22). Pandulph does not take *order* in Philip's sense, but = ordered government, a sacrosanct Tudor conception (for which see *Troil.*, I. iii. 75–137).

181. *champion*] Cf. III. i. 193, note.

184. *a . . . tongue*] So *Ado*, v. i. 90. Tilley (p. 739) took the common origin of ll. 184–6 to be the proverb "He holds a Wolf by the ears."

A cased lion by the mortal paw,  185 [259]
A fasting tiger safer by the tooth,
Than keep in peace that hand which thou dost hold.
*K. Phi.* I may disjoin my hand, but not my faith.
*Pand.* So mak'st thou faith an enemy to faith,
And like a civil war set'st oath to oath,  190 [264]
Thy tongue against thy tongue. O, let thy vow
First made to heaven, first be to heaven perform'd,
That is, to be the champion of our church.
What since thou swor'st is sworn against thyself
And may not be performed by thyself,  195 [269]
For that which thou hast sworn to do amiss
Is not amiss when it is truly done,
And being not done, where doing tends to ill,
The truth is then most done not doing it:
The better act of purposes mistook  200 [274]

185. *cased*] F1; *chased* Pope; *chafed* Theobald, edd.; *caged* Collier conj.  197. *not*]
F1; *most* Hanmer; *yet* Warburton; *but* Collier ii (MS.).

185. *cased lion*] Theobald's "chafed lion" was a common phrase (as in *H 8*, III. ii. 207), and may be right. Some defend *cased lion* = a lion irritated by confinement (Steevens). But surely the point is due to Austria's lion's-skin; a *cased lion* is one still wearing his *case* (= skin), i.e. a live lion. Cf. *T.R.* "the *Lyons case*, / Which here he *holds*" (I. iv. 31–2; cf. I. ii. 128–30).
   *mortal*] deadly.
   188. *but . . . faith.*] "and yet keep my faith", or "but my faith I may not disjoin (break)."
   189–223. *So . . . weight.*] In this speech, said T. W. Baldwin (*William Shakspere's Small Latine*, II, 277), Shakespeare follows exactly the form of ratiocinatio prescribed by Erasmus for "argumentatio perfectissima". Pandulph propounds the doctrine of equivocation, hated by Protestants, for which cf. *Ham.*, v. i. 148, *Mac.*, II. iii. 10–13.
   193. *champion*] "The King of France was styled the Eldest Son of the Church

and the Most Christian King" (Wright).
   196–9. *For . . . it*] Tilley (p. 511) quoted the proverb "An unlawful Oath is better broken than kept", with many Shakespearean uses, as *2 H 6*, v. i. 182.
   197–9. *Is . . . it*] "is *not amiss* (i.e., becomes right) when it is *done truely* (that is, as he explains it, not done at all); and being *not done*, where it would be a *sin* to *do it*, the *truth* is *most done* when you *do it not*" (Ritson). In *truly* (l. 197), *truth* (l. 199) there are quibbles on the meaning "righteous(ness)", "faithful(ness)".
   200–2. *The . . . direct*] Cf. *Ham.*, II. i. 66: "By indirections find directions out", where *indirections* and *directions* parallel *falsehood* and *truth* as here. "When we have turned aside from the straight path the best thing to do is not to retrace our steps but to take another turning which is a short cut to the direction we ought to go" (Wilson, comparing *Ham.*, v. ii. 398).

Is to mistake again; though indirect,
Yet indirection thereby grows direct,
And falsehood falsehood cures, as fire cools fire
Within the scorched veins of one new-burn'd.
It is religion that doth make vows kept,          205 [279]
But thou hast sworn against religion:
By what thou swear'st against the thing thou swear'st,
And mak'st an oath the surety for thy truth!
Against an oath the truth thou art unsure
To swear—swears only not to be forsworn!—   210 [284]
Else what a mockery should it be to swear?
But thou dost swear only to be forsworn,
And most forsworn, to keep what thou dost swear.
Therefore thy later vows against thy first
Is in thyself rebellion to thyself;                  215 [289]
And better conquest never canst thou make
Than arm thy constant and thy nobler parts
Against these giddy loose suggestions:
Upon which better part our prayers come in,

208. *truth!*] F3 (*truth:*); *truth*, F1, edd.     209. *oath*] F1; *oath.* Heath, edd.
210. *swear—. . . forsworn!—*] This ed.; *sweare, . . . forswore*, F1.     *swears*] F1;
*swear* Rowe iii.     214. *later*] F1; *latter* F3.     *vows*] F1; *vow* Dyce ii.

203. *And . . . cures*] Tilley (p. 147) quoted the proverb "One Deceit (falsehood) drives out another."

*fire cools fire*] Cf. *Gent.*, II. iv. 193, *Cor.*, IV. vii. 54, *Rom.*, I. ii. 47, *Caes.*, III. i. 171. Tilley (p. 215) quoted the proverb "One Fire drives out another."

205. *It . . . kept*] Cf. *LLL.*: "It is religion to be thus forsworn" (IV. iii. 363), and cf. these two treatments of perjury.

206. *against religion*] = "irreligiously", or "against the interests of religion (i.e. siding with heretics)".

207. *By . . . swear'st,*] By the truth (faithfulness) which you swear to John (you commit yourself) against your own truth (integrity).

208–10. *And . . . forsworn!—*] "(Having forsworn thy truth) thou hast the effrontery to make an oath the pledge of thy truth!" (l. 208). Ll. 209, 210 are

sarcastic (especially *art unsure*): "Thou art unlikely to swear the truth (if thy oath runs) against an (earlier) oath:— (He) swears only to avoid being forsworn (who has heard the like)!" Our punctuation is less confusing than that of the *textus receptus* and closer to F1.

210. *swears*] Usually taken as second person. The form (= *swearest*) is used elsewhere by Shakespeare, but the syntax is then un-English. We prefer *swears* as third person. Elliptic exclamation was common—cf. *A Knacke to Know an Honest Man* (1596): "*Eta serua vostra fettisima seruidore siniore.* | *For:* Speakes in parables." (sig. C^v).

215. *Is*] "*Therefore* (to put) *thy later vows*, whence the singular verb" (Moberly); "singular on account of 'rebellion'" (Wright).

218. *giddy*] foolish.

*suggestions*] temptations (Furness).

If thou vouchsafe them. But if not, then know   220 [294]
The peril of our curses light on thee
So heavy as thou shalt not shake them off,
But in despair die under their black weight.

*Aust.* Rebellion, flat rebellion!

*Bast.*                              Will't not be?
Will not a calve's-skin stop that mouth of thine? 225 [299]

*Lew.* Father, to arms!

*Blanche.*                    Upon thy wedding-day?
Against the blood that thou hast married?
What, shall our feast be kept with slaughter'd men?
Shall braying trumpets and loud churlish drums,
Clamours of hell, be measures to our pomp?   230 [304]
O husband, hear me! ay, alack, how new
Is "husband" in my mouth! even for that name,
Which till this time my tongue did ne'er pronounce,
Upon my knee I beg, go not to arms
Against mine uncle.

*Const.*                    O, upon my knee,        235 [309]
Made hard with kneeling, I do pray to thee,
Thou virtuous Dolphin, alter not the doom
Forethought by heaven!

*Blanche.* Now shall I see thy love: what motive may
Be stronger with thee than the name of wife?   240 [314]

*Const.* That which upholdeth him that thee upholds,
His honour: O, thine honour, Lewis, thine honour!

*Lew.* I muse your majesty doth seem so cold,
When such profound respects do pull you on.

---

224. *Will't*] F1 (*Wil't*); *Wilt* Capell.   231. *ay,*] F1; *ah!* Theobald ii.   235-8. *O
. . . heaven!*] Pope; three lines F1 (ending *kneeling,* / .   . Daulphin, / . . .
heauen./*).

222-3. *heavy . . . black*] Transferred
epithets; *heavy curse, black curse* are
implied.

224. *Will't not be?*] "Is everything in
vain?"—Onions compared *Rom.,* IV. v
11, *1 H 6,* I. v. 33.

229. *braying trumpets*] Probably a recent coinage; cf. *Answer to the Vntruthes*
(1589), by D. F. R. de M.: "braieng
trumps" (sig. H,ᵛ); cf. *R 2,* I. iii. 135;

*Ham.,* I. iv. 11.
*churlish drums*] Cf. II. i. 76.
230. *measures*] melodies.
237-8. *Thou . . . heaven!*] Protestants
held "it is impossible for any of the
elect to fall away"; the Roman
Catholics "Men cannot bee saued,
though they bee predestinate, vnlesse
they keepe Gods commaundements."
244. *respects*] considerations.

*Pand.* I will denounce a curse upon his head.        245 [319]

*K. Phi.* Thou shalt not need. England, I will fall from
    thee.

*Const.* O fair return of banish'd majesty!

*Elea.* O foul revolt of French inconstancy!

*K. John.* France, thou shalt rue this hour within this
    hour.

*Bast.* Old time the clock-setter, that bald sexton time,
    Is it as he will? well then, France shall rue.        251 [325]

*Blanche.* The sun's o'ercast with blood: fair day, adieu!
    Which is the side that I must go withal?
    I am with both: each army hath a hand;
    And in their rage, I having hold of both,        255 [329]
    They whirl asunder and dismember me.
    Husband, I cannot pray that thou mayst win;
    Uncle, I needs must pray that thou mayst lose;

---

246. *I will*] F1; *I'll* Pope.        249. K. John.] Eng. F1.

---

246. *fall from*] forsake.

248. *O . . . inconstancy!*] Delius compared *1 H 6*: "Done like a Frenchman: turn, and turn again!" (III. iii. 85).

249. *France . . . hour.*] Cf. *1 H 6*: "France, thou shalt rue this treason with thy tears" (III. ii. 36).

*within this hour*] in a short time (common phrase). Possibly there was an emblem (figuring Time or Death) with the motto "Thou shalt rue this hour within this hour", in the popular "Ut hora, sic fugit vita" class.

250–1. *Old . . . rue*] The sexton was in charge of the church clock, and dug the graves. The mattock and hour-glass of Father Time are also alluded to. Shakespeare plays on a popular quibble, as in Greene's *Quip* (1592): "the Courtiers comfort, Time, an herb that many stumble on . . . [makes] a snaile . . . as swift as a swallow", "they lookte so proudly . . . that they stumbled on a bed of Rue, that grewe at the bottome of the banke where the Time was planted" (sigs. A₂, A₂ᵛ). The last page of Greene's *Mamillia*, Pt II (writ-

ten by 1583) shows that Tilley's proverb "Rue and thyme grow both in one garden" (p. 577) was pre-Shakespearean. Read: "If it is only a question of time (thyme), then France shall rue, because rue and thyme go together (grow in the same garden)."

252. *The . . . blood*] i.e. the red heat of *the glorious sun* (III. i. 3) is not an omen of joy at all. Cf. *Ham.*, I. i. 117, and Chapman's *Bussy*: "O, my heart is broken . . . / My sun is turn'd to blood" (v. iv. 131–5).

254–62. *I . . . play'd*] John and Lewis (the same men as here) put the pope in a like dilemma: "[Papa] dixit: Heu mihi, quia in hoc facto ecclesia Dei non potest euadere confusionem. Si enim Rex Angliae vincitur, in ipsius confusione confundimur . . . Si dominus Lodouicus vincitur, quod Deus auertat, in ipsius laesione laeditur Romana ecclesia. . . Et in fine dixit, quod melius vellet mori, quam aliquod malum vobis accideret" (M. Paris, p. 379).

256. *dismember*] Cf. II. i. 508.

Father, I may not wish the fortune thine;
Grandam, I will not wish thy wishes thrive:      260 [334]
Whoever wins, on that side shall I lose;
Assured loss before the match be play'd.

*Lew.* Lady, with me, with me thy fortune lies.

*Blanche.* There where my fortune li'es, there my life dies.

*K. John.* Cousin, go draw our puissance together.      265 [339]

[*Exit Bastard.*

France, I am burn'd up with inflaming wrath;
A rage whose heat hath this condition,
That nothing can allay, nothing but blood,
The blood, and dearest-valued blood, of France.

*K. Phi.* Thy rage shall burn thee up, and thou shalt turn
To ashes, ere our blood shall quench that fire: 271 [345]
Look to thyself, thou art in jeopardy.

*K. John.* No more than he that threats. To arms let's hie!

[*Exeunt.*

263. *lies*] F1; *lives* Capell.      264. *li'es*] Fleay; *liues* F1.      265. S.D.] Pope; om.
F1.      268. *allay*] F1; *allay't* Capell conj.      269. *The blood*] F1; *The best*
Walker.      *dearest-valued*] Theobald; no hyphen F1.

259. *fortune*] better fortune.

261–2. *Whoever . . . play'd*] Cf. the
proverb "Uncertain life, but certain
misery".

264. *li'es*] Fleay quoted many examples of dropped medial *v*. The only
probable example we know for *lives*
(N.B. noun not verb as in *John*) is
in T. D.'s *Life of the Dutches of Suffolke*
(1631): "in your hands it lies, / Either
to comfort, or confound our liues"
(sig. E). Cf. IV. ii. 57, note.

266–73. *France . . . threats.*] Cf. W.
Clever's *Flower of Phisicke* (1590):
"There is a choller burning in itselfe,
and conuerted to ashes" (sig. H₂).
John says: "I am burned up with

inflaming choler (*wrath*, *rage*) which
can only be allayed (quelled) by
blood. [Here he remembers that *the
humours allay each other*, and adds] And
I don't mean the humour blood in my
own body, but the blood of France—
the blood of Philip." Cf. R. W.'s
*Tancred and Gismund* (ed. 1592): "this
heart hath felt the fire/That cannot els
be quencht but with his bloud" (sig.
E₄); *3 H 6*, II. i. 79–80; *Rom.*, I. i. 90–1.

267. *condition*] quality.

272. *jeopardy*] Derived by Wright
from French "jeu parti", a game
where the risk was evenly divided—
a sense which would connect with
ll. 261–2.

## SCENE II.—[*Plains near Angiers.*]

*Alarums, excursions. Enter the* BASTARD, *with* AUSTRIA'S *head.*

*Bast.* Now, by my life, this day grows wondrous hot;
Some airy devil hovers in the sky,
And pours down mischief. Austria's head lie there,

*Enter* KING JOHN, ARTHUR, *and* HUBERT.

While Philip breathes.
*K. John.* Hubert, keep this boy. Philip, make up:          5
My mother is assailed in our tent,
And ta'en, I fear.
*Bast.*                    My lord, I rescued her;
Her highness is in safety, fear you not:
But on, my liege; for very little pains          9
Will bring this labour to an happy end.          [*Exeunt.*

*Scene* II

Scene II.] Scaena Secunda. F1; III. Pope; IV. Hanmer; *Act* III *Scene* I. Donovan.
Plains . . . Angiers.] Malone; om. F1.          S.D.] Allarums, Excursions: Enter
Bastard with Austria's head. F1.          4. S.D.] Enter Iohn, Arthur, Hubert. F1;
after *breathes* l. 4 Capell.          5. *Hubert*] F1; *There* Hubert Pope; Here, *Hubert*
Keightley.          *keep*] F1; *keep thou* Tyrwhitt.          10. S.D.] Rowe; Exit. F1.

S.D. *Austria's* head.] A head was a
stock property owned by most companies. In the *T.R.* Philip, having
won Austria's lion's-skin, presents this
to Blanche, who commands him "To
weare the same as earst thy Father
did" (1. iv. 46); and perhaps Philip
ought to wear it in the rest of *John.* In
*The Famous History of* . . . *Fauconbridge*
Richard's bastard son wears the lion's-
skin in honour of his father (cf. Introduction, p. xxiii).

2–3. *Some* . . . *mischief.*] "i.e. A thun-
derstorm threatens. According to the
demonologists there were devils of air,
fire, water, and earth . . . those of the
air being specially responsible for tem-
pests and thunderstorms" (Wilson).
But the tense of the verb is queer. Perhaps Shakespeare means: "this *battle*
grows wondrous *fierce*; some *invisible*
devil is pouring down (providing) *hard
fighting*". With *pours down* cf. IV. ii. 109,

and *LLL*.: "Thus pour the stars down
plagues for perjury" (v. ii. 395); for
*day* = battle, cf. II. i. 314, 393; v. iii. 1,
etc.

4. *breathes*] recovers his breath (cf.
*1 H 4*, I. iii. 102).

5. *make up*] advance, hurry to the
fore.

6–7. *My* . . . *her;*] A curious conflation. Arthur was captured at Mirabeau while besieging Eleanor, who
was in a tower when the town fell to
John (Hol., 164). The tower becomes a
tent, and Faulconbridge, not John,
gets the credit for the rescue (one of
John's most determined exploits).

7. *ta'en, I fear.*] Shakespeare felt unsure about facts, and pretended that
his character was unsure. Holinshed
(164, ii) mentions that the authorities
disagreed whether Eleanor was captured or only besieged. Cf. II. ii. 14,
IV. ii. 123–4, V. iii. 3, V. vi. 23, notes.

*Alarums, excursions, retreat. Re-enter* KING JOHN, ARTHUR, *the*
BASTARD, HUBERT, *with* ELEANOR *and Lords.*

*K. John.* [*To Eleanor.*] So shall it be; your grace shall   [Sc. iii]
    stay behind
So strongly guarded. [*To Arthur.*] Cousin, look not sad:
Thy grandam loves thee; and thy uncle will
As dear be to thee as thy father was.
*Arth.*  O, this will make my mother die with grief!        15 [5]
*K. John.* [*To the Bastard.*] Cousin, away for England! haste
    before:
And, ere our coming, see thou shake the bags
Of hoarding abbots; imprison'd angels
Set at liberty: the fat ribs of peace
Must by the hungry now be fed upon:                          20 [10]
Use our commission in his utmost force.
*Bast.*  Bell, book, and candle shall not drive me back
    When gold and silver becks me to come on:
I leave your highness. Grandam, I will pray—
If ever I remember to be holy—                               25 [15]
For your fair safety; so, I kiss your hand.
*Elea.*  Farewell, gentle cousin.

11.] F1; *Scene* IV. Pope; V. Hanmer; III. Capell; *Act* III *Scene* I. Donovan.
11. S.D.] This ed.; Alarums, excursions, Retreat. Enter Iohn, Eleanor, Arthur,
Bastard, Hubert, Lords. F1.     S.D. [To Eleanor.] Hanmer; om. F1.     12. *So*]
F1; *More* Lettsom conj.; *And* Sisson.    12. S.D.] Pope; om. F1.    16. S.D.] Pope;
om. F1.    18–19. *imprison'd . . . liberty*] F1; *set at liberty Imprison'd angels* Walker
conj.    20. *now*] F1; *War* Warburton conj.    21. *his*] F1; *its* Rowe.    22–3.
*back/ . . . on:*] This ed.; *back,/ . . . on.* F1.    27. *gentle*] F1; *my gentle* Pope.

12. *So*] Eleanor may have asked for
a specific number of men, cf. l. 80
below (Marshall).

17. *shake the bags*] "Shake-bag" was
cant for thief, scoundrel (cf. *O.E.D.*
and the character "Shakebag" in
*Arden of Feversham*). John's order is to
*ruffianize it* among the abbots; the
word implies consciousness of wrong-
doing (cf. III. iii. 175, note).

18. *angels*] The usual pun; cf. II. i.
590, note.

20. *hungry*] Malone compared *Psalms*,
cvii, *Luke*, 1. 53.

22. *Bell . . . candle*] "A form of excommunication ending with the
words, 'Do to (close) the book, quench
the candle, ring the bell!' " (Tilley,
p. 42).

24. *I . . . highness.*] The F1 stop after
*on* may mean that this line should follow quickly, to imply "When gold
beckons me—I leave your highness"
(spoken facetiously, viz. *commodity* before loyalty).

26. *so . . . hand.*] It is not likely
that Faulconbridge, contemptuous of
formalities, would kiss the queen's
hand. He only says "I take my leave"
in the "I kiss your feet, your humble
servant" jargon. Cf. I. i. 154–6, 240,
notes.

*K. John.*                    Coz, farewell.    [*Exit Bastard.*
*Elea.* Come hither, little kinsman; hark, a word.
                              [*She takes Arthur aside.*
*K. John.* Come hither, Hubert. O my gentle Hubert,
        We owe thee much! within this wall of flesh        30 [20]
        There is a soul counts thee her creditor,
        And with advantage means to pay thy love:
        And, my good friend, thy voluntary oath
        Lives in this bosom, dearly cherished.
        Give me thy hand. I had a thing to say,           35 [25]
        But I will fit it with some better tune.
        By heaven, Hubert, I am almost asham'd
        To say what good respect I have of thee.
*Hub.* I am much bounden to your majesty.
*K. John.* Good friend, thou hast no cause to say so yet, 40 [30]
        But thou shalt have; and creep time ne'er so slow,
        Yet it shall come for me to do thee good.
        I had a thing to say, but let it go:
        The sun is in the heaven, and the proud day,

27. S.D.] Pope; om. F1.    28 S.D.] Malone; om. F1.    36. *tune*] F1; *time*
Pope.    37. *I am*] F1; *I'm* Pope.    40. *so yet,*] F1; *so—yet—* Pope.

28. *hither*] here. Regular for "to this place" in 1590.

30. *We . . . much*] Referring to Hubert's service in bringing about the Lewis-Blanche match (Wilson). But the usefulness of the match has gone: Hubert's support of John in the last battle is probably meant (cf. l. 33 n.).

30-1. *within . . . creditor*] "intended to recall the part which the First Citizen [Hubert], the soul within the walls of Angiers, had played while the two kings stood disputing without" (Wilson, p. xlvii). The commoner phrasing was "these walls of flesh" (plural); cf. *Tit.*, IV. ii. 99, *R 2*, III. ii. 167, Glapthorne's *Ladies Priviledge* (1640), sig. H₃ᵛ.

32. *advantage*] = interest; opportunity (cf. III. iii. 151).

33. *voluntary oath*] Cf. Intro., p. xli.
35. *hand*] Cf. III. i. 118, note.
35-6. *I . . . tune*] Cecropia similarly

manipulated her temptations in Sidney's *Arcadia* (1590): "I had a thing to say to you, but it is no matter . . . [she] staied indeede, thinking *Philoclea* would have had a female inquisitivenesse of the matter" (p. 377).

36. *tune*] Pope's *time* could easily be misread as *tune*, would agree with *time* (l. 41) and John's next speech. But *tune* (= style, *O.E.D.* tune, 4) is here idiomatic, as in *Mac.*, "the self-same tune and words" (I. iii. 88), *Ado*, "do you speak in the sick tune?" (III. iv. 42). Read: "But I will adorn my words (or, fit my purposes) when I can say it in better style (i.e. not only speak, but give)."

39. *much bounden*] greatly indebted. A frequent phrase in epistles dedicatory (archaic).

41-2. *and . . . come*] and however slowly time creeps forward, my *opportunity* shall come.

Attended with the pleasures of the world,  45 [35]
Is all too wanton and too full of gauds
To give me audience: if the midnight bell
Did, with his iron tongue and brazen mouth,
Sound on into the drowsy race of night;
If this same were a churchyard where we stand,  50 [40]
And thou possessed with a thousand wrongs;
Or if that surly spirit, melancholy,
Had bak'd thy blood and made it heavy, thick,
Which else runs tickling up and down the veins,
Making that idiot, laughter, keep men's eyes  55 [45]
And strain their cheeks to idle merriment,
A passion hateful to my purposes;
Or if that thou couldst see me without eyes,

---

49. *on into*] F1; *One unto* Theobald; *one into* Variorum 1821; *On! into* Delius conj.
*race*] F1; *ear* Collier conj.; *face* Sisson.     53. *heavy, thick,*] F1; hyphened Pope.
54. *tickling*] F1; *trickling* Rowe.

46. *gauds*] showy ornaments (Steevens); "gaudy spring" was a poetic
cliché.
48. *iron tongue*] Cf. *M.N.D.*, v. i. 372.
*brazen*] "used with a sub-reference
to its metaphorical sense of shameless,
unabashed" (Deighton).
49. *on*] F1 *on* could = "on" or "one".
To an Elizabethan 1 a.m. could be
midnight: cf. *Ham.*, I. i. 39 and I. ii.
198; *John a Kent*: "The houre is one at
midnight" (M.S.R., l. 298). Malone
compared the *one-on* quibble in *Gent.*,
II. i. 1–2. But here *on* is surely the primary sense, even if confusion was possible.
*race*] "course" is the usual gloss.
Keightley[*Shakespeare-Expositor* (1867),
p. 223] compared Spenser's Night,
who must "run her timely race"
(*F.Q.*, I. v. 44). Spenser had helped to
familiarize the cliché *drowsy night*.—
Sisson thinks the *r* in *race* may be a
broken *f*. Both *face* and *ear* agree with
the face-images of the speech. But *race*
may = huge compass (derivation unknown) as in "whom hell it selfe com-
plaines to keep within her race" [*Rare
Triumphes of Loue and Fortune* (1589),

sig. A₂]. Read: "If, at dead of night,
the passing-bell were sounding on and
on into the drowsy, vast stillness of the
night".
51. *possessed*] "wholly taken up with
. . . with an allusion to the 'possession'
of a man by an evil spirit" (Deighton).
52. *melancholy*] ill-temper, sullen-
ness. Melancholy was thought due to
the thickening of the blood, and *vice
versa* as here.
54. *tickling*] tingling; tickling to
laughter. So in *The Returne of the Renowned Caualiero Pasquill* (1589): "I
needed no Minstrill to make me mer-
rie, my hart tickled of it selfe" (sig.
C₂ᵛ); Furness noted the same pun in
Spenser's *Muiopotmos* (1590).
55. *idiot, laughter*] Cf. Dekker, *Old
Fortunatus*: "cheekes, / Wrinckled with
Idiot laughter" (III. i).
56. *strain*] stretch; constrain.
57. *passion*] emotion.
58–61. *Or . . . words;*] So in Mas-
singer's *Duke of Milan*: "O you
Powers, / That can convey our
thoughts to one another / Without
the aid of eyes or ears, assist me"
(v. i).

Hear me without thine ears, and make reply
Without a tongue, using conceit alone,                    60 [50]
Without eyes, ears, and harmful sound of words;
Then, in despite of brooded watchful day,
I would into thy bosom pour my thoughts:
But, ah, I will not. Yet I love thee well;
And, by my troth, I think thou lov'st me well.            65 [55]

*Hub.*  So well, that what you bid me undertake,
Though that my death were adjunct to my act,
By heaven, I would do it.

*K. John.*                    Do not I know thou wouldst?
Good Hubert, Hubert, Hubert, throw thine eye
On yon young boy; I'll tell thee what, my friend, 70 [60]
He is a very serpent in my way;
And wheresoe'er this foot of mine doth tread,
He lies before me: dost thou understand me?
Thou art his keeper.

*Hub.*                    And I'll keep him so
That he shall not offend your majesty.                    75 [65]

*K. John.*  Death.

*Hub.*                    My lord?

*K. John.*                              A grave.

*Hub.*                                        He shall not live.

*K. John.*                                                  Enough.
I could be merry now. Hubert, I love thee.
Well, I'll not say what I intend for thee:

---

62. *brooded*] F1; *broad-ey'd* Pope.      68. *I would do it*] F1; *I'd do't* Theobald.
75-6. *That . . . Death.*] One line Walker conj.      76. *Death . . . Enough.*] One line
Steevens; separate lines F1.      *lord?*] Rowe; *Lord.* F1.

---

60. *conceit*] conception, thought,
imagination.

62. *brooded*] brooding. The sense, not
the form, has puzzled edd. The vigi-
lance of brooding birds was Steevens's
explanation (comparing *L'Allegro*:
"Where brooding Darkness spreads
his jealous wings"): *young Arthur* might
be thought as defenceless as a chick.
The night-death-thick blood, day-life-
fresh blood contrasts make the word
effective.

71. *He . . . way*] Carter compared

*Genesis*, xlix. 17: "Dan shall be a serpent by the way".

76. *Death.*] In Holinshed John gives
way to his counsellors, but Shakespeare makes him alone responsible
for the idea of murder.

*My lord?*] Cf. IV. ii. 230.

77. *I . . . thee.*] Other villains expressed love of their "tools" thus; cf.
*The Alchemist*: "*Lungs*, my *Lungs!* / I
loue thee." (II. iii); *The Revengers Tragædie* (1607): "Thou art a pretious
fellow, faith I loue thee" (II. ii).

Remember.—Madam, fare you well:
I'll send those powers o'er to your majesty.          80 [70]
*Elea.* My blessing go with thee!
*K. John.*                      For England, cousin, go:
Hubert shall be your man, attend on you
With all true duty. On toward Calais, ho!          [*Exeunt.*

SCENE III.—[*The French King's Pavilion.*]   [Sc. iv]

*Enter* KING PHILIP, LEWIS, PANDULPH, *and Attendants.*

*K. Phi.* So, by a roaring tempest on the flood,
A whole armado of convicted sail
Is scatter'd and disjoin'd from fellowship.
*Pand.* Courage and comfort! all shall yet go well.
*K. Phi.* What can go well, when we have run so ill?          5
Are we not beaten? Is not Angiers lost?
Arthur ta'en prisoner? divers dear friends slain?
And bloody England into England gone,
O'erbearing interruption, spite of France?
*Lew.* What he hath won, that hath he fortified:          10
So hot a speed with such advice dispos'd,
Such temperate order in so fierce a cause,

82. *attend*] F1; *to attend* F3.     83. *Calais*] Rowe iii; Callice F1.

*Scene* III

*Scene* III.] F1; V. Pope; VI. Hanmer; IV. Capell; II. Donovan.     The . . .
Pavilion.] As Malone; om. F1; the *French* Court. Theobald.     S.D.] Enter
France, Dolphin, Pandulpho, Attendants. F1.     2. *armado*] F1; *Armada*
Theobald iii.     *convicted*] F1; *collected* Pope; *conjuncted* Maxwell conj. (*N. & Q.*,
28 Oct. 1950).     12. *cause*] F1; *course* Hanmer.

   1. *flood*] open sea.
   2. *armado*] More common than the
form"armada" in 1590; cf. Armado in
*LLL.*
   *convicted*] "defeated" (usual gloss).
We prefer the Cowden Clarkes' "condemned, doomed to perdition". The
1588 Armada was smitten by a tempest, popularly believed (in England)
the work of God, who had doomed the
foes of the true faith. The *T.R.* echo
bears this out: "Thus hath the God of

Kings with conquering arme / Dis-
pearst the foes to true succession" (1.
vii. 1–2).
   5. *run*] "a double meaning, *run our
course* and *run away*" (Smith).
   11–12. *So . . . cause*] As *such advice dispos'd* goes with *Such temperate order*, *So
hot a speed* would go with *so fierce a
course*. But *cause* (= dispute, quarrel)
often quibbles on *course*: cf. v. ii. 30,
and *Alchemist*, III. i ("The *sanctified
cause* / Should haue a *sanctified course*").

>       Doth want example: who hath read or heard
>       Of any kindred action like to this?
> *K. Phi.* Well could I bear that England had this praise      15
>       So we could find some pattern of our shame.

*Enter* CONSTANCE.

>       Look, who comes here! a grave unto a soul;
>       Holding th' eternal spirit, against her will,
>       In the vild prison of afflicted breath.
>       I prithee, lady, go away with me.                       20
> *Const.* Lo! now—now see the issue of your peace!
> *K. Phi.* Patience, good lady! comfort, gentle Constance!
> *Const.* No!—I defy all counsel, all redress,
>       But that which ends all counsel, true redress:
>       Death! death, O amiable, lovely death!                  25
>       Thou odoriferous stench! sound rottenness!
>       Arise forth from the couch of lasting night,

14. *kindred action*] Theobald; hyphened F1.      17. S.D.] F1; Enter Lady *Constance*, her Hair dishevel'd. Capell; after l. 19 Dyce.      17. *here!*] F1 (*heere?*).
18. *spirit*] F1; *sprite* Fleay.      21. *Lo! now—now*] This ed.; *Lo; now: now* F1; *Lo, now! now* Capell.      24–5. *redress:/Death! death,*] As Pope; *Redresse:/Death, death,* F1; *redress,/Death, Death;* Theobald, edd.

16. *pattern*] example.

17–19. *Look . . . breath.*] Some take *spirit = soul*, with *her* alluding to *soul*. We take *eternal spirit =* the Holy Ghost, held in Constance's soul, which is held in the vile body of her afflicted life (= *breath*). Cf. note on *1 Corinthians*, xv. 45 in an old Bible: "Christ is called a Spirite . . . Adam is called a liuing soule, by reason of the soule which is the best part in him." Note how *spirit* mediates between *soul* and *breath* (cf. I. i. 17, III. i. 154, III. iii. 146, etc.).

19. *vild prison*] body (popular cliché). Cf. *Tarltons Newes* (1590): "After thy breath hath left thy bodye, and thy soule is set free from this vile prison of earth" (p. 4); *Celestina* (1596): "the poore soule which must . . . passe out of his vile prison" (p. 203).

23. *defy*] renounce, disdain.

25–36. *Death . . . me!*] Cf. *Rom.*, III. ii. 73–85 for the style, IV. v. 35–40 for

the imagery. Apostrophe of Death was a popular poetic figure, cf. Harington's *Orlando Furioso* (1591): "Come death & close mine eyes, & stop my breath" (Bk xxxiii, st. 58).

25. *lovely*] Could mean "amorous" (cf. *Shr.*, III. ii. 126).

27. *Arise . . . night*] Cf. *Zepheria* (1594): "From forth dead sleep of everlasting dark; / Fame, with her trump's shrill summon, hath awaked / The Roman Naso" [ed. Arber (1904), p. 155]. A *couch* is any place of rest: here *lasting night* is the couch. Shakespeare means Hell, where Death is at rest since he cannot function. *Everlasting night* was the more usual cliché—as in *Soliman and Perseda* (Death says) "I will not downe to euerlasting night / Till I haue moralliz'd this Tragedie" (Kyd, p. 165); "To send them down to euerlasting night" (Kyd, p. 220). Note the fitting

Thou hate and terror to prosperity,
And I will kiss thy detestable bones
And put my eyeballs in thy vaulty brows,　　　　　　30
And ring these fingers with thy household worms,
And stop this gap of breath with fulsome dust,
And be a carrion monster like thyself:
Come, grin on me, and I will think thou smil'st,
And buss thee as thy wife. Misery's love,　　　　　　35
O, come to me!

*K. Phi.*　　　　　　　O fair affliction, peace!
*Const.* No, no, I will not, having breath to cry:
O, that my tongue were in the thunder's mouth!
Then with a passion would I shake the world;
And rouse from sleep that fell anatomy　　　　　　40
Which cannot hear a lady's feeble voice,
Which scorns a modern invocation.

*Pand.* Lady, you utter madness, and not sorrow.
*Const.* Thou art holy to belie me so!—
I am not mad: this hair I tear is mine;　　　　　　45

---

34. *smil'st*] F1; *smilest* Cambridge.　　35. *buss*] F1; *kiss* Pope.　　42. *modern*] F1; *mother's* Heath.　　44. *holy*] F1; *not holy* F4; *unholy* Variorum 1773; *too holy* Maxwell conj. (*N. & Q.*, 28 Oct. 1950).

---

cumbrousness of *forth from* instead of the usual *from forth*.

28. *prosperity*] Carter compared *Ecclesiasticus*: "O Death, how bitter is the remembrance of thee to a man that ... hathe prosperitie" (xli. 1); cf. *Job*: "in his prosperitie the destroyer shal come vpon him" (xv. 21).

32. *stop*] stop up.
*fulsome*] nauseous.

34. *grin . . . smil'st*] A *grin* is fixed, showing the teeth; a *smile* vivacious, with the play of the features.

35. *buss*] kiss wantonly.

39. *shake the world*] "The sorowes of the graue haue compassed me about: the snares of death ouertooke me. (But) in my trouble did I call vpon the Lorde.... Then the earth trembled ... the mountaines moued and shooke, because he was angry. . . . The Lorde also thundred in the heauen" (*Psalms*, xviii. 5–13).

40. *fell anatomy*] fierce, cruel skeleton.

42. *modern*] trite, ordinary [Steevens, citing "wise saws and modern instances" (*A.Y.L.*, II. vii. 156)].

*invocation*] supplication; incantation (*O.E.D.* 1, 2).

44. *holy*] Constance's venom needs a disrupted line. Read: "You are a good churchman (but inhuman) to tell this lie about me (viz. to pretend I am mad, therefore not responsible for my unchristian wish): Preach (l. 51) some philosophy to make (= render; prove) me mad and you will be made a saint." Suicides were rejected by the Church, but madness took away responsibility for oneself; *holy* and *canonis'd* thus go together (ll. 44, 52).

45–8. *I . . . mad:*] J. C. Bucknill [*Mad Folk of Shakespeare* (1867), p. 281] compared *Tw.N.*, IV. iii. 1, *Oth.*, II. iii. 118.

My name is Constance; I was Geoffrey's wife;
Young Arthur is my son, and he is lost!
I am not mad: I would to heaven I were!
For then 'tis like I should forget myself:
O, if I could, what grief should I forget!          50
Preach some philosophy to make me mad,
And thou shalt be canoniz'd, cardinal;
For, being not mad but sensible of grief,
My reasonable part produces reason
How I may be deliver'd of these woes,              55
And teaches me to kill or hang myself:
If I were mad, I should forget my son,
Or madly think a babe of clouts were he.
I am not mad; too well, too well I feel
The different plague of each calamity.              60
*K. Phi.* Bind up those tresses. O, what love I note
In the fair multitude of those her hairs!
Where but by chance a silver drop hath fall'n,
Even to that drop ten thousand wiry friends
Do glue themselves in sociable grief,              65
Like true, inseparable, faithful loves,
Sticking together in calamity.
*Const.* To England, if you will.
*K. Phi.*                    Bind up your hairs.
*Const.* Yes, that I will; and wherefore will I do it?

64. *friends*] Rowe iii; *fiends* F1.    68.] F1; [Giving some of her hairs to the wind. Rann.

48–9. *I . . . myself:*] Tilley (p. 229) quoted the proverb "He is a Fool that forgets himself."

53. *sensible*] capable.

55. *deliver'd of*] "= delivered from" (Wilson). But cf. ll. 93–8, where *Grief* is a child-substitute. Constance described Death as a lover (ll. 25–36, 40) and now talks of giving birth to (being *deliver'd of*) her Grief-child; the *babe of clouts* (l. 58) also belonging to this madly sane sequence. Cf. *R 2*, ii. ii. 62 ("midwife to my woe").

58. *babe of clouts*] "rag doll" (usual gloss). But "(person) of clouts" was an idiom for "inferior (person)": cf.

*Mother Bombie*: "I had as liefe haue one [a husband] of clouts" (Lyly, iii, 224); *Rare Triumphes of Loue and Fortune* (1589): "a maister of clowtes" (sig. C₃). Shakespeare may intend the figurative sense too, for in ll. 93–8 Grief becomes the inferior substitute.

64. *wiry*] "strong, and with a reference to the likeness between hair and wire" (Deighton); "wire" was a popular metaphor for hair (cf. Sonnet 130).

68. *To . . . will.*] Cf. Introduction, p. xli.

69. *Yes . . . will;*] "(You will not do a little thing like invade England to please me but) I will bind up my hair to

I tore them from their bonds and cried aloud,                    70
"O that these hands could so redeem my son,
As they have given these hairs their liberty!"
But now I envy at their liberty,
And will again commit them to their bonds,
Because my poor child is a prisoner.                              75
And, father cardinal, I have heard you say
That we shall see and know our friends in heaven:
If that be true, I shall see my boy again;
For since the birth of Cain, the first male child,
To him that did but yesterday suspire,                           80
There was not such a gracious creature born.
But now will canker-sorrow eat my bud
And chase the native beauty from his cheek
And he will look as hollow as a ghost,
As dim and meagre as an ague's fit,                              85
And so he'll die; and, rising so again,
When I shall meet him in the court of heaven
I shall not know him: therefore never, never
Must I behold my pretty Arthur more.
*Pand.* You hold too heinous a respect of grief.                90
*Const.* He talks to me that never had a son.
*K. Phi.* You are as fond of grief as of your child.

76. *And*] F1; *Oh* Pope.    78. *true*] F1; om. Pope.    *I shall*] F1; *I'll* Walker conj.
79. *male child*] Pope; hyphened F1.    81. *born*] F1 (*borne*).    85. *ague's fit*] As
F1; *ague-fit* Dyce ii.

please you"; "*I* will" resumes "*you will*", bracketing an invasion of England and the tying of her hair as equally simple.

76. *And*] i.e. "As for you (I have not finished with you yet)". Having insulted Philip obliquely (ll. 68–75), she turns on Pandulph again to condemn his mad philosophy.

77. *see . . . heaven*] The Anglican Church also accepted this doctrine, but it was disputed: cf. P. S., *Christal Glasse for Christian Women* (1591), sig. C^v ff.

78. *If . . . again;*] Constance makes the popular objection that our friends may change after we knew them (ll.

82–6), that sight and normal powers of recognition are not enough, but that sight without recognition is valueless.

80. *suspire*] breathe.

81. *gracious*] godly, holy.

83. *native*] natural.

88–9. *never . . . more*] Instead of *pretty Arthur* she will see a *hollow ghost* which she will not recognize. Cf. Marlowe's *Edward the Second* (1594): "I shall neuer see / My louely *Pierce*, my *Gaueston* againe" (sig. F₃).

90. *heinous*] wicked; terrible.

91. *He . . . son.*] Cf. *3 H 6*, v. v. 63, *Mac.*, IV. iii. 216 (Tilley, p. 99).

92. *fond of*] foolishly tender (about); eager for, desirous of.

*Const.* Grief fills the room up of my absent child,
    Lies in his bed, walks up and down with me,
    Puts on his pretty looks, repeats his words,             95
    Remembers me of all his gracious parts,
    Stuffs out his vacant garments with his form;
    Then have I reason to be fond of grief?
    Fare you well: had you such a loss as I
    I could give better comfort than you do.            100
    I will not keep this form upon my head,
    When there is such disorder in my wit.
    O Lord! my boy, my Arthur, my fair son!
    My life, my joy, my food, my all the world!     104
    My widow-comfort, and my sorrows' cure!      *[Exit.*
*K. Phi.* I fear some outrage, and I'll follow her.     *[Exit.*
*Lew.* There's nothing in this world can make me joy:
    Life is as tedious as a twice-told tale
    Vexing the dull ear of a drowsy man;
    And bitter shame hath spoil'd the sweet word's taste, 110

---

98. *grief?*] F1; *Grief.* Rowe.     101.] F1; [Tearing off her head-cloaths. Pope;
[Dishevelling her hair. Dyce ii.     105. *sorrows'*] F1 (*sorrowes*).     107.] F1;
*Scene* VI. Pope; VII. Hanmer.     110. *word's*] F1; *world's* Pope.

93. *Grief . . . child,*] Malone compared "Perfruitur lachrymis, et amat *pro conjuge luctum. Lucan.* lib. ix."

93–100. *Grief . . . do.*] Some edd. think Shakespeare remembers the death of his son Hamnet (*ob.* 1596).

98. *grief?*] ? often = ! in F1; but frenzied Constance loves to triumph in her logic, and a question here withers all retort.

101–2. *form . . . disorder*] Cf. III. i. 179, which suggests that *form* here = order, not a head-dress; i.e. Constance again disorders her hair.

104. *My . . . world!*] The four metaphors of this line were familiar from love-poetry. In II. ii. 53–4 Constance also applied a courtly lover's comparisons to her son. This suggests that a particular fixation was meant.

108. *Life . . . tale*] Malone compared *Psalms,* xc. 9, *Mac.,* v. v. 24–8; Noble added *Wisdom,* ii. 1 ("Our life is short and tedious"); cf. *Ecclesiasticus,* xxii

("6. A tale out of time is as musicke in mourning: but wisedome knoweth the seasons of correction and doctrine. 7. Who so teacheth a foole, is as one that . . . waketh one that sleepeth. . . . 10. Who so telleth a foole of wisdome, is as a man which speaketh to one that is asleepe"). Cf. IV. ii. 18–20, where *time unseasonable* appears too.

110. *word's*] "The *sweet word* is *life*" (Malone). Dyce called this "sheer foolishness", and Pope's *world's* has stood. But if *sweet word's taste* = enjoyment of (the praise of) one's achievements [sweet word(s) = praise, flattery was common] then F1 means: Hearing his life-story told a second time (looking back after having lived it) *his very successes* are his bitterest shames when he recalls that he has now failed so miserably. See also G. Baldini, *Letterature Moderne,* II (1951), 555–60.

That it yields nought but shame and bitterness.
*Pand.*  Before the curing of a strong disease,
Even in the instant of repair and health,
The fit is strongest; evils that take leave,
On their departure most of all show evil.                    115
What have you lost by losing of this day?
*Lew.*  All days of glory, joy and happiness.
*Pand.*  If you had won it, certainly you had.
No, no; when fortune means to men most good
She looks upon them with a threat'ning eye.                  120
'Tis strange to think how much King John hath lost
In this which he accounts so clearly won:
Are not you griev'd that Arthur is his prisoner?
*Lew.*  As heartily as he is glad he hath him.
*Pand.*  Your mind is all as youthful as your blood.        125
Now hear me speak with a prophetic spirit;
For even the breath of what I mean to speak
Shall blow each dust, each straw, each little rub,
Out of the path which shall directly lead
Thy foot to England's throne; and therefore mark.           130
John hath seiz'd Arthur; and it cannot be
That, whiles warm life plays in that infant's veins,
The misplac'd John should entertain an hour,
One minute, nay, one quiet breath of rest.
A sceptre snatch'd with an unruly hand                       135
Must be as boisterously maintain'd as gain'd;

---

133. *misplac'd John*] *mis-plac'd*-Iohn F1.        *an*] F1; *one* Collier ii (MS.).        134.
*One*] F1; *A* Rowe.

---

112–15. *Before . . . evil.*] "This passage unquestionably refers to the medical doctrine of crises which was universally prevalent" [Bucknill, *Medical
Knowledge of Shakespeare* (1860), p. 134].

114–15. *evils . . . evil*] Shakespeare
follows the proverbs grouped together
by Tilley (p. 28) as "When Bale is
highest boot is next."

119–20. *No . . . eye.*] For the "false
Fortune's frown" *sententia* cf. *Pilgr.*:
"Whilst as fickle Fortune smil'd / Thou
and I were both beguil'd" (Sonnets,
vi), *Troil.*, I. iii. 22–8.

128. *dust*] grain of dust.

*rub*] In bowls, an obstacle hindering
the bowl's course; hence, obstacle.

135–8. *A . . . up*] J. W. Cunliffe [*Influence of Seneca* (1893)] compared *Hercules Furens*: "rapta sed trepida manu /
sceptra obtinentur. omnis in ferro est
salus. / quod ciuibus tenere te inuitis
scias, / strictus tuetur ensis. alieno in
loco / haut stabile regnum est" (ll.
345–9). Here (said Cunliffe) *obtinentur*
= *servantur* = Shakespeare's *maintain'd*. Perhaps *haut stabile* led Shakespeare to the biblical parallel (cf.
l. 137, note).

136. *boisterously*] violently, roughly.

And he that stands upon a slipp'ry place
Makes nice of no vild hold to stay him up:
That John may stand, then, Arthur needs must fall;
So be it, for it cannot but be so.                                    140
*Lew.* But what shall I gain by young Arthur's fall?
*Pand.* You, in the right of Lady Blanche your wife,
May then make all the claim that Arthur did.
*Lew.* And lose it, life and all, as Arthur did.
*Pand.* How green you are and fresh in this old world!      145
John lays you plots; the times conspire with you;
For he that steeps his safety in true blood
Shall find but bloody safety and untrue.
This act so evilly borne shall cool the hearts
Of all his people, and freeze up their zeal,                      150
That none so small advantage shall step forth
To check his reign, but they will cherish it;
No natural exhalation in the sky,
No scope of nature, no distemper'd day,
No common wind, no customed event,                             155
But they will pluck away his natural cause
And call them meteors, prodigies and signs,
Abortives, presages, and tongues of heaven,
Plainly denouncing vengeance upon John.

---

146. *you plots*] F1; *your plots* Malone conj.      152. *reign*] F1; *rein* Capell conj.
154. *scope*] F1; *scape* Pope.      156. *his*] F1; *its* Pope.

137. *slipp'ry place*] "Surely thou hast set them [the wicked] in slipperie places, (and) castest them downe into desolation. 19. Howe suddenly are they destroyed, perished (and) horribly consumed" (*Psalms*, lxxiii).

138. *Makes . . . up:*] Is not fussy how vilely he supports himself.

140. *So be it*] Amen. In the Genevan Bible *amen* is always *so be it*, also in some catechisms etc. Pandulph thus pretends submission to Providence (i.e. his *prophetic spirit*, i.e. Church interests).

146. *lays you plots*] Ethic dative. "To lay a plot for" could = teach, prescribe a course for, as in P. Barrough's *Methode of Phisicke* (1583), epistle to Burghley: "[I would be a fool] to lay

a plot for your Honor, from whence you may deriue an example of gouernment". The sense *teach* goes with *green* (l. 145), and *plots* (= traps, schemes) with *conspire*.

147–8. *For . . . untrue*] Noble compared *Genesis*, ix. 5, 6 ("Whoso shedeth mans blood, by man shall his blood be shed . . .").

149. *borne*] A quibble on *born* (having such an evil birth) and *borne* (carried out): cf. *Mac.*, III. vi. 3.

151. *advantage*] opportunity.

153. *exhalation*] meteor.

154. *scope*] "circumstance within the limits of nature's operations" (Wright).

158. *Abortives*] Abortions of nature.

*Lew.*  Maybe he will not touch young Arthur's life,          160
　　But hold himself safe in his prisonment.
*Pand.*  O, sir, when he shall hear of your approacn,
　　If that young Arthur be not gone already,
　　Even at that news he dies; and then the hearts
　　Of all his people shall revolt from him,          165
　　And kiss the lips of unacquainted change,
　　And pick strong matter of revolt and wrath
　　Out of the bloody fingers' ends of John.
　　Methinks I see this hurly all on foot:
　　And, O, what better matter breeds for you          170
　　Than I have nam'd! The bastard Faulconbridge
　　Is now in England ransacking the church,
　　Offending charity: if but a dozen French
　　Were there in arms, they would be as a call
　　To train ten thousand English to their side,          175

170-1. *O, . . . The*] As F1; *O!—what . . . nam'd—the* Maxwell conj. (*N. & Q.*, 28 Oct. 1950).          173. *a dozen*] F1; *twelve* Pope.

164-8. *and . . . John.*] "To pick out of (one's own) fingers' ends" = to use one's mother-wit about [cf. *Gammer Gurton's Needle*: "I picke not this geare, hearst thou, out of my fingers endes; / But he that hard it told me" (v. ii); *Greenes Newes* (1593) by B. R.: "my wife . . . had picked out at her fingers endes the whole drift of my pretence" (sig. F₃)]. Shakespeare departs from this use. Perhaps he knew the *Heroicall Devises* of C. Paradin (1591; S.R. Aug. 1590) in which a full-page picture of a hand with needles under the finger-nails and blood streaming forth is explained: When Dionysius the Tyrant was expelled, his daughters were ravished, then put to death "by driuing sharpe needles, or pinnes vnder the nayles of their fingers" (p. 126). Shakespeare has a tyrant-revolt context, alters a set phrase, and ll. 166, 167-8 seem to follow Paradin.
166. *And . . . change*] As in the parallel of IV. ii. 5-8 revolt is "stain", here it is "rape" (equivalent images: Introduction, p. lxii); *unacquainted change* (l. 166) = *long'd-for change* (IV. ii. 8).

The subaudition is "Ravish the lips of virgin change".
167. *matter*] corrupt matter, pus; argument. Cf. IV. i. 64, v. ii. 85.
169. *hurly*] tumult.
170-1. *O . . . The*] Maxwell wants *what* subject and *better matter* object of *breeds*, not intransitive *breeds* [N.B. Cf. Jonson's *Alchemist*: "No clime breeds better matter" (Prologue)].
173. *charity*] good-will (I. John). Or perhaps alluding to the Roman Catholic cry that closing the monasteries ends all charity. Onions quoted E. K. (gloss on Spenser) that "sweete Saint Charitee" was "the Catholiques comen othe".
174. *call*] decoy. Birds were often caught by placing a decoy in a net, then imitating their calls.
175. *train*] "attract, draw on" (usual gloss). The verb was influenced by the substantive *train* = treachery, guile, trap. After *call* this suggests "a decoy to trap 10,000 English into treachery": Shakespeare's comment is there behind Pandulph's words (cf. notes on III. ii. 17, v. i. 20, v. vii. 46).

Or as a little snow, tumbled about,
Anon becomes a mountain. O noble Dolphin,
Go with me to the king: 'tis wonderful
What may be wrought out of their discontent,
Now that their souls are topful of offence.        180
For England go; I will whet on the king.

*Lew.*  Strong reasons makes strange actions. Let us go:
If you say ay, the king will not say no.        [*Exeunt.*

---

177. *O*] F1; om. Pope.        179–80. *discontent, . . . offence.*] As Knight; *discontent,
. . . offence*, F1; *Discontent. . . . Offence*, Rowe.        182. *makes*] F1; *make* Capell.
*strange*] F1; *strong* F2, edd.

---

176–7. *Or . . . mountain.*] "*Bacon*, in
his history of *Henry* VII. speaking of
*Perkin's* march, observes, that *their*
snow-ball *did not gather as it rolled*"
(Johnson). So in Savile's *Tacitus*
(1591): "vindex first stirred the stone,
which rowling along tumbled Nero
out of his seate" (p. 7). A commonplace.

177. *Anon*] Immediately.
180. *topful*] brimful; cf. *Mac.*, I. v. 43.
*offence*] John's offence, or their own

offending thoughts. Intentional ambiguity (cf. l. 175).

182. *strange*] Cf. the last speeches of
Acts I and II: that strong motives de-
flect us into strange courses is a basic
theme in *John*. The strangeness (foolishness) of invading England emerges
in II. i. 23–30, III. iii. 1–3, 68, v. vii.
112–18. *Strong reasons* causing strange
action reappear in IV. ii. 40–1.

*actions*] deeds; military engage-
ments.

# ACT IV

SCENE I.—[*A Room in a Castle. Coals burning in a brazier.*]

*Enter* HUBERT *and Executioners.*

*Hub.* Heat me these irons hot; and look thou stand
    Within the arras: when I strike my foot
    Upon the bosom of the ground, rush forth
    And bind the boy which you shall find with me
    Fast to the chair. Be heedful: hence, and watch.     5
*First Exec.* I hope your warrant will bear out the deed.
*Hub.* Uncleanly scruples! fear not you; look to't.
                     [*The Executioners withdraw.*
    Young lad, come forth; I have to say with you.

*Enter* ARTHUR.

ACT IV
*Scene* 1

*Act* IV *Scene* I.] F1; *Act* III *Scene* III. Donovan.     A . . . Castle.] Staunton; om.
F1.     Coals . . . brazier.] Wilson; om. F1.     S.D.] F1; . . . two *Attendants.*
Malone, edd.     6. First Exec.] Cambridge; Exec. F1.     7. *scruples! fear not
you;*] Rowe iii; *scruples feare not you:* F1.     7. S.D.] This ed.; om. F1; Exeunt
*Attendants.* Malone.

*Scene*] Various locations have
been proposed—Northampton (Capell), Dover (Halliwell), Canterbury
(White), Tower of London (Wilson).
But Shakespeare probably gave no
thought to this.—For the source of the
scene cf. Appendix A (2).

S.D. Executioners] "tormentors" in
Holinshed (p. 165). *John* and *T.R.*
assign the "execution" to Hubert;
*T.R.* calls Hubert's helpers *Attendants*
(i. xii. 12), but Shakespeare's "Executioners" suggests their role in Holinshed.

1. *irons*] Cf. iv. i. 39, 59, 61, 67, 74,
81, 119, 124. Shakespeare uses *iron* =

(*a*) iron metal, (*b*) searing-iron. Two
searing-irons are needed.

3. *bosom*] Cf. v. ii. 28, iii. i. 171–2.

7. *Uncleanly*] Improper.—Smith
read F1 as "Let no unbecoming
scruples frighten you". Or we might
read: "Uncleanly scruples! fear not!
(*To the last speaker*).—You: look to't.
(*To the other two*)." *T.R.* has three attendants.

S.D.] The illustration in Theobald ii shows why the *exit* could be
omitted. The irons are heated on-
stage. And the man behind the *arras*
(curtain to the inner stage) could be
visible watching, not really "off".

89

*Arth.* Good morrow, Hubert.
*Hub.*                          Good morrow, little prince.
*Arth.* As little prince, having so great a title          10
    To be more prince, as may be.—You are sad.
*Hub.* Indeed, I have been merrier.
*Arth.*                          Mercy on me!
    Methinks nobody should be sad but I:
    Yet, I remember, when I was in France,
    Young gentlemen would be as sad as night,          15
    Only for wantonness. By my christendom,
    So I were out of prison and kept sheep,
    I should be as merry as the day is long;
    And so I would be here, but that I doubt
    My uncle practises more harm to me.          20
    He is afraid of me and I of him:
    Is it my fault that I was Geoffrey's son?
    No, indeed, is't not; and I would to heaven
    I were your son, so you would love me, Hubert.
*Hub.* [*Aside.*] If I talk to him, with his innocent prate          25
    He will awake my mercy, which lies dead:
    Therefore I will be sudden and dispatch.
*Arth.* Are you sick, Hubert? you look pale to-day.
    In sooth, I would you were a little sick,
    That I might sit all night and watch with you:          30

18. *be as*] F1; *be* Pope.     23. *No*] F1; om. Pope.     *is't*] F1; *it's* F2.     25. S.D.]
Rowe; om. F1.

9. *Good morrow*] Good morning. *T.R.*
makes the time *euening* (1. xii. 14). The
sad, long night (IV. i. 15, 30, 45–7) is
not only a symbol of darkness (blindness). It is early morning; Arthur perhaps enters in his night-shirt from bed,
returning back to bed at the end (IV. i.
129, note).
  10–11. *As . . . be*] "Considering my
great title . . . I am at present as little a
prince as may be" (I. John). Or:
"True, I am a little prince—in so far as
anyone having so great a claim to be a
great prince may be 'little prince'"
(quibbling on physical and feudal
stature).

  15. *Young gentlemen*] Holinshed more
than once calls Arthur a "yoong gentleman" (p. 165); Shakespeare means
"young gentlemen such as I".
  16. *for wantonness*] through a whim-
sical affectation.
  *By my christendom*] "= *As I am a
Christian!*" (*O.E.D.*). Malone took
*christendom* = baptism, as in *All's W.*,
1. i. 190.
  17. *kept sheep*] Cf. *3 H 6*, II. v.
1–54.
  18. *as . . . long*] A proverb; so *Ado*, II.
i. 52 (Tilley, p. 140).
  19. *doubt*] fear.
  25. *prate*] prattle.

I warrant I love you more than you do me.

*Hub.* [*Aside.*]  His words do take possession of my bosom.
Read here, young Arthur.                    [*Showing a paper.*
         [*Aside.*]  How now, foolish rheum!
Turning dispiteous torture out of door!
I must be brief, lest resolution drop                    35
Out at mine eyes in tender womanish tears.—
Can you not read it? is it not fair writ?

*Arth.*  Too fairly, Hubert, for so foul effect:
Must you with hot irons burn out both mine eyes?

*Hub.*  Young boy, I must.

*Arth.*                    And will you?

*Hub.*                              And I will.    40

*Arth.*  Have you the heart? When your head did but ache,
I knit my handkercher about your brows,
The best I had, a princess wrought it me,
And I did never ask it you again;
And with my hand at midnight held your head,                    45
And, like the watchful minutes to the hour,
Still and anon cheer'd up the heavy time,
Saying, "What lack you?" and "Where lies your grief?"
Or "What good love may I perform for you?"

---

31. *do*] F1; om. Vaughan conj.    32. S.D.] Capell; om. F1.    33. S.D.
[Showing a paper.] As Rowe iii; om. F1.    S.D. [Aside.] Rowe iii; om. F1.
33–4. *rheum!* . . . *door!*] F1 (*rheume?* . . . *doore?*).    37. *fair*] F1; *fairly* Keightley.
39. *hot*] F1; om. Pope.

31. *I warrant*] Cf. l. 6, John's murderous warrant.

32. *bosom*] Cf. l. 3: Arthur's words strike into Hubert's bosom.

33. *rheum*] Arthur's words take *room* in Hubert's bosom (l. 32), so that no *room* for the idea of torture remains (l. 34). The quibble on *rheum* (= tears) supports the conceit.

33–4. *rheum!* . . . *door!* F1 *?* may = *!* or *?* in both cases.

34. *dispiteous*] merciless.

37. *fair writ*] "clearly written"; or "clear writing".

38. *effect*] meaning, purpose.

42. *knit*] tied. As Arthur speaks Hubert's *brows* are probably *knit*.

The image plays on the blinding-theme.

43. *wrought*] embroidered.

46. *watchful . . . hour*] "the minutes that watch the progress of the hour" (On.). But this may be a parenthood image (cf. ll. 24, 50): *midnight* and *watchful* resume III. ii. 47, 62, and minutes-hour may resume *brooded* (III. ii. 62, note), viz. minutes = the brood or chicks of the hen-hour.

47. *Still and anon*] Continually.

48. *Where . . . grief?*] A set phrase; cf. *If You Know Not Me* (1605): "*Winch*: Oh, I am sicke. / *Con.* Where lyes your greife?" (sig. F₄).

49. *love*] loving deed.

Many a poor man's son would have lien still          50
And ne'er have spoke a loving word to you;
But you at your sick-service had a prince.
Nay, you may think my love was crafty love,
And call it cunning: do, and if you will.
If heaven be pleas'd that you must use me ill,          55
Why then you must. Will you put out mine eyes?
These eyes that never did nor never shall
So much as frown on you.

*Hub.*                    I have sworn to do it;
And with hot irons must I burn them out.

*Arth.* Ah, none but in this iron age would do it!          60
The iron of itself, though heat red-hot,
Approaching near these eyes, would drink my tears
And quench this fiery indignation
Even in the matter of mine innocence;
Nay, after that, consume away in rust,          65
But for containing fire to harm mine eye.
Are you more stubborn-hard than hammer'd iron?
And if an angel should have come to me

---

52. *sick-service*] Delius; no hyphen F1.     58. *I have*] F1; *I've* Pope.     63. *this*] F1; *his* Capell, edd.     64. *matter*] F1; *water* W.W. (*Parthenon*, 16 Aug. 1862). 66. *eye*] F1; *eyes* Dyce ii.     67. *stubborn-hard*] Theobald ii; no hyphen F1.

---

55–6. *If . . . must*] Tilley (p. 486) quoted the proverb "What Must be must be", and *Rom.*, iv. i. 21.

60. *this iron age*] this cruel world. As metals were thought to degenerate (from gold to silver to iron etc.) so the one-time "golden age" had coarsened. A traditional phrase. Cf. iii. i. 5, note.

61. *The iron*] That an inanimate weapon could be more humane than its wielder was a popular conceit: "Seemed, the senselesse yron did feare, / Or to wrong holy eld did forbeare" (Spenser's *Shepheardes Calender*).

*heat*] heated.

63. *this fiery indignation*] "the indignation *thus* produced by the iron being made red-hot for such an inhuman purpose" (Malone); or *indignation* may simply = wrath (as in ii. i. 212).

Walker thought that *this* and *his* were often confused in Shakespeare, citing this line and v. ii. 145 in *John*.

64. *matter*] substance; exudation. H. Constable's *Diana* contains a curious parallel: "Thyne eye a fire is both in heate and light, / Myne eye of teares a river doth become; / O that the matter of myne eye had might / To quench the flames that from thyne eye doe come" [*Harleian Miscellany*, ix (ed. 1812), p. 493, from an early MS. Instead of *matter* the printed text (1592) read *water*].

67. *hammer'd iron*] "iron beaten into strongest consistency by the hammer" (Deighton).

68. *angel*] "Sapience" was thought the essential quality of angels, who were also the announcers of decrees of the Deity.

And told me Hubert should put out mine eyes,
I would not have believ'd him,—no tongue          70
But Hubert's.
*Hub.*                Come forth!                    [*Stamps.*

*The Executioners come forth, with a cord, irons, etc.*

                        Do as I bid you do.
*Arth.* O, save me, Hubert, save me! my eyes are out
Even with the fierce looks of these bloody men.
*Hub.* Give me the iron, I say, and bind him here.
*Arth.* Alas, what need you be so boist'rous-rough?    75
I will not struggle, I will stand stone-still.
For heaven sake, Hubert, let me not be bound!
Nay, hear me, Hubert, drive these men away,
And I will sit as quiet as a lamb;
I will not stir, nor winch, nor speak a word,          80
Nor look upon the iron angerly:
Thrust but these men away, and I'll forgive you
Whatever torment you do put me to.
*Hub.* Go, stand within; let me alone with him.
*First Exec.* I am best pleas'd to be from such a deed.   85
                        [*Exeunt Executioners.*
*Arth.* Alas, I then have chid away my friend!
He hath a stern look, but a gentle heart:
Let him come back, that his compassion may
Give life to yours.
*Hub.*                Come, boy, prepare yourself.
*Arth.* Is there no remedy?

70–1. —*no . . . Hubert's.*] This ed.; *no tongue but* Huberts. F1; *a tongue but* Hubert's.
Pope; *no . . . Hubert's*— Steevens conj.    71. S.D.] This ed.; om. F1; Re-enter
*Officers* with a Cord, the Irons, *&c.* Capell, edd.    71. *do.*] F1; *do.* [Stamps, and
the men enter. Pope; om. Theobald ii.    75. *boist'rous-rough*] Theobald; no
hyphen F1.    77. *heaven sake*] F1; *heav'n's sake* Theobald ii, edd.    85. S.D.]
Cambridge; om. F1; Exit. Pope.

70–1. *no . . . Hubert's.*] i.e. I would
not have believed *any* tongue but
Hubert's; *no* is a double negative.

77. *heaven sake*] A distinct form; the
"s" of "heaven's" was dropped before
the following "s".

79. *as . . . lamb*] Pre-Shakespear-

ean proverb (Tilley, p. 366).

80. *winch*] Variant of *wince*, as in
*Ham.*, iii. ii. 256 (Q3).

81. *angerly*] angrily.

84. *let . . . him.*] "leave me to deal
with him alone" (Wright, comparing
*Tw.N.*, ii. iii. 146).

*Hub.*                           None, but to lose your eyes.          90
*Arth.* O heaven, that there were but a mote in yours,
        A grain, a dust, a gnat, a wandering hair,
        Any annoyance in that precious sense!
        Then, feeling what small things are boisterous there,
        Your vild intent must needs seem horrible.          95
*Hub.* Is this your promise? go to, hold your tongue.
*Arth.* Hubert, the utterance of a brace of tongues
        Must needs want pleading for a pair of eyes:
        Let me not hold my tongue, let me not, Hubert!
        Or, Hubert, if you will, cut out my tongue,          100
        So I may keep mine eyes: O, spare mine eyes,
        Though to no use but still to look on you!
        Lo, by my troth, the instrument is cold
        And would not harm me.
*Hub.*                           I can heat it, boy.
*Arth.* No, in good sooth; the fire is dead with grief,          105
        Being create for comfort, to be us'd
        In undeserv'd extremes; see else yourself:
        There is no malice in this burning coal;
        The breath of heaven hath blown his spirit out
        And strew'd repentant ashes on his head.          110

90. *to*] F1; om. Vaughan.       91. *mote*] F1 (*moth*).       108. *in this burning*] F1;
*burning in this* Z. Grey.       109, 110. *his*] F1; *its* Pope.

91. *mote*] Upton compared *Matthew*,
vii. 3. So *Luke*, vi. 41. Mote and moth
could stand for each other.

92. *A . . . hair*] Cf. III. iii. 128.
*a gnat*] Suggested by *moth* (l. 92), as
in *LLL.*, IV. iii. 161–6.

93. *precious sense*] Sight was thought
the principal sense; cf. III. i. 5, and
*LLL.*, V. ii. 446.

94. *boisterous*] intractable, hence irri-
tating.

97–8. *the . . . eyes:*] "the words used
by a pair of tongues must necessarily
plead inadequately for", or "the
words of a pair of tongues must needs
be used to plead when two eyes are at
stake" (the latter an appeal to "argue
it out between us").

99. *let me not*] (*a*) Repetition; (*b*)
= do not stop (*let*) me (pleading).

102. *Though . . . you!*] "I pray you
(said she) even by these dying eies of
mine (which are onely sorrie to dye,
because they shall lose your sight)"
(Sidney's *Arcadia*, p. 297).

105. *dead with grief*] Cf. l. 128, note
(the rumour that Arthur *died of grief*).

107. *In . . . extremes*] "In cruel deeds
which I have not deserved", with a
quibble on *in extremes* (Latin *in extre-
mis*) = in one's last agony (cf. *O.E.D.*,
extreme, 4, 2).

108. *malice*] power to harm.
*burning*] glowing.

109. *breath of heaven*] air; divine influence.

110. *repentant ashes*] Referring to the
ceremonial manner of Jewish repen-
tance (Carter, citing *Job*, xlii. 6, etc.).
Deighton compared *R 2*, v. i. 46–9.

*Hub.* But with my breath I can revive it, boy.

*Arth.* And if you do, you will but make it blush
  And glow with shame of your proceedings, Hubert:
  Nay, it perchance will sparkle in your eyes;
  And, like a dog that is compell'd to fight,   115
  Snatch at his master that doth tarre him on.
  All things that you should use to do me wrong
  Deny their office: only you do lack
  That mercy which fierce fire and iron extends—
  Creatures of note for mercy lacking uses!   120

*Hub.* Well, see to live; I will not touch thine eye
  For all the treasure that thine uncle owes:
  Yet am I sworn and I did purpose, boy,
  With this same very iron to burn them out.

*Arth.* O, now you look like Hubert! all this while  125
  You were disguis'd.

*Hub.*       Peace; no more. Adieu.
  Your uncle must not know but you are dead.
  I'll fill these dogged spies with false reports:
  And, pretty child, sleep doubtless and secure

---

119. *extends*] F1; *extend* Pope.  120. *mercy lacking*] This ed.; *mercy, lacking* F1;
hyphened Pope, edd.  121. *eye*] F1; *eyes* ed. 1735.  122. *owes*] F1; *owns* Pope.
126. *disguis'd*] F1; *disguisèd* Dyce.

114. *sparkle in*] send out sparks into.

115–16. *And . . . on.*] Tilley (p. 419) quoted the proverb "A Man may cause his own dog to bite him", comparing *2 H 6*, v. i. 151–2, *H 5*, II. ii. 83.

116. *Snatch*] Snap, bite.

*tarre*] urge; so *Ham.*, II. ii. 379.

118. *office*] proper function.

120. *Creatures . . . uses!*] Creatures = anything created, animate or inanimate. Pope rounds off a sense already clear (taking *uses* = customs). But F1 also means: "(How strange that) Creatures of note for mercy (such as Hubert) (should be) lacking in their ability to use (mercy)!" (Cf. *O.E.D.*, use, 10b: "The power of using some faculty").

121. *Well, . . . live;*] "*Well*, take you thought how *to live*" (Capell). The idiom "See to do" puzzled some edd. in view of the blinding context.

*I . . . eye*] *LLL.*, IV. iii. 183–4 and many other rhymes show that, as now, *I* and *eye* were pronounced alike.

122. *owes*] owns. Also quibbling on "owes me" (cf. III. ii. 30–42, 78).

128. *dogged*] cruel; with play on "dogging" = hot on the trail.

*false reports*] "[Hubert] caused it to be bruted abroad through the countrie, that the kings commandement was fulfilled, and that Arthur also through sorrow and greefe was departed out of this life" (Hol., 165, ii).

129. *sleep*] May mean "*always* sleep", or "go back *now* to sleep" (cf. IV. i. 9, note).

*doubtless and secure*] "free from fear and care", or (in view of l. 131 *not*) "certain and assured".

That Hubert, for the wealth of all the world,          130
    Will not offend thee.

*Arth.*                  O heaven! I thank you, Hubert.

*Hub.*  Silence; no more. Go closely in with me:
    Much danger do I undergo for thee.          [*Exeunt.*


### SCENE II.—[*The Court of England.*]

*Enter* KING JOHN, PEMBROKE, SALISBURY, *and other Lords.*

*K. John.*  Here once again we sit, once again crown'd,
    And look'd upon, I hope, with cheerful eyes.

*Pem.*  This "once again", but that your highness pleas'd,
    Was once superfluous: you were crown'd before,
    And that high royalty was ne'er pluck'd off,          5
    The faiths of men ne'er stained with revolt;
    Fresh expectation troubled not the land
    With any long'd-for change or better state.

*Sal.*  Therefore, to be possess'd with double pomp,
    To guard a title that was rich before,          10
    To gild refined gold, to paint the lily,

*Scene* II

*Scene* II] F1; *Act* IV *Scene* I. Donovan.    The . . . England.] Pope; om. F1.
S.D.] Enter Iohn, Pembroke, Salisbury, and other Lordes. F1; King *John* upon
his Throne, . . . discovered. Kemble.    1. *again*] F3; *against* F1.    8. *long'd-
for change*] *long'd-for-change* F1.    10. *guard*] F1; *gard* Halliwell.

132. *closely*] secretly.

*Scene* II

1. *again*] Yet *against* (as in F1) was a
variant of *again* (*O.E.D.*, against, C).

2. *cheerful eyes*] Dramatic irony after
IV. i.

4. *superfluous*] Shakespeare may recall M. Paris: "Reuersus itaque Cantuariam Rex cum Regina sua . . .
coronati sunt ambo ibidem, vbi
Archiepiscopus Cantuariensis copiosas
eis, ne dicam superfluas, ministrauit
expensas" (p. 275).

*crown'd before*] This is John's *fourth*
coronation (Z. Grey).

8. *long'd-for change*] Cf. III. iii. 166,
note.

9. *pomp*] ceremony.

10. *guard*] ornament a garment with
trimming [a sense continued in *rich* =
splendid (of dress)]; defend.

11. *gild . . . gold*] To "gild gold" was
a common phrase, as in Sidney's *Arcadia*, p. 467.

11–12. *lily . . . violet*] These flowers
were associated for their opposite
qualities: "let lillies wither on the
stalke and weare violets in thy hand,
the one faire and vnsauory, the other
blacke but of sweete verdure" [R.
Greene, *Ciceronis Amor* (1589), sig. G₁].
Note the climax: (*a*) from part-perfect
to wholly perfect (gold has to be refined, the lily and violet are only half-
perfect); (*b*) motion upwards [gold

To throw a perfume on the violet,
To smooth the ice, or add another hue
Unto the rainbow, or with taper-light
To seek the beauteous eye of heaven to garnish,          15
Is wasteful and ridiculous excess.

*Pem.* But that your royal pleasure must be done,
This act is as an ancient tale new told,
And, in the last repeating, troublesome,
Being urged at a time unseasonable.                      20

*Sal.* In this the antique and well-noted face
Of plain old form is much disfigured;
And, like a shifted wind unto a sail,
It makes the course of thoughts to fetch about,
Startles and frights consideration,                      25
Makes sound opinion sick and truth suspected,
For putting on so new a fashion'd robe.

*Pem.* When workmen strive to do better than well
They do confound their skill in covetousness;
And oftentimes excusing of a fault                       30

26. *suspected*] F1; *suspect* Anon. conj. *ap.* Cambridge.          29. *covetousness*] F1;
*covetize* Capell conj.

within the earth (cf. III. i. 5, note),
flowers and ice (on the earth's surface),
rainbow, sun].

14–16. *or . . . excess*] Edd. compared
"to burn daylight" (*Rom.*, I. iv. 43,
*Wiv.*, II. i. 54) = to do the superfluous.
Tilley (p. 641) quoted the proverb
"To set forth the Sun with a candle
(taper)". Perhaps also a glance at
primitive eclipse ritual: "the Ro-
MAINES beganne to make a noyse
with basons and pannes . . . to call her
[the moon] againe, and to make her
come to her light, lifting vp many
torches lighted" [Plutarch's *Lives* (ed.
1595), p. 270]. John fears an eclipse o.
himself.

15. *eye*] Cf. III. i. 5, IV. ii. 2, notes.
18–19. *This . . . troublesome*] Cf. III.
iii. 108, note.
21. *well-noted*] familiar; much observed.
22. *form*] order (cf. III. i. 179, III. iii.
101–2).

*disfigured*] *disfigur'd* would read
better.

23–4. *like . . . about*] Cf. *Ephesians*, iv.
14: "wauering and caryed about with
euerie winde of doctrine".

24. *fetch about*] change their tack.

26. *sick . . . suspected*] A natural transition, since houses with the plague were
"suspected places".

27. *robe*] See l. 10, note. The attack
on ceremony inevitably veers to "vest-
ment", the deepest issue. J. W. Allen
[*History of Political Thought in the 16th
Century* (1941), p. 213] showed why
Elizabeth's government regarded an
attack on ceremony as one on royal
supremacy. John's nobles here indirectly attack *his* supremacy.

28–9. *When . . . covetousness*] Malone
compared *Lr.*, I. iv. 371, Sonnet 103.
"Confound" = mingle indistinguish-
ably; waste, consume; destroy. Alluding to the proverb "He that coveteth
all, loseth all."

Doth make the fault the worse by th' excuse:
As patches set upon a little breach
Discredit more in hiding of the fault
Than did the fault before it was so patch'd.

*Sal.* To this effect, before you were new crown'd,                35
We breath'd our counsel: but it pleas'd your highness
To overbear it, and we are all well pleas'd,
Since all and every part of what we would
Doth make a stand at what your highness will.

*K. John.* Some reasons of this double coronation                40
I have possess'd you with, and think them strong;
And more, more strong than lesser is my fear,
I shall indue you with: meantime but ask
What you would have reform'd that is not well,
And well shall you perceive how willingly                        45
I will both hear and grant you your requests.

*Pem.* Then I, as one that am the tongue of these,
To sound the purposes of all their hearts,
Both for myself and them, but, chief of all,
Your safety, for the which, myself and them,                     50

---

31. *worse*] F1; *worser* Maxwell conj. (*N. & Q.*, 28 Oct. 1950).    37. *it*] F1;
'*t* Anon. conj. *ap.* Cambridge.    *we are*] F1; *we're* Pope.    42. *than*] F1 (*then*);
*when* Tyrwhitt, edd.    50. *safety, . . . which, . . . them,*] This ed.; *safety: . . .
which, . . . them* F1.    *them*] F1; *they* Pope.

---

32-4. *As . . . patch'd.*] "no man
pieceth an olde garment with a piece
of newe clothe: for that that shuld fil it
vp, taketh awaye from the garment,
and the breache is worse" (*Matthew*,
ix. 16; cf. *Mark*, ii. 21, *Luke*, v. 36) [G.
Colton, *Shakspeare and the Bible* (1888),
p. 38]. Genevan bibles note that the
example refers to a *ceremony*.

33. *fault*] defect.

37. *we . . . pleas'd*] "Salisbury concludes politely . . . the nobles are well
pleased since their will must corre-
spond with his" (Wilson, taking *make
a stand at* (l. 39) = pause, stop short
at).—Or is Salisbury ironic ["make
a stand at" = conflict with (*O.E.D.*,
stand, 4)]?

39. *will*] wishes; commands.

42. *than lesser*] "reasons stronger

than my fear is less, or as strong as my
fear is little . . . comparing the degree
of two things . . . entirely different in
kind" (White). In F1 *then* often =
"than".

43. *indue*] supply.

48. *sound . . . purposes*] "express . . .
proposals", or "proclaim (as with a
trumpet) . . . intentions". The alter-
natives in IV. ii. 10, 37-9, 48, 63 rise
to barely concealed threatening.

49-50. *but . . . safety*] "The F. pauses
before and after these words give them
a sinister emphasis that is almost a
threat" (Wilson).

50. *them*] Condemned as ungram-
matical. But if *them* stands for "they"
(whether due to repetition of l. 49, or
the form *them(selves)* after *myself*), we
expect "our", not *their*, in l. 51. If *my-*

Bend their best studies, heartily request
Th' enfranchisement of Arthur: whose restraint
Doth move the murmuring lips of discontent
To break into this dangerous argument:
If what in rest you have in right you hold,                    55
Why then your fears, which, as they say, attend
The steps of wrong, should move you to mew up
Your tender kinsman, and to choke his days
With barbarous ignorance, and deny his youth
The rich advantage of good exercise?                    60
That the time's enemies may not have this
To grace occasions, let it be our suit
That you have bid us ask his liberty;
Which for our goods we do no further ask
Than whereupon our weal, on you depending,                    65
Counts it your weal he have his liberty.

*Enter* HUBERT.

55. *rest*] F1; *wrest* Steevens conj.    56–7. *then . . . should*] F1; *shou'd . . . then* Pope.
63. *ask*] F1; *ask,* Rowe iii.    64. *goods*] F1; *good* Pope.    *further*] F1; *farther*
Collier.    67. S.D.] As F1; after l. 67 Johnson, edd.

*self* and *them* are governed by *for* we
can assume a subject "They" for
*Bend* (l. 51), suggested by *these, their,*
*them, them* (ll. 47–50). The subject *I*
(l. 47) of *request* (l. 51) would thus be
further obscured, but l. 50, with the
subject-confusion of l. 51, then emphasizes the identity of interests that is
Pembroke's theme (as in iv. ii. 64–6).

51. *Bend . . . studies*] "direct their (or
our) best efforts" (Smith).

55. *rest*] Steevens' *wrest* = an act of
seizure or violence. Wright thought *in*
*rest* = "in quiet possession". Both have
found backers and critics.—We think
*rest* = the (not uncommon) aphetic
form of "arrest". But cf. p. 152, l. 12.

56–7. *then . . . should*] Pope's transposition is needless: the syntax is correct for an indirect question (Wright).

57. *move*] Perhaps the *v* was dropped
to pronounce *mo'e* (cf. iii. i. 264, note),
playing on *mo'e* and *mew*—John's
fears *force* him to use *force* against

Arthur (they are in a similar position).

*mew up*] coop up, imprison.

60. *exercise*] Not only martial exercise, but the practice of all gentlemanly
qualities. Edd. compare *AYL.*, i. i. 5–
22, 72–80.

62. *grace occasions*] take the stigma
from attack, or fault-finding.

62–3. *suit . . . liberty*] Cf. Introduction, p. xiii. "The custom of asking
and granting *suits* at these seasons [i.e.
coronations], was once general"
(Capell).

63. *That . . . ask*] Ambiguous: "let
his liberty be the suit *which* you have
told us to ask", or "let it be our suit
*that* (it may be given out that) *you* asked
us to ask for his liberty."

64. *our goods*] our own good.

65. *whereupon*] in so far as.

67. S.D.] John grants the suit as
soon as Hubert's entry assures him
Arthur is dead. To bring on Hubert
later than F1 changes John's tac-

*K. John.*  Let it be so: I do commit his youth
        To your direction. Hubert, what news with you?
                                                [*Taking him apart.*
*Pem.*  This is the man should do the bloody deed:
        He show'd his warrant to a friend of mine.                70
        The image of a wicked heinous fault
        Lives in his eye; that close aspect of his
        Do show the mood of a much troubled breast;
        And I do fearfully believe 'tis done,
        What we so fear'd he had a charge to do.                   75
*Sal.*  The colour of the king doth come and go
        Between his purpose and his conscience,
        Like heralds 'twixt two dreadful battles set:
        His passion is so ripe, it needs must break.
*Pem.*  And when it breaks, I fear will issue thence               80
        The foul corruption of a sweet child's death.
*K. John.*  We cannot hold mortality's strong hand:
        Good lords, although my will to give is living,
        The suit which you demand is gone and dead:
        He tells us Arthur is deceas'd to-night.                   85

68. S.D.] Capell; om. F1.    73. *Do*] F1; *Does* F4; *Doth* Dyce.    78. *set*] F1; *sent* Theobald.

tical surrender into mere weakness.
  *it be so*] Cf. III. iii. 140.
  71. *heinous fault*] monstrous offence.
A common tag (cf. *Faerie Queene*, III.
viii. 36).
  76. *The . . . go*] In the old *King Leir*
(1605) Ragan, reading a letter, is thus
described: "See how her colour comes
and goes agayne, / Now red as scarlet,
now as pale as ash:" (sig. E^v).
  78. *heralds*] Wilson thought the
coloured coats of heralds are meant.
—John's alternate paleness and red-
ness declare his *purpose* (to kill Arthur)
and his (regard for the dictates of)
*conscience* (to refrain)—as heralds
come and go to declare the wishes of
two powers ready to fight.
  *set*] Edd. now take with *battles* (=
armies in battle array). White insisted
that *"coming and going*, could not be
compared to any thing *set*". But *set*

may = stationed to perform duties
(*O.E.D.*, set, 45; as *set sentries*), referring to *function*, not *place*.
  79–81. *His . . . death.*] "the rancor
which king Henrie the sonne had conceiued . . . was so ripened, that it
could not but burst out . . . the sooner
to powre out his poison which he had
sucked before" (Holinshed, life of
Henry II, 86, i). The impostume
image recurs in l. 101.
  82. *We . . . hand:*] Cf. the cliché "to
shake hands with death" = to die
(*O.E.D.*, shake, 9a; *3 H 6*, I. iv. 102).
He means (*a*) We (the king) cannot
save anyone from Death; (*b*) We (man-
kind) cannot hold Death's hand (without dying, i.e. we must all die). Cf.
v. ii. 22.
  84. *gone and dead*] "dead and gone"
was the cliché: cf. *1 H 6*, I. iv. 93,
*2 H 6*, II. iii. 37, *Ham.*, IV. v. 29.

*Sal.* Indeed we fear'd his sickness was past cure.

*Pem.* Indeed we heard how near his death he was,
 Before the child himself felt he was sick:
 This must be answer'd, either here or hence.

*K. John.* Why do you bend such solemn brows on me?  90
 Think you I bear the shears of destiny?
 Have I commandment on the pulse of life?

*Sal.* It is apparent foul-play; and 'tis shame
 That greatness should so grossly offer it:
 So thrive it in your game! and so, farewell.  95

*Pem.* Stay yet, Lord Salisbury; I'll go with thee,
 And find th' inheritance of this poor child,
 His little kingdom of a forced grave.
 That blood which ow'd the breadth of all this isle
 Three foot of it doth hold: bad world the while!  100
 This must not be thus borne: this will break out
 To all our sorrows, and ere long I doubt.  [*Exeunt Lords.*

*K. John.* They burn in indignation. [*Enter a Messenger.*]
 I repent:
 There is no sure foundation set on blood,
 No certain life achiev'd by others' death.  105

---

99. *ow'd*] F1; *own'd* Pope.  102. S.D.] Capell; Exeunt F1.  103.] F1;
*Scene* III. Pope.  103-5. *They . . . death.*] F1; Aside. Rowe iii.  103. S.D.]
This ed.; Enter Mes. F1 (after *repent:*; after l. 105 Johnson, edd.).

---

89. *answer'd*] accounted or atoned for.

*here or hence*] on earth or in heaven; cf. III. i. 113, v. iv. 29.

91. *Think . . . destiny?*] Alluding to the Fates, i.e. Atropos, who cut the thread of life.

93. *apparent*] obvious.

94. *grossly offer*] plainly, flagrantly attempt or dare.

95. *So . . . game*] "*So thrive it* with you *in your game* as your game deserves" (Capell). Or perhaps: "May you have the like fortune."

98. *forced*] = (*a*) brought about by violent means; (*b*) artificially or carefully raised (of soils). Vaughan compared a similar use, referring to a tomb, in North's Plutarch.

99-100. *That . . . hold:*] Following

the conventionalized monarch's epitaph. Cf. that of Henry II: "And yet while all the earth could scarse my greedie mind suffice, / Eight foot within in the ground now serues, wherein my carcase lies" (Hol., 116, ii).

100. *bad . . . while!*] It's a bad world while such things are suffered. Cf. IV. iii. 116, *R 3*, III. vi. 10.

101. *break out*] Cf. l. 80.

103. S.D.] The F1 entrance can be defended: John does not dare to ask at once for more bad news.

*I repent*] Cf. note to IV. ii. 208-14. The line ("They are indignant *therefore* I repent") suggests that John repents his policy, not his crime; cf. IV. ii. 220, note.

104-5. *There . . . death.*] Cf. Appendix A, p. 166.

[*To the Messenger.*] A fearful eye thou hast: where is that
    blood
That I have seen inhabit in those cheeks?
So foul a sky clears not without a storm:
Pour down thy weather: how goes all in France?

*Mess.*  From France to England. Never such a power          110
    For any foreign preparation
Was levied in the body of a land.
The copy of your speed is learn'd by them;
For when you should be told they do prepare
The tidings comes that they are all arriv'd.          115

*K. John.*  O, where hath our intelligence been drunk?
    Where hath it slept? Where is my mother's care,
That such an army could be drawn in France,
And she not hear of it?

*Mess.*                                  My liege, her ear
Is stopp'd with dust: the first of April died          120
Your noble mother; and, as I hear, my lord,
The Lady Constance in a frenzy died
Three days before: but this from rumour's tongue
I idly heard; if true or false I know not.

*K. John.*  Withhold thy speed, dreadful occasion!          125
    O, make a league with me, till I have pleas'd
My discontented peers! What! mother dead!

---

106.] F1; *Scene* III. Kemble.    106. S.D.] As Rowe iii; om. F1.    110. *England.*]
Roderick, edd.; *England*, F1.    115. *comes*] F1; *come* F4, edd.    117. *care*] F1;
*ear* Walker conj. *ap.* Dyce.

109. *weather*] tempest.

110. *From . . . England.*] "All *in*
France goes *from* France *to* England"
(Roderick).

113. *copy*] example. Cf. Introduction, p. lxv.

116–17. *O, . . . slept?*] Malone compared *Mac.*: "Was the hope drunk, /
Wherein you dress'd yourself? hath it
slept since," (I. vii. 35–6).

116. *intelligence*] spies.

117. *care*] The first letter is broken in
F1. Some thought it an "e", but Furness showed that it was a "c".

119–20. *her . . . dust*] Death stopping

the ears of men is a biblical image.

120. *first of April*] Cf. Introduction,
p. xvii.

121–4. *and . . . not.*] She died three
*years* before (Constance in 1201,
Eleanor in 1204). Perhaps Shakespeare remembered that Constance
died three somethings before, and the
messenger's disclaimer (ll. 123–4) indicates *Shakespeare's* uncertainty: cf. III.
ii. 7, note.

124. *idly*] without paying proper
attention.

125. *occasion*] Cf. Introduction, p.
lxi.

> How wildly then walks my estate in France!
> Under whose conduct came those powers of
>      France
> That thou for truth giv'st out are landed here?            130
*Mess.*  Under the Dolphin.

*Enter the* BASTARD *and* PETER *of Pomfret.*

*K. John.*                    Thou hast made me giddy
>      With these ill tidings.—Now, what says the world
>      To your proceedings? do not seek to stuff
>      My head with more ill news, for it is full.
*Bast.*  But if you be afeard to hear the worst,            135
>      Then let the worst unheard fall on your head.
*K. John.*  Bear with me, cousin; for I was amaz'd
>      Under the tide: but now I breathe again
>      Aloft the flood, and can give audience
>      To any tongue, speak it of what it will.            140
*Bast.*  How I have sped among the clergymen
>      The sums I have collected shall express.
>      But as I travaill'd hither through the land
>      I find the people strangely fantasied;
>      Possess'd with rumours, full of idle dreams,            145
>      Not knowing what they fear, but full of fear.
>      And here's a prophet, that I brought with me
>      From forth the streets of Pomfret, whom I found

131. S.D.] As F1; after *tidings* l. 132 Johnson, edd.

128. *wildly*] chaotically
*walks*] proceeds (cf. I. i. 172, note).
131. S.D. Pomfret] Pontefract.
137. *amaz'd*] Cf. IV. iii. 140, note.
138. *Under the tide*] "Thy wrathful displeasure goeth ouer me: and the feare of thee hath vndonne me. They came rounde about me dayly lyke water: and compassed me tegeather on euery syde. My louers and frends hast thou put away fro me: and hyd mine acquaintance out of my sight" (*Psalms*, lxxxviii. 16–18, Book of Common Prayer); "all thy waues and thy

floods are gone ouer me" (*Psalms*, xlii. 7).
139. *Aloft*] Not used elsewhere by Shakespeare as a preposition.
141. *sped*] fared; succeeded; hastened.
143. *travaill'd*] Travel and travail were only differentiated after Shakespeare who here means *toiled* and *journeyed*.
144–5. *I . . . dreams*] Cf. Intro., p. xiv.
145. *idle dreams*] A cliché, as in *Faerie Queene*, I. i. 46, II. vi. 27, *Meas.*, IV. i. 65.
146. *Not . . . fear*] Cf. *Mac.*, IV. ii. 20.

With many hundreds treading on his heels;
To whom he sung, in rude harsh-sounding
   rhymes,                                                    150
That, ere the next Ascension-day at noon,
Your highness should deliver up your crown.
*K. John.* Thou idle dreamer, wherefore didst thou so?
*Peter.* Foreknowing that the truth will fall out so.
*K. John.* Hubert, away with him; imprison him:            155
And on that day at noon, whereon he says
I shall yield up my crown, let him be hang'd.
Deliver him to safety, and return,
For I must use thee.            [*Exit Hubert with Peter.*
        O my gentle cousin,
Hear'st thou the news abroad, who are arriv'd?            160
*Bast.* The French, my lord: men's mouths are full of it.
Besides, I met Lord Bigot and Lord Salisbury,
With eyes as red as new-enkindled fire,
And others more, going to seek the grave
Of Arthur, whom they say is kill'd to-night            165
On your suggestion.
*K. John.*            Gentle kinsman, go,
And thrust thyself into their companies.
I have a way to win their loves again;
Bring them before me.
*Bast.*            I will seek them out.
*K. John.* Nay, but make haste: the better foot before!            170

---

150. *harsh-sounding*] Pope; no hyphen F1.
om. F1.            165. *whom*] F1; *who* Pope.
Rowe iii; with l. 165 F1.

159. S.D.] Theobald (after l. 159);
166. *On . . . suggestion.*] New line

149. *on*] at.

150. *sung*] declared in verse (*O.E.D.*,
sing, 12). Shakespeare probably read
M. Paris on the Children's Crusade
(during John's reign): "Quidam enim
puer . . . per ciuitates vadens & castella
in regno Francorum, quasi a Domino
missus, cantillabat gallice modulando
. . . . sequebantur eum infiniti" (p.
324).

153. *dreamer*] A dreamer could be a
recognized prophet, as in B. & F.'s
*Women Pleased*: "Diviners, Dreamers,
Schoolemen, deep Magitians" (ed.

1647, p. 37); but John is contemptuous. H. F. Brooks refers me to *Caes.*:
"He is a dreamer; let us leave him:
pass." (I. ii. 24.)

158. *safety*] safe custody.

163. *With . . . fire*] Tilley (p. 214)
quoted the proverb "As red as
Fire".

165. *whom*] Confusion of construction with "whom they say (report)
killed".

170. *the . . . before*] Already proverbial (Tilley: p. 234) when used by
Shakespeare in *Tit.*, II. iii. 192.

O, let me have no subject enemies,
When adverse foreigners affright my towns
With dreadful pomp of stout invasion!
Be Mercury, set feathers to thy heels,
And fly like thought from them to me again.          175
*Bast.* The spirit of the time shall teach me speed.          [*Exit.*
*K. John.* Spoke like a sprightful noble gentleman.
Go after him; for he perhaps shall need
Some messenger betwixt me and the peers;
And be thou he.
*Mess.*                    With all my heart, my liege. [*Exit.* 180
*K. John.* My mother dead!

*Re-enter* HUBERT.

*Hub.* My lord, they say five moons were seen to-night:
Four fixed, and the fift did whirl about
The other four in wondrous motion.
*K. John.* Five moons?
*Hub.*                    Old men and beldams in the streets  185
Do prophesy upon it dangerously:
Young Arthur's death is common in their mouths:
And when they talk of him, they shake their heads
And whisper one another in the ear;
And he that speaks doth gripe the hearer's wrist,          190
Whilst he that hears makes fearful action,
With wrinkled brows, with nods, with rolling eyes.

171. *subject*] As F1; *subjects* F2.      180. S.D.] Rowe; om. F1.      182.] F1;
*Scene* IV. Pope.      182. S.D.] Re-enter Capell; Enter F1.

174. *Be Mercury*] E. I. Fripp [*Shake-speare Studies* (1930), p. 106] compared Ovid's *Metam.*, I. 671 ff.

175. *like thought*] "As swift as thought" was proverbial (Tilley, p. 663) as in *Lucr.*, l. 1216, *LLL.*, IV. iii. 330.

177. *sprightful*] spirited. Punning on l. 176 (*spright* being a contraction of *spirit*).

182. *five moons*] So Holinshed. (Appendix A, p. 152.)

183. *fift*] Common variant of *fifth*.

185–202. *Old...death.*] Shakespeare amplifies Holinshed's comment on Arthur's death "For the space of fifteene daies this rumour incessantlie ran through both the realmes of England and France" (165, ii).

185. *beldams*] grandmothers; hags.

186. *prophesy*] "used not so much in the sense of foretelling the future events predicted by this phenomenon as in that of commenting upon and expounding the phenomenon itself, making it the text of a dangerous discourse" (Wright).

I saw a smith stand with his hammer, thus,
The whilst his iron did on the anvil cool,
With open mouth swallowing a tailor's news;          195
Who, with his shears and measure in his hand,
Standing on slippers, which his nimble haste
Had falsely thrust upon contrary feet,
Told of a many thousand warlike French
That were embattailed and rank'd in Kent:           200
Another lean unwash'd artificer
Cuts off his tale and talks of Arthur's death.

*K. John.* Why seek'st thou to possess me with these fears?
Why urgest thou so oft young Arthur's death?
Thy hand hath murd'red him: I had a mighty cause 205
To wish him dead, but thou hadst none to kill him.

*Hub.* No had, my lord! why, did you not provoke me?

*K. John.* It is the curse of kings to be attended
By slaves that take their humours for a warrant
To break within the bloody house of life,           210
And on the winking of authority
To understand a law, to know the meaning
Of dangerous majesty, when perchance it frowns
More upon humour than advis'd respect.

*Hub.* Here is your hand and seal for what I did.     215

205. *I had*] F1; *I'd* Vaughan.    *a*] F1; om. Steevens.    *mighty*] F1; om. Pope.
207. *No had*] F1; *Had none* Rowe iii, edd.

197. *slippers*] "tailors generally work
barefooted" (Malone).
198. *contrary*] Accent on second
syllable.
200. *embattailed*] set in order of
battle.
203. *Why . . . fears?*] Cf. II. ii. 11–18.
207. *No had*] Arrowsmith (*ap.* Furness) showed that constructions such
as *No had?, No does?, No will?,* were
common, as in "the whole world
Yields not a workman that can frame
the like. *Fort.* No does?" (Dekker's
*Old Fortunatus,* II. i).
*provoke*] incite.
208. *It . . . to*] An idiom = Kings are
cursed (condemned) to.
208–14. *It . . . respect.*] Holinshed

says that Hubert did not murder
Arthur because he thought the command due to John's "heat and furie
. . . and that afterwards, vpon better
*aduisement,* he would both *repent* himselfe so to haue commanded, and giue
them small thanke that should see it
put in execution" (165, ii). Cf. IV. ii.
103.
212. *To*] Influenced by *To,* l. 210.
214. *humour*] moodiness. This follows Holinshed's hint of *heat and furie*
(cf. l. 208, note).
215. *Here . . . did.*] Cf. *R 2,* V. vi. 34 ff.
(Deighton). For the Davison allusion
cf. Introduction, p. xxviii; for the mur-
der-blinding confusion Appendix B,
p. 168.

*K. John.* O, when the last accompt 'twixt heaven and earth
  Is to be made, then shall this hand and seal
  Witness against us to damnation!
  How oft the sight of means to do ill deeds
  Make deeds ill done! Hadst not thou been by,   220
  A fellow by the hand of nature mark'd,
  Quoted and sign'd to do a deed of shame,
  This murther had not come into my mind;
  But taking note of thy abhorr'd aspect,
  Finding thee fit for bloody villainy,   225
  Apt, liable to be employ'd in danger,
  I faintly broke with thee of Arthur's death;
  And thou, to be endeared to a king,
  Made it no conscience to destroy a prince.
*Hub.* My lord—   230
*K. John.* Hadst thou but shook thy head or made a pause
  When I spake darkly what I purposed,
  Or turn'd an eye of doubt upon my face,
  As bid me tell my tale in express words,   234
  Deep shame had struck me dumb, made me break off,
  And those thy fears might have wrought fears in me:
  But thou didst understand me by my signs
  And didst in signs again parley with sin;

220. *Make*] F1; *Makes* Theobald, edd.  *deeds ill*] F1; *ill deeds* Capell conj. *Hadst*] F1; *for hadst* Pope; *Hadest* Capell.  229. *Made*] F1; *Mad'st* Pope. 230. *lord—*] Rowe iii; *Lord.* F1.  234. *As*] F1; *Or* Pope.  238. *sin*] F1; *sign* Collier MS.

216. *accompt*] account. This variant is used also in *Wint.*, II. iii. 197, *Mac.*, v. i. 42, etc.

220. *Make*] Plural influenced by *means*, *deeds*.

*ill done*] unskilfully performed. John equates the *evil deed* (l. 219) and *inefficient doing* to suggest that sin is intellectually untenable. He submits to accepted values since they pay best: cf. IV. ii. 103, v. vii. 82, notes, v. i. 5.

222. *Quoted*] Noted.

226. *liable*] fit.

227. *broke with*] confided to.

229. *conscience*] matter of conscience.

230. *My lord—*] Cf. III. ii. 76.

232–4. *darkly . . . express*] Cf. Introduction, p. xxix.

234. *As*] Which (Vaughan); Such as (Abbott, sect. 280).

238. *signs . . . sin*] *Sin* and *sign* were punned upon in Middleton's *Tricke to Catch the Old-One* (1608): "Henceforth for euer I defie, / The Glances of a sinnefull eye, / Wauing of Fans, which some suppose, / Tricks of Fancy, Treading of Toes, / . . . Taking false Phisicke, and nere start, / To be let blood, tho signe be at heart" (sig. H₃ᵛ). In Tourneur's *Revengers Tragædie* (1607) "sin" is spelt "signe" (sig. E₄ᵛ). Cf. *Paradise Lost*, II. 760.

Yea, without stop, didst let thy heart consent,
And consequently thy rude hand to act                    240
The deed, which both our tongues held vild to name.
Out of my sight, and never see me more!
My nobles leave me, and my state is brav'd,
Even at my gates, with ranks of foreign powers:
Nay, in the body of this fleshly land,                    245
This kingdom, this confine of blood and breath,
Hostility and civil tumult reigns
Between my conscience and my cousin's death.

*Hub.* Arm you against your other enemies,
I'll make a peace between your soul and you.            250
Young Arthur is alive: this hand of mine
Is yet a maiden and an innocent hand,
Not painted with the crimson spots of blood.
Within this bosom never ent'red yet
The dreadful motion of a murderous thought;            255
And you have slander'd nature in my form,
Which, howsoever rude exteriorly,
Is yet the cover of a fairer mind
Than to be butcher of an innocent child.

*K. John.* Doth Arthur live? O, haste thee to the peers,  260
Throw this report on their incensed rage,
And make them tame to their obedience!
Forgive the comment that my passion made
Upon thy feature; for my rage was blind,
And foul imaginary eyes of blood                        265
Presented thee more hideous than thou art.

---

247. *reigns*] F1; *reign* Hanmer.

240. *to*] Cf. Abbott, sect. 349 (*to* inserted after *let*). Vaughan thought *to* could = *too* here, which is more probable than Furness's "take the infinitive 'to act' as directly dependent on the verb 'consent'".

245. *fleshly land*] His own body.

246. *confine*] territory; prison.

247–8. *Hostility . . . death*] Cf. IV. ii. 76–8.

254–5. *Within . . . thought*] But cf. III. ii. 76, IV. i. 123.

255. *motion*] impulse, inclination.

261. *Throw*] i.e. as water, to quench their rage.

265–6. *And . . . art*] After l. 264 the foul *imaginary* (= imaginative) eyes seem to be John's. But as the foul blood which John had thought disfigured Arthur's eyes now turns out to be *imaginary* (= unreal), Arthur's eyes might be meant. And the *image* of the blinding is visible in Hubert's eye (IV. ii. 71), viz. Hubert's guilty eyes *reflecting* his crime might present him more hideous, etc. (Cf. *imaginary* in *O.E.D.*).

O, answer not, but to my closet bring
The angry lords with all expedient haste.
I conjure thee but slowly: run more fast!          [*Exeunt.*


SCENE III. —[*Before the Castle.*]

*Enter* ARTHUR, *on the walls.*

*Arth.* The wall is high, and yet will I leap down:
Good ground, be pitiful and hurt me not!
There's few or none do know me: if they did,
This ship-boy's semblance hath disguis'd me quite.
I am afraid; and yet I'll venture it.                          5
If I get down, and do not break my limbs,
I'll find a thousand shifts to get away:
As good to die and go, as die and stay.
          [*He leaps, and lies momentarily in a trance.*
O me! my uncle's spirit is in these stones:
Heaven take my soul, and England keep my bones!   10
                                                        [*Dies.*

*Enter* PEMBROKE, SALISBURY, *and* BIGOT.

*Sal.* Lords, I will meet him at Saint Edmundsbury:
It is our safety, and we must embrace
This gentle offer of the perilous time.

*Scene* III

Scene III] F1; V. Pope; II. Donovan.     Before . . . Castle.] Capell; om. F1;
A Prison. Rowe.     8. S.D.] This ed.; om. F1; Leaps down. Rowe, edd.
9. *spirit*] F1; *sprite* Fleay.

1. *leap*] Shakespeare read various theories about Arthur's death, two being: "proouing to clime ouer the wals of the castell, he fell" (Hol. 165, ii); "leaping into the ditch thinking to make his escape" (Foxe, 250, i).

7. *shifts*] stratagems; changes of clothing. A common pun, as in *2 H 6*: "My shame will not be shifted with my sheet" (II. iv. 108).

8. S.D.] Our S.D. follows the *T.R.*, which probably imitated *John* here: cf. Appendix C, p. 175.

10. *Heaven . . . bones!*] Rushton [*Shakespeare's Testamentary Language* (1869), pp. 4–5] noted the resemblance to the regular opening of wills, e.g. Shakespeare's own: "ffirst I Comend my Soule into the handes of god my Creator . . . And my bodye to the Earth whereof yt ys made."

11. *Saint Edmundsbury*] Shakespeare conflates the nobles' pilgrimage to St Edmundsbury where they "vttered their complaint of the kings tyrannicall maners" in 1214, and the Dauphin's landing (1216).

*Pem.* Who brought that letter from the cardinal?
*Sal.* The Count Melun, a noble lord of France;      15
    Whose private with me of the Dolphin's love
    Is much more general than these lines import.
*Big.* To-morrow morning let us meet him then.
*Sal.* Or rather then set forward; for 'twill be
    Two long days' journey, lords, or ere we meet.      20

*Enter the* BASTARD.

*Bast.* Once more to-day well met, distemper'd lords!
    The king by me requests your presence straight.
*Sal.* The king hath dispossess'd himself of us:
    We will not line his thin bestained cloak
    With our pure honours, nor attend the foot      25
    That leaves the print of blood where'er it walks.
    Return and tell him so: we know the worst.
*Bast.* Whate'er you think, good words, I think, were best.
*Sal.* Our griefs, and not our manners, reason now.
*Bast.* But there is little reason in your grief;      30
    Therefore 'twere reason you had manners now.
*Pem.* Sir, sir, impatience hath his privilege.

---

16. *with me*] F1; *warrant* Wilson conj.; *notice* Sisson.     17. *general than these*] F1; *than these gen'ral* Hanmer.     24. *thin bestained*] Rowe; hyphened F1.     32, 33. *his*] F1; *its* Pope.

15. *Count Melun*] Cf. Introduction, pp. xiii, xviii, n. 4.

16. *private*] Though *private* = "privacy, private affairs, etc." is found, this is the only use = private communication.

17. *general*] comprehensive.

20. *or ere*] before (as in *Mac.*, IV. iii. 173).

21. *Once more*] Cf. IV. ii. 162 (Delius).

*distemper'd*] ill-tempered. Faulconbridge probably means "deranged", i.e. making their disloyalty a disease.

24. *line*] "(*a*) furnish a lining to, (*b*) reinforce" (Wilson).

25–6. *nor . . . walks.*] Cf. III. ii. 72, IV. ii. 57.—A commonplace? Cf. E. Daunce, *Briefe Discourse* (1590): "Mac-

chiauel . . . maintaineth that where the Pope and Cardinals set footing, they leaue most fearefull printes of confusion" (sig. D₂ᵛ). So in the *Psalms*: "That thy foote may be dipped in the blood . . . of the enemies" (lxviii. 23); "the mighty people . . . haue reproched the footsteppes of thine Anointed" (lxxxix. 50–1).

28. *good words*] Cf. *T.R.* "Good words sir sauce, your betters are in place" (I. ii. 129). Faulconbridge means "it would be best to speak fair words," and "it would be best not to speak so fiercely" (cf. *O.E.D.*, good, 7b).

29. *reason*] talk.

30. *But . . . grief;*] Cf. III. iii. 43.

*Bast.* 'Tis true, to hurt his master, no manners else.
*Sal.* This is the prison. [*Seeing Arthur.*] What is he lies here?
*Pem.* O death, made proud with pure and princely beauty!
    The earth had not a hole to hide this deed.               36
*Sal.* Murther, as hating what himself hath done,
    Doth lay it open to urge on revenge.
*Big.* Or, when he doom'd this beauty to a grave,
    Found it too precious-princely for a grave.               40
*Sal.* Sir Richard, what think you? You have beheld.
    Or have you read, or heard? or could you think,
    Or do you almost think, although you see,
    That you do see? could thought, without this object,
    Form such another? This is the very top,                  45
    The heighth, the crest, or crest unto the crest,

33. *manners*] This ed.; *mans* F1; *man* F2, edd.    34. S.D.] Pope; om. F1.    40. *precious-princely*] Capell; no hyphen F1.    41. *You have beheld.*] Fleay; *you haue beheld,* F1; *have you beheld,* F3, edd.    42. *read, or heard?*] Capell; *read, or heard,* F1. 42–4. *think, . . . think, . . . see?*] Pope; *thinke? . . . thinke, . . . see?* F1, edd.    45. *This is*] F1; *'tis* Pope.

33. *to . . . master*] For the "iracundia sibi nocet" proverb see Tilley (p. 14), *Ecclesiasticus,* i. 27.

*manners*] *mans* is nonsense. The contiguous play on *manners* suggests "man's" (a possible spelling of *manners,* with the *-er* suspension), copied unintelligently from the MS. to make a familiar phrase [as in Holinshed: "to his naturall brother, and to no man else" (146, ii)]. Perhaps a play on "good manners" (as in ll. 29, 31), and "customary mode of acting or behaviour" (*O.E.D.,* manner, 3), i.e. the only quality (or good manners) that impatience has is to hurt its master.

35. *death . . . proud*] Death's pride in exceptional victims was a common conceit.

40. *grave*] "The bodies of princes were not buried in the ground, but embalmed and placed in a sepulchre or vault" (Wilson).

41. *You have beheld.*] You have had a good look. The syntax seems to have confused the edd.

42–4. *Or . . . see?*] We take as two *or . . . or* (= either . . . or) constructions. The speech revolves round *thinking* and *seeing. Reading* and *hearing* anticipate thinking (l. 42), and two degrees of thought follow (ll. 42–4). Perhaps an echo of legal interrogatories (cf. III. i. 73), which often tried thus to cover all the possibilities: "*Imprimis,* whither do you know, or haue you herd, seene or red that...".

43. *almost*] Used to intensify a rhetorical question (On.); = with difficulty (Vaughan, comparing *R 3,* III. v. 34).

44. *That*] The relative, though the conjunction is possible. Read: "Have you either read or heard (of the like)? could you either conceive, or do you get near the verge of conceiving, even with the aid of your eyes, that which you actually see before you?"

46. *heighth*] Variant of "height".

*crest*] Crests were not generally used, and a "crest unto the crest" not at all in John's time [C. W. Scott-Giles, *Shakespeare's Heraldry* (1950), p. 42].

Of murther's arms: this is the bloodiest shame,
The wildest savagery, the vildest stroke,
That ever wall-ey'd wrath or staring rage
Presented to the tears of soft remorse.                    50
*Pem.* All murthers past do stand excus'd in this:
And this, so sole and so unmatchable,
Shall give a holiness, a purity,
To the yet unbegotten sin of times;
And prove a deadly bloodshed but a jest,                    55
Exampled by this heinous spectacle.
*Bast.* It is a damned and a bloody work;
The graceless action of a heavy hand,
If that it be the work of any hand.
*Sal.* If that it be the work of any hand!                    60
We had a kind of light what would ensue:
It is the shameful work of Hubert's hand,
The practice and the purpose of the king:
From whose obedience I forbid my soul,
Kneeling before this ruin of sweet life,                    65
And breathing to his breathless excellence
The incense of a vow, a holy vow,
Never to taste the pleasures of the world,
Never to be infected with delight,

---

54. *sin of times*] F1; *sins of Time* Pope.        60. *hand!*] F1 (*hand?*).        66. *his*] F1;
*this* Rowe.

49. *wall-ey'd*] with glaring eyes (so
*Tit.*, v. i. 44), literally an eye with a
discoloured iris. *O.E.D.* (wall-eyed, 2)
notes that the adjective could be applied specifically to jealousy (John's
motive).

50. *remorse*] pity.

51–4. *All . . . times*] Cf. A. Colynet,
*True History* (1591): "yee that are
famous for any notorious wickednes,
reioyce, for your infamy is iustified by
the raging cruelty of . . . Dominican
Fryers" (p. 402), *Lr.*, II. iv. 259–60.

52. *sole*] unique.

54. *times*] future times.

55. *And . . . jest*] Cf. *Arden of Feversham*: "My death to him is but a
merryment, / And he will murther me
to make him sport" (sig. E).

56. *Exampled by*] Compared with.

58. *heavy*] wicked, grievous.

61. *light*] inkling.

63. *practice*] machination.

64–72. *From . . . revenge.*] The idea
may come from K. Philip's reactions:
"seeking reuenge of his death . . .
swearing that he would not ceasse to
pursue the warre against king Iohn,
till he had depriued him of his whole
kingdome" (Hol., 167, i). But the
elaborate *vow* copies the new Revenge
Tragedy. Cf. also Appendix A, p. 165.

67. *The . . . vow*] "Prayer" or *vow* =
"incense" was a common figure [cf.
*Psalms*: "Let my prayer be directed in
thy sight (as) incense" (cxli. 2)].

69. *infected*] "as though *delight* in
such circumstances would be a disease,

Nor conversant with ease and idleness,                70
Till I have set a glory to this hand,
By giving it the worship of revenge.

*Pem.* ⎱
*Big.* ⎰ Our souls religiously confirm thy words.


*Enter* HUBERT.


*Hub.* Lords, I am hot with haste in seeking you:
Arthur doth live; the king hath sent for you.        75
*Sal.* O, he is bold and blushes not at death.
Avaunt, thou hateful villain, get thee gone!
*Hub.* I am no villain.
*Sal.*                        Must I rob the law? [*Drawing his sword.*
*Bast.* Your sword is bright, sir; put it up again.
*Sal.* Not till I sheathe it in a murtherer's skin.  80
*Hub.* Stand back, Lord Salisbury, stand back, I say;
By heaven, I think my sword's as sharp as yours.
I would not have you, lord, forget yourself,
Nor tempt the danger of my true defence;
Lest I, by marking of your rage, forget             85
Your worth, your greatness and nobility.
*Big.* Out, dunghill! dar'st thou brave a nobleman?
*Hub.* Not for my life: but yet I dare defend

71. *hand*] F1; *head* Farmer.    74.] F1; *Scene* VI. Pope.    78. S.D.] Pope; om. F1.

something that would pollute him"
(Deighton).

71. *glory*] splendour (?). Or an
aureole, with which early painters
adorned hands, might be meant
(Fleay).

*hand*] Mason thought this Arthur's
hand. But Salisbury probably means
his own, which he lays on his sword as
on a cross (cf. *Ham.*, I. v. 160), so that
*worship* = honour, dignity.

76. *death*] the murder which he has
committed.

79. *Your . . . again.*] Malone compared *Oth.*: "Keep up your bright
swords, for the dew will rust them"
(I. ii. 59).

84. *tempt*] put to the test; venture
upon, risk; entice, solicit.

*true defence*] "*Honest* defence; defence
in a *good cause*" (Johnson); skilful defence, good swordsmanship (Davies).
A quibble.

85. *marking*] observing; aiming a
blow at (cf. *O.E.D.*, mark, 12, 13).

87. *Out . . . nobleman?*] Cf. Marlowe's
*Edward the Second*: "Away base vpstart,
brau'st thou nobles thus." (sig. G₂ᵛ).
Rushton [*Shakespeare Illustrated* (1867),
1, 64] showed that villein service included the carrying of dung for the
lord, whence such jibes. Wilson de-
duced that Hubert is not of noble birth
(cf. Introduction, p. xxxvii).

88–9. *Not . . . emperor*] So Dekker's
*Match Mee in London* (1631): "*King.*
'Shart doe I lye! doe you braue me!
you base Peasant! / *Mart.* No my

My innocent life against an emperor.
*Sal.* Thou art a murtherer.
*Hub.*                     Do not prove me so:            90
Yet I am none. Whose tongue soe'er speaks false,
Not truly speaks; who speaks not truly, lies.
*Pem.* Cut him to pieces!
*Bast.*                     Keep the peace, I say.
*Sal.* Stand by, or I shall gall you, Faulconbridge.
*Bast.* Thou wert better gall the divel, Salisbury:            95
If thou but frown on me, or stir thy foot,
Or teach thy hasty spleen to do me shame,
I'll strike thee dead. Put up thy sword betime—
Or I'll so maul you and your toasting-iron
That you shall think the divel is come from hell.            100
*Big.* What wilt thou do, renowned Faulconbridge?
Second a villain and a murtherer?
*Hub.* Lord Bigot, I am none.
*Big.*                     Who kill'd this prince?
*Hub.* 'Tis not an hour since I left him well:
I honour'd him, I lov'd him, and will weep            105

90. *not*] F1; *but* Keightley.

Lord, but I must guard my life against an Emperor" (sig. C).

90–1. *Do . . . none.*] "Do not make me a murderer by compelling me to kill you; I am *hitherto* not a murderer" (Johnson). Singer took *prove* = provoke.

91–2. *Whose . . . lies.*] Cf. W. Segar's *Booke of Honor and Armes* (1590): "who soeuer being offered iniurious speach, shall say to the offerer thereof *Thou liest*, or thou saiest not truelie, doth therby repulse the iniurie, and force the Iniurer to challenge" (sig. B₂ᵛ). In ll. 81–6 Hubert suggests that he will *fight*, Bigot scornfully rejects the challenge as an inferior's *brave* (l. 87) or impudence, which makes Hubert give the lie direct (cf. *AYL.*, v. iv. 94 ff.).

93. *Cut . . . pieces!*] The nobles pretend they are too far above Hubert to need to consider his claim to a duel—a grave insult.

94. *by*] aside.
*gall*] hurt.

95, 100. *divel*] Cf. II. i. 567, note.

97. *spleen*] fiery temper.
*do me shame*] treat me shamefully like an inferior, as you have done Hubert.

99. *toasting-iron*] "Iron" was slang for "sword". Z. Grey compared *H 5*: "I will wink and hold out mine iron. It is a simple one; but what though? it will toast cheese" (II. i. 8–10). Perhaps the mockery of Salisbury's sword is in allusion to his nickname: "Salisburie . . . surnamed Long Espée", "William Longspée earle of Salisburie base brother to king Iohn" (Hol., 150, ii, 179, i).

102. *Second*] Support; act as second to. The ambiguity is placatory, granting the *right to duel* (by implication), which was previously denied (cf. notes on ll. 91, 93).

My date of life out for his sweet live's loss.
*Sal.* Trust not those cunning waters of his eyes,
For villainy is not without such rheum;
And he, long traded in it, makes it seem
Like rivers of remorse and innocency.                    110
Away with me, all you whose souls abhor
Th' uncleanly savours of a slaughter-house;
For I am stifled with this smell of sin.
*Big.* Away toward Bury, to the Dolphin there!            114
*Pem.* There tell the king he may inquire us out.
                                        [*Exeunt Lords.*
*Bast.* Here's a good world! Knew you of this fair work?
Beyond the infinite and boundless reach
Of mercy, if thou didst this deed of death,
Art thou damn'd, Hubert.
*Hub.*                    Do but hear me, sir—
*Bast.* Ha! I'll tell thee what;                          120
Thou'rt damn'd as black—nay, nothing is so black;
Thou art more deep damn'd than Prince Lucifer:
There is not yet so ugly a fiend of hell
As thou shalt be, if thou didst kill this child.
*Hub.* Upon my soul—
*Bast.*                If thou didst but consent          125

110. *innocency*] F1; *innocence* Pope.    116.] F1; *Scene* VII. Pope.    117-19.]
Pope; two lines F1 (ending *mercie*,/... Hubert./).    124-6. *child.... If ... act,*]
As Rowe; *childe.... If ... Act:* F1; *child—... —If ... act.* Maxwell (*N. & Q.*,
28 Oct. 1950).

106. *date*] duration.
*live's*] life's.
109. *traded in*] accustomed to; driv-
ing a trade in.
112. *uncleanly*] Stronger than in IV. i.
7, perhaps = the "unclean flesh" sac-
rifices of the Old Testament (*Leviticus*, v,
etc.); *savours* and *smell* may also be biblical: "The Lorde looke vpon you and
iudge: for ye haue made our sauour to
stinke before Pharaoh ... ye haue put
a sword in their hand to slay vs"
(*Exodus*, v. 21; cf. *Genesis*, xxxiv. 30).
116. *Here's ... world!*] Common exclamation = "It's a bad world!" Cf.
IV. ii. 100.

117-19. *Beyond ... Hubert.*] "Thy
mercie, O Lord, (reacheth) vnto the
heauens" (*Psalms*, xxxvi. 5).
121-4. *Thou'rt ... child.*] That blackness = damnation was not disputed
["Damn'd as thou art" said to Othello
(I. ii. 63); "Damn'd as he is" said of
Aaron (*Tit.*, v. iii. 124)]. The white
angel Lucifer was thrown into deepest
hell, i.e. blackest, i.e. ugliest (cf. *Isaiah*,
xiv, *Luke*, x).
123. *ugly*] "The emphasis upon
Hubert's ugliness (cf. 4. 2. 220-25,
266) suggests that the actor who played him possessed uncomely features"
(Wilson).

> To this most cruel act, do but despair;
> And if thou want'st a cord, the smallest thread
> That ever spider twisted from her womb
> Will serve to strangle thee; a rush will be a beam
> To hang thee on; or wouldst thou drown thyself,    130
> Put but a little water in a spoon,
> And it shall be as all the ocean,
> Enough to stifle such a villain up.
> I do suspect thee very grievously.

*Hub.*  If I in act, consent, or sin of thought,    135
> Be guilty of the stealing that sweet breath
> Which was embounded in this beauteous clay,
> Let hell want pains enough to torture me!
> I left him well.

*Bast.*            Go, bear him in thine arms.
> I am amaz'd, methinks, and lose my way    140
> Among the thorns and dangers of this world.
> How easy dost thou take all England up

---

129. *Will . . . beam*] F1; *Will . . . be/A beam* Steevens.    *serve to*] F1; om. Pope.
130. *thyself*] F1; om. Steevens conj.    142–3. *up . . . royalty!*] F1 (*vp, . . . Royaltie?*); *up! . . . Royalty,* Theobald, edd.

126. *do but despair*] "only despair is left for you" (I. John). Despair was sinful, as the Cave of Despair shows (*Faerie Queene*, Bk I, canto ix).

127–33. *And . . . up.*] Vaughan suggested an allusion to the superstition that criminals are less immune to ill fortune than others, citing from Holinshed (744, i, Life of Richard III) an example of "drowning in a small puddle", which Holinshed thought God's judgement.

130. *hang*] A reference to Judas's hanging himself after betraying Christ? (Delius).

133. *up*] Intensive.

134. *I . . . grievously*] Holinshed says of Arthur's death "king Iohn was had in great suspicion" (165, ii), "king Philip . . . tooke the matter verie greeuouslie" (166, i), and Shakespeare adapts to Hubert. This "very grievously" is unique in Shakespeare (cf. Bartlett's *Concordance*).

135. *If . . . thought*] Cf. iv. ii. 254, note. Hubert echoes the "general confession" in use before Holy Communion: "wee knowledge and bewaile our manifolde sinnes and wickednesse, which we from tyme to tyme most grieuously haue committed, by thought, word, and deede."

137. *embounded*] enclosed.

140. *amaz'd*] bewildered. This word was connected with *maze* = labyrinth.

140–1. *lose . . . world*] Thorns = riches, and losing one's way among thorns is a biblical commonplace. *Proverbs*, xxii. 3–5, *Matthew*, xiii. 22 have been compared. This resumes the commodity motif.

142. *How . . . up*] Here *take up* must refer to l. 139; and Hubert's innocence is suggested since the body does not bleed near its supposed murderer (cf. J. Masefield: *William Shakespeare*, p. 83). But *take up* = "levy, raise in arms"

From forth this morsel of dead royalty!
The life, the right and truth of all this realm
Is fled to heaven; and England now is left          145
To tug and scamble, and to part by th' teeth
The unow'd interest of proud swelling state.
Now for the bare-pick'd bone of majesty
Doth dogged war bristle his angry crest
And snarleth in the gentle eyes of peace:           150
Now powers from home and discontents at home
Meet in one line; and vast confusion waits,

147. *proud swelling*] F1; hyphened Pope.

as well (cf. *2 H 4*, IV. ii. 26), anticipating ll. 145–54.

142–3. *How . . . royalty!*] The speech quibbles on the identity of king and country (cf. II. i. 91, 202, notes). In l. 142 *England* = (*a*) the nation, (*b*) Arthur. The *right* that has *fled to heaven* (l. 145) = (*a*) the nation's law and order (cf. II. i. 86–8), (*b*) Arthur's soul. Theobald's removal of F1 ? (= !) to l. 142 destroys the quibble, which shows Faulconbridge *almost* recognizing Arthur's right. The idea of England taken up *From forth* Arthur's body parallels that of his soul *fled to heaven* (from his body).

144. *The . . . truth*] Alluding to the words of Jesus (*John*, xiv. 6)? The sovereign was traditionally the *life* of his land, but Faulconbridge does not necessarily recognize Arthur's claims here: he says that *sovereignty* has departed, since Arthur's death will cause revolt from John.

145, 148, 151, 155. *now . . . Now*] Such summaries of the state of things were common in the moralities (cf. Introduction, p. lxxi), e.g. Bale's *King Iohan*: "now maye we realmes confounde / Our holye father, maye now lyue at hys pleasure / . . . He is now able, to kepe downe Christe and hys gospell / . . . Now shall we ruffle it . . . / . . . now maye we synge Cantate" (M.S.R., ll. 1702–9).

146. *scamble*] scramble.

147. *unow'd interest*] (*a*) unowned title

or right; (*b*) the accruing interest or power of the nobles *unowed* to a king. For the owe-own pun cf. IV. i. 123.

148. *bone*] The common dissention figure, as in Dekker's *Newes from Hell* (1606): "the *Diuell* . . . has . . . throwne heresies (like bones for dogges to gnaw vpon) amongst the Doctors" (sig. B₂), and *Troil.*, I. iii. 391–2.

151. *Now . . . home*] Here *from home, at home* may = "out of their element", "in their element" (cf. v. vii. 115; *O.E.D.*, home, 11c, 12). This would emphasize disorder, viz. nobles uniting *unnaturally* with the rabble (taking *powers* = nobles, as in *H 8*, II. iv. 111). But many take *powers from home* = "armies from abroad". There was much talk in 1590 of Roman Catholic "discontents" joining the feared invaders. Cf. the same ambiguity in v. i. 8–9, and *T.R.*: "The multitude (a beast of many heads) / Doo wish confusion to their Soueraigne; / The Nobles blinded with ambitions fumes, / Assemble powers to beat mine Empire downe, / And more than this, elect a forren King" (II. ii. 124–8).

152. *Meet . . . line*] "When in one line two crafts directly meet" (*Ham.*, III. iv. 210) has been compared. Schmidt glossed as "go the same way." Wilson added "The image involved is not clear, but I suggest that of two knights meeting at full tilt". But "meeting in one line" could have the opposite sense, as in *The Proceedings of*

As doth a raven on a sick-fall'n beast,
The imminent decay of wrested pomp.
Now happy he whose cloak and ceinture can          155
Hold out this tempest. Bear away that child
And follow me with speed: I'll to the king.
A thousand businesses are brief in hand,
And heaven itself doth frown upon the land.          [*Exeunt.*

155. *ceinture*] F1 (*center*); *cincture* Pope.          159. S.D.] Rowe; Exit. F1.

*he Earle of Leycester for* . . . *Sluce* (1590):
Leicester tried to reconcile all his
allies, "to recure all seditious wounds,
and to drawe all in one line to the re-
liefe of this beseiged Towne" (sig. B₂).
It all depends whether *powers* and *discontents* (l. 151) are friends or not.

154. *wrested*] Some think that Faulconbridge now "wavers in his allegiance", recognizing John's authority
as *wrested* (usurped from Arthur). We
think Shakespeare continues the ambiguity of ll. 142 ff., that Faulconbridge talks of England first, of John
only secondly, i.e. Arthur's death will
cause revolt (cf. l. 144, note). Read:
"Now armies from abroad and discontents at home join forces; and an all-
embracing chaos, like a raven hover-
ing above a dying beast, awaits the
imminent general dissolution consequent upon the wresting of power
from John."

155. *cloak* . . . *ceinture*] "Let it be unto
him as the cloke that he hath vpon

him: and as the gyrdle that he is
alway gyrded withall" (*Psalms*, cix.
19, in *Book of Common Prayer*). Shakespeare follows the common protection-
image, as in *Isaiah*, xi. 5, xxii. 21, lix.
17, etc. J. C. Maxwell suggests (privately) that *ceinture* = "centre" and
"ceinture", as in *1 H 6*, II. ii. 6 ("the
middle centre of this cursed town").

156. *this tempest*] "SVb eadem tem-
pestate conuenerunt ad colloquium
apud sanctum Eadmundum Comites
& Barones Anglie" (M. Paris, p. 337).
Cf. v. i. 17, 20, etc. (the common war-
tempest image).

158. *brief*] "Rife; common; prevalent: often used of epidemic dis-
eases" (*O.E.D.*).

159. *And* . . . *land*.] "the generall
scourge wherewith the people were
afflicted, chanced not through the
princes fault, but for the wickednesse
of his people, for the king was but the
rod of the Lords wrath" (Hol., 173, ii).
Cf. v. ii. 84.

# ACT V

## SCENE I. [*The Court of England.*]

*Enter* KING JOHN, PANDULPH, *and Attendants.*

*K. John.* Thus have I yielded up into your hand
    The circle of my glory.         [*Giving the crown.*
*Pand.*               Take again [*Giving back the crown.*
    From this my hand, as holding of the pope,
    Your sovereign greatness and authority.
*K. John.* Now keep your holy word: go meet the French,    5
    And from his holiness use all your power
    To stop their marches 'fore we are inflam'd.
    Our discontented counties do revolt;
    Our people quarrel with obedience,
    Swearing allegiance and the love of soul         10

ACT V

*Scene* I

Act V *Scene* I.] Rowe; Actus Quartus, Scaena prima. F1; *Act* IV *Scene* III. Donovan. The . . . England.] Pope; om. F1.    S.D.] Enter King Iohn and Pandolph, attendants. F1; King *John*, . . . discovered. Kemble.    2. S.D. [Giving the crown.] Pope; om. F1.    2. *Take*] F1; *Take't* Lettsom conj. 2. S.D. [Giving back . . .] Capell; om. F1.    3. *From this*] F1; *This from* Heath. 7. *'fore*] F1; *for* J. M. Mason [*Comments* (1785), p. 160].

1–4. *Thus . . . authority.*] For the source cf. Introduction, p. xiv; for the motivation, p. xxvii.

   2. *circle . . . glory*] For *crown* = *glory* cf. *R 2*, III. iii. 90; for *glory* = *circle* cf. *1 H 6*, I. ii. 133–7; for the magic of the circle cf. *AYL.*, II. v. 60, v. iv. 34.

   3. *pope,*] Shakespeare probably took l. 4 as vague object of "Take" and "holding".

   7. *'fore*] Mason emended since "the nation was already as much inflamed as it could be".—Shakespeare probably intended *for* and *'fore*, taking *we* =

England or John, *inflam'd* = sick or roused.

   8. *counties*] shires. Some edd. interpret "nobles", but Shakespeare only used the word in this sense in "Italian" plays. Smith noted that military organization was in counties, comparing *Kent*, l. 30. Cf. IV. iii.151, note.

   10. *love of soul*] *Faerie Queene* has been compared: "love of soule doth love of bodie passe / No lesse than perfect gold surmounts the meanest brasse" (IV. ix. 2). Schmidt (*Lex.*, soul) cited examples where the soul is "the seat of real, not only professed, sentiments".

To stranger blood, to foreign royalty.
This inundation of mistemp'red humour
Rests by you only to be qualified:
Then pause not; for the present time's so sick
That present med'cine must be minist'red                    15
Or overthrow incurable ensues.
*Pand.* It was my breath that blew this tempest up,
Upon your stubborn usage of the pope;
But since you are a gentle convertite
My tongue shall hush again this storm of war,              20
And make fair weather in your blust'ring land.
On this Ascension-day, remember well,
Upon your oath of service to the pope,
Go I to make the French lay down their arms.        [*Exit.*
*K. John.* Is this Ascension-day? Did not the prophet       25
Say that before Ascension-day at noon
My crown I should give off? Even so I have:
I did suppose it should be on constraint;
But, heaven be thank'd, it is but voluntary.

*Enter the* BASTARD.

*Bast.* All Kent hath yielded: nothing there holds out       30

11. *stranger blood*] Theobald; hyphened F1.        29. *heaven*] F1 (*heau'n*).

12–13. *This . . . qualified:*] Alluding
to the physiology of humours, in
which, if one humour preponderated
(making an *inundation*), it had to be
*qualified* (abated) to restore health (H.
Belden); *mistemp'red* = disordered.

14–15. *present . . . present*] existing . . .
immediate.

15. *present . . . minist'red*] Medical
cliché: "*Gangrena . . . comes . . . because
the inflamation was not defended . . .
the aboundance of humours . . . choake
and extinguish the naturall heate . . .
except present helpe be ministred
[mortification will follow]*" [*The Sclo-
potarie of Iosephus Quercetanus* (1590),
sig. K₂]. Cf. v. i. 7, 12.

17. *breath*] Cf. III. iii. 127.
*this tempest*] Cf. IV. iii. 156.
18. *stubborn*] Cf. *wilfully* (III. i. 68),

and Holinshed: "The pope perceiuing
that king Iohn continued still in his
former mind (which he called obstinacie)" (171, ii).

19. *convertite*] convert.

20–1. *My . . . land*] Make fair
weather = (*a*) be conciliatory, (*b*) pretend that something is better than it is.
Also *fair weather* was a cliché for pacifi-
cation (cf. *O.E.D.*, weather). Shakespeare comments on Pandulph's hypocrisy, as in III. iii. 175.

21. *blust'ring*] blowing violently (of
winds); threatening bluffingly; agitated.

28–9. *I . . . voluntary*] Holinshed says
that John "voluntarilie submitteth
himselfe" (186, ii).

30–6. *All . . . friends.*] Cf. Appendix
A, p. 166.

But Dover Castle; London hath receiv'd,
Like a kind host, the Dolphin and his powers;
Your nobles will not hear you, but are gone
To offer service to your enemy;
And wild amazement hurries up and down    35
The little number of your doubtful friends.

*K. John.* Would not my lords return to me again
After they heard young Arthur was alive?

*Bast.* They found him dead and cast into the streets,
An empty casket, where the jewel of life    40
By some damn'd hand was robb'd and ta'en away.

*K. John.* That villain Hubert told me he did live.

*Bast.* So, on my soul, he did, for aught he knew.
But wherefore do you droop? why look you sad?
Be great in act, as you have been in thought;    45
Let not the world see fear and sad distrust
Govern the motion of a kingly eye!
Be stirring as the time, be fire with fire,
Threaten the threat'ner, and outface the brow
Of bragging horror: so shall inferior eyes,    50
That borrow their behaviours from the great,
Grow great by your example and put on
The dauntless spirit of resolution.
Away, and glister like the god of war

35. *hurries*] F1; *harries* Staunton conj.    40. *jewel of life*] F1; *jewel, life,* Pope.
53. *spirit*] F1; *sprite* Fleay.

35. *amazement*] bewilderment.

*hurries*] Transitive, with *up and down* adverbial (Wright); intransitive with *up and down* prepositional (Delius). Cf. *The Golden Age*: "Feare and amazement hurry through each chamber" (Heywood, III, 23).

40. *jewel of life*] i.e. the soul; cf. *Mac.*, III. i. 68: "mine eternal jewel"; *2 H 6,* III. ii. 409: "A jewel, lock'd into the woefull'st cask". Or Shakespeare may mean "the jewel *that is* life".

44–61. *But . . . nigh!*] Shakespeare follows M. Paris: John's advisers "Dixerunt enim grunniendo & derisionibus multiplicatis subsannando: Ecce vigesimus quintus Rex in Anglia:

ecce iam non Rex, nec etiam regulus, sed Regum opprobrium . . . Heu miser & seruus vltimae conditionis, ad quam seruitutis miseriam deuolutus es? Fuisti Rex, nunc fex . . . Et sic iram prouocantes . . . [irae] scintillas excitarunt" (pp. 352–3).

45. *act . . . thought*] Cf. IV. iii. 135.

46. *sad*] grave, serious; sorrowful, despondent.

48. *stirring*] energetic.

49. *outface*] Cf. II. i. 97, note.

50. *bragging*] threatening (*O.E.D.,* brag, 3).

53. *dauntless . . . resolution*] The cliché was "undaunted resolution".

54. *glister*] Cf. *Ven.,* 273–6.

When he intendeth to become the field:            55
Show boldness and aspiring confidence!
What, shall they seek the lion in his den,
And fright him there? and make him tremble there?
O, let it not be said: forage, and run
To meet displeasure farther from the doors,        60
And grapple with him ere he come so nigh!

*K. John.*  The legate of the pope hath been with me,
And I have made a happy peace with him;
And he hath promis'd to dismiss the powers
Led by the Dolphin.

*Bast.*                    O inglorious league!        65
Shall we, upon the footing of our land,
Send fair-play orders and make comprimise,
Insinuation, parley and base truce
To arms invasive? shall a beardless boy,
A cock'red silken wanton, brave our fields,        70
And flesh his spirit in a warlike soil,
Mocking the air with colours idlely spread,

---

60. *farther*] F1; *further* Steevens.    61. *come*] F1; *comes* ed. 1735.    67. *fair-play orders*] Ed. 1735; *fayre-play-orders* F1.    70. *cock'red silken*] Fleay; hyphened F1.    72. *idlely*] F1; *idly* Hanmer, edd.

---

55. *become*] adorn.

57. *the lion*] John bore the English lion in his arms. If Faulconbridge wears the lion-skin this symbolizes his ascendancy here (cf. III. ii. 1, note).

59. *forage*] "range abroad", "seek for prey" have been suggested; cf. *LLL.*, IV. i. 94, *H 5*, I. ii. 110.

63. *happy*] propitious, favourable; dexterous, skilful.

65–73. *O . . . arms!*] Armada rhetoric. Cf. *Cornelia* (1594): "Shall we then, that are men and Romains borne,/Submit vs to vnurged slauerie?/Shall Rome that hath so many ouer-throwne / Now make herselfe a subiect to her owne? / O base indignitie: a beardles youth . . ." (Kyd, p. 138).

66. *upon . . . of*] standing upon.

67. *fair-play orders*] Cf. IV. ii. 93–5, v. ii. 118. "Orders" probably = arrangements, measures, though

Schmidt takes it = stipulations.

*comprimise*] This variant form of compromise was Shakespeare's favourite.

68. *Insinuation*] Self-ingratiation.

70. *cock'red*] pampered.

*wanton*] spoilt child.

*brave*] "the ordinary sense of 'defy,' with a side reference to the meaning of the adjective 'brave,' showy, or splendid; as if 'to brave our fields' signified to display his finery in our fields" (Wright).

71. *flesh*] initiate or inure to bloodshed (On.), as in *Lr.*, II. ii. 50. But the senses "inflame" (cf. *2 H 4*, I. i. 149), "gratify" (cf. *All's W.*, IV. iii. 19) are also present.

72. *idlely*] carelessly. An expressive variant of *idly*, once common.— Shakespeare repeats the image in *Mac.*: "the Norweyan banners flout the sky" (I. ii. 50) (Johnson).

And find no check? Let us, my liege, to arms!
Perchance the cardinal cannot make your peace;
Or if he do, let it at least be said                    75
They saw we had a purpose of defence.
*K. John.* Have thou the ordering of this present time.
*Bast.* Away, then, with good courage! yet, I know,
Our party may well meet a prouder foe.                    [*Exeunt.*


SCENE II.—[*The Dauphin's Camp at St Edmundsbury.*]

*Enter, in arms,* LEWIS, SALISBURY, MELUN, PEMBROKE, BIGOT,
*and Soldiers.*

*Lew.* My Lord Melun, let this be copied out,
And keep it safe for our remembrance:
Return the precedent to these lords again;
That, having our fair order written down,
Both they and we, perusing o'er these notes,                    5

---

74. *cannot*] F 1 ; *can't* Pope.

*Scene* 11

*Scene* II] F 1 ; *Scene* IV. Donovan.    The . . . Edmundsbury.] Theobald; om. F 1.
S.D.] Enter (in Armes) Dolphin, Salisbury, Meloone, Pembroke, Bigot,
Souldiers. F 1.

77. *Have . . . time.*] "Ipso eodem tempore, Rex Iohannes . . . qui quendam armigerum Falconem imposuerat custodie cuidam in Marchia Walliae, sciens illum nullum facinus abhorrere, vocauit ipsum vt in Barones baccharetur. Erat autem ruptarius nequissimus, Neuster natione, & spurius" (M. Paris, p. 311).

78. *yet*] "now as always"; or "none the less", viz. "(Though I am heartening you) *yet* (this is unnecessary since) our side (*party*) may well cope with a more spirited (*prouder*) foe."

*Scene* 11

1–63. *My . . . mine.*] Shakespeare dramatizes the lament of the barons after John's submission to *Rome* (Introduction, p. xvi), whence the dis-

courtesy of Salisbury's grief after the barons' submission to *Lewis*. In Holinshed (186, ii, 48) the *stranger* (l. 27) is the pope.

1. *this*] Shakespeare conflates the lords' pilgrimage to St Edmundsbury of 1214 and the landing of Lewis in 1216. No reform document is ascribed to either occasion by Holinshed, but the climax of these years was Magna Carta (1215), signed to restore old liberties to the nobles (cf. *our right*, l. 21). Holinshed implies that Lewis subscribed to Magna Carta: "[Lewis] tooke an oth to maintaine and performe the old lawes and customes of the realme" (191, ii).

3. *precedent*] original. Some take = first draft (as in *R 3*, III. vi. 7).

4. *fair order*] Cf. III. i. 176–7, note.

  May know wherefore we took the sacrament
  And keep our faiths firm and inviolable.
*Sal.* Upon our sides it never shall be broken.
  And, noble Dolphin, albeit we swear
  A voluntary zeal and an unurg'd faith     10
  To your proceedings; yet believe me, prince,
  I am not glad that such a sore of time
  Should seek a plaster by contemn'd revolt,
  And heal the inveterate canker of one wound
  By making many. O, it grieves my soul,   15
  That I must draw this metal from my side
  To be a widow-maker! O, and there
  Where honourable rescue and defence
  Cries out upon the name of Salisbury!
  But such is the infection of the time,   20
  That, for the health and physic of our right,
  We cannot deal but with the very hand
  Of stern injustice and confused wrong.
  And is't not pity, O my grieved friends,
  That we, the sons and children of this isle,  25
  Was born to see so sad an hour as this;
  Wherein we step after a stranger, march
  Upon her gentle bosom, and fill up

---

10. *and an*] F1; *and* Pope; *an* Capell.  13. *contemn'd*] F1; *condemn'd* Heath.
16. *metal*] F1 (*mettle*).  26. *Was*] F1; *Were* F2.  27. *stranger, march*] F1;
hyphened Hanmer.

6–7. *May . . . inviolable.*] At St Edmundsbury the nobles "receiued a solemne oth vpon the altar" that they would force John to confirm their rights "vnder his seale, for euer to remaine most stedfast and inuiolable" (Hol., 183–4).

12–15. *I . . . many.*] A Tudor commonplace, as in *The Book of Homilies*: "rebellion is an vnfit and vnwholesome medicine . . . far worse than any other maladies and disorders that can be in the body of a commonwealth" (Homily against Wilful Rebellion).

13. *contemn'd revolt*] Wright compared "despised arms" (*R 2*, II. iii. 95).

19. *Cries out upon*] Exclaims against; or (more probably) appeals to; cf.

*AYL.*, II. vii. 70, IV. iii. 151 (Wright).

21–3. *right . . . wrong*] "play upon *right* (that which is due) . . . [and] *right* (that which is morally good) as opposed to *wrong* (that which is morally evil) makes the sentence difficult" (Deighton).

22. *We . . . hand*] "in such extremitie of despaire they [the barons in 1216] resolued with themselues to seeke for aid at the enimies hands" (Hol., 190, i).

27. *stranger, march*] Theobald took *stranger* = adjective, comparing *R 2*, I. iii. 143, *march* = martial music. But cf. next note.

27–8. *march . . . bosom*] Cf. III. i .172, IV. i. 2–3; *R 2*, II. iii. 92–3.

Her enemies' ranks—I must withdraw and weep
Upon the spot of this enforced cause—       30
To grace the gentry of a land remote,
And follow unacquainted colours here?
What, here? O nation, that thou couldst remove!
That Neptune's arms, who clippeth thee about,
Would bear thee from the knowledge of thyself—    35
And cripple thee—unto a pagan shore,
Where these two Christian armies might combine
The blood of malice in a vein of league,
And not to spend it so unneighbourly!
*Lew.* A noble temper dost thou show in this;      40

30. *spot of*] F1; *spot, for* Pope.      36. *cripple*] F1; *grapple* Pope, edd.; *gripple*
Steevens conj.      39. *to spend*] F1; *mis-spend* Hanmer.

29. *I . . . weep*] So Chettle's *Hoffman* (1631): "I must withdraw, and weepe, my heart is full" (sig. E₄ᵛ).

30. *Upon . . . cause*] Spot = (a) stain, disgrace (as v. vii. 107), (b) place; Upon = (a) because of, (b) on; cause = (a) course, (b) cause (cf. III. iii. 12, note).

31. *grace*] adorn; do honour to.

33–9. *What . . . unneighbourly!*] M. Paris quotes the pope's letter to the barons saying that their revolt endangered the Crusade (p. 385), and discusses plans for the Crusade (pp. 357, 362).

34. *That . . . about*] Fripp [*Shakespeare Studies* (1930), p. 100] compared Ovid, *Metam.*, I. 13, II. 270; *clippeth* = embraceth, surroundeth.

35. *bear*] F1 *beare* = bear (after *remove*, l. 33), bare (heralding *cripple*, l. 36). For the same pun cf. *Meas.*: "Would bark your honour from that trunk you bear, / And leave you naked" (III. i. 70–1), Middleton's *Mad World* (1608): "She gets but her allowance, thats bare one" (sig. Bᵛ).

*from . . . thyself*] (away,) so that thou wouldst not know thyself. Smith compared *Ant.*: "poison'd hours had bound me up / From mine own knowledge" (II. ii. 94–5). Wilson glossed "i.e. to self-forgetfulness". Cf. The

*Two Noble Ladies*: "my father who did change his name, / and kept him from the knowledge of himselfe" (M.S.R., ll. 2056–7).

36. *cripple*] "Grapple" assumes the variant "gripple" (never used by Shakespeare) corrupted to *cripple*. But *cripple* (= disable) makes sense. "Nation" = (a) Englishmen, (b) England. Read: "O Englishmen, that you could depart! That Neptune . . . would strip England of its people (so that it would no longer recognize itself without them), bearing them to a pagan shore, and actually cripple the *nation* in this separation of people and land (if this would only cure it)!" The "separation of people and land" idea precedes in l. 31 and the "disease must cure disease" commonplace in ll. 12–15, 20–3. Shakespeare follows the proverb "A desperate Disease must have a desperate cure" (Tilley, p. 158). Cf. also *Lucr.*: "Who, like a late-sack'd island, vastly stood, / Bare and unpeopled in this fearful flood" (ll. 1740–1).

38. *malice*] Cf. II. i. 251.

*vein*] "(a) blood-vessel, (b) mood, humour" (Wilson).

39. *to*] For Shakespeare's insertion of *to* cf. Abbott, pp. 248–52, and I. i. 135, IV. ii. 212, 240, V. ii. 31, 139–42.

And great affections wrastling in thy bosom
Doth make an earthquake of nobility.
O, what a noble combat hast thou fought
Between compulsion and a brave respect!
Let me wipe off this honourable dew,　　　　　　45
That silverly doth progress on thy cheeks:
My heart hath melted at a lady's tears,
Being an ordinary inundation;
But this effusion of such manly drops,
This shower, blown up by tempest of the soul,　　50
Startles mine eyes, and makes me more amaz'd
Than had I seen the vaulty top of heaven
Figur'd quite o'er with burning meteors.
Lift up thy brow, renowned Salisbury,
And with a great heart heave away this storm:　　55
Commend these waters to those baby eyes
That never saw the giant world enrag'd,
Nor met with fortune other than at feasts,

41. affections] F1; affection Pope.　　42. Doth] F1; Do Hanmer, edd.　　43. hast
thou] F4; hast F1.　　56. baby eyes] Capell; hyphened F1.　　57. giant world]
Theobald; hyphened F1.

41. affections] passions, viz. loyalties.
Perhaps we should read affection's.
　　wrastling] Variant of "wrestling".
　　42. earthquake] Cf. Tamburlaine, Pt 1:
"windy exhalations / Fighting for passage, tilt within the earth" (i. ii); this
was the usual explanation of earth-
quakes.
　　43–4. O . . . respect!] Cf. Wint., v. ii.
80, also the old King Leir (1605): "Oh,
what a combat feeles my panting
heart, / 'Twixt childrens loue, and
care of Common weale!" (sig. A4v),
and W. Fulke's Sermon of Faith (1574)
"if God him selfe seeme to wrestle wyth
vs . . . hys purpose is in thys most noble
combate . . . to geue vs strength" (sigs.
Dv, D2).
　　44. brave] fine; courageous.
　　respect] discrimination (viz. a combat between a recognition of a personal compulsion, and a fair consideration of the motives for and against
revolt).
　　46. progress] Perhaps the noun, viz.

"makes a progress": Salisbury's tears
symbolize his honour, which, having
won the sovereignty in his nature,
makes a (royal) procession. Cf. ii. i.
339–40.
　　48. inundation] Recalls v. i. 12.
　　50. This . . . soul] Cf. Lucr., l. 1788
(Malone), 3 H 6, ii. v. 85 (Wright).
　　55. great heart] your great heart, full
as it is; or your great-heartedness.
　　heave] = utter (a groan) (cf. AYL.,
ii. i. 36, Lr., iv. iii. 27); thrust away.
　　56. Commend] Do not hide your face
(l. 54), but express your passions un-
ashamedly (l. 55): recommend such
tears (through your shedding them) to
those baby eyes.—Lewis thus approves
of Salisbury's tears. But the opposite is
possible too: Do not be dejected (l. 54);
thrust this passion behind you with
your great-heartedness (l. 55), and
commit (or leave) these tears to those
baby eyes (but abandon them yourself)—.
　　58. fortune . . . at feasts] The popular
"bountiful Fortune" image.

Full warm of blood, of mirth, of gossiping.
Come, come; for thou shalt thrust thy hand as deep          60
Into the purse of rich prosperity
As Lewis himself: so, nobles, shall you all,
That knit your sinews to the strength of mine.

*Enter* PANDULPH.

And even there, methinks, an angel spake:
Look, where the holy legate comes apace,          65
To give us warrant from the hand of heaven,
And on our actions set the name of right
With holy breath.
*Pand.*                    Hail, noble prince of France!
The next is this: King John hath reconcil'd
Himself to Rome; his spirit is come in,          70
That so stood out against the holy church,
The great metropolis and see of Rome.
Therefore thy threat'ning colours now wind up,
And tame the savage spirit of wild war,
That, like a lion foster'd up at hand,          75
It may lie gently at the foot of peace,
And be no further harmful than in show.
*Lew.* Your grace shall pardon me, I will not back:

59. *warm of*] F1; *of warm* Heath, edd.        64.] F1; *Scene* III. Pope.        64. S.D.]
Enter Pandulpho. F1; He sees *Pandulph* coming at a distance. Hanmer; after
l. 64 Halliwell; after *breath* l. 68 Dyce.        68.] F1; *Scene* III. Enter *Pandulph*.
Hanmer.        77. *further*] F1; *farther* ed. 1735.

59. *Full warm*] *Full* is an intensive;
*warm* (= friendly, loving, heated) continues the Fortune imagery of II. i. 391,
II. ii. 54–61.
*of* ] with.
*blood*] emotion, passion; the fleshly
nature of man ["the fire i' the blood"
(*Tp.*, IV. i. 53)].
64. *And . . . spake :*] Wright explained
as a pun on *angel* (the coin) after *purse*,
*nobles*. "There spake an angel" was a
proverb (Tilley, p. 14, quoted an early
gloss to it: "Ironically spoken oft
times, as if one would say, There spake
Wisdom it self"). The proverb was

often used punningly, as in Middleton's *Famelie of Love* (1608): "*Pur.*
Myne is very currant sir, I can shew
you good gilt. *Dry.* I marry, there
spoke an Angell, guilt's currant" (sig.
H₃).
67. *set*] "*i.e.* as a seal, carrying on the
metaphor in *warrant*" (Deighton).
69. *reconcil'd*] "reconciled, both to
God and his church" (Hol., 176, ii;
cf. 178, ii).
70. *is come in*] has submitted.
73. *wind*] furl.
78. *shall*] must.
*back*] go back.

I am too high-born to be propertied,
To be a secondary at control,                                    80
Or useful serving-man and instrument
To any sovereign state throughout the world.
Your breath first kindled the dead coal of wars
Between this chastis'd kingdom and myself,
And brought in matter that should feed this fire;   85
And now 'tis far too huge to be blown out
With that same weak wind which enkindled it.
You taught me how to know the face of right,
Acquainted me with interest to this land,
Yea, thrust this enterprise into my heart;          90
And come ye now to tell me John hath made
His peace with Rome? What is that peace to me?
I, by the honour of my marriage-bed,
After young Arthur, claim this land for mine;
And, now it is half-conquer'd, must I back          95
Because that John hath made his peace with Rome?
Am I Rome's slave? What penny hath Rome borne,
What men provided, what munition sent,
To underprop this action? Is't not I
That undergo this charge? who else but I,           100
And such as to my claim are liable,
Sweat in this business and maintain this war?
Have I not heard these islanders shout out

83. *coal of wars*] F1 ; *coals of war* Capell conj.

79. *propertied*] made a tool of. So
*Tw.N.*: "They have here propertied
me" (IV. ii. 101).

83–7. *Your . . . it.*] Tilley (p. 728)
quoted the proverb "A little Wind
kindles, much puts out the fire," and
*Shr.*, II. i. 135.

83. *kindled . . . wars*] The "blowing
the coals of contention" cliché recurs
in Hol., 204, i, and *H 8*, II. iv. 77, 92.

84. *chastis'd*] Cf. IV. iii. 159, note.

85, 88–9. *matter, . . . You . . . land*] Cf.
III. iii. 166–7.

88–9. *right . . . interest*] Lewis "with
frowning looke beheld the legat . . .
disprouing not onelie the right which
king Iohn had to the crowne, but also

alledging his owne interest" (Hol.,
191, i) ; *interest* = claim, title.

90–100. *enterprise . . . charge*] Shakespeare conflates Lewis's and King
Philip's answers to Pandulph: Philip
"determined not so to breake off his
enterprise, least it might be imputed to
him for a great reproch to haue beene
at such charges" (Hol., 178, ii).

98. *What . . . sent*] Shakespeare was
now reading Holinshed (p. 191) (cf.
note on ll. 88–9), where John's "furnishing the castell of Douer, with men,
munition, and vittels" is also noted.

100. *charge*] = expense (cf. l. 90,
note) ; burden.

101. *liable*] Cf. II. i. 490.

"Vive le roi!" as I have bank'd their towns?
Have I not here the best cards for the game                105
To win this easy match play'd for a crown?
And shall I now give o'er the yielded set?
No, no, on my soul, it never shall be said.
*Pand.* You look but on the outside of this work.
*Lew.* Outside or inside, I will not return                110
Till my attempt so much be glorified
As to my ample hope was promised
Before I drew this gallant head of war,
And cull'd these fiery spirits from the world,
To outlook conquest and to win renown                115
Even in the jaws of danger and of death. [*Trumpet sounds.*
What lusty trumpet thus doth summon us?

*Enter the* BASTARD, *attended.*

*Bast.* According to the fair-play of the world,
Let me have audience; I am sent to speak:
My holy lord of Milan, from the king                120
I come, to learn how you have dealt for him;
And, as you answer, I do know the scope
And warrant limited unto my tongue.
*Pand.* The Dolphin is too wilful-opposite,
And will not temporize with my entreaties;                125

108. *No, no*] F1; *No,* Pope.      116. S.D.] Rowe; om. F1.      118. S.D.] As
Capell; Enter Bastard. F1.      119–20. *speak:* . . . *king*] F1; *speak,* . . . *King:*
Theobald.      124. *wilful-opposite*] Theobald; no hyphen F1.      125. *entreaties*]
F1; *entreats* Walker.

104. *"Vive le roi!"* . . . *bank'd*] Card-
playing terms (cf. Appendix B, p. 169);
*Vive* is disyllabic.
106. *crown*] The common pun, as in
*H 5,* I. ii. 263.
113. *drew*] assembled.
*head of war*] *head* = armed force is
common, but Shakespeare may here
translate "caput belli" = flower, nuc-
leus of an army.
114. *cull'd*] chose.
115. *outlook*] Cf. *outface* (II. i. 97, v. i.
49) and *outstare* (*Mer.V.,* II. i. 27 etc.).
116. *jaws . . . of death*] So *Tw.N.,*

III. iv. 396.
118. *fair-play*] Cf. v. i. 67.
119. *I . . . speak:*] This clause goes
with the preceding ("Let me have
audience: *for* I am sent") *and* the following ("I am sent . . . from the king").
Similarly, the pause at the end of l. 120
allows *from the king* to go with *I . . . him;*
(l. 121) as well as with *I . . . speak:*
(l. 119).
123. *limited*] appointed.
124. *wilful-opposite*] stubbornly hos-
tile.
125. *temporize*] compromise.

He flatly says he'll not lay down his arms.
*Bast.*  By all the blood that ever fury breath'd,
          The youth says well. Now hear our English king,
          For thus his royalty doth speak in me:
          He is prepar'd, and reason too he should—                    130
          This apish and unmannerly approach,
          This harness'd masque and unadvised revel,
          This unhair'd sauciness and boyish troops,
          The king doth smile at; and is well prepar'd
          To whip this dwarfish war, this pigmy arms,                  135
          From out the circle of his territories.—
          That hand which had the strength, even at your door,
          To cudgel you and make you take the hatch,
          To dive like buckets in concealed wells,
          To crouch in litter of your stable planks,                   140
          To lie like pawns lock'd up in chests and trunks,
          To hug with swine, to seek sweet safety out
          In vaults and prisons, and to thrill and shake
          Even at the crying of your nation's crow,

---

133. *unhair'd*] F1 (*vn-heard*).     *troops*] F1; *troop* Capell conj.     135. *this*] F1;
*these* Rowe, edd.     142. *hug*] F1; *herd* Rowe iii.     144. *crying . . . crow*] F1;
*crowing . . . cock* Collier MS.     *your*] F1; *our* Rowe ii.

127. *blood . . . fury*] Either noun could
be subject or object.

129. *For . . . me:*] Cf. I. i. 3.

132. *harness'd masque*] masque in
armour.

133. *unhair'd*] Cf. *beardless* (v. i. 69);
*hair* was commonly spelt *heare*.

136. *circle*] compass.

137–48. *That . . . No:*] Armada rhetoric, as in W. Averell's *Exhortation* [in
*A Meruailous Combat* (1588)]: "Consider the auncient fame you haue often
won in the field . . . where are nowe the
noble heartes that haue so much
honoured your English land? Shall
the enemie thinke they are gone . . . ?
No, no, they shall I hope finde them
redoubled" (sig. E^v).

138. *take . . . hatch*] Cf. I. i 171, *Lr.*,
III. vi. 76.

139–40. *To . . . planks*] The proverb
"Like two Buckets of a well, if one go
up the other must go down" (Tilley,

p. 69) may lie behind l. 139. Cf. *R 2*,
IV. i. 184.

139–42. *To*] Cf. v. ii. 39, note.

140. *litter*] bedding (for animals or
men).

141. *To . . . trunks*] *pawns* = articles
in pawn (cf. *Wint.*, I. ii. 436); *chests* (=
chess) and *trunks* (a kind of billiards)
were games, chests involving *pawns*, so
he hints that the English *played with* the
French.

143. *thrill*] shiver.

144. *crow*] cock, "*your* nation's crow"
(Douce, since *gallus* meant cock and
Frenchman). Furness thought cock
did not = France till after Shakespeare. But cf. G. Lynne's *Beginning . . .
of all Popery* (1548), sig. E₄, B. Aneau's
*Alector* (1560), *passim*, for cock =
France Z. Grey compared *1 H 6*, I. iv.
43 (Talbot = the "scarecrow" of the
French). Or is the crow as omen
meant? Omens could be *for* one side,

Thinking this voice an armed Englishman;                    145
Shall that victorious hand be feebled here,
That in your chambers gave you chastisement?
No: know the gallant monarch is in arms
And like an eagle o'er his aery towers,
To souse annoyance that comes near his nest.          150
And you degenerate, you ingrate revolts,
You bloody Neroes, ripping up the womb
Of your dear mother England, blush for shame:
For your own ladies and pale-visag'd maids
Like Amazons come tripping after drums,                  155
Their thimbles into armed gauntlets change,

145. *this*] F1 ; *his* Rowe, edd.      148. *No : know*] F1 ; *No, no* Lettsom conj.      153. *mother England*] Theobald; hyphened F1.      156. *change*] F1 ; *chang'd* Dyce.

*against* the other (*R 3*, v. iii. 282–8; *Cym.*, IV. ii. 348–52): Faulconbridge mocks French panic at the omen that supports them.

145. *this*] Cf. IV. i. 63, note.

*voice*] John Newnham talks of the "crie or voice" of a crow [*Nightcrowe* (1590), sig. A₃]. Or is *voice* a verb? ("Thinking this *announces* an armed E.", i.e. the crow anticipates carrion.)

148. *No : know*] Cf. v. ii. 108.

149. *eagle*] The French are crows (l. 144): cf. *Cor.*, III. i. 138, *Troil.*, I. ii. 263 for the traditional comparison of crows and eagles.

*aery*] nest or brood of a bird of prey.

*towers*] (In falconry) "to rise in circles of flight till she reaches her 'place'" (On.), hence "soar".

150. *souse*] Usually glossed as "swoop upon, a hawking term". But hawking *souse* was constructed with *on, upon,* or *down*. Though the hawking sense is there, the sense "smite" (also common) is there too.

151–3. *And . . . England*] Armada commonplaces, as in G. D.'s *Briefe Discoverie* (1588): "he that will not sticke to rippe vp the wombe, and to teare and rake out the bowels of his owne mother, he that will endeuour to bring in an inuasion, to the vtter spoyle, ruine, and depopulation of his deare

countrye: . . . what impietye, will hee leaue vnattempted?" (sig. H₂).

151. *revolts*] rebels.

154–8. *For . . . inclination.*] Armada commonplaces, as in A. Marten's *Exhortation, To Stirre vp the Mindes of all Her Maiesties Faithfull Subiects, to defend their Countrey* (1588): "Conuert your ploughes into speares, and your sithes into swordes. Turne your boules into bowes, and al your pastimes into musket shot" (sig. E); cf. Hol., 61, ii, and *Joel*, iii. 10, *Micah*, iv. 3; also L. Wright's *Display of Dutie* (1589): "changing their trapt Mules, into bard horses: sylken cotes, into arming corslets: golden hats, into steeled helmets . . . dauncing in chambers, into marching in the field" (sig. B₂ᵛ).

156–7. *thimbles . . . needl's*] Fifty years later the Parliamentary Army was nicknamed "the Thimble and Bodkin Army", since even thimbles and bodkins were accepted for the cause.

156. *armed*] Perhaps Shakespeare thinks of leather thimbles, or the plates over the fingers of gauntlets. Furness noted that "many forms of the early thimble were open at the end, thus the resemblance to an 'armed gauntlet' was not so unlike."

*change*] A second present is wanted,

Their needl's to lances, and their gentle hearts
To fierce and bloody inclination.

*Lew.*  There end thy brave, and turn thy face in peace;
We grant thou canst outscold us: fare thee well;    160
We hold our time too precious to be spent
With such a brabbler.

*Pand.*                    Give me leave to speak.

*Bast.*  No, I will speak.

*Lew.*                    We will attend to neither.
Strike up the drums; and let the tongue of war
Plead for our interest and our being here.    165

*Bast.*  Indeed, your drums, being beaten, will cry out;
And so shall you, being beaten: do but start
An echo with the clamour of thy drum,
And even at hand a drum is ready brac'd
That shall reverberate all, as loud as thine:    170
Sound but another, and another shall
As loud as thine rattle the welkin's ear
And mock the deep-mouth'd thunder: for at hand—
Not trusting to this halting legate here,
Whom he hath us'd rather for sport than need—    175
Is warlike John; and in his forehead sits
A bare-ribb'd death, whose office is this day
To feast upon whole thousands of the French.

---

157. *needl's*] F1 (*Needl's*); *Needles* F3; *neelds* Variorum 1778.    159. *There end*]
F1; *There; end* Collier ii.    170. *all,*] F1; *all* Pope, edd.

---

for two distinct actions, marching and
riding, are described.

157. *needl's*] *Needle* was often monosyllabic.

158. *inclination*] mental tendency,
character; leaning or slanting position
(of a charging knight with lance).

159. *brave*] defiant threat, bravado.

160. *outscold*] Cf. II. i. 191, note.

162. *brabbler*] brawler, quarreller.

163-5. *We . . . here.*] Cf. *R 3*, IV. iv.
149-54.

169. *brac'd*] with tightened skin;
perhaps quibbling on *brace* = pair.

172. *welkin's ear*] Cf. *LLL.*, IV. ii. 5.
Shakespeare usually used *welkin* in
"extravagant" poetry.

173. *deep-mouth'd*] loud and sonor-
ous; cf. *H 5*, v. chor. 11, *Shr.*, Ind. i.
18.

174. *halting*] "wavering, shifting (cf.
I *Kings*, xviii. 21)" (Wilson).

176-8. *and . . . French*] The idiom
differs from the suggested "echo" in
*R 2*, III. ii. 160-2; cf. *Good Newes from
Fraunce* (written 1591): "Terror and
maiestie sitteth in the forehead of this
christian King" (sig. A₃ᵛ); *The
Famous History of . . . Fauconbridge* (ed.
1635): "such newes that . . . the signi-
fication thereof, sate like characters in
their foreheads, & as it were made
dumb shewes of discontent" (p. 24).

178. *feast*] Cf. II. i. 354, note.

*Lew.*  Strike up our drums, to find this danger out.        179
*Bast.*  And thou shalt find it, Dolphin, do not doubt.  [*Exeunt.*


SCENE III.—[*The Field of Battle.*]

*Alarums. Enter* KING JOHN *and* HUBERT.

*K. John.*  How goes the day with us? O, tell me, Hubert.
*Hub.*  Badly, I fear. How fares your majesty?
*K. John.*  This fever, that hath troubled me so long,
  Lies heavy on me; O, my heart is sick!

*Enter a Messenger.*

*Mess.*  My lord, your valiant kinsman, Faulconbridge,        5
  Desires your majesty to leave the field
  And send him word by me which way you go.
*K. John.*  Tell him, toward Swinstead, to the abbey there.
*Mess.*  Be of good comfort; for the great supply
  That was expected by the Dolphin here,                    10
  Are wrack'd three nights ago on Goodwin Sands.

179. *our*] F1; *your* I. John.

*Scene* III

*Scene* III.] F1; *Scene* V. Pope; *Act* V *Scene* I. Donovan.    The . . . Battle.] Pope
om. F1.        S.D.] Alarums. Enter Iohn and Hubert. F1.

180. *find it*] find it with a vengeance.
Cf. M. Hurault's *Discourse vpon the pre-sent estate of France* (1588): "Carrie thither the fire of war, seeing it is there that thou shouldest finde thine eni-mies, and thou shalt finde them in deede" (p. 54).


*Scene* III
S.D. Alarums.] " 'Alarums' may possibly represent the decisive battle of Lincoln . . . when the French and their English allies were defeated by William Marshal Earl of Pembroke, who commanded the army of the boy-king Henry III . . . we may suppose this "great supply" [mentioned l. 9] to be the reinforcements sent by Philip of France, about three months after the battle of Lincoln" [Boswell-Stone,

*Shakspere's Holinshed* (1896), p. 71].
  3. *fever*] Holinshed (p. 194, ii) gives various theories for John's death, fever and poison (cf. v. vi. 23) among them: cf. III. iii. 7, note.
  8. *Swinstead*] Swinstead (where there was no abbey) is twenty-five miles from Swineshead Abbey (where John rest-ed) (Reed, Halliwell). For Shake-speare's source cf. Introduction, p. xx.
  9. *supply*] Cf. v. iii. 1, note. Holin-shed says "a new supplie of men was readie to come and aid Lewes" (p. 201, i).
  10–11. *was . . . Are*] Shakespeare must be responsible for this confusion of tense and number: cf. v. v. 13.
  11. *wrack'd*] wrecked. The major chronicles agree that Hubert de Burgh

This news was brought to Richard but even now:
The French fight coldly, and retire themselves.

*K. John.* Ay me! this tyrant fever burns me up,
And will not let me welcome this good news.                    15
Set on toward Swinstead; to my litter straight:
Weakness possesseth me, and I am faint.          [*Exeunt.*


SCENE IV.—[*Another part of the Field.*]

*Enter* SALISBURY, PEMBROKE, *and* BIGOT.

*Sal.* I did not think the king so stor'd with friends.
*Pem.* Up once again; put spirit in the French:
If they miscarry, we miscarry too.
*Sal.* That misbegotten divel, Faulconbridge,
In spite of spite, alone upholds the day.                      5
*Pem.* They say King John sore sick hath left the field.


*Enter* MELUN, *wounded.*

*Mel.* Lead me to the revolts of England here.
*Sal.* When we were happy we had other names.
*Pem.* It is the Count Melun.
*Sal.*                    Wounded to death.
*Mel.* Fly, noble English, you are bought and sold;           10

14. *Ay me!*] F1 (*Aye me,*); *Ah me!* Pope.

### Scene IV

*Scene* IV.] F1; *Scene* VI. Pope; scene contd. Donovan.    Another ... Field.] As
Capell; om. F1.        7. S.D.] F1; Enter *Melun*, led. Capell.

sank the French navy. Shakespeare
may have got his version from R.
Coggeshall (Appendix A, p. 166), not
wishing to glorify Hubert.

13–14. *The ... up*] The French are
*cold* through most of the play: cf. Introduction, p. lxv.

16. *litter*] "not able to ride, [John]
... was faine to be carried in a litter"
(Hol., 194, i). *T.R.* does not name the
litter, but opens II. vi with "Enter
*King Iohn carried betweene 2. Lords.*"

### Scene IV

4. *divel*] Cf. II. i. 567, note.

5. *In ... spite*] "against all odds.
Compare *3 Henry VI*, II. iii. 5" (I.
John).

8. *When ... names.*] He means (*a*)
When we had other names we were
happy; (*b*) We were happy before we
became rebels; (*c*) When things were
going well with us you gave us other
names. The line veils resentment.

10. *bought ... sold*] Foul play has

Unthread the rude eye of rebellion
And welcome home again discarded faith.
Seek out King John and fall before his feet;
For if the French be lords of this loud day
Lewis means to recompense the pains you take          15
By cutting off your heads: thus hath he sworn
And I with him, and many moe with me,
Upon the altar at Saint Edmundsbury;
Even on that altar where we swore to you
Dear amity and everlasting love.                      20

*Sal.* May this be possible? may this be true?

*Mel.* Have I not hideous death within my view,
Retaining but a quantity of life,
Which bleeds away, even as a form of wax
Resolveth from his figure 'gainst the fire?           25
What in the world should make me now deceive,
Since I must lose the use of all deceit?
Why should I then be false, since it is true

---

11. *Unthread . . . eye*] F1; *Untread . . . way* Theobald.     *rude eye of*] F1; *eye of
rude* Hudson ii.     14. *the French be lords*] As F1; *the Prince be lord* Keightley;
*French Lewis be lord* Donovan.     15. *Lewis*] This ed.; *He* F1, edd.     17. *moe*] F1;
*more* Rowe.     25. *his*] F1; *its* Pope.

---

been used (Malone, comparing *R 3*,
v. iii. 306). Tilley (p. 75) gives this as a
proverb = to be tricked.

11. *Unthread*] Cf. *untread* (v. iv. 52).
In *Cor.*, III. i. 123 *thread* (the gates) =
pass through the gates [Steevens compared *Lr.*: "*threading* dark-*ey'd* night"
(II. i. 121)]. Rebellion is thought as
effective as needle and thread together.

*rude*] Transferred epithet (Malone).

12. *discarded*] After *Unthread* this may
be a quibble on "to card" = to prepare
(wool, etc.) for spinning (by disen-
tangling threads with a "card"); ll.
10–12 then suggest that *faith* (= wool)
is a natural product abused in organ-
ized society.

15. *Lewis*] Wright compared *H 5*,
IV. iv. 82: "the French might have a
good prey of us, if he knew of it." But
in *John* not only concord (*French* and
*He*), but syntax is queer [*He* (l. 15) =

John]. If we suppose the form "Le" for
"Lewis" (a monosyllable), "He"
would be an easy misreading in Secretary hand.

17. *moe*] more. Common in Shakespeare (e.g. *R 3*, IV. iv. 200, 503).

18. *Saint Edmundsbury*] Shakespeare
follows Holinshed closely, except for
the location at St Edmundsbury:
cf. IV. iii. 11, note, Appendix A,
p. 161.

23. *quantity*] small quantity; cf. *Shr.*,
IV. iii. 112, *2 H 4*, v. i. 69.

24. *form of wax*] Wax images of one's
enemies were melted before a fire,
usually by witches, to destroy the real
persons by sympathy. Shakespeare
hints that Melun is doubly doomed
(by his wounds, by destiny).

25. *Resolveth*] Dissolves.

26–9. *What . . . truth?*] Tilley (p. 434)
compared *R 2*, II. ii. 5 ff.

27. *use*] profit, advantage.

That I must die here and live hence by truth?
I say again, if Lewis do win the day,                          30
He is forsworn if e'er those eyes of yours
Behold another day break in the east:
But even this night, whose black contagious breath
Already smokes about the burning crest
Of the old, feeble and day-wearied sun,                        35
Even this ill night, your breathing shall expire,
Paying the fine of rated treachery
Even with a treacherous fine of all your lives,
If Lewis by your assistance win the day.
Commend me to one Hubert with your king:                       40
The love of him, and this respect besides,
For that my grandsire was an Englishman,
Awakes my conscience to confess all this.
In lieu whereof, I pray you, bear me hence
From forth the noise and rumour of the field,                  45
Where I may think the remnant of my thoughts
In peace, and part this body and my soul
With contemplation and devout desires.
*Sal.*  We do believe thee; and beshrew my soul

30. *do*] F1; om. Pope.        34. *crest*] F1; *cresset* Anon. conj. *ap.* Cambridge.

29. *hence*] Cf. iv. ii. 89, note.
*by truth*] "by telling the truth" (Furness). Or *truth* may = the Deity, as often at this time.
33. *But . . . breath*] Furness compared *Caes.*, ii. i. 265 ("the vile contagion of the night") for "this idea that the night air was dangerous to health".
34. *smokes*] grows misty: cf. "smoke and dusky vapours of the night" (*1 H 6*, ii. ii. 27).
*crest*] helmet. The conjecture "cresset" = beacon.
36. *expire*] Lat. *exspiro*, breathe out.
37–8. *fine . . . fine*] penalty; end. Wright quoted *Ham.*, v. i. 113: "is this the fine of his fines?"
37. *rated*] Perhaps the sense "rebuked, blamed" is implied (Smith); "(a) assessed, (b) estimated at its true value, exposed" (Wilson).
41. *love of him*] If Hubert was a leading citizen of Angiers (Introduction,

p. xxxvi) he might well be the friend of a French lord.
42. *For . . . Englishman*] One of the two lines identical in *T.R.* (ii. v. 28) and *John* (cf. ii. i. 528, note). The genealogy is probably wrong (Melun's maternal grandfather is untraceable), but Shakespeare may have associated this Melun with Robert de Melun, Bishop of Hereford, d. 1167.
42–3. *Englishman . . . conscience*] In Foxe (not in Holinshed) Melun mentions England and conscience as motives for his disclosure: "I was one of them, which was sworn to [kill you]. I haue great conscience therof, and therfore I geue you this warning. I pittie poore England, which hath bene so noble a region, that now it is come to so extreme misery" (p. 255, ii; cf. Foxe, p. 258, i).
45. *rumour*] confused din.
49. *beshrew*] Cf. v. v. 14.

But I do love the favour and the form                    50
Of this most fair occasion, by the which
We will untread the steps of damned flight,
And like a bated and retired flood,
Leaving our rankness and irregular course,
Stoop low within those bounds we have o'erlook'd,     55
And calmly run on in obedience
Even to our ocean, to our great King John.
My arm shall give thee help to bear thee hence;
For I do see the cruel pangs of death
Right in thine eye. Away, my friends! New flight;      60
And happy newness, that intends old right!
                    [*Exeunt, leading off Melun.*

SCENE V.—[*The French Camp.*]

*Enter* LEWIS *and his train.*

*Lew.* The sun of heaven methought was loath to set,
But stay'd and made the western welkin blush,

60. *Right*] F1; *Fight* Capell; *Bright* Collier MS.       61. S.D.] As Theobald;
Exeunt F1.

Scene v

*Scene* V.] F1; *Scene* VII. Pope.    The . . . Camp.] Capell; om. F1; *Night comes
on; retreat sounded.* Donovan.    S.D.] *Enter Dolphin, and his Traine.* F1.

50. *But*] *If* I do *not* love the favour.
Cf. *Oth.*,III.iii.91.

*favour*] appearance, look (as *Lr.*, I.
iv. 260); attraction, charm (as *Ham.*,
IV. v. 188).

52. *untread*] retrace (steps); cf. *Mer.
V.*,II. vi. 10.

*damned flight*] = *contemn'd revolt* (v.
ii.13).

53. *bated*] diminished.

54. *rankness*] "*Rank* . . . signifies *ex-
uberant, ready to overflow*" (Malone).

55. *Stoop*] The nobles will kneel for
pardon.

*o'erlook'd*] Cf.II. i. 441–5,II.ii. 23.

57. *ocean*] Shakespeare adapts a
commonplace. Cf. J. Prime's *Sermon*
(1585): "*All autoritie is of God*, and

therefore kinglie most of all, euen as all
the waters ishue from the Ocean, but
more immediatlie the great riuers"
(sig. A₆).

60. *Right*] Clearly; immediate
(Steevens); unmistakably (Wilson).

61. *happy*] = (*a*) propitious, (*b*)
appropriate. Read: "A new flight
must be our course; and its newness is
appropriate, seeing it *aims at* the re-
storation of the old (former) right; and
is propitious, seeing it *signifies* old
(ancient) right." Cf. III. i. 196–7, and
v. iv. 8, note.

Scene v

1–2. *The* . . . *stay'd*] Cf. III. i. 3–4,
note.

When English measure backward their own ground
In faint retire. O, bravely came we off,
When with a volley of our needless shot,                                    5
After such bloody toil, we bid good-night,
And wound our tott'ring colours clearly up,
Last in the field, and almost lords of it!

*Enter a Messenger.*

*Mess.* Where is my prince, the Dolphin?
*Lew.*                                         Here: what news?
*Mess.* The Count Melun is slain; the English lords          10
By his persuasion are again fall'n off,
And your supply, which you have wish'd so long,
Are cast away and sunk on Goodwin Sands.
*Lew.* Ah, foul shrewd news! beshrew thy very heart!
I did not think to be so sad to-night                               15
As this hath made me. Who was he that said
King John did fly an hour or two before
The stumbling night did part our weary powers?
*Mess.* Whoever spoke it, it is true, my lord.
*Lew.* Well; keep good quarter and good care to-night:        20
The day shall not be up so soon as I,
To try the fair adventure of to-morrow.          [*Exeunt.*

3. *English*] F 1; *th'* English Rowe iii; *the* English Capell, edd.     *measure*] F 1;
*measur'd* Pope, edd.     7. *clearly*] F 1; *chearly* Capell conj.; *cleanly* Cambridge conj.
12. *supply*] F 1; *supplies* Capell.     13. *Are*] F 1; *Is* Halliwell.

3. *English*] Englishmen; cf. *R 2*, IV. i.
137.

*measure*] traverse, tread. "The western welkin blushes . . . in sympathy
with the discomfiture of the most western race and kingdom. . . . The general and indefinite word 'English' and
the present tense 'measure' seem to me
appropriate to the double meaning"
(Vaughan). Final *e* and *d* were often
confused, but F 1 seems sound.

4. *retire*] Cf. v. iv. 53.

*came we off*] retired we from the en-
gagement.

7. *tott'ring*] Totter (variant of *tatter*)
was associated with *totter* = swing to
and fro (cf. *O.E.D.*). Both "waving"
and "tattered, in rags" may be meant,
for ragged ensigns (*colours*) were no

disgrace but implied hard fighting.

*clearly*] "without obstruction from
the enemy" (Collier). The gloss "entirely or totally" is lame, while Collier's agrees with *O.E.D.*, clear, 18:
"Free from encumbering contact; dis-
engaged, unentangled, out of reach,
quite free", and *Tw.N.*: "Let me be
clear of thee" (IV. i. 4).

12. *supply*] Cf. v. iii. 9, note.

14. *shrewd*] bad, grievous; *beshrew*
comes from the same root, which =
curse.

18. *stumbling*] "causing stumbling"
(On.).

20. *keep . . . quarter*] "guard carefully
the posts assigned to you" (Wright,
comparing *1 H 6*, II. i. 63).

22. *adventure*] hazard, chance.

SCENE VI.—[*An open place in the neighbourhood of Swinstead Abbey.*]

*Enter the* BASTARD *and* HUBERT, *severally.*

*Hub.* Who's there? speak, ho! speak quickly, or I shoot.
*Bast.* A friend. What art thou?
*Hub.*                              Of the part of England.
*Bast.* Whither dost thou go?
*Hub.* What's that to thee? [*Pause.*] Why, may not I demand
   Of thine affairs as well as thou of mine?          5
*Bast.* Hubert, I think.
*Hub.*                        Thou hast a perfect thought:
   I will upon all hazards well believe
   Thou art my friend, that know'st my tongue so well.
   Who art thou?
*Bast.*                    Who thou wilt: and if thou please
   Thou mayst befriend me so much as to think          10
   I come one way of the Plantagenets.
*Hub.* Unkind remembrance! thou and endless night
   Have done me shame: brave soldier, pardon me,
   That any accent breaking from thy tongue
   Should 'scape the true acquaintance of mine ear.     15
*Bast.* Come, come; sans compliment, what news abroad?

*Scene* VI

*Scene* VI.] F1; VIII. Pope; II. Donovan.     *An ... Abbey.*] Theobald; om. F1.
S.D.] As F1.     1–5. Hub. ... *mine?*] As F1; Bast. *Who's ... shoot.* Hub. *A friend.*
Bast. *What ... thou?* Hub. *Of ... go?* Bast. *What's ... thee?* Hub. *Why ... mine?*
K. Elze [*Notes on Eliz. Dram.* (1880), p. 65].     2–5.] Hub. *Of ... go?* Bast. *What
is that to thee?* Hub. '*What's that to thee?*'—*Why may ... mine?* Vaughan.     4. S.D.]
This ed.; om. F1.     4. *Why,*] This ed.; *Why* F1.     4–5.] Capell; three lines F1
(ending *thee?/... affaires,/... mine?/*).     *Why ... mine?*] As F1; Bast. *Why ...
mine?* Lloyd (*ap.* Dyce ii).     12. *endless*] F1; *eyeless* Theobald, edd.

1–5. Hub. ... *mine?*] The speech
headings are altered by some since
Faulconbridge is "hot-headed", Hubert "sedate". But this is one of Faulconbridge's laconic moods (cf. I. i.
154–6, note)—his coolness in danger
is not out of character.
   4. S.D.] The pause is needed to make
Hubert angry.
   *Why,*] Exclamative, not a question;
*why,* is often *why* in F1.

6. *perfect*] correct; cf. 2 *H* 4, III. i. 88
7. *hazards*] Cf. I. i. 119.
12. *remembrance*] memory.
   *endless night*] Common cliché: cf.
*R* 2, I. iii. 177, 222; *Faerie Queene*, III. v.
22; *Tamburlaine*, Pt II, II. iv. 7; Du
Bartas, *Iudith* (tr. T. Hudson, 1584),
p. 81. "Endless" was a common intensive (cf. the last lines of *The Spanish
Tragedy*).
14. *accent*] word, speech.

*Hub.*  Why, here walk I in the black brow of night,
    To find you out.
*Bast.*                Brief, then; and what's the news?
*Hub.*  O, my sweet sir, news fitting to the night,
    Black, fearful, comfortless and horrible.           20
*Bast.*  Show me the very wound of this ill news:
    I am no woman, I'll not swound at it.
*Hub.*  The king, I fear, is poison'd by a monk:
    I left him almost speechless; and broke out
    To acquaint you with this evil, that you might      25
    The better arm you to the sudden time,
    Than if you had at leisure known of this.
*Bast.*  How did he take it? who did taste to him?
*Hub.*  A monk—I tell you, a resolved villain—
    Whose bowels suddenly burst out: the king      30
    Yet speaks and peradventure may recover.
*Bast.*  Who didst thou leave to tend his majesty?
*Hub.*  Why, know you not? the lords are all come back,
    And brought Prince Henry in their company;
    At whose request the king hath pardon'd them,    35
    And they are all about his majesty.
*Bast.*  Withhold thine indignation, mighty heaven,

---

25. *To*] F1; *T'* Pope.    29. *monk—...you,...villain—*] This ed.; *Monke...you,
...villaine* F1; *Monk, ...you; ...Villain,* Theobald, edd.    32. *Who*] F1;
*Whom* Hanmer.    33–4. *not?...company;*] Theobald, edd.; *not?...companie,*
F1; *not,...company?* Malone conj.

---

17. *black brow*] frowning brow; blackness. Hinting at the malevolence of this night. Cf. *black-brow'd night* (*MND.*, III. ii. 387; *Rom.*, III. ii. 20).

22. *swound*] Later form of *swoon*, with excrescent *d*.

23. *I fear*] Holinshed says that John died through fever *or* poison (cf. v. iii. 3, note): *I fear* betrays Shakespeare's uncertainty (cf. III. ii. 7).

26. *sudden time*] emergency.

28. *taste*] A *taster* ate part of every dish set before his master, to detect poison.

29. *A...villain—*] The usual punctuation suggests "A monk, as I've already told you." But (a) would Hubert show impatience with his superior? (b) Hubert has not told Faulconbridge about the *tasting*; (c) *I tell you* draws attention to the monk's resolution. We take *I tell you* = "I dare be sworn," as in *Err.*, IV. iv. 7, *Wint.*, III. ii. 114, etc.

30. *bowels...burst out*] Shakespeare follows J. Foxe (Introduction, p. xiv).

32. *tend*] take care of, look after; wait or attend upon.

35. *pardon'd*] Holinshed says Melun's speech moved the nobles to make peace with Henry III (after John's death); Foxe, like Shakespeare, gives it an immediate effect—the nobles returned to John, and so "were a great number of them pardoned" (p. 256, i).

And tempt us not to bear above our power!
I'll tell thee, Hubert, half my power this night,
Passing these flats, are taken by the tide;               40
These Lincoln Washes have devoured them;
Myself, well mounted, hardly have escap'd.
Away before: conduct me to the king;
I doubt he will be dead or ere I come.              [*Exeunt.*

SCENE VII.—[*The Orchard in Swinstead Abbey.*]

*Enter* PRINCE HENRY, SALISBURY, *and* BIGOT.

*P. Hen.*  It is too late: the life of all his blood
Is touch'd corruptibly, and his pure brain,
Which some suppose the soul's frail dwelling-house,
Doth by the idle comments that it makes
Foretell the ending of mortality.                        5

*Enter* PEMBROKE.

*Pem.*  His highness yet doth speak, and holds belief
That, being brought into the open air,
It would allay the burning quality
Of that fell poison which assaileth him.
*P. Hen.*  Let him be brought into the orchard here.      10

*Scene* VII

*Scene* VII.] F1; IX. Pope; III. Donovan.          The . . . Abbey.] Theobald; om. F1.
2. *corruptibly*] F1; *corruptedly* Capell.

38. *tempt*] put to the test. So L.
Wright's *Display of Dutie* (1589): "God
. . . neuer fayleth his children in necessity: nor suffereth them to be tempted
aboue their power" (sig. E�ᵛ). Carter
compared *1 Corinthians*: "God . . .
shall not suffer you to be tempted
aboue your strength: but shall with the
temptation make a way, that ye may
be able to beare it" (x. 13, Bishops'
Bible; cf. *Genesis*, iv. 13).

39–42. *I'll . . . escap'd*] Shakespeare
follows M. Paris (Introduction, p.
xv); cf. v. vii. 61–4.

43. *Away before*] Lead the way.

*Scene* VII

1. *life*] essence, or vitality.
2. *touch'd*] infected.
*corruptibly*] causing corruption.
*pure*] clear. Halliwell noted that
Deloney imitated these lines in his
*Lamentable Death of King Iohn* [in
*Strange Histories* (1602)]: the poison
distempered John's "pure vnspotted
braine".

3. *some suppose*] The location of the
soul was disputed, but the brain was
thought to house the "reasonable
soul".

4. *idle comments*] nonsensical remarks.

Doth he still rage?                    [*Exit Bigot.*
*Pem.*                    He is more patient
Than when you left him; even now he sung.
*P. Hen.* O vanity of sickness! fierce extremes
In their continuance will not feel themselves.
Death, having prey'd upon the outward parts,        15
Leaves them invisible, and his siege is now
Against the mind, the which he pricks and wounds
With many legions of strange fantasies,
Which, in their throng and press to that last hold,
Confound themselves. 'Tis strange that death should
     sing.                    20
I am the cygnet to this pale faint swan
Who chants a doleful hymn to his own death
And from the organ-pipe of frailty sings
His soul and body to their lasting rest.

---

11. S.D.] Capell; om. F1.    16. *invisible*] F1; *insensible* Hanmer; *invincible*
Steevens conj.; *invasible* Wilson conj.; *enfeebl'd* Maxwell conj. (*N. & Q.*, 18 Feb.
1950); *unusable* Sisson.    17. *mind*] Rowe iii; *winde* F1.    20. *Confound*] *Coun-*
*found* F1.    21. *cygnet*] Rowe iii; *Symet* F1.

11. *rage*] rave.

13–17. *sickness . . . mind*] Mrs Bone
refers me (privately) to Holinshed:
"through anguish of mind, rather
than through force of sicknesse, he departed this life" (p. 194, i).

15–17. *Death . . . mind*] Cf. H.
Chettle's *Hoffman*: "How cold thou
art; death now assailes our hearts, /
Hauing triumph't ouer the outward
parts" (sig. E₃).

16. *invisible*] The invisibility of death
was a commonplace: Malone compared *Ven.*, 1004 (Death is called "invisible commander") and took *invisible*
as adverb; but "invincible" or "unusable" might well have been misread.

18. *legions*] Goes with the images of
*war* and of *numberlessness.*
*fantasies*] fancies; whims.

19. *press*] Malone compared *H 8*:
"many maz'd considerings did throng,/
And press'd in with this caution" (II.
iv. 183–4), and *Lucr.*, 1301.

*last hold*] Possibly so called because
the mind was often located in the
heart, as in W. Clever's *Flower of
Phisicke* (1590): "the minde and the
heart mutually inhabite one with another" (sig. K^v). The heart would be
pricked by the trembling caused by the
dying man's fancies. Cf. l. 3, note.

20. *Confound*] Confuse; destroy.

21. *cygnet*] Did Shakespeare write
"Sycnet"?

*swan*] Cf. *Mer.V.*, III. ii. 44, *Lucr.*,
1611. Tilley (p. 644) quoted the proverb "Like a Swan, he sings before his
death." Ovid's "carmina iam moriens
canit exequialia cygnus" (*Metam.*,
xiv. 430) has been compared.

23. *organ-pipe*] W. Vallans explained
"swan-song" in 1590: "The Philo-
sophers say it is because of the spirit,
which, labouring to passe thorow the
long and small passage of her necke,
makes a noise as if she did sing" ["To
the Reader" in *A Tale of Two Swannes*
(1590), ed. Hearne].

*Sal.* Be of good comfort, prince; for you are born                    25
    To set a form upon that indigest
    Which he hath left so shapeless and so rude.

*Enter Attendants, and* BIGOT, *bringing in* KING JOHN *in a chair.*

*K. John.* Ay, marry, now my soul hath elbow-room
    It would not out at windows nor at doors.
    There is so hot a summer in my bosom,                    30
    That all my bowels crumble up to dust:
    I am a scribbled form, drawn with a pen
    Upon a parchment, and against this fire
    Do I shrink up.
*P. Hen.*           How fares your majesty?
*K. John.* Poison'd, ill fare; dead, forsook, cast off:                    35
    And none of you will bid the winter come
    To thrust his icy fingers in my maw,
    Nor let my kingdom's rivers take their course
    Through my burn'd bosom, nor entreat the north
    To make his bleak winds kiss my parched lips                    40
    And comfort me with cold. I do not ask you much,

28. S.D.] Capell; Iohn brought in. F1.    28–9. *elbow-room . . . doors.*] This ed.;
*elbow roome, . . . doores,* F1 ; *elbow-room; . . . doors.* Pope, edd.    35. *fare*] F1 ; *fate*
Pope.    41. *I . . . you*] F1 ; *I ask not* Pope.

26. *form*] Holinshed marvels how soon England under Henry III was "from a troubled fourme reduced to a flourishing and prosperous degree: chiefelie by the diligent heed . . . of the king himselfe" (p. 203, ii); *form* = order.

26–7. *indigest . . . rude*] Ovid's "rudis indigestaque moles" (*Metam.*, I. 7) was a familiar tag, e.g. R. H. in *A Sermon* (1589) called his book "this my *Rudis indigestaque moles*" (sig. A₅).

28–9. *Ay . . . doors.*] i.e. "now *that* my soul". John wants to die quickly, but now that his soul does not need to labour for passage (cf. l. 23, note) it prefers to stay. Some think Shakespeare alludes to the superstition that it is easier to die out of doors, taking *windows, doors* literally; but surely the

*mouth* is imagined as *windows* etc. of the body (cf. *this wall of flesh*, III. ii. 30).

33. *parchment*] Cf. Chapman's *Alphonsus*: "Mine entrails shrink together like a scroll / Of burning parchment" (IV. ii. 9–10) (Bagley).

35. *ill fare*] For the same pun cf. *Ham.*, III. ii. 97–100.

36–41. *And . . . cold.*] Much imitated, closest in B. and F.'s *Wife for a Month* (ed. 1647, sig. 6H₃ᵛ). Shakespeare may follow *Faerie Queene*, II. vi. 44. Malone compared *Lusts Dominion* (1657) ("Written by Christofer Marloe"): "the cold hand of sleep / Hath thrust his Icie fingers in my brest" (sig. D₅ᵛ); so earlier: "Deaths frozen hand hold's Royal *Philip's* heart" (sig. B₅ᵛ).

37. *maw*] throat; belly.

39. *north*] north wind.

I beg cold comfort; and you are so strait,
And so ingrateful, you deny me that.
*P. Hen.* O that there were some virtue in my tears
That might relieve you!
*K. John.*                    The salt in them is hot.          45
Within me is a hell; and there the poison
Is as a fiend confin'd to tyrannize
On unreprievable condemned blood.

*Enter the* BASTARD.

*Bast.* O, I am scalded with my violent motion,
And spleen of speed to see your majesty!          50
*K. John.* O cousin, thou art come to set mine eye:
The tackle of my heart is crack'd and burn'd,
And all the shrouds wherewith my life should sail
Are turned to one thread, one little hair;
My heart hath one poor string to stay it by,          55
Which holds but till thy news be uttered;
And then all this thou seest is but a clod
And module of confounded royalty.
*Bast.* The Dolphin is preparing hitherward,

---

49.] F1; *Scene* X. Pope.     49. S.D.] As F1 (Enter Bastard.).     51. *eye*] F1; *eyes* Keightley.     58. *module*] F1; *model* Hanmer.

---

42. *cold comfort*] poor comfort (idiom), as in *Shr.*, IV. i. 33.

*strait*] narrow, i.e. niggardly.

44. *virtue*] power, efficacy.

45. *The* . . . *hot.*] John does not simply reject Henry's tears as *hot* (i.e. unpleasant). He recalls the medical theory that *salt* is essential to preserve the *blood* from corruption, and rejects tears quibblingly (his blood cannot be saved even by salt).

46. *Within* . . . *hell*] The biblical idea that the sinner has a hell within him was commonplace, as in R. Some's *Godly Sermon* (1580): "his sinnes had so galled his heart, that he felt . . . a greeuous hell within him" (sig. B₃). This idea (not in John's but in Shakespeare's mind) is reinforced through the legal *unreprievable, condemned* (l. 48).

49. *scalded*] heated, burnt.

50. *spleen*] Cf. II. i. 448, note.

51. *set*] close (after death).

52. *tackle*] Wright compared *3 H 6*, v. iv. 18. Perhaps Shakespeare follows *Isaiah*: "Thy tackling is loosed . . ." (xxxiii. 23, Bishops' Bible. The Genevan Bible called this chapter "The destruction of them, by whome God hath punished his Church", and commented on v. 23: "Hee derideth the . . . enemies of the Church, declaring their destruction, as they that perish by shipwracke").

53. *shrouds*] ropes of the mast.

54. *thread*] The thread spun by the Fates?

55. *string*] The physiology of "heart-strings" was generally accepted.

58. *module*] counterfeit, image.

Where God He knows how we shall answer him;      60
For in a night the best part of my power,
As I upon advantage did remove,
Were in the Washes all unwarily
Devoured by the unexpected flood.        [*The King dies.*

*Sal.* You breathe these dead news in as dead an ear.      65
My liege! my lord!—But now a king, now thus.

*P. Hen.* Even so must I run on, and even so stop.
What surety of the world, what hope, what stay,
When this was now a king, and now is clay?

*Bast.* Art thou gone so? I do but stay behind      70
To do the office for thee of revenge,
And then my soul shall wait on thee to heaven,
As it on earth hath been thy servant still.
Now, now, you stars that move in your right spheres,
Where be your powers? show now your mended
    faiths,      75
And instantly return with me again,
To push destruction and perpetual shame
Out of the weak door of our fainting land.
Straight let us seek, or straight we shall be sought;
The Dolphin rages at our very heels.      80

*Sal.* It seems you know not, then, so much as we:

---

60. *God*] Walker; *heauen* F1.      64. S.D.] Rowe; om. F1.      74. *right*] F1;
*bright* Pope.

---

60. *God*] Cf. III. i. 81, note.

61–4. *For . . . flood.*] Cf. v. vi. 39–44.
Shakespeare follows M. Paris (Introduction, p. xv), but *the best part of my
power* (l. 61) follows Holinshed: "a
great part of his armie" (194, i)—for
this *T.R.* reads "the most of all our
men" (II. vi. 50).

62. *upon advantage*] to seize an advantage.

65. *dead news*] deadly, terrible news.

66. *now . . . now*] "but even now
worth this, / And now worth nothing"
*Mer.V.*, I. i. 35–6).

68–9. *What . . . clay?*] "For what
suerty is in stone or timber? What
strength? Nor is any house for the gor-
geousnes the safer" [L. Humfrey,

*Nobles or of Nobilitye* (1563), sig. T₈ᵛ)].
Moralist commonplace.

68. *stay*] prop, support (On.); continuance in a state (as Sonnet 15).

69. *clay*] Cf. the "Kings are clay"
proverbs.

72. *And . . . heaven*] But cf. ll. 103–5.

74. *stars*] Various edd. thought that
Faulconbridge addresses John's stars
—"John's fortune had broken faith
with him" (Wright). But Shakespeare
may follow M. Paris (Introduction,
p. xvii), with *stars* = nobles (who move
round the king as stars round a sun).
Cf. *Per.*, II. iii. 39–40 ("Had princes
sit, like stars, about his throne, / And
he the sun"), *H 8*, IV. i. 54.

78. *door*] Cf. v. i. 60, v. ii. 137.

The Cardinal Pandulph is within at rest,
Who half an hour since came from the Dolphin,
And brings from him such offers of our peace
As we with honour and respect may take,                    85
With purpose presently to leave this war.

*Bast.* He will the rather do it when he sees
Ourselves well sinew'd to our defence.

*Sal.* Nay, 'tis in a manner done already,
For many carriages he hath dispatch'd                    90
To the sea-side, and put his cause and quarrel
To the disposing of the cardinal:
With whom yourself, myself and other lords,
If you think meet, this afternoon will post
To consummate this business happily.                    95

*Bast.* Let it be so: and you, my noble prince,
With other princes that may best be spar'd,
Shall wait upon your father's funeral.

*P. Hen.* At Worcester must his body be interr'd;
For so he will'd it.

*Bast.*                    Thither shall it then:                    100
And happily may your sweet self put on
The lineal state and glory of the land!
To whom, with all submission, on my knee
I do bequeath my faithful services
And true subjection everlastingly.                    105

*Sal.* And the like tender of our love we make,
To rest without a spot for evermore.

---

88. *sinew'd*] F1; *sinewèd* Dyce.    89. *'tis*] F1; *it is* Pope.    91. *sea-side*] As F2; no hyphen F1.    97. *princes*] F1; *nobles* K. Elze [*Notes on Eliz. Dram.* (1880), p. 66].

---

82. *The . . . rest*] Unhistorical. Shakespeare emphasizes John's spiritual independence.

84. *such . . . peace*] Lewis, after the loss of his supply (v. v. 12), "inclined he sooner vnto peace . . . he tooke such offers of agreement as were put vnto him" [Hol., 201, ii, noted by A. S. Cairncross, *Problem of Hamlet* (1936), p. 141].

85. *respect*] self-respect.

90. *carriages*] With the impedimenta of his army.

99–100. *At . . . it.*] Cf. Intro., p. xii.

101. *happily*] propitiously; contentedly; fittingly, appropriately.

102. *lineal*] Cf. II. i. 85.—"As the heir of a crowned king, Henry had a better title than John; just as Henry V's was better than his father's" (Wilson). Cf. I. i. 40, note.

106. *tender*] offer.

*P. Hen.*  I have a kind soul that would give thanks
  And knows not how to do it but with tears.
*Bast.*  O, let us pay the time but needful woe,                    110
  Since it hath been beforehand with our griefs.
  This England never did, nor never shall,
  Lie at the proud foot of a conqueror,
  But when it first did help to wound itself.
  Now these her princes are come home again                    115
  Come the three corners of the world in arms
  And we shall shock them! Nought shall make us rue
  If England to itself do rest but true!                    [*Exeunt.*

108. *give*] *give you* Rowe, edd.    110. *time*] *time:* F1.    118. S.D.] F1; Exeunt,
bearing in the Body. Capell.

108. *kind*] proper, appropriate;
loving.
  *give thanks*] Henry's temporary in-
sufficiency is expressed in an imperfect pentameter.
  110–11. *O . . . griefs.*] "Let us now
indulge in sorrow, since there is
abundant cause for it. England has
been long a scene of confusion, and its
calamities have anticipated our tears"
(Malone); "As previously we have
found sufficient cause for lamentation,
let us not waste the present time in
superfluous sorrow" (Steevens). The
F1 colon, bringing a pause after *time*,
brackets *give (you) thanks* (l. 108) and
*pay the time.*
  *woe . . . griefs*] lamentation . . . suf-
ferings.
  111. *beforehand*] Wilson glosses as a
"commercial metaphor", since "to
be beforehand" = to draw money in
advance (*O.E.D.*, 1d).
  115. *home*] Cf. iv. iii. 151, v. iv. 12.
  116. *three . . . world*] "the four *corners*

of the world" (*Isaiah*, xi. 12) and "the
three *parts* of the world" (cf. *Ant.*, iv.
vi. 6, *Caes.*, iv. i. 14) were both
clichés = the whole world. Furness
thought *three* corners means that England was the fourth ["that utmost
corner of the west" (ii. i. 29)]. *T.R.*
(ii. ix. 54) supports him, taking the
three to be the pope, France, Spain.
  117. *shock*] meet force with force,
throw into confusion.
  117–18. *Nought . . . true!*] Armada
pamphleteers (citing *Matthew*, xii. 25,
*Mark*, iii. 24, *Luke*, xi. 17) popularized
this watch-word. Cf. G. D.'s *Briefe
Discoverie* (1588): "our realme . . . was
neuer conquered by any, so long as it
was true within it selfe" (sig. R₂ᵛ);
G. B.'s *Fig for the Spaniard* (1591): "If
England feare God, and be true within
it selfe, it may boldly bid a fig for the
Spaniard" (sig. B₃ᵛ); also *3 H 6*, iv. i.
40, *The True Tragedie of Richard Duke of
Yorke* (1595), sig. D₂ᵛ, *T.R.*, ii. ix.
45–6.

# Appendix A

## HOLINSHED AND COGGESHALL

### (1) Holinshed

The sources of *John* were discussed in the Introduction, where Shakespeare's debts to his minor sources were outlined in full. A detailed comparison of the play and Holinshed, the principal source, was not possible there: we now subjoin extracts from the chronicle, covering the story as Shakespeare used it. Some of Shakespeare's purely verbal debts are not included, however: these can be traced through the footnotes.

A.D. 1191. Richard I "had instituted his nephue Arthur duke of Britaine to be his heire and successour" (Hol., 129, ii).

1199. Richard I died. He "ordeined his testament . . .
"Vnto his brother Iohn he assigned the crowne of England, and all other his lands and dominions, causing the Nobles there present to sweare fealtie vnto him . . ." (155, ii–156, i). Cf. *John*, II. i. 191–4.

"IOhn the yoongest son of Henrie the second . . . so soone as his brother Richard was deceassed, sent Hubert archbishop of Canturburie, and William Marshall earle of Striguill (otherwise called Chepstow) into England, both to proclaime him king, and also to see his peace kept, togither with Geffrey Fitz Peter lord cheefe iustice, and diuerse other barons of the realme, whilest he himselfe went to Chinon where his brothers treasure laie, which was foorthwith deliuered vnto him by Robert de Turneham: and therewithall the castell of Chinon and Sawmer and diuerse other places, which were in the custodie of the foresaid Robert. But Thomas de Furnes nephue to the said Robert de Turneham deliuered the citie and castell of Angiers vnto Arthur duke of Britaine. For by generall consent of the nobles and peeres of the countries of Aniou, Maine, and Touraine, Arthur was receiued as the liege and souereigne lord of the same countries.

"For euen at this present, and so soone as it was knowne that king Richard was deceased, diuerse cities and townes on that side of the sea belonging to the said Richard whilest he liued, fell at ods among themselues, some of them indeuouring to preferre king

Iohn, other labouring rather to be vnder the gouernance of Arthur duke of Britaine, considering that he seemed by most right to be their cheefe lord, forsomuch as he was sonne to Geffrey elder brother to Iohn . . ." (157, i, ii).

"Now whilest king Iohn was thus occupied in recouering his brothers treasure, and traueling with his subiects to reduce them to his obedience, queene Elianor his mother . . . trauelled as diligentlie to procure the English people to receiue their oth of allegiance to be true to king Iohn . . ." (157, ii).

John established himself in England: ". . . this was doone cheeflie by the working of the kings mother, whom the nobilitie much honoured and loued. For she being bent to prefer hir sonne Iohn, left no stone vnturned to establish him in the throne, comparing oftentimes the difference of gouernement betweene a king that is a man, and a king that is but a child. For as Iohn was 32 yeares old, so Arthur duke of Britaine was but a babe to speake of. In the end, winning all the nobilitie wholie vnto hir will . . ." (158, i).

"Surelie queene Elianor the kings mother was sore against hir nephue Arthur, rather mooued thereto by enuie conceiued against his mother, than vpon any iust occasion giuen in the behalfe of the child, for that she saw if he were king, how his mother Constance would looke to beare most rule within the realme of England, till hir sonne should come to lawfull age, to gouerne of himselfe . . ." (158, i). Cf. II. i. 122–3.

"When this dooing of the queene was signified vnto the said Constance, she doubting the suertie of hir sonne, committed him to the trust of the French king, who receiuing him into his tuition, promised to defend him from all his enimies . . ." (158, i, ii).

"In the meane time . . . queene Elianor, togither with capteine Marchades entred into Aniou, and wasted the same, bicause they of that countrie had receiued Arthur for their souereigne lord and gouernour. And amongst other townes and fortresses, they tooke the citie of Angiers, slue manie of the citizens, and committed the rest to prison . . ." (158, ii).

"Whilest these things were a dooing in England, Philip K. of France hauing leuied an armie, brake into Normandie. . . . In an other part, an armie of Britains . . . tooke the citie of Angiers, which king Iohn had woon from duke Arthur, in the last yeare passed. These things being signified to king Iohn, he thought to make prouision for the recouerie of his losses there, with all speed possible . . ." (160, i).

". . . king Philip made Arthur duke of Britaine knight, and receiued of him his homage for Aniou, Poictiers, Maine, Touraine, and Britaine. Also somewhat before the time that the truce should expire . . . the two kings . . . came togither personallie, and communed at full of the variance depending betweene them. But the French king shewed himselfe stiffe and hard in this treatie, demanding the whole countrie of Veulquessine to be restored vnto him . . . Moreouer, he demanded, that Poictiers, Aniou, Maine, and Touraine, should be deliuered and wholie resigned vnto Arthur duke of Britaine.

"But these, & diuerse other requests which he made, king Iohn would not in any wise grant vnto . . ." (160, ii). Cf. II. i. 151–5.

"All this while was William de Roches busilie occupied about his practise, to make king Iohn and his nephue Arthur freends, which thing at length he brought about, and therevpon deliuered into king Iohns hands the citie of Mauns which he had in keeping. . . But in the night folowing, vpon some mistrust and suspicion gathered in the obseruation of the couenants on K. Iohns behalfe, both the said Arthur, with his mother Contance . . . fled awaie secretlie from the king, and got them to the citie of Angiers, where the mother of the said Arthur refusing hir former husband the earle of Chester, married hir selfe to the lord Guie de Tours . . . by the popes dispensation. The same yere, Philip bastard sonne to king Richard, to whome his father had giuen the castell and honor of Coinacke, killed the vicount of Limoges, in reuenge of his fathers death . . ." (160, ii). Cf. II. ii. 14, note, III. ii. 3.

1200. King John and King Philip "came eftsoones to a communication betwixt the townes of Vernon and Lisle Dandelie, where finallie they concluded an agreement, with a marriage to be had betwixt Lewes the sonne of king Philip, and the ladie Blanch, daughter to Alfonso king of Castile the 8 of that name, & neece to K. Iohn by his sister Elianor.

"In consideration whereof, king Iohn, besides the summe of thirtie thousand markes in siluer, as in respect of dowrie assigned to his said neece, resigned his title to the citie of Eureux, and also vnto all those townes which the French king had by warre taken from him, the citie of Angiers onelie excepted. . . The French king . . . receiued of king Iohn his homage for all the lands, fees and tenements which at anie time his brother king Richard, or his father king Henrie had holden of him, the said king Lewes (sic) or any his predecessors, the quit claims and marriages alwaies excepted. The king of England likewise did homage vnto the French king for Britaine, and againe (as after you shall heare) receiued homage for the same countrie, and for the countie of Richmont of his nephue Arthur . . ." (161, i, ii).

"By this conclusion of marriage betwixt the said Lewes and Blanch, the right of king Iohn went awaie, which he lawfullie before pretended vnto the citie of Eureux, and vnto those townes in the confines of Berrie . . . likewise vnto the countrie of Veuxin or Veulquessine . . . the right of all which lands, townes and countries was released to the king of France by K. Iohn, who supposed that by his affinitie, and resignation of his right to those places, the peace now made would haue continued for euer. And in consideration thereof, he procured furthermore, that the foresaid Blanch should be conueied into France to hir husband with all speed . . ." (161, ii). Cf. II. i. 416–560.

"King Iohn being now in rest from warres with forren enimies, began to make warre with his subiects pursses at home, emptieng them by taxes and tallages, to fill his coffers, which alienated the minds of a great number of them from his loue and obedience . . ." (161, ii).

John dealt severely with the white monks. "The cause that mooued the king to deale so hardlie with them was, for that they refused to helpe him with monie, when . . . he demanded it of them towards the paiment of the thirtie thousand pounds which he had couenanted to pay the French king . . ." (162, i). Cf. III. ii. 16–23.

"About the moneth of December, there were seene in the prouince of Yorke fiue moones, one in the east, the second in the west, the third in the north, the fourth in the south, and the fift as it were set in the middest of the other, hauing manie stars about it, and went fiue or six times incompassing the other, as it were the space of one houre, and shortlie after vanished awaie . . ." (163, i). Cf. IV. ii. 182–5.

1202. "In the yeare 1202 king Iohn . . . and the French king met togither, neere vnto the castell of Gulleton, and there in talke had betweene them, he commanded king Iohn with no small arrogancie, and contrarie to his former promise, to restore vnto his nephue Arthur duke of Britaine, all those lands now in his possession on that side the sea, which king Iohn earnestlie denied to doo, wherevpon the French king immediatlie after, began war against him, . . . he besieged the castell of Radepont for the space of eight daies, till king Iohn came thither, and forced him to depart with much dishonor . . ." (164, i).

Arthur led an army against the English and won a small victory. "Queene Elianor that was regent in those parties being put in great feare with the newes of this sudden sturre, got hir into Mirabeau a strong towne, . . . Arthur following the victorie, shortlie after followed hir, and woone Mirabeau, where he tooke his grandmother within the same, whom he yet intreated verie honorablie, and with great reuerence (as some haue reported.) But other write far more trulie, that she was not taken, but escaped into a tower, within the which she was straitlie besieged . . ." (164, ii). Cf. III. ii. 5–8.

"King Iohn . . . was maruellouslie troubled with the strangenesse of the newes, and with manie bitter words accused the French king as an vntrue prince, and a fraudulent league-breaker: and in all possible hast speedeth him foorth, continuing his iournie for the most part both day and night to come to the succour of his people. To be briefe, he vsed such diligence, that he was vpon his enimies necks yer they could vnderstand any thing of his comming, or gesse what the matter meant . . ." (164, ii). Cf. III. i. 266–70, II. i. 79.

Arthur's force was routed "and Arthur with the residue of the armie that escaped with life from the first bickering was taken, who being herevpon committed to prison, first at Falais, and after within the citie of Rouen, liued not long after as you shall heare . . ." (164, ii).

"It is said that king Iohn caused his nephue Arthur to be brought before him at Falais, and there went about to persuade him all that he could to forsake his freendship and aliance with the French king, and to leane and sticke to him being his naturall vncle. But Arthur like one that wanted good counsell . . . made a presumptuous answer . . ." (165, i).

"Shortlie after king Iohn comming ouer into England, caused himselfe to be crowned againe . . . and then went backe againe into Normandie, where immediatlie vpon his arriuall, a rumour was spred through all France, of the death of his nephue Arthur. True it is that great suit was made to haue Arthur set at libertie, as well by the French king, as by William de Riches a valiant baron of Poictou, and diuerse other Noble men of the Britains, who when they could not preuaile in their suit, they banded themselues togither, and . . . began to leuie sharpe wars against king Iohn in diuerse places, insomuch (as it was thought) that so long as Arthur liued, there would be no quiet in those parts: wherevpon it was reported, that king Iohn through persuasion of his councellors, appointed certeine persons to go vnto Falais, where Arthur was kept in prison, vnder the charge of Hubert de Burgh, and there to put out the yoong gentlemans eies.

"But through such resistance as he made against one of the tormentors that came to execute the kings commandement (for the other rather forsooke their prince and countrie, than they would consent to obeie the kings authoritie heerein) and such lamentable words as he vttered, Hubert de Burgh did preserue him from that

iniurie, not doubting but rather to haue thanks than displeasure at
the kings hands, for deliuering him of such infamie as would haue
redounded vnto his highnesse, if the yoong gentleman had beene
so cruellie dealt withall. For he considered, that king Iohn had resolued vpon this point onelie in his heat and furie (which moueth
men to vndertake manie an inconuenient enterprise, vnbeseeming
the person of a common man, much more reprochfull to a prince,
all men in that mood being meere foolish and furious, and prone
to accomplish the peruerse conceits of their ill possessed heart . . .)
and that afterwards, vpon better aduisement, he would both repent
himselfe so to haue commanded, and giue them small thanke that
should see it put in execution. Howbeit to satisfie his mind for the
time, and to staie the rage of the Britains, he caused it to be bruted
abroad through the countrie, that the kings commandement was
fulfilled, and that Arthur also through sorrow and greefe was departed out of this life. For the space of fifteene daies this rumour incessantlie ran through both the realmes of England and France . . ."
(165, i, ii). Cf. iv. i.

"But when the Britains were nothing pacified, but rather kindled
more vehementlie to worke all the mischeefe they could deuise, in
reuenge of their souereignes death, there was no remedie but to signifie abroad againe, that Arthur was as yet liuing and in health.
Now when the king heard the truth of all this matter, he was nothing displeased for that his commandement was not executed. . .
But now touching the maner in verie deed of the end of this Arthur,
writers make sundrie reports. . . Some haue written, that as he
assaied to haue escaped out of prison, and proouing to clime ouer
the wals of the castell, he fell into the riuer of Saine, and so was
drowned. . . But some affirme, that king Iohn secretlie caused him
to be murthered . . . verelie king Iohn was had in great suspicion,
whether worthilie or not, the lord knoweth . . ." (165, ii). Cf. iv. ii.
249–69, iv. iii. 1–10.

1203–4. John gathered huge sums in subsidies. "Neither were the
bishops, abbats, nor any other ecclesiasticall persons exempted, by
meanes whereof he ran first into the hatred of the clergie . . ." (167,
i). Cf. iii. ii. 16–23.

1204. "King Philip vnderstanding that king Iohn remained still
in England, rather occupied in gathering of monie amongst his
subiects, than in making other prouision . . . thought now for his
part to lose no time. . . With this swiftnesse of speed, he brought also
such a feare into the hearts of most men, that he wan all the countrie of Normandie . . ." (167, i, ii).

"About this time queene Elianor the mother of king Iohn departed this life, consumed rather through sorow and anguish of mind, than of any other naturall infirmitie . . ." (167, ii–168, i). Cf. IV. ii. 116–21.

1206. King John, making an expedition in France, "entred into Aniou, and comming to the citie of Angiers, appointed certeine bands of his footmen, & all his light horssemen to compasse the towne about, whilest he, with the residue of the footmen, & all the men of armes, did go to assault the gates. Which enterprise with fire and sword he so manfullie executed, that the gates being in a moment broken open, the citie was entered and deliuered to the souldiers for a preie. So that of the citizens some were taken, some killed, and the wals of the citie beaten flat to the ground . . ." (170, i).

"After this it chanced that king Iohn remembring himselfe of the destruction of the citie of Angiers, which (bicause he was descended from thence) he had before time greatlie loued, began now to repent him, in that he had destroied it, and therefore with all speed he tooke order to haue it againe repaired, which was doone in most beautifull wise . . ." (170, ii).

From 1205 onwards King John was in trouble because of the election of the Archbishop of Canterbury. The nominees of John and of the monks of Canterbury were both rejected by Innocent III, who promoted Stephen Langton, only to find that John refused to accept him. Holinshed's marginal gloss ["Stephan Langton chosen archbishop of Canturburie" (171, i)] was transcribed by Shakespeare. Cf. III. i. 69.

1207. King John wrote to the pope "that he maruelled not a little what the pope ment, in that he did not consider how necessarie the freendship of the king of England was to the see of Rome, sith there came more gains to the Romane church out of that kingdome, than out of any other realme on this side the mountaines. He added hereto, that for the liberties of his crowne he would stand to the death, if the matter so required . . .

"Moreouer, he declared that if he might not be heard and haue his mind, he would suerlie restraine the passages out of this realme, that none should go to Rome, least his land should be so emptied of monie and treasure . . ." (171, i). Cf. III. i. 73–97.

1208. "The pope perceiuing that king Iohn continued still in his former mind (which he called obstinacie) sent ouer his bulles into England, directed to William bishop of London [and others] . . . commanding them that vnlesse king Iohn would suffer peaceablie the archbishop of Canturburie to occupie his see, and his moonks their abbie, they should put both him and his land vnder the sentence of interdiction, denouncing him and his land plainelie accurssed..." (171-2).

King John "in a great rage sware, that if either they or any other presumed to put his land vnder interdiction ... what Romans so-euer he found within the precinct of any his dominions, he would put out their eies, and slit their noses..." (172, i).

The king was cursed by the bishops and, "taking this matter in verie great displeasure, seized vpon all their temporalties, and con-uerted the same to his vse..." (172, i).

1209. "King Iohn notwithstanding that the realme was thus wholie interdicted and vexed, ... made no great account thereof as touching any offense towards God or the pope: but rather mistrust-ing the hollow hearts of his people, he tooke a new oth of them for their faithfull allegiance..." (173, i). Cf. IV. ii. 1.

"There liued in those daies a diuine named Alexander Cem-entarius ... [who declared] that the generall scourge where-with the people were afflicted, chanced not through the princes fault, but for the wickednesse of his people, for the king was but the rod of the Lords wrath ...

"[Cementarius also asserted] that it apperteined not to the pope, to haue to doo concerning the temporall possessions of any kings or other potentats touching the rule and gouernment of their subiects, sith no power was granted to Peter (the speciall and cheefe of the apostles of the Lord) but onlie touching the church..." (173, ii–174, i). Cf. III. i. 73–97.

"In the same yeare also, the pope sent two legats into England, the one named Pandulph a lawier, and the other Durant a templer, who comming vnto king Iohn, exhorted him with manie terrible words to leaue his stubborne disobedience to the church, and to re-forme his misdooings. The king for his part quietlie heard them ... when they perceiued that they could not haue their purpose ... the legats departed, leauing him accursed, and the land interdicted, as they found it at their comming..." (175, i). Cf. III. i. 61 ff.

"In the meane time pope Innocent, after the returne of his legats out of England, perceiuing that king Iohn would not be ordered by him, determined ... to depriue king Iohn of his kinglie state, and so first absolued all his subiects and vassals of their oths of allegiance made vnto the same king, and after depriued him by solemne pro-testation of his kinglie administration and dignitie, and lastlie sig-nified that his depriuation vnto the French king and other christian princes, admonishing them to pursue king Iohn, being thus de-priued, forsaken, and condemned as a common enimie to God and his church. He ordeined furthermore, that whosoeuer imploied goods or other aid to vanquish and ouercome that disobedient prince, should remaine in assured peace of the church . . . not onlie in their goods and persons, but also in suffrages for sauing of their soules . . ." (175, ii). Cf. III. i. 100–5.

The pope "appointed Pandulph . . . to go into France . . . giuing him in commandement, that repairing vnto the French king, he should communicate with him all that which he had appointed to be doone against king Iohn, and to exhort the French king to make warre vpon him, as a person for his wickednesse excommunicated . . ." (175, ii). Cf. III. i. 117–19.

1213. "Ye shall vnderstand, the French king being requested by Pandulph the popes legat, to take the warre in hand against king Iohn, was easilie persuaded thereto of an inward hatred that he bare vnto our king, and therevpon with all diligence made his pro-uision. . . Pandulph vpon good considerations thought first to go eftsoones, or at the least wise to send into England, before the French armie should land there, and to assaie once againe, if he might induce the king to shew himselfe reformable vnto the popes pleasure . . ." (176, ii).

King John assembled an army to defend England, "so that if they had beene all of one mind, and well bent towards the seruice of their king and defense of their countrie, there had not beene a prince in christendome, but that they might haue beene able to haue defended the realme of England against him . . ." (176, ii). Cf. v. vii. 112–18.

Pandulph convinced John that he was in a hopeless position. John "vtterlie despairing in his matters, when he saw himselfe con-streined to obeie, was in a great perplexitie of mind . . . oppressed with the burthen of the imminent danger and ruine, against his will, and verie loth so to haue doone, he promised vpon his oth to stand to the popes order and decree. Wherefore shortlie after (in like manner as pope Innocent had commanded) he tooke the crowne from his owne head, and deliuered the same to Pandulph the legat, neither he, nor his heires at anie time thereafter to re-ceiue the same, but at the popes hands . . ." (177, i).

"Then Pandulph keeping the crowne with him for the space of fiue daies in token of possession thereof, at length (as the popes vicar) gaue it him againe . . ." (177, ii). Cf. v. i. 1 ff.

"Pandulph . . . sailed backe into France, & came to Roan, where he declared to king Philip the effect of his trauell, and what he had doone in England. But king Philip hauing in this meane while con-sumed a great masse of monie, to the summe of sixtie thousand pounds, as he himselfe alledged, about the furniture of his iournie,

which he intended to haue made into England . . . was much
offended for the reconciliation of king Iohn, and determined not so
to breake off his enterprise, least it might be imputed to him for a
great reproch to haue beene at such charges and great expenses in
vaine . . ." (178, ii). Cf. v. ii. 65–116.

"An hermit named Peter of Pontfret, or Wakefield as some
writers haue." This gloss introduces a series of events briefly recorded in the play: "There was in this season an heremit, whose
name was Peter, dwelling about Yorke, a man in great reputation
with the common people, bicause that either inspired with some
spirit of prophesie as the people beleeued, or else hauing some notable skill in art magike, he was accustomed to tell what should follow after. And for so much as oftentimes his saiengs prooued true,
great credit was giuen to him as to a verie prophet . . . [but he was]
rather a deluder of the people, and in instrument of satan raised vp
for the inlargement of his kingdome: as the sequele of this discourse
importeth. This Peter about the first of Ianuarie last past, had told
the king, that at the feast of the Ascension it should come to passe,
that he should be cast out of his kingdome. And (whether, to the
intent that his words should be the better beleeued, or whether
vpon too much trust of his owne cunning) he offered himselfe to
suffer death for it, if his prophesie prooued not true. Herevpon being committed to prison within the castell of Corf, when the day by
him prefixed came, without any other notable damage vnto king
Iohn, he was by the kings commandement drawne from the said
castell, vnto the towne of Warham, & there hanged, togither with
his sonne.

"The people . . . thought, that he had much wrong to die, bicause the matter fell out euen as he had prophesied: for the day before the Ascension day, king Iohn had resigned the superioritie of
his kingdome (as they tooke the matter) vnto the pope . . ." (180,
i, ii). Cf. iv. ii. 143–58, v. i. 22–9.

1214. A large section of John's nobles, goaded by the king's in-
fringements upon their ancient rights, were plotting against him.
"The Nobles supposing that longer delaie therein was not to be
suffered, assembled themselues togither at the abbeie of Burie
(vnder colour of going thither to doo their deuotions to the bodie
of S. Edmund which laie there inshrined) where they vttered their
complaint of the kings tyrannicall maners. . ."

The nobles "receiued a solemne oth vpon the altar there, that if
the king would not grant to the same liberties, with others which
he of his owne accord had promised to confirme to them, they
would from thencefoorth make warre vpon him, till they had ob-

teined their purpose, and inforced him to grant, not onelie to all these their petitions, but also yeeld to the confirmation of them vnder his seale, for euer to remaine most stedfast and inuiolable..." (183, ii–184, i). Cf. IV. iii. 11, V. ii. 2, 7.

1215. "The king soone after also, to assure himselfe the more effectuallie of the allegiance of his people in time to come, caused euerie man to renew his homage, and to take a new oth to be faithfull to him against all other persons..." (184, ii). Cf. IV. ii. 1.

The barons began to make war against King John. "The chiefe ringleaders of this power were these... Richard earle de Bigot... G. de Maundeuile earle of Essex..." (185, i).

The barons captured London, and the remainder of the nobility left John, viz. "William Marshall earle of Penbroke,... Nicholas earle of Salisburie..." (185, ii).

The barons "sore lamented the state of the realme, gessing what would follow...

"... they said among themselues, Wo be to vs, yea rather to the whole realme that wanteth a sufficient king, and is gouerned by a tyrant that seeketh the subuersion therof. Now hath our souereigne lord made vs subiect to Rome... [John] of his owne accord voluntarilie submitteth himselfe to become vassall to euerie stranger..." (186, ii). Cf. V. ii. 1–63.

1216. Because of John's successes the barons appealed for help to the French. "Therefore considering that they were in such extremitie of despaire they resolued with themselues to seeke for aid at the enimies hands..." (190, i). Cf. V. ii. 22, 29.

To put heart into the English barons, Lewis "sent ouer a certeine number of armed men, vnder the leading of [various French lords including]... Giles de Melun... Moreouer the said Lewes wrote to the barons, that he purposed by Gods assistance to... passe ouer with all speed vnto their succours..." (190, i, ii). Cf. IV. iii. 15–17.

John, hearing of the alliance of the barons and Lewis, "dispatched a messenger in all hast to the pope, signifieng to him what was in hand and practised against him, requiring furthermore the said pope by his authoritie to cause Lewes to staie his iournie... This he needed not haue doone, had he beene indued with such prudence and prowesse as is requisit to be planted in one that beareth rule... he bare too low a saile, in that he would be so foolified as being a king, to suffer vsurped supremasie to be caruer of his kingdome... The pope desirous to helpe king Iohn all that he might (bicause he was now his vassall) sent his legat Gualo into France, to disswade king Philip from taking anie enterprise in hand against the king of England. But king Philip though he was content

to heare what the legat could saie, yet by no meanes would be turned from the execution of his purpose . . ." (190, ii–191, i).

"Lewes on the morrow following . . . came into the councell
chamber, and with frowning looke beheld the legat, where by his
procurator he defended the cause that moued him to take vpon him
this iournie into England, disprouing not onelie the right which
king Iohn had to the crowne, but also alledging his owne interest
. . ." (191, i). Cf. v. ii. 64–116.

Lewis landed at Sandwich and camped there for three days. "In
which meane time there came vnto him a great number of those
lords and gentlemen which had sent for him, and there euerie one
apart and by himselfe sware fealtie and homage vnto him, as if he
had beene their true and naturall prince.

"King Iohn about the same time that Lewes thus arriued, came
to Douer, meaning to fight with his aduersaries by the way as they
should come forward towards London. But yet vpon other aduisement taken, he changed his purpose. . . Therefore furnishing the
castell of Douer, with men, munition, and vittels, he left it in the
keeping of Hubert de Burgh, a man of notable prowesse & vali-
ancie. . . Lewes being aduertised that king Iohn was retired out of
Kent, passed through the countrie without anie incounter, and
wan all the castels and holds as he went, but Douer he could not
win.

"At his comming to Rochester, he laid siege to the castell there. . .
This doone, he came to London, and there receiued the homage of
those lords and gentlemen which had not yet doone their homage
to him at Sandwich. On the other part he tooke an oth to main-
teine and performe the old lawes and customes of the realme, and
to restore to euerie man his rightfull heritage and lands, requiring
the barons furthermore to continue faithfull towards him . . ." (191,
ii). Cf. v. i. 30–6, v. ii. 1–7.

"The rumour of this pretended outward courtesie being once
spred through the realme, caused great numbers of people to come
flocking to him" among whom were William Earl of Salisbury,
William Marshall the Younger, and others (191, ii.).

Gualo, the papal legate, returned to England after the landing
of Lewis. He went at once to see John, "of whome he was most
ioifullie receiued, for in him king Iohn reposed all his hope of victorie. This legat immediatlie after his comming did excommunicate Lewes by name, with all his fautors and complices, but speci-
allie Simon de Langton, with bell, booke, and candle, as the maner
was . . ." (192, i). Cf. v. i. 62–5, III. ii. 22.

"About the same time, or rather in the yeare last past as some

hold, it fortuned that the vicount of Melune a French man, fell
sicke at London, and perceiuing that death was at hand, he called
vnto him certeine of the English barons, which remained in the
citie, vpon safegard thereof, and to them made this protestation:
I lament (saith he) your destruction and desolation at hand, bicause ye are ignorant of the perils hanging ouer your heads. For
this vnderstand, that Lewes, and with him 16 earles and barons of
France, haue secretlie sworne (if it shall fortune him to conquere
this realme of England, & to be crowned king) that he will kill,
banish, and confine all those of the English nobilitie (which now
doo serue vnder him, and persecute their owne king) as traitours
and rebels, and furthermore will dispossesse all their linage of such
inheritances as they now hold in England. And bicause (saith he)
you shall not haue doubt hereof, I which lie here at the point of
death, doo now affirme vnto you, and take it on the perill of my
soule, that I am one of those sixteene that haue sworne to performe
this thing: wherefore I aduise you to prouide for your owne safeties,
and your realmes which you now destroie, and keepe this thing
secret which I haue vttered vnto you. After this speech was vttered
he streightwaies died.

"When these words of the lord of Melune were opened vnto the
barons, they were, and not without cause, in great doubt of themselues . . . so that manie of them inwardlie relented, and could haue
bin contented to haue returned to king Iohn, if they had thought
that they should thankfullie haue beene receiued . . ." (193, ii).
Cf. v. iv.

John decided to fight back against his enemies. "So that hauing
gotten togither a competent armie for his purpose, he brake foorth
of Winchester, as it had beene an hideous tempest of weather, beating downe all things that stood in his waie . . ." (193, ii).

"Thus the countrie being wasted on each hand, the king hasted
forward till he came to Wellestreme sands, where passing the
washes he lost a great part of his armie, with horsses and carriages,
so that it was iudged to be a punishment appointed by God, that
the spoile which had beene gotten and taken out of churches,
abbeies, and other religious houses, should perish, and be lost by
such means togither with the spoilers. Yet the king himselfe, and a
few other, escaped the violence of the waters, by following a good
guide. But as some haue written, he tooke such greefe for the losse
susteined at this passage, that immediatlie therevpon he fell into an
ague, the force and heat whereof, togither with his immoderate
feeding on rawe peaches, and drinking of new sider, so increased
his sicknesse, that he was not able to ride, but was faine to be carried

in a litter . . . the disease still so raged and grew vpon him, that . . .
through anguish of mind, rather than through force of sicknesse, he
departed this life . . .

"There be which haue written, that after he had lost his armie,
he came to the abbeie of Swineshead in Lincolnshire . . . a moonke
. . . being mooued with zeale for the oppression of his countrie, gaue
the king poison in a cup of ale, wherof he first tooke the assaie, to
cause the king not to suspect the matter, and so they both died in
manner at one time . . ." (194, i, ii). Cf. v. vi. 39–42, v. vii. 59–64;
v. vi. 23–31, v. vii.

John's men "marching foorth with his bodie, each man with his
armour on his backe, in warlike order, conueied it vnto Worcester,
where he was pompouslie buried in the cathedrall church before
the high altar, not for that he had so appointed (as some write) but
bicause it was thought to be a place of most suertie for the lords . . ."
(194, ii). Cf. v. vii. 99–100, note.

"Here therefore we see the issue of domesticall or homebred
broiles, the fruits of variance . . . no greater nor safer fortification
can betide a land, than when the inhabitants are all alike minded
. . . [this being the real] sinewes of a realme . . ." (195, i). Cf. v. vii.
112–18, v. vii. 88.

Holinshed describes King John: "He was comelie of stature, but
of looke and countenance displeasant and angrie, somewhat cruell
of nature, as by the writers of his time he is noted, and not so hardie
as doubtfull in time of perill and danger . . . he was a great and
mightie prince, but yet not verie fortunate, much like to Marius the
noble Romane, tasting of fortune both waies . . ." (196, i).

"HEnrie, the third of that name, the eldest sonne of K. Iohn, a
child of the age of nine yeres, began his reigne ouer the realme of
England the nineteenth day of October, in the yeare of our Lord
1216 . . ." (197, i).

"Immediatlie after the death of his father king Iohn, William
Marshall earle of Penbroke, generall of his fathers armie, brought
this yoong prince . . . vnto Glocester . . . a great number of the lords
and cheefe barons of the realme hasted thither (I meane not onelie
such as had holden with king Iohn, but also diuerse other, which
vpon certeine knowledge had of his death, were newlie reuolted
from Lewes) in purpose to aid yoong king Henrie, to whome of
right the crowne did apperteine . . ." (197, i).

Pembroke made an oration in support of Henry. ". . . Wherefore,
in so much as euerie man is charged onelie with the burthen of his
owne works and transgressions, neither shall the child (as the scripture teacheth vs) beare the iniquitie of his father: we ought there-

fore of dutie and conscience to pardon this yoong and tender prince... let vs remooue from vs this Lewes the French kings sonne, and suppresse his people, which are a confusion and shame to our nation: and the yoke of their seruitude let vs cast from off our shoulders..." (197, i, ii). Cf. II. i. 179–82, v. vii. 74–80.

The barons "with one consent, proclaimed the yoong gentleman king of England..." (197, ii).

"It is reported by writers, that amongst other things, as there were diuerse which withdrew the hearts of the Englishmen from Lewes, the consideration of the confession which the vicount of Melune made at the houre of his death, was the principall..." (197, ii). Cf. v. iv.

1218. A "new supplie of men was readie to come and aid Lewes". Hubert de Burgh, captain of Dover Castle, attacked the French fleet at sea... "in the end the Englishmen bare themselues so manfullie, that they vanquished the whole French fleet, and obteined a famous victorie..." (201, i). Cf. v. iii. 9–11, v. v. 12–13.

"Lewes, after he vnderstood of this mischance happening to his people that came to his aid, began not a litle to despaire of all other succour to come vnto him at any time heerafter: wherfore he inclined the sooner vnto peace, so that at length he tooke such offers of agreement as were put vnto him..." With the help of the legate Gualo peace was finally effected (201, ii.). Cf. v. vii. 84–95.

"But a maruell it was to consider here at home, in how short a space the state of the English common-wealth was changed, and from a troubled fourme reduced to a flourishing and prosperous degree: chiefelie by the diligent heed and carefull prouision of the king himselfe..." (203, ii). Cf. v. vii. 26.


## (2) COGGESHALL

In some ways IV. i is the climax of *John*. Shakespeare may have known Coggeshall's account of the attempted blinding and death of Arthur, and we therefore reprint it below [from *Radulphi de Coggeshall Chronicon Anglicanum* (1875), ed. Joseph Stevenson].

"Cernentes autem regis consiliarii quod multas strages et seditiones facerent ubique Britones pro Arturo domino suo, et quod nulla firma pacis concordia posset fieri, Arturo superstite, suggesserunt regi quatinus praeciperet ut nobilis adolescens oculis et genitalibus privaretur, et sic deinceps ad principandum inutilis redderetur, ut vel sic pars adversa ab insania sedulae expugnationis conquiesceret et regi se subderet. Exacerbatus itaque indefessa

congressione adversariorum, et minis eorum et impropriis lacessi-
tus, praecepit tandem in ira et in furore tribus suis servientibus
quatinus ad Falesiam quantocius pergerent, atque hoc opus detestabile perpetrarent. Duo vero ex servientibus tam execrabile opus
in tam nobili adolescente committere detestantes, a curia domini
regis diffugerunt; tertius vero ad castellum pervenit in quo puer
regius a domino Huberto de Burch, regis camerario, diligenter cus-
todiebatur, triplices annulos circa pedes habens. Cumque mandatum domini regis Huberto detulisset, exortus est fletus et planc-
tus nimius inter milites qui custodiebant illum, utpote nimia miseratione super nobili adolescente permoti. Arturus autem diram avun-
culi sui sententiam super se datam cognoscens, atque de salute pro-
pria omnino diffidens, totus effluxit in lacrymas et in lamentabiles
querimonias. At cum astaret ille praesens qui a rege missus fuerat
ad hoc opus exsequendum, et persona gementi et flenti puero in-
notuisset, inter lamenta subito concitus surrexit, et manus suae de-
jectionis ultrices in personam illam violenter injecit, ad milites cir-
cumstantes voce lacrymabili vociferans: "O domini mei carissimi!
pro Dei amore sinite paulisper, ut me de isto facinoroso ulciscar
antequam mihi oculos eripiat; nam hic ultimus omnium existet
quem in praesenti saeculo conspiciam." Ad hunc vero tumultum
sedandum ocius surrexere milites, et manus utriusque cohibuerunt,
atque, ex praecepto domini Huberti, juvenis ille qui advenerat de
thalamo illo eiectus est; ex cujus expulsione atque ex assistentium
consolatoria collocutione Arturus aliquantulam, sedata cordis
moestitia, recepit consolationem.

"Hubertus autem regis camerarius, honestati et famae regiae
deferre volens, et indemnitati regis prospiciens, puerum regium
servavit illaesum, perpendens quod dominus rex super tali edicto
statim poeniteret, ac semper postmodum haberet exosum qui ejus
tam crudeli imperio obtemperare praesumpissset (*sic*); quod magis
ex subitaneo furore quam ex perpendiculo aequitatis et justitiae
emanare credidit. Volens itaque et domini regis iram ad tempus
mitigare ac Britonum saevitiam cohibere, fecit per castellum et per
totam provinciam divulgari quod sententia regis effectui esset man-
cipata, et quod dominus Arturus prae cordis tristitia et vulnerum
acerbo dolore diem clausisset extremum: quae fama, per xv. dies,
per utrumque regnum volitabat incessanter. Denique classicum
per vicos et castella, quasi pro anima ejus, pulsatum est; vestes ejus
hospitali leprosorum distributae. Divulgatum est etiam quod cor-
pus ejus ad abbatiam de Sancto Andrea, ordinis Cisterciensis, de-
latum sit, ibique sepultum. Ad tales igitur rumores, Britones non
animis sedati sed magis magisque exacerbati, ferocius quam prius,

ubi poterant, debacchati sunt; jurantes quod nunquam deinceps ab expugnatione regis Angliae conquiescerent, qui tam detestabile facinus in dominum suum et nepotem proprium exercere praesumpsisset. Sicque factum est quod necesse erat iterum praedicare Arturum adhuc viventem et incolumem, quem ubique diffamaverant mortuum, ut vel sic efferata Britonum ferocitas aliquantulum mitigaretur. Quod cum regi intimatum esset, nequaquam displicuit ei ad praesens quod mandatum ejus exsecutum non esset. Dicebant etiam quidam militum domino regi, nequaquam ulterius milites se inventurum qui castella sua custodirent, si tam infaustum judicium de domino Arturo nepote suo exercere praesumpsisset; nam, si contingeret aliquos deinceps capi milites a rege Franciae, vel ab adversariis suis, similem statim absque miseratione sortirentur vindictam." (pp. 139–41).

Holinshed, in his account of the end of Arthur, refers to Coggeshall in the margin as his authority. Elizabethan chroniclers knew this work well, but it was only available to them in MS. The Waverley *Chronicle*, however, was also unprinted; and modern studies of Shakespeare's sources have shown that printed books do not necessarily tell us the whole story.

As Holinshed condensed Coggeshall we might conclude that any convergence of Coggeshall and *King John*, where Holinshed is silent, argues Shakespeare's debt to Coggeshall. In isolated instances of convergence this argument would scarcely hold. Any single point listed below could be explained as a coincidence, one or two as Shakespeare's conventional technique. But do they carry any cumulative weight? It is not easy to decide. We think they do, but admit that the balance is very evenly poised.

(i) In Shakespeare and Coggeshall Arthur is informed of his fate, and utters lamentable words, before the entry of the executioners, or messenger. He pleads for a delay ["For heaven sake, Hubert, let me not be bound!" (IV. i. 77); "pro Dei amore sinite paulisper"]. *Hubert orders the executioners, or messenger, out of the room.* Arthur is consoled by the compassion of the executioners (IV. i. 85–9), or attending soldiers. Holinshed's conflation omits all these details.

(ii) Shakespeare, who identifies his Salisbury, Pembroke, Bigot, with the nobles of Brittany, makes them swear a solemn vow to revenge Arthur's death (IV. iii. 64–73). Holinshed merely says that

the Britains were nothing pacified, but rather kindled more vehementlie to worke all the mischeefe they could deuise, in reuenge of their souereignes death (165, ii).

Coggeshall repeatedly emphasizes the rage of the nobles (cf. *John*, IV. ii. 103, 261, 268; IV. iii. 21), mentioned only once by Holinshed, and like Shakespeare makes his nobles vow revenge.

(iii) Possible verbal contacts with Shakespeare in the above passage may be noted:

(*a*) The formula "dominum suum et nepotem proprium", "de domino Arturo nepote suo", may have led to Shakespeare's "Thy nephew and right royal sovereign" (I. i. 15).

(*b*) In Coggeshall the murder of Arthur was suggested to John because "nulla firma pacis concordia posset fieri" on account of Arthur. In the play John also weighs "no firm peace" against the death of Arthur:

> There is no sure foundation set on blood,
> No certain life achiev'd by others' death (IV. ii. 104–5)

(*c*) When the nobles were not pacified by the rumour of the death of Arthur "there was no remedie," says Holinshed, "but to signifie abroad againe, that Arthur was as yet liuing and in health" (165, ii). In Coggeshall Arthur is proclaimed alive "ut vel sic efferata Britonum ferocitas aliquantulum mitigaretur". Compare *John*, IV. ii. 261–2, especially "their incensed rage".

(iv) Besides the account of the attempted blinding of Arthur, one or two fugitive Shakespeare–Coggeshall contacts may be suggested.

(*a*) In *John* we read twice that the French supply to aid Lewis was lost on Goodwin Sands (V. iii. 11, V. v. 13). Holinshed, Foxe, M. Paris etc. say that the French navy was defeated by an English force. Only Coggeshall also mentions the storm: "reduxit Dominus super quosdam eorum diffugientes aquas maris, et submersi sunt quasi plumbum" (p. 185).

(*b*) *John*, V. i. 30–6 corresponds closely to Hol., 191, ii (cf. p. 160), but even more so to Coggeshall: "Lodovicus . . . civitatem Cantuariam cum castello in deditionem accepit; postea alia castella Cantiae, praeter solam Doveram munitissimam. Inde Londonias veniens, honorifice a proceribus et civibus susceptus est, et in fidelitatem ejus et homagium omnes pariter juraverunt . . . [Lewis proceeded to Winchester]. Ibi venerunt ad eum fere omnes comites et barones regni, qui eatenus Johanni adhaeserant . . . pauci vero adhuc Johanni pertinaciter adhaeserunt" (pp. 181–2). Note (1) Shakespeare and Coggeshall refer to the *yielding* of Kent—Holinshed says that Lewis "wan all the castels and holds"; (2) Shakespeare's "But Dover Castle" has "But" as a preposition, like Coggeshall's "praeter"—Holinshed's "but" is conjunctive; (3) in Shakespeare and Coggeshall we read of Lewis *being received*, and Shakespeare's "like a kind host" resembles "honorifice"—in Holinshed, Lewis (active) *received* homage; (4) Shakespeare's conclusion of this short summarizing passage about "the little number" of John's "doubtful friends" reminds one of Coggeshall's "pauci vero adhuc Johanni pertinaciter adhaeserunt".

# Appendix B

## STRUCTURAL INCONSISTENCIES IN *JOHN* AND *THE TROUBLESOME RAIGNE OF IOHN*

From time to time critics have noted "structural inconsistencies" in *John* which, they claim, are due to Shakespeare's hurry while revising the *T.R.* The most important attacks were made by Edward Rose,[1] Prof. Moore Smith,[2] Prof. F. Liebermann,[3] and Prof. J. D. Wilson.[4] As Prof. Wilson summarized the key arguments of his predecessors it is convenient to restrict comment mainly to his case.—Prof. Wilson contends that

there are a number of points common to the two plays which are far clearer in *The Troublesome Reign* than in *King John*, some of them indeed being quite unintelligible in the latter without reference to the former.

If we prefer to date the *T.R.* after *John* it is our duty, of course, to defend *John* against Prof. Wilson's points.

(i) Prof. Wilson finds the Bastard's "insulting parody of the Dauphin's lovemaking . . . both impolitic and excessive".—But as the speech (II. i. 504–9) is an aside, even in Prof. Wilson's edition, the Bastard scarcely took an impolitic risk with it. And as he was "spoiling for a fight" he is naturally annoyed by the proposed marriage which would bring peace, as Prof. Wilson agreed. What is more, is not the Bastard habitually "excessive"? Rose observed

---

1. 'Shakespeare as an Adapter' [*Macmillan's Mag.* (1878)]; reprinted in the Introduction to the Praetorius facsimile of *T.R.*, Pt I.
2. See Smith's *King John* (1900), Introduction; and *An English Miscellany presented to Dr Furnivall* (1901), p. 335.
3. See Herrig's *Archiv*, CXLII, 177; CXLIII, 17, 190.
4. The C.U.P. *John*, pp. xxi–xxxiv.

that the *T.R.* had a better reason for the Bastard's behaviour, because Blanche had been previously promised in marriage to him (*T.R.*, I. iv. 121–5). But a "better reason" in the *T.R.* does not make *John* inconsistent, nor even unclear.

Prof. Moore Smith subjoined that the Bastard's threat in the *T.R.* that he will cuckold his rival, the Dauphin, loses point when directed, as by Shakespeare, against Austria.[1] But in fact the lionlioness quibble, which the editors have so far overlooked, gives the *John* threat a very neat point.[2]

(ii) "Shakespeare never accounts for the poisoning of John."—As this was one of the details of the John story familiar to Elizabethans, we suggest that Shakespeare expected his audience to look forward to the poisoning, therefore motivation was less necessary.[3] In any case, repeated passages describing John's anti-monastic policy (I. i. 48–9, III. ii. 17–23, IV. ii. 141–2) would surely make matters plain.

(iii) In *John*, IV. iii. 11 the English nobles give no reason why they should meet at Saint Edmundsbury.—Our reply is that there are other persons in other Shakespeare plays who do not give reasons for going on their various journeys. Why should reasons always be given?

(iv) Shakespeare's John does not inform us of the reasons for his second coronation (IV. ii. 40–3).—Nevertheless, John's motives are not "unclear", his desire to turn over a new leaf, now that he thinks Arthur dead, being emphasized by his offer of a boon (IV. ii. 43–6). And as the new coronation is lifted straight out of Holinshed (165, i), in a context very close to the source, another argument why Shakespeare states no clear-cut reasons is that Holinshed provided none. If Shakespeare is unclear, the fault is Holinshed's in the first place.

(v) The "glaring inconsistency" that Shakespeare's John suggests the *assassination* of Arthur to Hubert (III. ii. 76), but that Hubert, executing the king's command, has in mind only *blinding* (IV. i. 39), already puzzled Thomas Edwards[4] two hundred and T. P. Courtenay[5] one hundred years ago. In the *T.R.* John delivers Arthur to Hubert with the words:

> *Hubert* keepe him safe,
> For on his life doth hang thy Soueraignes crowne,
> But in his death consists thy Soueraignes blisse (I. ix. 31–3)

1. See *T.R.*, I. iv. 128–30, *John*, II. i. 290–3.   2. See II. i. 291, note.
3. See Introduction, p. xxvii.   4. *Canons of Criticism* (1765), p. 254.
5. *Commentaries on the Historical Plays of Shakspeare* (1840), vol. I, pp. 18–19.

In the *T.R.*, says Wilson, John is obliged "to content himself with putting out his rival's eyes, which would at least render him incapable of ruling"—and this Shakespeare misunderstood, taking John's hinted desire for Arthur's death as an order to murder him, but quite forgetting this order whilst rapidly revising the blinding-scene.

In our opinion, Prof. Wilson misconstrues both plays. Shakespeare, if he differs from the *T.R.* "source-play", must be following Holinshed (p. 165), who shows how the necessity of Arthur's *death* led to an order for his *blinding*, and how Hubert pretended that Arthur *died* after the blinding, as John had intended. In short, we think that Holinshed and Shakespeare (and the *T.R.* too, by the way) interpret John's overt order to blind Arthur as a concealed order to kill him in the process—exactly as Hubert's pretence of Arthur's death indicates. Shakespeare in Act IV, Sc. i has not *forgotten* the earlier order: he still pursues one and the same plan.

(vi) Constance calls Philip and John "perjur'd kings" (III. i. 33), though only Philip has perjured himself by promising her aid. In the *T.R.* Constance curses "the traytors . . . Whose periurie . . . Beleaguers all the Skie with misbeliefe" (I. iv. 208–10), and probably thinks of Philip, Lewis and Austria, while Shakespeare, it is said, took her to mean the two kings.—But "perjured" was sometimes used more loosely than now, in the sense "acting against the law, wrong-doing, false",[1] which would explain this minute "inconsistency". Apart from which, Constance's suggestion that *both* kings are *perjured* (=forsworn), a meaning also present, harmonizes with her vein of exaggeration, and indeed follows up a well-prepared idea.[2]

(vii) Some "obscure expressions" in *John* are explained through the *T.R.*, the two main ones being "and the territories" (I. i. 10), and "bank'd" (v. ii. 104). The former is discussed in our footnote; the latter can now be explained, with the help of a discovery by Mrs F. M. H. Bone (who has generously given permission for its publication here).

Staunton once suggested that "bank'd" was "an allusion to card-playing; and by 'bank'd their towns' is meant, *won their towns, put them in bank*". Furness countered, however, that *O.E.D.* records no such use of "bank" before the nineteenth century. Despite the fact

1. Thus Cassander is reviled as "periurde villaine, homicide vniust" in F. Sabie's *Fissher-mans Tale* (1595), sig. E₂ᵛ, though neither a murderer nor an oath-breaker.
2. "False blood to false blood join'd" (II. ii. 2); "you think *them* false" (II. ii. 27).

that Shakespeare continues at once with a card-playing allusion, Staunton's idea was therefore dropped. Mrs Bone has now found that Shakespeare probably uses a card-playing term immediately before "bank'd":

> Have I not heard these islanders shout out
> "Vive le roi!" as I have bank'd their towns?
> Have I not here the best cards for the game ... (v. ii. 103–5)

For many early playing-cards had "Vive le roi" and similar expressions inscribed on them.[1] Moreover, Mrs Bone contends, "bank" was known as a card-playing term in other languages in the sixteenth century:[2] since cards and card-terms were nearly all imported in England at that time, and v. ii. 105 definitely mentions card-playing, Staunton's theory can no longer be brushed aside.

If Staunton and Mrs Bone are right, the crux gives us further help with the problem of the precedence of *John* and the *T.R.* (cf. p. lviii). For the *T.R.* also assigns a "vive le roi" speech to Lewis:

> Your Citie Rochester with great applause
> By some deuine instinct layd armes aside:
> And from the hollow holes of Thamesis
> Eccho apace replide *Viue la roy.*
> From thence, along the wanton rowling glade
> To *Troynouant* your fayre *Metropolis,*
> With luck came *Lewes* to shew his troupes of *Fraunce,*
>
> (II. iii. 170–6)

The point of interest is that the sources do not indicate that Lewis proceeded by water up the Thames, as the *T.R.* states: but this

---

1. H.-R. D'Allemagne's *Les Cartes à Jouer* (2 vols., 1906) reproduces 16th-century French cards, one inscribed "VIVE LE ROY" (II, 445); 17th-century French cards inscribed "VIVE LE ROY", "ET LA COVR" etc. (I. 91); "VIVE LA REYNE" (I. 89). R. Merlin's *Origine des Cartes à Jouer* (1869) reproduces a 16th-century French card inscribed "vive le ro" (Plate 36). W. Gurney Benham's *Playing Cards* (1931) reproduces 17th-century French cards inscribed "VIVE LE ROY", "ET LA COVR", "VIVE LA RAINE", "MAYME LAMOVR" (p. 135).

2. Cf. Florio's *Worlde of Wordes* (1598): "Banco fallito, *a game at cards*" (p. 38); C. Cotton's *Compleat Gamester* (1674): "BANKAFALET, a Game on the Cards" (p. 153).—Passages in T. M.'s *Blacke Booke* (1604) suggest that "bank" was also an English gambling term in Shakespeare's time: "I giue and bequeath to you, old *Bias, Alias, Humfrey Hollow-banke,* true cheating Bowler, and Lurcher, the one halfe of all false Bettes" (sig. Fᵛ); "Moreouer, *Humfrey,* I giue you the lurching of all yong Nouices ... that are hookt in by the winning of one Twelue-penny Game at first, lost vppon policy, to bee cheated of Twelue-pounds worth-a Bets afterward" (sigs. Fᵛ, F₂); "Your cheating Bowler that will bancke false of purpose, and loose a game of twelue=pence to purchase his Partner twelue shillings in Bettes, and so share it after the Play" (sigs. D₄, D₄ᵛ).

journey might have been suggested by "bank'd their towns" (*John*, v. ii. 104). Editors of *John*, not understanding the card-playing allusion, have similarly explained "bank'd" as "sailed past". As *T.R.*, II. iii. 170 *sqq.* either imitates *John*, v. ii. 103 *sqq.*, or *vice versa*, it is most significant that Shakespeare's "bank'd" and "Vive le roi", if technical, can only be associated with "*Viue la roy*" in the *T.R.* (with a change of meaning);—while the *T.R.* departure from history is most simply explained as a misunderstanding of Shakespeare's two technicalities. However this may be, it can no longer be argued that Shakespeare's "bank'd" is unclear without reference to the *T.R.*[1]

The "inconsistencies" in *John* can all be rejected, we think, on one or more of four counts: (i) Shakespeare's vocabulary was not fully appreciated; (ii) some of the "inconsistencies" are actually subtleties, and the editors and not Shakespeare must be blamed for working too hurriedly; (iii) the sources have been followed—without "misunderstandings"—so that Shakespeare himself did not originate inconsistencies; (iv) various "inconsistencies", laboriously searched for to prove the priority of the *T.R.*, have numerous parallels in Shakespeare's other plays, and would never have been so named if his customary techniques had been compared.

It has not yet occurred to anyone to reverse the "inconsistency" test, but clearly the argument can be turned. Are there not self-contradictions in the *T.R.* which might be due to the priority of *John*?

(i) The age of Arthur.—In the *T.R.*, as in Holinshed, Arthur appears as a young soldier aged sixteen or seventeen: "*Arthur*, bestirre thee man" (*T.R.*, I. v. 136); "Duke *Arthur* . . . To armes in hast" (I. vii. 24–5). In *John* he is a boy aged eight or ten, not more than three feet tall (IV. ii. 100). Shakespeare obviously made Arthur younger so that his helplessness would be more pathetic. Addressed as "pretty Arthur" (III. iii. 89), and "boy" (II. i. 18, 30, 43, 115, etc.) the child of eight or ten cannot complain. But what young warrior of sixteen or seventeen (a less immature age in Shakespeare's time than in ours) would like to be called "Poore helples boy" (*T.R.*, I. iv. 225) or "louely boy" (*T.R.*, I. iv. 232)? In view of the close verbal contact of the plays, the version which altered Arthur's age would have introduced the "pretty Arthur" jargon more naturally than *vice versa*, and unintelligent echoing seems the likeliest explanation of the language of the *T.R.*

(ii) The prophecy of Peter of Pomphret.—In *John*, IV. ii. 151–2,

1. I am indebted to Mrs Bone for the argument of this paragraph.

v. i. 25–7 we find that Peter predicted John's surrender of the crown "ere the next Ascension-day at noon". The *noon* of the day does not come from Holinshed or Foxe, both of whom the two playwrights probably consulted for the episode.—In Part I of the *T.R.* the prophecy dates John's "surrender" precisely as Shakespeare:

> ere Ascension day
> Haue brought the Sunne vnto his vsuall height,
> Of Crowne, Estate, and Royall dignitie,
> Thou shalt be cleane dispoyld and dispossest
> (*T.R.*, I. xiii. 184–7)

In Part II it has been forgotten that the *noon* of Ascension day is the fatal hour, the whole day itself being taken as the time-limit:

> The Diall tells me, it is twelue at noone.
> Were twelue at midnight past, then might I vaunt
> False seers prophecies of no import (*T.R.*, II. ii. 11–13)

> *Peter* King *Iohn*, although the time I haue prescribed
> Be but twelue houres remayning yet behinde
> (*T.R.*, II. ii. 24–5)

Why has "noone" (*T.R.*, II. ii. 11) been dragged in by the hairs? The writer seems to realize that it has some significance, but to have forgotten what that significance is. Just as the Duke of York, in the piracy of *Henry VI*, Part II, builds up an elaborate claim to the crown on a false assumption which would ironically be sufficient claim by itself if it were true:[1] so in the *T.R.* an elaborate prophecy is "planted", its point is forgotten, the prepared "facts" are confused, and then, best of all, *Shakespeare's* threat to hang Peter on Ascension day at noon (IV. ii. 155–7), a threat not made in the *T.R.*, is put into execution (*T.R.*, II. ii. 43–5), though the *T.R.* at this stage envisages another twelve hours before the end of the danger!

(iii)  Old Faulconbridge's attitude to the Bastard.—In the *T.R.* Robert Faulconbridge reports that his father accepted Philip as his son (I. i. 122). Yet he continues later that Lady Faulconbridge was delivered "Sixe weekes before the account my Father made" (I. i. 167)—which contradicts his father's blindness. In *John* we do not hear that old Faulconbridge ever thought Philip his own son: but the father's calculation that Philip was born "Full fourteen weeks before the course of time" (I. i. 113) has some connection with the "Sixe weekes" of the *T.R.* Here *John* is logical, the *T.R.* self-contradictory.

---

1. See Prof. P. Alexander, *Shakespeare's Henry VI and Richard III*, p. 62.

(iv) The Bastard's ignorance of his father.—In the *T.R.* Philip asks his mother who his father was (I. i. 325 *sqq.*). In *John* the same question puzzles us less (I. i. 233 *sqq.*), because Philip had not already named his father (*T.R.*, I. i. 278), nor had he done so in the presence of his mother, whom Shakespeare brought on after John's hearing of the dispute.

(v) The behaviour of the citizens of Angiers.—In the *T.R.* the citizens ask for a parley (I. iv. 9–11), though in fact they have nothing to say (I. iv. 51–2). In *John* the citizen asks for audience after the Bastard's proposal to sack Angiers (II. i. 373–96), which seems more natural. Confusion of the sequence of events, as in the *T.R.*, we know to be the hallmark of piratical memorization.

(vi) King Philip's betrayal of Constance.—In the *T.R.* King Philip, while inclining to the proposed reconciliation with John, denies that he betrays Constance, blatantly untrue though it is:

> The King of *Fraunce* respects his honor more
> Than to betray his friends and fauourers (I. iv. 117–18)

He assures Constance very similarly in *John* that she

> shall have no cause
> To curse the fair proceedings of this day:
> Have I not pawn'd to you my majesty? (III. i. 22–4)

Here Philip speaks after the marriage, for Shakespeare took Constance off during the "marriage-proposal" episode (II. i. 416 *sqq.*): and the king seems a less bare-faced liar than in the *T.R.* because he makes vague promises for the future, and is not glossing over his past promises to Constance as he actually breaks them.

Countless other inconsistencies crop up in the *T.R.* Once our suspicions are aroused they stare us in the face. Whereas in the *T.R.* these are *structural*, two conflicting versions of one character or event being apparently conflated, the "inconsistencies" that have been detected in *John* are entirely due to the commentators' failure to consider Shakespeare's regular techniques, or unfamiliar Elizabethan idioms.

## Appendix C

### THE TEXT OF *THE TROUBLESOME RAIGNE OF IOHN* (1591)

We observed (p. lvi) that the *T.R.* has textual features common in "bad quartos". A short selection will make this clear.

(i) *Omission of exits and entrances.* This also happens in good texts (omission of entrances being much the rarer of the two), but not in the profusion offered by the *T.R.* In I. i. 73 the (first) entrance of the Faulconbridges passes unnoted; so in I. ii. 74 the (first) entrance of Blanche. In I. x. 16 Constance is brought on a second time, though already brought on in I. x. 1. In I. i. 60, xii. 28, xiii. 144 etc. exits are unnoted.

(ii) *Speeches without headings.* See II. i. 1, II. i. 52, II. ii. 219, II. iii. 150, II. iv. 1.

(iii) *Ambiguous speech headings.* In I. v the third and fifth speech headings both read "*Philip*": the third standing for Faulconbridge, the fifth for France. Other speech heading variations are perhaps no more extraordinary than those of some good texts (France is *King* in I. ii. 1, *K. Philip* in I. ii. 46, *Philip* in I. iv. 14; Pandulph is *Pandulph* and *Legat* in II. viii; and so on).

(iv) *Descriptive and summarizing directions.* This is an important clue for a decision about the provenance of the text. Some cases can be parallelled in "good" texts, e.g.

Enter *Philip* leading a Frier, charging him to show where the Abbots golde lay (I. xi. 1).

Others remind one of "bad quarto" presentation:

Excursions. The Bastard chaseth *Lymoges* the Austrich Duke, and maketh him leaue the Lyons skinne. (I. iii. 1)
Excursions. The Bastard pursues *Austria*, and kills him. (I. vi. 1)
Excursions. *Elianor* is rescued by *Iohn*, and *Arthur* is taken prisoner. *Exeunt*. Sound victorie. (I. viii. 1)

Compare similar compression in the bad quarto of *Romeo*:

They draw, to them enters *Tybalt*, they fight, to them the Prince, old *Mountague*, and his wife, old *Capulet* and his wife, and other Citizens and part them.

where the dialogue and action of I. i. 66–86 (Oxford text) is summarized in one direction. Good texts do not call for prolonged action without dialogue except under unusual circumstances.

Some directions actually appear to describe action already witnessed:

There the fiue Moones appeare (I. xiii. 131)

He leapes, and brusing his bones, after he was from his traunce, speakes thus; (II. i. 12)

The text of the *T.R.* is very "foul". "Permissive directions"[1] at I. xi. 110, II. ii. 1, II. iv. 1 confirm that we are dealing with foul papers. Repetition of words and phrases *ad nauseam* suggests that the writer (or writers) worked under pressure.

At least two styles are noticeable, the one pretentious, using many blustering words and larded with Latin tags. S. Rowley, whom various *T.R.* tricks recall, may have had a hand in the writing.[2] Munday (or Chettle, the co-author), whose Robin Hood plays also contain verbal peculiarities which can be parallelled in the *T.R.*, may be associated with the *T.R.* more confidently, if any significance may be attached to a freak spelling.[3] The form "Hughbert" (for "Hubert") occurs three times on one page of the *T.R.* (Part II, sig. A₄), but on no other page; in *The Death of Robert, Earle of Huntington* (1601) it is common, the most revealing corruption being: "Its Lord *Hugh Burgh* alone, *Hughberr*, what newes?" (sig. H₂).

It has been argued that the printer, hoping for a double profit, was responsible for the two-part publication of the *T.R.* Chambers noted that the lines "To the Gentlemen Readers" prefixed to both parts do not claim to be prologues.[4] Wilson agreed that the division into two parts could have no dramatic reason:[5] and there are strong reasons against the production of the *T.R.* in two parts. It should be added that both the title-page and lines "To the Gentlemen Readers" of Part I promise the death of John, which takes

1. Cf. Greg, *The Editorial Problem in Shakespeare*, p. 36. The *T.R.* directions are "Enter *Peter* a Prophet, with people"; "Enter King *Iohn* with two or three and the Prophet"; "Enter K. *Iohn, Bastard, Pandulph*, and a many priests with them" respectively.

2. Pope asserted in 1723 that the *T.R.* was by "W. Shakespear *and* W. Rowley" (Pope's Shakespeare, III, 115). Perhaps a tradition that Shakespeare and "Rowley" were connected with it reached Pope. For S. Rowley's early hackwork cf. Introduction, p. lv.

3. *The Death of Robert* is probably a bad quarto, in which case Munday himself would not be responsible for the *T.R.*

4. *The Elizabethan Stage*, IV, 23.     5. *King John*, p. xvii.

place in Part II. Such overlapping can be parallelled *c.* 1590 in two-part learned works with separate title-pages and signatures, but seems suspicious in plays.

Only one scene (I. xi) in the *T.R.* wholly lacks its opposite number in *John*. The *T.R.* (nearly 2,900 lines) is also slightly longer than *John* (nearly 2,600 lines). Part I of the *T.R.* is disproportionately long (1,750 lines approximately) in comparison with Part II (1,150 lines approximately), which, again, discountenances two-part production.—Part I seems to have been written on 45-line pages, and Part II on 55-line pages: the lines per scene, at least, fall in quite neatly with these figures. This need have no significance, but systematic divergence between the two parts [cf. (ii) above] deserves thought.

Whether or not only one man wrote the *T.R.* is hard to decide. The two styles may be due to the lapses of one author at times falling below his best. But the printer's copy may have been padded with interpolations to disguise the shortness of the two parts. The lines "To the Gentlemen Readers", almost certainly written for the press, resemble the style of much of the text. And if the theatrical foul papers were not expanded for the press the *T.R.* was somewhat longer than the other one-part plays owned by the same company at the same time.

Bearing all these textual pecularities in mind it is as well to ponder again Prof. Alexander's misgivings about the *T.R.*:

It is difficult to understand how this work, so well digested in the scenes as to permit Shakespeare to follow it nearly scene by scene, should yet show so little corresponding modesty or cunning in its writing as to appear like a tissue of borrowed and only half-assimilated phrases from *Henry VI, Richard III*, as well as *King John* itself. This reasoning would date all these pieces before 1591 ...[1]

For the disparity between clever plotting and very uneven verse (or prose) was a standard feature of "bad" and "derivative" play-texts in the Elizabethan period.

1. *Shakespeare's Life and Art*, p. 85.

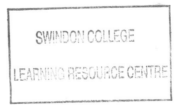